Tom Owen Edmunds

About the Author

KATIE HICKMAN was born into a diplomatic family and has spent more than twenty-five years living abroad in Europe, the Far East, and Latin America. She is the author of the *London Times* bestseller *Daughters of Britannia* and two previous works of nonfiction, *A Trip to the Light Fantastic: Travels with a Mexican Circus* and *Dreams of the Peaceful Dragon: A Journey Through Bhutan*, as well as a novel, *The Quetzal Summer*. She is featured in *Wayward Women*, the Oxford University Press guide to women travelers.

Katie Hickman

COURTESANS

Money, Sex and Fame in the
Nineteenth Century

Perennial

An Imprint of HarperCollinsPublishers

This title was originally published in Great Britain in 2003 by HarperCollins Publishers.

The first U.S. edition was published in 2003 by HarperCollins Publishers.

HarperCollins books may be purchased for educational, business, or sales promotional use. For information please write: Special Markets Department, HarperCollins Publishers Inc., 10 East 53rd Street, New York, NY 10022.

FIRST PERENNIAL EDITION PUBLISHED 2004.

The Library of Congress has catalogued the hardcover edition as follows:

Hickman, Katie.
    Courtesans : money, sex and fame in the nineteenth century / Katie Hickman.—1st U.S. ed.
        p. cm.
    Includes bibliographical references and index.
    ISBN 0-06-620955-2 (acid-free paper)
    1. Courtesans—Great Britain—History—19th century.
    2. Courtesans—Great Britain—Biography.
    3. Baddeley, Sophia, 1745?–1786. 4. Fox, Elizabeth, 1750–1842. 5. Wilson, Harriette, 1786–1846.
    6. Pearl, Cora, 1837–1886. I. Title.

HQ185.A5H53   2003
306.74'0941—dc22

2003059389

ISBN 0-06-093514-6 (pbk.)

04 05 06 07 08 QW 10 9 8 7 6 5 4 3 2 1

This book is for A.C. Grayling

'Ask not how many young men their fortunes let slip, and careers,
Chancing one night on her couch (and it was worth it, they said);
Neo-Platonic sages failed to show up at their lectures –
Dream of the touch of her lips, metaphysics go hang!'

From 'Epitaph for Thaïs', by John Heath-Stubbs.
From *John Heath-Stubbs, Collected Poems 1943–1987*.
Carcanet, 1988

CONTENTS

ILLUSTRATIONS

The sixteenth-century Venetian courtesan Veronica Franco (1546–91), painted by Tintoretto, was almost as celebrated for her artistic and poetic gifts as for her fabled eroticism. *(Worcester Art Museum, Worcester, Massachusetts. Austin S. and Sarah C. Garver Fund)*

Kitty Fisher painted by Nathaniel Hone (1765). Such was her fame that crowds of eager sightseers flocked to watch her eat supper in her box at Vauxhall Gardens. *(© Philip Mould/Historical Portraits)*

Three examples of the '*Tête-à-Tête*' series from the *Town and Country Magazine*, featuring Sophia Baddeley and Elizabeth Armistead. *(By permission of The British Library)*

Sophia and Robert Baddeley in Garrison and Colman's play *The Clandestine Marriage*, painted by John Zoffany (1733–1810). *(© The Art Archive)*

Grace Dalrymple Eliot by Thomas Gainsborough (1778). Having committed a *faux pas* and been rejected by her husband, the aristocratic Grace (1754–1823) had no choice but to embark on a career 'on the town' simply in order to survive. *(The Metropolitan Museum of Art. Bequest of William K. Vanderbilt, 1920. (20.155.1). Photograph © 1998 The Metropolitan Museum of Art)*

Elizabeth Armistead by Sir Joshua Reynolds. Her contemporaries found her looks charming, rather than classically beautiful. *(© The Trustees of The British Museum)*

Elizabeth Bridge Bane, The Hon. Mrs Charles James Fox (Elizabeth Armistead), by Sir Joshua Reynolds. *(© Christie's Images)*

Charles James Fox by Karl Anton Hickel (1793). Fox, the Whig parliamentarian and statesman, was, in Edmund Burke's phrase, 'a man born to be loved'. *(By Courtesy of the National Portrait Gallery, London)*

A caricature of Fox as Demosthenes. Much lampooned in his day for his dark, hairy looks and his unkempt appearance, Fox was also justly famous for his powers of oratory. *(© Hulton Archive)*

'A St James's Beauty' gazes out of the window, through which the outline of St James's Palace can clearly be seen. *(© The Trustees of The British Museum)*

Emily Warren as Thaïs, by Joshua Reynolds. At the age of twelve Emily was found begging on the streets by one of London's most notorious madams, Charlotte Hayes, who was so struck by the child's 'uncommon beauty' that she set about training her up. *(Waddesdon Manor, The Rothschild Collection. Photograph © 1994 Mike Fear/The National Trust/Waddesdon Manor)*

'The Cyprian's Ball at the Argyle Rooms'. This engraving by Robert Cruikshank (c.1825) shows a ball given by Harriette Wilson and her three sisters for their patrons. *(By permission of The British Library)*

Lord Ponsonby, by Henry Pierce Bone, after Thomas Lawrence. Widely regarded as the handsomest man in England, Ponsonby was the love of Harriette Wilson's life. *(By Courtesy of the National Portrait Gallery, London)*

'King's Place, or a View of Mr Fox's Best Friends' (1784). The Prince of Wales (later George IV) is shown with two of his mistresses, Perdita Robinson and Elizabeth Armistead. *(© The Trustees of The British Museum)*

'Employment!'. For a time Harriette Wilson was the kept mistress of the young Marquis of Worcester, who set up a house for her in Brighton. *(© The Trustees of The British Museum)*

'Cupid Conducting the Three Graces to the Temple of Love'. Harriette's patrons the Reverend Lord Frederick Beauclerk, the Duke of Wellington and the Marquis of Lorne. *(© The Trustees of The British Museum)*

'La Côterie Débouché' (1825). Harriette Wilson's former patrons were invited to buy themselves out of her *Memoirs* for £200. *(© The Trustees of The British Museum)*

Detail from *Derby Day*, by William Frith (1858) shows a fashionable courtesan, at once at the centre of a large crowd, and yet both physically and spiritually separate from it. *(© Tate, London 2003)*

Cora Pearl. Many thought her vulgar, even ugly; but to the men she chose as her patrons she was a mistress of genius, 'the last word in luxury'. *(© The Board of Trustees of the Victoria & Albert Museum)*

Portrait of Laura Bell by Ernest Girard (1873–97). Laura Bell was one of the few courtesans of the mid-nineteenth century who could rival the success of Catherine Walters. *(By kind permission of the Trustees of the Wallace Collection)*

Cora Pearl c.1863, wearing one of the extravagant crinolines popularised by the English couturier Charles Worth. *(© Hulton Archive)*

An early photograph of Catherine Walters, possibly taken when she was still the kept mistress of 'Harty Tarty', the Marquis of Hartington (later the 8th Duke of Devonshire). *(© Hulton Archive)*

The English poet, diplomat and traveller Wilfrid Scawen Blunt (1840–1922) fell in love with Catherine when he met her in France in 1863, when he was just twenty-three, and she twenty-four. *(© Hulton Archive)*

An unpublished photograph of Catherine which Blunt kept secretly until his death in 1922. *(Fitzwilliam Museum, Cambridge)*

Catherine's classical beauty, and her great elegance and good taste, made her as successful in Paris as in England. *(© Hulton Archive)*

Another previously unpublished photograph from Blunt's collection. Catherine was renowned for the perfect fit of her 'Princess' riding habit, into which she had to be sewn. *(Fitzwilliam Museum, Cambridge)*

ACKNOWLEDGEMENTS

Many people helped me with advice and encouragement during the writing of this book. My greatest thanks go to my partner, Anthony Grayling, whose inspired idea this book was, and also, as ever, to my parents: sterling footwork was done by my mother, Jenny Hickman, who traced sources and pictures for me, as, before his death, did my beloved father, John Hickman, whose unfailing enthusiasm for all my projects can never be replaced. Thank you both so much for everything. I would also like to thank the librarians of the British Library, UCL Library, the Wellcome Institute, the London Library, Colindale Newspaper Library, and the Fitzwilliam Library. I am most grateful also to the archivists at Chatsworth House and the Royal Archives at Windsor Castle for their help, and also to Henry Gillett at the Bank of England for helping me through the confusing maze of monetary conversion tables. I am deeply indebted to Alexander Russell, whose perfect French has saved me from many mistakes in my own (any errors that remain are of course mine). Warm thanks are due also to Tom Owen Edmunds, Roger Katz, Karin Scherer, Emma Walkers, Elizabeth Shenton, Douglas Matthews, Lucrezia Stewart, John Saumarez-Smith, Charlie Ellingworth, Lucy Luck and my agent Gill Coleridge; at HarperCollins I am extremely grateful to Juliet Davis, Vera Brice, Robert Lacey, Helen Ellis, and most of all to my very dear and wonderful editor, Michael Fishwick.

This book would not have been possible without the erudition of many other writers and scholars: I thank them all, but would like to pay special tribute to I.M. Davis, whose work *The Harlot and the Statesman* first drew my attention to the extraordinary bitter-sweet love story of Charles James Fox and Elizabeth Armistead. My own version of their story would not have been possible without it.

Katie Hickman
London, 2003

AUTHOR'S NOTE

When I was a young girl my parents, who were diplomats, lived abroad, and I was sent away to boarding school in England. Unlike diplomatic children of earlier generations, I was lucky enough to be able to join my family every holiday, in Ireland and later in South America. There was one holiday, however, which I did not spend with them, and it stands out with special vividness: I was sent to Paris to stay with my French grandmother.

This grandmother, Lucie Nathan, was in fact no blood relation at all, but an old and dear friend of my mother's from her own schooldays, when in 1949 she too had been sent to Paris to learn French. Life with Lucie and her husband Hubert had been a turning point in my mother's life. It opened her eyes to a way of living which then seemed quite as exotic as anything she would later experience during her long career as a diplomat's wife.

The Nathans were well-to-do rather than rich, but they lived like true Parisians, in a style upon which the war seemed to have had little impact. Hubert taught my mother to drink wine; Lucie, to cook with garlic. They took her to the fashion shows at Dior, to beauty parlours, bistros and nightclubs. My grandfather, a staunchly middle-class Englishman, deplored it all. My grandmother, who was ambitious for her daughters, and who on my mother's return was gratified to hear her speak like a Frenchwoman, as well as dress and eat like one, approved. And, naturally, she carried the day.

I was fifteen in the spring of 1975 when I went to stay with Lucie. She looked exactly the same to me then as she had done all my life: a small, stout, energetic woman with perfect skin, dancing eyes, and a rasping, cigarette-pocked voice like Edith Piaf. Hubert, who was famed in our family for his single sentence of English – 'Ze sky iz blu' – had died several years previously. Lucie spoke no English at all. For the next few weeks, in every waking hour other than those (fairly numerous) in which she was being administered to by her beautician or her masseuse, we saw Paris.

One night, after dinner at one of Lucie's favourite restaurants in Montmartre, she said that as the night was warm we should walk home. If we went by the route which she proposed, there was something she thought I would like to see. We walked along the cobbled back streets for some time. It was very dark. Then, at one point I looked up and saw a beautiful woman standing in a doorway in a floor-length black cloak. There was a bright light shining from the lintel, but the woman had positioned herself in such a way that she was mysteriously illuminated, half in and half out of the light. As we drew level with her, the black cloak fell back to reveal the full regalia beneath: high heels, black stockings, suspender belt, a scarlet and black basque.

Lucie gripped my arm, as I thought to speed me decorously past this dangerous apparition. But not a bit of it; instead, she was slowing me down. *'Regarde!'* she said as we drew level with the woman. *'Qu'elle-est belle!'*

PROLOGUE

O<small>N THE SULTRY EVENING</small> of 26 June 1771 a new play by the comic actor-playwright Samuel Foote opened at the Little Theatre* in the Haymarket. *The Maid of Bath* was a satirical comedy inspired by the true-life story of a young actress, Elizabeth Linley, whose parents had forced her into a marriage contract with the elderly Sir William Long, a man old enough to be her grandfather.

On the opening night the house was packed, not only by crowds of regular theatre-goers, but by friends and colleagues of the playwright, amongst them as many London luminaries as he had been able to muster. As well as being a clever comedian, Foote was a brilliant showman. In the audience that night sat Dr Johnson, Oliver Goldsmith, Sir Joshua Reynolds and David Garrick (who had written the prologue for Foote's play himself).

Chief among them, however, carefully positioned by Foote in the most ostentatiously public of the theatre's boxes, was Sophia Baddeley, the most fashionable and beautiful actress and courtesan of the day.

Despite the improvements in theatre design innovated by David Garrick the previous decade, in the 1770s a London theatre was still an exceptionally rowdy place. The areas around the two principal theatres, Covent Garden and Drury Lane, were dangerous stews infested with brothels, *bagnios*† and accommodation houses.‡ Despite

---

* Foote had been granted the patent to stage dramas at the Little Theatre in 1766. Before then the only two theatres in London licensed to stage plays were Covent Garden and Drury Lane. Foote was granted this privilege by special request of the Duke of York and some of his friends, whose rowdy behaviour had caused a riding accident in which Foote had lost a leg. He was only allowed to use the theatre in the summer, however, when Covent Garden and Drury Lane were not in use.
† A *bagnio* was a Turkish bath, first popularised in London in the early eighteenth century. When private 'retiring rooms' were introduced they soon became used for other purposes, and by the late eighteenth century the term was synonymous with brothel.
‡ A type of brothel in which rooms were available for hire by the hour.

this, all classes avidly attended the theatre, even the King and Queen. The most fashionable aristocrats and their ladies, primped, pomaded and patched, filled the expensive private boxes, while their servants and the ordinary London folk, from the orange-sellers to the painted pimps and ladies of the town, squeezed into the pit or the upper galleries, where they sang, jeered, ate, spat, threw fruit at one another, and chatted the whole night long. The English theatre-going public was an opinionated, argumentative, and occasionally violent mob, passionate in its enthusiasms, devilish when riled. Its uninhibited interaction with the players on the stage was a peculiarly English habit which often shocked foreign visitors to London. But Mrs Baddeley, surveying this seething, smelly, rowdy scene from her private box that midsummer night, was as cool and resplendent as a duchess.

At twenty-six years old, Sophia Baddeley was at the very height of her *demi-mondaine* glory. Made famous first by her exquisite beauty, and then by the scandalousness of her many amours, she was a notorious figure. And, as was only to be expected, when she went to the theatre she went not just to see, but to be seen. 'The box reserved for us was next to the stage box,' remembered Mrs Eliza Steele, Sophia's constant companion in those days, 'that commanded a sight of the whole house.'

And what a sight she was. Her dress and jewels, and the good taste which she displayed in wearing them, made her appearance 'equal to a woman of the first rank'. Her brilliants alone were worth a small fortune. She always wore two watches, 'an expensive one' and 'a little beautiful French watch, that hung by way of a trinket to a chain, set with diamonds, the value of which could not be less than two hundred pounds'. In addition, she had 'four brilliant diamond necklaces, the least of which cost three hundred pounds; two were of near double the value each, and the fourth was the one Lord Melbourne paid Mr Tomkins four hundred and fifty pounds for. She had a pair of beautiful enamelled bracelets, as large as a half-crown piece, set round with brilliants, which cost a hundred and fifty pounds, and rings out of number.'*

* This amounts to more than £2500 – the equivalent of £1.5 million today.

But Sophia Baddeley's dress and jewels were as nothing to the incomparable allure of her face. She was 'absolutely one of the wonders of the age', the Duke of Ancaster once told her; 'no man can gaze on you unwounded. You are in this respect like the Basilisk, whose eyes kill those whom they fix on.'

It was not only men who were so beguiled. The ladies of the nobility, too, 'spoke of her with rapture: "There's that divine face! That beautiful creature!" Others would cry out "Here is Mrs Baddeley – what a sweet woman!"' 'Half the world is in love with you,' her admirer Lord Falmouth told her. And he was hardly exaggerating.

The play began at last, with Samuel Foote himself performing. It went off with immediate *éclat*. Encouraged by his success, Foote began to improvise: 'About the middle of the piece,' recalled Mrs Steele, 'where Mr. Foote enlarged much on the beauty of the Maid of Bath, he added, "Not even the beauty of the nine Muses, nor even that of the divine Baddeley herself, who there sits (pointing to the box where we sat,) could exceed that of the Maid of Bath."' At his words a 'thunder of applause' burst from all parts of the house. Such was the delight of the audience that Foote was encored not once, not twice, but three times. Thrice he repeated the words, to the same ecstatic applause. 'Every eye was on Mrs Baddeley,' wrote Mrs Steele, 'and I do not recollect ever seeing her so confused before.' Blushing at this 'trick of Mr. Foote's', Sophia rose to her feet and curtsied to the audience, 'and it was near quarter of an hour before she could discontinue her obedience, the plaudits lasting so long'.[1]

By 1785 – just fifteen years later – the notorious courtesan was dead: a pauper and a hopeless laudanum addict, the fabulous riches bestowed upon her by her many lovers blown, the jewels, the diamonds, the silks, the carriages, squandered or sold. But all that was in the future. In 1771, on Samuel Foote's opening night, Sophia's candle burned steadily and bright.

INTRODUCTION

IN HIS ESSAY *La Vie Parisienne* Sacheverell Sitwell tells a story of two small boys who were taken for a walk by Prince Paul Murat one Sunday morning in Paris in the 1860s. In their stiffly starched sailor-suits they followed the Prince into a big house in the Bois de Boulogne, where they found the famous English courtesan Cora Pearl relaxing on a sofa,

> *the focus of a hemicycle of diplomats, senators, and academicians, all seated with their chins leaning on gold-knobbed walking sticks, their yellow gloves placed in the 'cylinders' at their side, upon the floor. The Prince presented his jeunes amis, and they joined the hemicycle. When they returned home their mother asked if the Bois had been nice and whether they had seen any animals, to which the reply was* 'Mais non, Maman, beaucoup plus que ça; une femme toute nue!'[1]*

It is a wonderful story, but it is very unlikely to be true. Cora Pearl, although indeed a famous courtesan, would have been horrified to appear in company in such a state. She was much too grand – and much too expensive (very few, if any, of the men described would have been able to afford the exorbitant sum the privilege of seeing Cora naked would have cost). 'Zed',† that great and affectionate chronicler of

---

* It is interesting to speculate on what constituted 'nudity' in this period. The society beauty the Countess de Castiglione, who was a contemporary of Cora Pearl's in Paris, several times had her naked feet and legs photographed – a scandalous impropriety by the standards of the day, when more ordinary *demi-mondaines*, such as actresses and dancers, usually wore stockings even in their more daring poses. In one photograph, the Countess, who delighted in displaying herself in erotic, courtesan-like guises, reclines on a *chaise longue*, her hair loose, her body apparently covered only by a quilt or bedspread. Although to modern eyes she is completely covered up, this photograph is thought to have been the source of a rumour that she had been photographed naked.

† The pseudonym for the Comte de Maugny.

the Parisian *demi-monde*, gives an altogether more telling vignette when he describes how Cora and her friends, the biggest stars of that strange firmament, would take a box at the Opéra, or the Théâtre des Italiens, where they would appear once a week '*en grande toilette*', covered in jewels, and graciously consent to receive a few of the more humble of their ordinary admirers '*de l'air grave et imposant d'ambassadrices en exercise*' (with the grave and imposing bearing of ambassadresses taking the air).

I like this description very much: it connects the courtesan to one of the categories of women that most people would think she was least likely to resemble, yet it is very apt. All but forgotten now, in their own lifetimes English courtesans of the stature of Cora Pearl, Sophia Baddeley, Elizabeth Armistead, Harriette Wilson and Catherine Walters – the five women whose stories I tell in this book – were important people. Whatever the narrow bourgeois view of their profession might have been, they felt they were worthy of respect, and they demanded it. They had a right to. These were highly cultured women; rich, famous and, most remarkably, independent females in an era in which this was almost an impossibility.

But to a large segment of society they were also invisible. In Lady Augusta Fane's hunting memoirs of the 1880s she describes how Catherine Walters – 'Skittles' as she was popularly known – caused an uproar because she dared to ride in the daily parade in Rotten Row,* Hyde Park, which until then had been the unspoken preserve of 'society'.

> In the eighties and before, Rotten Row was packed with riders on weekdays (no one rode on the Sabbath), the fashionable hour being from eleven 'till one o'clock. Everybody who was anybody had a hack, and turned out dressed to the nines. Sir Augustus Lumley, who was the 'Beau Nash' of the Mid-Victorian days, and gave parties to the select few in his studio in William Street, would pass by in a well-padded coat pulled in at the waist, his hair carefully divided at the back and brushed towards his ears, carrying a big silk hat in his hand to save taking it off his head for

---

* The name derives from 'rotan', a kind of wheeled vehicle.

his continual bows! Then Lady Cardigan marvellously attired,
wearing a golden wig and a three-cornered hat and a Louis XVI
coat and leopard skin over her shoulder, would trip along arm-in-
arm with General Sir Henry Stracey, followed by a tall footman
carrying her pet dog on a cushion.[2]

Skittles, on the other hand, drew all eyes by her perfect simplicity. A brilliant natural horsewoman, she would canter up the Row on her chestnut horse, 'dressed in a perfectly-fitting "Princess" habit made in one piece, which looked as if it were glued to the wearer, and showed off her slim figure to perfection'. She was a sensation. Ladies of the aristocracy rushed to copy the perfect cut of her riding habit, while their husbands wondered whether she could possibly be wearing any undergarments at all beneath its skin-tight folds. Scandalised letters were written to *The Times*. Crowds of ordinary Londoners, who until this time had never been part of the aristocratic daily parade, came to stare.

And yet for most women, especially those of Lady Augusta's *milieu*, Skittles did not officially exist. 'A great deal of mystery was made about these ladies of the "half-world",' Lady Augusta explained. 'In conversation they were only mentioned in private and in a whisper ... It was an unheard-of thing for any respectable dame to acknowledge that she knew such ladies as "Skittles" existed, and the little squares and streets where they lived were completely out-of-bounds.' Even Skittles's famous chestnut hunter was damned by association. The Behrens brothers who kept her mount at Melton Mowbray for her during the winter months did so with such secrecy that they only exercised it at night, and for years only a few close friends ever knew the horse was there at all.

Who were these women, these ghosts of society? And what was this strange 'half world' that they inhabited – the *demi-monde*, in the memorably coined phrase of Alexandre Dumas *fils*. Part of the allure of the courtesan, I think, is that she has always been an ambiguous figure. She is not a mere prostitute, although she is unequivocally a 'professional' woman who accepts money in return for sexual favours.*

---

* Although noting that many courtesans were extremely clever at arithmetic, mastering 'all the difficulties of compound interest and multiplication', Frédéric Loliée, another

Neither is she a mistress, who usually considers herself the lover of just one man – although many courtesans, such as Elizabeth Armistead, were much-beloved mistresses at some point in their careers. Unlike a prostitute, prepared to sell her favours to all-comers, a courtesan always chose her patrons, very often for her own pleasure as well as theirs. Her gifts – of company and conversation as well as of erotic pleasure – were only ever bestowed upon a favoured few, who paid fabulous – sometimes ruinous – sums for them. Laura Bell, the toast of London during the 1850s, was allegedly once given £250,000, the equivalent today of nearly £12 million, to spend a single night with the Nepalese Prince Jung Bahadoor. This may or may not have been literally true,* but such stories, of which there are many, were like oxygen to the courtesan, transforming women of flesh and blood into fabulous, semi-mythical creatures.

The extraordinary physical allure of these women was a various, complex thing. Definitions of female beauty in our own times – usually confined to the face and the figure – seem crude by comparison. Courtesans were prized for many things: for the beauty of their complexions; the eloquence of their eyes; the dazzling whiteness of a neck and shoulders; for their tiny feet and hands, or a ravishing *tournure*. 'Has she thighs?' sighs one of the admirers of Nana, Emile Zola's ficitional portrait of the Parisian actress Blanche d'Antigny (and, yes, she did). More poetically, in sixteenth-century Rome, Tullia d'Aragona was loved for her sweetness, that could 'still the winds of heaven', and for the special way she laughed; Léonide Leblanc, in the Parisian *demi-monde* of the Second Empire, for her irresistible dimples; while the Victorian *fille de joie* Nelly Fowler was much sought-after for her delicious smell. A handkerchief pressed for several nights under 'Sweet

---

French commentator on the Parisian *demi-monde*, wrote that others preferred to be paid in kind. One, who he does not name, 'had seven friends, one for each day in the week, and they had all to provide her with some special commodity of life. One replenished her cellar, the other saw to the fuel, a third paid the milliner's bill, and so forth. The seventh was not endowed with the wealth of this world, as he was a tenor in a small theatre, but he, too, had to pay his way, for he was the chiropodist and manicurist of his mistress. So much was saved.'

* It has been suggested that this was actually the total sum the Prince spent on Laura during the whole period of their acquaintance. The single night is a better story, though.

Nelly's' pillow was considered almost as rare a prize as the lady herself.

It is a striking fact that many courtesans were not conventionally beautiful at all. Harriette Wilson, whose wit and vitality illuminate every sentence of her notorious memoirs, was not especially flatteringly described by Sir Walter Scott as 'a smart, saucy girl with good eyes and dark hair, and the manners of a wild schoolboy'. Cora Pearl was considered by some to be positively ugly: '*l'inexplicable Cora Pearl*' was Zed's unusually dusty opinion; 'I swear that it is a success I have never understood – it existed, but nothing justifies it.' English by birth, in character and in charm, Cora had, according to him, '*la tête d'une ouvrière de la cité*' (the head of a factory worker), hair of a violent yellow colour, '*une voix rauque, des manières excessivement canailles et un ton de valet d'écurie*' (a raucous voice, excessively vulgar manners, and all the style of a stableboy). 'A clown's head', wrote another contemporary. Yet the beauty of Cora's breasts and neck were legendary, as Marie Colombier, her fellow *demi-mondaine*, describes: '*Son buste était irréprochable, sa gorge merveilleuse et digne d'être monlée par quelque illustre artiste de l'antiquité*' (Her bust was faultless, her throat marvellous and worthy of being sculpted by some illustrious artist of antiquity).[3]

Whatever her detractors found to say about her, and there was much, Cora's best revenge was her quite phenomenal success. Her lovers included kings and princes. Her stables – for she too used her equestrian skills to great effect – were the envy of Paris. Her pearls alone (what else?) were said to be worth more than £40,000: a single strand given to her by a besotted lover was bought for £28,000. '*Quel attrait caché, quel philtre secret pourait-elle bien avoir?*' asked Zed, not entirely rhetorically. 'What hidden charm, what secret love philtre could she have had?' Such was the grip that courtesans exercised on the imaginations of the men who loved them, that to the rest of the world, even in recent times, sorcery often seemed the only explanation.

Although I cannot agree with Zed about Cora's ugliness – photographs, although not always the most reliable guide, show her to have had a certain puckish prettiness rather than the Wagnerian handsomeness then in vogue – what is certain is that she, like all successful courtesans, had the gift of being able to make men think she was beautiful. The attitude of mind necessary for this is something Balzac captures brilliantly in his portrait of the courtesan Valerie Marneffe in *La Cousine Bette*, contrasting her with Baroness Hulot, the beautiful but virtuous wife of one of Madame Marneffe's lovers, who no matter how hard she tries will never be able to emulate her rival.

> The next day, Valerie put on her armour, dressing in the way Parisian women contrive to do when they want to make the most of their advantages. She studied her appearance for her work, as a man about to fight a duel rehearses his feints and his parries . . . People think that eighteenth-century beauty spots have been forgotten or are out of fashion; they are mistaken. Today women more skilled than those of past ages, use daring devices to incite men to turn their opera-glasses on them.
>
> One woman is the first to invent the knot of ribbons with a diamond placed in the centre, and she monopolises all eyes for a whole evening. Another revives the hair-net or sticks a dagger in her hair in a way that makes you think of her garter. Another wears black velvet wristbands . . . These supreme efforts, the Austerlitzes of coquetry or love, then become fashionable in lower spheres, just when their happy creators are looking round for new ideas.
>
> For that evening, when Valerie was concerned to be successful, she arranged three beauty spots. First she had her hair rinsed with a lotion which, for a few days, turned her fair hair ash-blonde . . . Then she put on a black velvet neck-band, wide enough to set off the whiteness of her bosom.
>
> The third beauty spot could be compared to the black silk patches that our grandmothers used to wear. Valerie placed the prettiest little rosebud in the middle of her bodice, just above the whalebone, in the daintiest of little hollows. It was enough to make any man under thirty lower his eyes.
>
> 'I look good enough to eat,' she said to herself.[4]

It was indeed a kind of sorcery; and only an exceptional woman could pull it off. Physical beauty might have been enough to attract a lover, but on its own it was not enough to keep him. Intelligence, wit and style counted just as much. 'A goose like Nana would do very bad business,' wrote the journalist Georges Ohnet sourly of Zola's heroine; 'it requires more intelligence to succeed in being a whore kept in luxury than to make a future in a respectable business.'[5] And for many women, of course, it was just that: a business. Adèle Courtois, a contemporary and friend of Cora Pearl's, once frankly confessed that she had no real vocation for her occupation, nor the requisite attainments for it. A professional lover, she used to say, required two digestions and the strength of four seamstresses.

Continual inventiveness was another requirement. Skittles, with her famous pork pie hat and Poole *paletot*,* was by no means the first courtesan to set fashions. The eighteenth-century actress† Ann Cately was so elegant in her dress that a new word was coined to describe her effect: 'She wore her hair plain over her forehead, in an even line almost to her eyebrows . . . and the word was with all the ladies to have their hair Cately-fied.'[6] Her contemporary and fellow actress Mrs Abingdon was also regarded as a barometer of taste. If Mrs Abingdon adopted such *outré* fashions as the French custom of sprinkling red powder in the hair, or adopted the outrageously tall head-dress known as the *ziggurat*, then all the ladies of rank and fashion immediately rushed to copy her. 'As she possesses an exquisite taste, she is constantly employed in driving about the capital to give her advice concerning the modes and fashion of the day,' wrote one commentator. 'She is called in like a physician, and recompensed as if she were an artist . . . A great number of people of fashion treat her in the most familiar manner, and as if she were their equal.'[7] Also in the eighteenth century Gertrude Mahon, the 'Bird of Paradise', was famous for her extravagant hats. Perdita Robinson, at one time the paramour of the Prince of Wales, drew all eyes the first time she went to Ranelagh Gardens in her 'singularly plain and Quaker-like' habit. Cora Pearl even had a drink named after her, 'The Tears of Cora Pearl' (although I don't know whether she herself ever drank it).

Courtesans did not follow the fashion; they *were* the fashion. For the young bloods of the nineteenth century, to be seen riding in the

---

* A kind of loose cloak.
† At this time the words 'actress' and 'courtesan' were virtually synonymous; see page 39.

Park with Skittles, or attending the opera with one of 'the Three Graces', as Harriette Wilson and her companions were known, was the apogee of social success: 'It was the fashion for young men to procure letters from any celebrated demirep, and shew them amongst friends, boasting of their success,' wrote Harriette's friend, and later implacable enemy, Julia Johnstone.[8]

When Skittles first made her appearance in Hyde Park in 1861, some twenty years before the period of Lady Augusta's recollections, she was not riding a horse at all, but daringly driving herself in a miniature phaeton drawn by 'two of the handsomest brown ponies eye ever beheld'. In those days the fashionable parade did not take place along Rotten Row, which marks the southern perimeter of the Park, but along Ladies' Mile, as it is still called, beside the Serpentine. The fashionable hours then were between five and seven. The Park was always crowded at this time, and when the press became too much for Skittles and her phaeton, she would take herself off to a more deserted thoroughfare, the road leading from Apsley House to Kensington, 'where she could more freely exhibit her ponies' marvellous action, and talk to her male acquaintances with becoming privacy'.

But as the fame of her beauty and her equipage spread, so too did the crowds. A letter to *The Times* the following year complained in mock-serious tones of the congestion she was causing in Hyde Park,[9] and everywhere that they were able to flourish, fashionable courtesans became the celebrities of their day. A hundred years earlier, eager sightseers had regularly flocked to watch Skittles's eighteenth-century sister, Kitty Fisher, eat supper in her box at Vauxhall Gardens, while it is said that when Laura Bell attended the opera in the 1850s, the entire house would rise to watch her leave. In Italy in the sixteenth century huge crowds would gather to watch Rome's famous courtesans as they made their way to Mass on Sundays. In his '*Ragionamenti*', the poet Aretino describes the enormous entourages, as richly dressed and liveried as possible, that accompanied the wealthiest and most favoured. He mentions Matrema,* 'the first courtesan in Rome' in the

---

* 'Matrema' was short for '*Matrema non voi*,' which in the Roman dialect of the day means, with somewhat ironic charm, 'My mother does not want me to.'

early 1620s, as the most ostentatious: 'And when Matrema goes there, with more than ten maids and as many pages and girls, she is accompanied by great princes, marquesses, ambassadors and dukes.'[10]

As these public displays suggest, a courtesan's notoriety and her wealth were both important aspects of her dangerous appeal. In the *Vanto della Cortigiana Ferrarese* (The Boast of the Ferrarese Courtesan – attributed to Giambattista Verini) Beatrice of Ferrara's* marvellous house is described in detail, full of such quantities of jewels, gold and other luxuries that its entrance had a specially-made iron door to safeguard them. Inside was a sideboard laden with silver, and walls and benches covered with the richest hangings and tapestries, while Beatrice's own apparel was of cloth of gold, velvet or silk richly encrusted with pearls and other precious stones. Her household linen alone, 'as delicate and white as snow' and sensuously perfumed with civet and musk, was worth a fortune; her bedcover so splendid 'no pope had ever possessed one to equal it'. Perhaps most striking of all her possessions, however, was her coach and six: 'The coach, a great luxury at the time, was carved and covered with gold and arabesques of blue and white, and the horses were "as white as snow". Indeed it seems likely that Beatrice did not exaggerate when she said that people crowded to their windows and balconies when she drove by.'[11]

Although these descriptions might involve some poetic licence, a comparison with the inventory of the possessions of Julia Lombardo, who like Beatrice was also a prominent courtesan during the Italian Renaissance (she is referred to, marvellously, as *'somtuosa meretrize'* – sumptuous courtesan), shows that the poet was not exaggerating. This extraordinary document, which dates from 1542, came to light in the archives of the Istituzionii di Ricòvero e di Educazione in Italy, and is thought to be the only existing inventory of a courtesan of this period. In Julia's sumptuously decorated house are carved, gilded and canopied beds embellished with hangings and richly embroidered coverlets, shelves crammed with glass, porcelain, majolica, books, sculpture, gold and enamelled *objets d'art*, twenty-eight paintings,

---

* Beatrice's real name was Beatrice de Bonis. Georgina Masson believes she may have been the model for Raphael's famous nude half-length picture of a courtesan, known as the *Fornarina*.

crystal chandeliers, a harpsichord and numerous items of jewellery.

The most striking items, however, are six enormous chests, or *cassoni*, in the principal bedroom, and eight slightly smaller chests in the adjoining dressing room, each one crammed with clothing and precious fabrics. In the smaller chests were found sixty-five *braccia** of fabric, and silk and lace trimmings. Of the six larger chests, two were filled with bed and table linen and sixteen rugs, while the rest were crammed with women's clothing, including fifteen pairs of shoes, a pair of gloves, seventeen *braghesse de donna* (pantaloons), five *velli* (veils), eight pairs of stockings, six purses, five pairs of sleeves, eighteen *fazuoli* or *fazoletti* (handkerchiefs), eleven *scuffie* (caps) and no fewer than sixty-four *camicie*. *Camicie* were the flowing, fine white blouses, usually beautifully embroidered, which peeped decoratively through the slashed sleeves and bodices of women's dresses. An upper-class *gentildonna* of the period might have expected to have thirty *camicie* in her trousseau.

It is not the sheer quantity of dresses and fabrics alone which amazes, but their extraordinary quality and opulence. The description of Julia Lombardo's wardrobe reads like a passage from the *Arabian Nights*:

> *A fabulous assortment of fabrics and furs filled her* cassoni: *silks, satins and velvets in a spectrum of colours, linen from Rheims, 'tabin' – taffeta imported from Baghdad, 'ormesin ganzante' – fine, iridescent silk made in the Persian city of Ormuz, 'camocha' – a precious oriental fabric, wools of different weight and texture, 'dimito' – a type of corduroy, muffs and garments lined with sable and fox. There were 'maneghe' à la mode: striped, slashed and cut. What to wear, what to wear! The 'scuffia d'oro a rede' or the one 'con sbalzo de tella d'arzento', or something simple, with a little embroidery?*[12]

In France during the Second Empire the profession of courtesan reached new heights of refinement – and expense. Zed attests to the extraordinary quantities of money that were required to keep up this luxury – '*une luxe qui dépasse tout ce que l'on peut rêver*' (a luxury which surpasses all one's wildest dreams) – and the elegance which

---

* A *braccio* = c.59 centimetres.

was so much the courtesan's trademark. Like the fictional Madame Marneffe, Parisian courtesans were supremely skilled at dressing the part, and they elevated the creation of the alluring semi-*déshabille* – dress for the boudouir or the bedroom – into nothing less than an art form. '*Les toilettes de boudoir, les déshabillés galants, les dessous émoustillants, les fouillis de dentelles, de soie et de batiste, le luxe de linge et d'accessoires à vous donner la chair de poule*', 'Zed' wrote almost feverishly. '*Je renonce à les décrire.*' (The toilettes for the boudoir, the romantic negligées and tantalising undergarments, the tangles of silks and muslin, the sheer luxury of lingerie and other accessories would give you goose pimples. I cannot even begin to describe them.)

> *Toute cette artillerie, tous ces piments, tous ces assaisonnements exquis, vulgarisés depuis, étaient, à cette époque, l'apanage exlusif de ces demoiselles, qui les avaient inventés, qui les possaient jusqu'au dernier degré de la perfection, qui en jouaient avec un science, avec un art de la mise en scène admirable, et elles parais-saient d'autant plus précieuses, d'autant plus désirables, d'autant plus charmant, que les femmes de la societé, même les plus éche-velées, n'en avaient encore qu'une trop vague et trop lointaine notion.*[13] (This whole artillery, all these spices and exquisite seasonings, which were later vulgarised, were at that time the exclusive preserve of these ladies, who had invented them, and who possessed them to the last degree of perfection, who played with them as if it were a science, but with such an admirable art for the *mise en scène*, that it made them all the more precious, all the more desirable, all the more charming, so much so that the respectable women of society, even the most daring, still have not even the vaguest and most distant notion of how it was done.)

The courtesans' extravagance knew no bounds. In the autumn of 1868, when the actress Blanche d'Antigny set off from Paris for the fashion-able watering hole at Baden, her departure was recorded in the *Gazette des Étrangers*. That morning the rue des Écuries-d'Artois was com-pletely jammed, the reporter noted, not by Blanche's entourage, but by the thirty-seven toilettes which she thought necessary to take with her on the sojourn, each one carefully arranged in its own carriage.[14]

To a courtesan there was only one thing which mattered more than her wardrobe, and that was her jewels. Many courtesans have been famed for their jewellery, but the prize must surely go to La Belle Otero, the Spanish dancer and courtesan of the *Belle Epoque*. 'No man who has an account at Cartier's could be regarded as ugly,' she is alleged to have said, and in her time she knew scores of such gentlemen, who over the years provided her with a fortune in jewels. The most famous of her pieces – which included three exquisite necklaces which had belonged, respectively, to the Empress Eugenie, the Empress of Austria and the courtesan Leonide Leblanc – was a diamond bolero created for her by Cartier from ten million francs' worth of jewels 'set into a gold frame with thirty large diamonds hanging at the end like huge tears, and a pair of diamond ropes each glistening with twenty stones, secured at the centre by a large diamond clasp'. During her dancing career this extraordinary garment – if it can be called such – was kept in the vaults of the Crédit Lyonnais and brought out only on special occasions, when it was carried in a special reinforced carriage, ostentatiously guarded by two armed policemen.

A courtesan was the ultimate luxury good, and advertising the fact made good business sense. But what did it take to maintain this kind of luxury? Courtesans were indeed exceptional women: forces of nature, as rare and scintillating as their fabulous jewels. When Zed, that experienced connoisseur of women, mused about the fascinations of Cora Pearl, he could have been speaking of any of the great courtesans of history: '*Ce fut une individualité à part, une spécimen d'un autre race, une phénomène bizarre et étonnant. Et c'est, peut-être, ce qui explique sa notoriété, ce qui a été cause de son prestige.*' (Hers was an extraordinary individuality, as if she were a specimen of another race, a bizarre, astonishing phenomenon. And it is this, perhaps, which explains her notoriety, which was in turn the reason for her prestige.)

Throughout history this has always been so. In ancient Greece, a period in which women were so rigorously confined to the private arenas of life that at times they appear hardly to have existed at all, some of the only individuals known to us by name are courtesans. The hetaeras, as these upper-class courtesans were known, formed a distinct class all of their own, clearly distinguishable from their more easily available sisters. This lower class of women began with the plain *pornai* (meaning 'common whore', from which our own word 'pornography' derives) and streetwalkers, and their homelessness (and therefore exposure to public gaze) is denoted by a number of baldly descriptive terms: 'bridge-woman' (*gephuris*), 'runner' (*dromas*), 'wanderer' (*peripolas*), 'alley-treader' (*spodesilaura*), 'ground-beater' and even 'foot-soldier'. Higher up the scale were the *auletrides*, or flute girls, who were musicians as well as prostitutes. The *auletrides* played an important role at the symposium, for which they were hired to entertain the guests with enticing music at the beginning of the drinking party, as well as with sex after it. The hetaeras, who also took part in symposia, had a far more personal role in these events. As their name, which in Greek literally means 'companion', suggests, hetaeras were hired not only for sex, but also to provide company for the male guests for the evening: to drink with them, flirt with them, but most importantly to provide witty and entertaining conversation.

Over and above the ordinary hetaeras, however, came another category of women, the great *megalomisthoi*, or 'big-fee' hetaeras. It is these women – among them Laïs the elder, Laïs the younger, Thaïs, Sinope and Aspasia, the mistress of Pericles – whose beauty and talents were so great that their names, doings and *bons mots* have come down to us in literature, so earning them a place in history. Uniquely amongst the women of ancient Greece, the *megalomisthoi* hetaeras were able to achieve some measure of independence, moral as well as financial. One famous courtesan, Neaera, was so beloved by her patrons that they clubbed together to buy her freedom. '*Autēn autēs kurian*', she was able to describe her status thereafter: 'Herself mistress of herself'.

Although it is debatable whether or not any woman was allowed to own property in ancient Athens, in practice the *megalomisthoi* were indeed women of substance, and there are many references in literature to their houses. In Xenophon's *Memoirs of Socrates* there is an account of the philosopher's visit to the house of the beautiful Theodote, a woman of mysteriously independent means. Socrates is amazed at the lavishness of her household, 'noticing that she was richly dressed, and that her mother at her side was also wearing fine clothes and jewellery, and that she had many lovely-looking maidservants also well-looked-after and that her house was furnished lavishly'.[15] She was, of course, a courtesan.

Perhaps the most famous, and certainly the richest, of all the great hetaeras of ancient Greece was Phryne. She is alleged to have modelled for the sculptor Praxiteles, whose revolutionary female nude, the first of its kind, became known as the *Venus of Cnidus*, and also for Apelles, whose *Birth of Venus* was the model for Botticelli's later version of the same scene. When Phryne was accused of profaning the Eleusinian mysteries, the orator Hyperides, who defended her, threw aside her robe in court, showing off her perfect loveliness, and so won the verdict in her favour. According to Callistratus in his work *On Hetaeras*, Phryne's many lovers made her so rich that after the Macedonians had laid waste the city of Thebes in 479 BC, she single-handedly paid for the city wall to be rebuilt out of her own funds. The citizens put up an inscription which read: 'Alexander may have knocked it down, but Phryne the hetaera got it back up again.'[16]

There is no doubt that the fierce rules governing the seclusion of the citizen-wives of Athens left an enormous emotional and intellectual arena open to the hetaera, a sphere of influence of far more subtlety and power than that which sexual availability alone could have achieved. These conditions find an exact parallel in sixteenth-century Venice, which has also been much vaunted as a 'golden age' of courtesanry.

While visiting the city-state at the end of the sixteenth century, the Elizabethan traveller Thomas Coryat was struck by the unusually severe restrictions imposed by Venetian husbands on their wives: 'For the Gentlemen do even coope up their wives alwaies within the walles of their houses ... So that you shall very seldome see a Venetian Gentleman's wife but either at the solemnization of a great marriage, or at the Christning of a Iew, or late in the evening rowing in a Gondola.'[17] Another English traveller and writer, Fynes Moryson, made the same observation, remarking with some insight that the huge number of prostitutes in Venice was directly linked to this practice, and was not merely a product of the republic's infamous '*luxuria*'. Men, he wrote, are driven

*with fierce affections to forbidden lusts, and to those most which
are forbidden, most kept from them, and with greatest cost and
danger to be obtayned. And because they are barred not only the
speech and conversation but the least sight of their love (all which
are allowed men of other nations) they are carryed rather with a
blynde rage of passion . . . to adore them as Images, rather than
love them as wemen. And as nowe they spare no cost, and will
runne great dangers to obtayne their lustfull desyres, so would
they persue them to very madnes, had they not the most naturall
remedy of this passion ready at hand to allay their desyres, namely
Harlotts, whom they call Curtizans, having beauty and youth and
whatsoever they can imagine in their mistres.*[18]

When Fynes Moryson was writing, in the early sixteenth century, the
term 'courtesan' was a relatively recent one. The word, which derives
from the female version of the Italian '*cortegiano*' or courtier, was
coined to describe the women associated with the luxurious and
dissolute world of the Papal Court in Rome a hundred years earlier.
The Renaissance popes, who had only ever been nominally celibate,
frequently took these women as their mistresses. The Master of Cere-
monies at the Papal Court, who was responsible for hiring them,
referred to them picturesquely as 'our respectable prostitutes', but they
frequently became much more than that.

Alexander VI, who was elected Pope in 1492 when he was sixty-one,
was already the father of no fewer than six children by his lover Vanozza
dei Catenei.* He later fell in love with Giulia Farnese, who joined him
in the Vatican when she was just seventeen, and later became the model
for Raphael's fresco of the Madonna in the Pope's private apartments.
By the beginning the sixteenth century the usual term for any high-
class prostitute, *meretrize*, was beginning to be replaced by the politer
cortegiana, irrespective of any position she might hold at court.

Politer still, and with important social and legal implications for the
woman concerned, was the term '*cortegiana honesta*', meaning 'honest'
or 'honoured' courtesan. The *cortegiani honesti* of late-sixteenth-
century Venice surpassed even the fame and beauty of the courtesans

---

* Two of these children became especially notorious: Lucrezia and Cesare Borgia.

of Rome. Some idea of the exquisite refinement of the world created by these women is given in a letter to a friend by a Florentine, Niccolo Martelli. He wrote of 'the royal way in which they treat you, their graceful manners, their courtesy and the luxury with which they surround you – dressed as they are in crimson and gold, scented, and exquisitely shod – with their compliments they make you feel another being, a great lord, and while you are with them you do not envy even the inhabitants of paradise'.[19]

It was not only for their sumptuous appearance and seductive manners that these women made their mark. Like the *megalomisthoi* hetaeras of ancient Greece two thousand years earlier, the *cortegiana honesta* was courted for her intellectual and musical talents; for the beauty of her mind quite as much as for her love-making skills.

The very cultivation of these talents, however, was a source of deep mistrust amongst the male writers and travellers to Venice who recorded them. A 'public tongue', it was widely believed, was synonymous with a dishonest woman. Even the propriety of playing music was questioned by some.* As Thomas Coryat warned his readers:

> *Moreover shee will endevour to enchaunt thee partly with her melodious notes that shee warbles out upon her lute, which shee fingers with as laudable a stroake as many men that are excellent professors in the noble science of Musicke; and partly with that hart-tempting harmony of her voice. Also thou wilt finde the Venetian Cortezan (if she be a selected woman indeede) a good Rhetorician, and a most elegant discourser, so that if shee cannot move thee with all these aforsaid delights, shee will assay thy constancy with her Rhetoricall tongue.*[20]

A source of still more anxiety was the fact that a successful courtesan's wealth and instinctive sense of style made her indistinguishable, as far

---

* In her essay on Julia Lombardo, 'A Portrait by Property', Cathy Santore notes the existence of a green harpsichord in the Casa Loncini. 'Can such an item be considered necessarily *cortigianesca*? It can, indeed, in both meanings of the word, first as pertaining to ladies of the court, and as pertaining to ladies of pleasure. There appears to have been a variance of opinion regarding the propriety of female musicianship, and curiously, it was, for the most part, reserved as a pastime of women of those two social groups.'

as appearances were concerned, from any chastely married woman of the upper classes. Cesare Vecellio's costume book of the period noted:

> *because of the way they dress, courtesans and* donne di partito *very much resemble married women; they wear rings on their fingers like married women and therefore anyone who is not more than aware can be deceived ... The train of their dress is very long; indeed at times some of these courtesans dress like widows and look very much like Venetian noblewomen to those who are not familiar with their condition.*[21]

Frequent attempts were made to redress this dangerous ambiguity. Sumptuary laws were passed which severely limited the grandeur of the clothes a courtesan could wear (although, as Julia Lombardo's inventory shows, they frequently went unheeded). A ruling of 1562 stated:

> *The prostitutes of this city are not allowed to wear gold, silver, or silk as part of their dress on any part of their body, exception being made for caps of pure silk. They are not allowed to wear chains, rings with or without gemstones, or any ornament in their ears, so that, in fact they are under all circumstances forbidden the use of gold, silver and silk, as well as that of jewels of any kind, genuine or false, inside and outside the house and even outside this city.*

Numerous attempts were also made to regulate their movements in public. A special decree, originally formulated in 1539 but reappearing in 1571, 1582 and 1613, related to church attendances:

> *Nor may the said courtesans or prostitutes enter a church on the day of its festival or during the principal celebration thereof ... On other truly ordinary days the above mentioned are in no church whatever allowed to stand, kneel, or sit on the benches that in the church are occupied by noblewomen and by our female citizens of good and honest standing, but they must keep apart and at a distance from them, taking care not to give offence to other decent persons.*[22]

The *cortegiana honesta*, however, considered herself to be quite distinct from an ordinary courtesan or *meretrize*, and refused to acknowledge that the strict sumptuary laws and other rules which so restricted the lives of those women should apply to them.

The greatest and most famous of all the Venetian *cortegiani honesti* was Veronica Franco. Born into a good bourgeois family in 1546, she first appears in the notorious catalogue which listed 'All the principal and most honoured Courtesans of Venice, with their names and those of their procuresses (in a number of cases their own mothers), the places where they live, the quarters of the city where they are, and how much money Gentlemen have to pay, who desire to enter into their favour.' Veronica and her mother Paola, who was also a courtesan, are listed here for the relatively low fee of two scudi (the lowest charge given is one scudo; the highest thirty scudi). But at the height of her fame it was said that just one kiss from her was worth six scudi, while '*la négociation entière*', as Montaigne once delicately put it, was a fabulous fifty scudi.

Veronica was not only charming and witty, she was extremely beautiful too. A portrait by Tintoretto shows her to have been a classical beauty, with a perfect heart-shaped face and reddish-gold hair. She was a noted poet and writer in her lifetime, the friend and confidante of some of the best-known and most powerful literary figures in Italy. She was also naturally passionate, and it was this, perhaps, more than all her other talents, which caused the twenty-two-year-old Henri de Valois – passing through Venice in 1574 on his way to France, where he was to be crowned King after the unexpected death of his brother Charles IX – to choose her, alone of all the courtesans in Venice, to entertain him during his visit.

> Cosi dolce e gustevole divento,
> quando mi trovo in letto,
> da cui amata e gradita mi sento,
> che quel mio piacer vince ogni diletto . . .
>
> (So sweet and appetising do I become,
> When I find myself in bed,

With he who loves and welcomes me,
That our pleasure surpasses all delight . . .)

Veronica wrote in one of her most tenderly erotic verses, which was addressed to her friend and lover, the poet Marco Vernier; 'Phoebus who served the goddess of love, received from her recompense so sweet that it meant more to him than to be a god . . . I too am versed in those same arts, and am so practised in the pleasures of the bed that there I surpass by far Apollo's mastery of the arts. And my singing and writing are forgotten by those who have tried me in this guise that Venus shares with her devotees.'[23]

In France half a century later, another remarkable woman, Ninon de l'Enclos, was to share both Veronica Franco's literary ambitions and her natural passions. Like Veronica, Ninon was so skilled in the pleasures of the bed that she came to be regarded as France's foremost authority on the matter. 'One needs a hundred times more *esprit* in order to love properly than to command armies,' she once said. Born in Paris in 1620, Ninon was the product of an unhappy marriage between a forbiddingly religious mother, Marie-Barbe de la Marche and a charming, but libertine, cavalry-officer father, Henri de l'Enclos. Henri, who was in love with a much younger married woman, committed a murder and was forced into exile when Ninon was twelve years old. The scandal, and Ninon's lack of a dowry, meant that she was unlikely to make a respectable marriage. The one thing which her father had bequeathed her, however, was an education: she was well-versed not only in music and dancing, but in philosophy and literature as well.

Ninon embarked on a series of affairs, choosing men who were both aristocratic and intellectual, and after the death of her mother she openly became a courtesan. Her patrons included the young Comte Gaspard de Coligny, the Abbé Dessiat, Saint-Evremond, La Rochefoucauld and the Marquis de Sévigné (his son would have liked to follow in his father's footsteps, but Ninon, who was an exacting lover, is said to have dismissed him contemptuously as having 'a soul of boiled beef, a body of damp paper, with a heart like a pumpkin fricasseed in snow'). Soon Ninon became famous not only for her many liaisons, but also for the brilliance of her *salon*, which was frequented by all the great thinkers and writers of the day, among them Molière, Scarron, Madame de Maintenon, Queen Christina of Sweden and the thirteen-year-old Voltaire (to whom Ninon left two thousand francs in her will with which to buy books).

'*Notre-Dame des Amours*', as Horace Walpole nicknamed her, was perhaps most famous of all for a *salon* of an altogether more exclusive kind. Later in life she was to put her own considerable *esprit* to good effect by creating a School of Gallantry, a kind of finishing school for young aristocrats. Ninon's bedroom was the principal classroom, but it was not only in the physical techniques of love-making that she passed on her expertise. She also advised these young men about the psychology of women: how to court and seduce them, with conversation and charm as well as with caresses, and how to handle and care for a mistress once the seduction was complete. 'Remember, there are moments when women would rather be treated a little roughly than with too much consideration.' She even advised on the best and most courteous way in which to end an affair: 'Should you be the one who ceases to love first,' she is said to have remarked, 'let the woman have the advantage of making the break and appearing cruel . . . A woman who is through with a man will give him up for anything except another woman.'[24]

Of course, it was not only men who longed to know these secrets. A courtesan's extraordinary sexual success made her quite as fascinating to women. 'Nothing equals the curiosity of virtuous women on this subject,' reflected Balzac, and Ninon, certainly, was often approached by young women, just as eager as their brothers to receive the benefits of her expertise in the arts of love. While she is not known to have given practical lessons to women, Ninon is said to have advised them whenever she could. 'How large should a woman's breast be to attract a lover?' she was once asked. To which she replied simply, 'Large enough to fill the hand of an honest man.'[25]

It is not surprising that one of the most memorable descriptions of a courtesan ever written should have been by another woman. In *My Apprenticeships* Colette describes her friendship, in her music-hall days, with La Belle Otero: 'I might have been able to garner, perhaps, from lips more august than hers, words of wisdom rich in echoes that would have led to my greater profit and enlightenment!' wrote Colette,

> *but august lips are not so prodigal. I have asked for compensations from the unknown and the come-by-chance, and they have some-times given them to me, rather in the way the coconut tree bestows its nuts – plump on the head! Madame Otero . . . had not the faintest resemblance to a coconut tree. She was purely ornamental. Like all luxuries, she was curiously and variously instructive, and merely to hear her made me rejoice that the early stages in one of my careers should have set her in my way.*

The public figure of Carolina Otero, rigid in her gala corsets and her famous breastplate of jewels (after dinner with her one night, Jean Cocteau wrote in his diary that she seemed to have as much chance of getting out of her impossible clothes as an oyster from its shell), was like an exotic wild animal escaped from a zoo. 'A motionless icon – alive as a tree laden with hoar frost is alive, only in its glittering,' was how Colette described her, although she infinitely preferred

> *another Lina, no less full of condescension, who used to call out to me familiarly: 'Coming to eat my puchero on Zaturday? Come early and I'll play you a game of bezique before dinner.'*
>
> *I answered her with the same vague familiarity, and from the moment I set foot upon her doorstep I was happy. A child seldom finds enchantment in the actual palace it has imagined for itself beforehand. Madame Otero's house never disappointed me. Its owner was like a caryatid, carved in the fashion of the period . . . You cannot be intimate with a caryatid, you can only gaze at it . . .*
>
> *To make everything perfect in my eyes it was enough that my hostess should be enjoying her late afternoon in silk stockings and well-worn mules, a chemise and a petticoat underneath her teagown, which she took off as often as not and replaced with a*

bathwrap. The 192 cards and the rosewood marker in front of her, an ashtray at her right hand, a glass of anisette at her left, and she was queen.

'Zit down,' she would say. 'Cut. Maria, give her a glass of anizette.' Her companion, Maria Mendoza, a decayed Spanish gentlewoman of good family . . . obeyed with great and slightly terrified haste, and the game of bezique, stern enemy of conversation, began.

'Two hundred and fifty to zay . . . Two hundred and fifty to zay . . . Two hundred and fifty zaid . . . Fifteen hundred!'

She was perfectly well able to pronounce her 's's' correctly, but she kept this small effort of articulation for the stage and her more select acquaintance.

As the excitement of the game increased, the bathwrap would fall carelessly open, and the chemise would slip.

Deep in the shadowy hollow between her breasts – which were of a curious shape, reminding one of elongated lemons, firm and upturned at the tips – a jewel drooped, hooked on apparently at random, sometimes real, sometimes false, seven rows of glowing, pinkish pearls, or a string of stage glass beads, or a heavy diamond. Only the smell of the puchero and an imperious appetite could tear Lina from her bezique. Standing up, tall and supply erect, her waist still slim above a rump that was her especial pride, she would yawn loudly, thump her exacting stomach with her fist and, followed by her guests, would go downstairs.

No men were invited to these intimate occasions. Over the *puchero*, a rich peasant pot of meat, beans and vegetables, Otero's queenliness would melt, 'and a kind of happy innocence took its place'. 'Her teeth, her eyes, her glossy lips shone like a girl's. There are few beautiful women who can guzzle without loss of prestige. Lina did not push away her plate until she had emptied it four or five times. A little strawberry water-ice, a cup of coffee, and up she sprang, fastening a pair of castanets to her thumbs.'

From ten o'clock until past two in the morning, Carolina Otero would dance and sing for her guests, although Colette always suspected that on these occasions she cared little for her guests' enjoyment, thinking only of her own. The transformation was extraordinary.

> *From a handsome forty she became a lively seventeen. The bath-wrap tossed aside, she danced in her petticoat, which was of brocaded silk with a flounce five metres round, the only garment essential to Spanish dancing. Soaked with sweat, her fine lawn chemise clung to her loins. Her moist skin gave off a delicate scent, a dusky scent, predominantly of sandalwood, that was more subtle than herself. There was nothing base in her violent and wholly selfish pleasure; it was born of a true passion for rhythm and music. She would snatch up her sauce-stained table-napkin and wipe herself vigorously, face, neck and damp armpits, then dance again, sing again: 'Ziz one? D'you know it?' Her feet were not very light, but her face tilted backwards over her shoulders, the muscles of her waist rippling above the powerful loins, the savage, swaying furrow of her naked back could defy the harshest glare. A body that had defied sickness, ill-usage and the passage of time – a well-nourished body, sleek of sinew, bright of skin, amber by day, white by night – I have always told myself that I would, some day, with due care and detachment, describe it and its arrogant decline.*[26]

Perhaps one of the definitions of a courtesan should be that she was a woman who dared to break the rules. The rules of sexual morality gave way first, but in their wake fell other, perhaps more far-reaching barriers: of class, society and female propriety. Courtesans were shunned by 'respectable' society, and yet, despite itself, society – men and women alike – was fascinated by them.

Here again is the scene as Skittles – or Katie, or Kitty, or Skittsie, as she was known to her lovers – waited to make her entrance along Rotten Row in Hyde Park in 1861:

> *Chairs are placed along it on either side; the best* partis *that England knows, the toadies who cling to them, the snobs who copy them – all sit there, watching for Anonyma. Expectation is*

raised to its highest pitch, a handsome woman drives rapidly by in a carriage drawn by thoroughbred ponies of surpassing shape and action, the driver is attired in the pork pie hat and the Poole paletot introduced by Anonyma, but, alas!, she caused no effect at all, for she is not Anonyma; she is only the Duchess of A–, the Marchioness of B–, the Countess of C–, or some other of Anonyma's many eager imitators. The crowd, disappointed, reseat themselves and wait. At last their patience is rewarded. Anonyma and her ponies appear, and they are satisfied. She threads her way dexterously, with an unconscious air, through the throng, commented upon by hundreds who admire and hundreds who envy her. She pulls up her ponies to speak to an acquaintance, and her carriage is instantly surrounded by a multitude; she turns, and drives back again towards Apsley House, and then – away into the unknown world, nobody knows whither.[27]

That unknown world – the English *demi-monde* – is the subject of this book. Much has been written about its counterparts in Paris, Venice or Rome, but this is not the case in England. Why is it that Zed and Frédéric Loliée, to name but two of the most affectionately prolix chroniclers of the French *grand bicherie*, have no equivalent in our literature? Even our vocabulary for it is a borrowed one. And yet such a thing most certainly existed. Englishmen, I suspect, did not care to remember their misspent youth with quite the same affection as their Continental brothers were inclined to do. When Mrs Arbuthnot asked the Duke of Wellington if what was written about him in Harriette Wilson's memoirs was true, he became conveniently vague. 'He had known Harriette Wilson, he admitted, "a great number of years ago, so long that he did not think he should remember her again, that he had never seen her since he married tho' he had frequently given her money when she wrote to beg for it".'[28]

Courtesans may have been admired, emulated and even courted in England, yet our thinking about them is confused. Like Wellington, we have chosen barely to remember them, far less celebrate them, despite the vivid testaments – in memoirs, journals and letters – that they have left behind. Harriette Wilson's *Memoirs*, it is true, are not conventionally reliable ('dates make ladies nervous, and stories dry'), but something else, some other genius, is undoubtedly at work in them. Written with an express intent to blackmail, they are exaggerated, partial, and frequently mischievous, but nonetheless there is something absolutely authentic about them. A distillation of that spirit – pure essence of Harriette – comes down to us which is perhaps more telling than plain facts.

Her contemporaries could not see it this way. Not only was Harriette a woman, but she was a woman of ill-repute, so her testament was doubly damned. Cora Pearl and Sophia Baddeley, who have also left memoirs, suffered the same fate. Despite the enormous *succès de scandale* of all three books when they were first published, they were at the same time dismissed in the most contemptuous terms. Their content alone – the life of 'vice' – was enough to condemn them. Cora Pearl's *Memoirs*, a curiously fastidious document by today's standards, was nothing more than a 'list of dirty laundry', complained one contemporary reader, while Sophia Baddeley's entrancing life story, complete with its shopping lists, household accounts and millinery bills, was also thought to have been written with a view to blackmail, although not one shred of evidence exists to support this view.

The fact that the authors earned money from their unedifying life stories was, in the eyes of many, just as bad. The few readers who could get past the books' scandalous contents, and were reluctantly forced to concede some of their qualities, could only conclude that a man must have been behind them. In Harriette's case it was her rackety husband, Colonel Rochfort; while Sophia Baddeley's *Memoirs*, written by the splendid Mrs Eliza Steele, have sometimes been attributed, for no particularly good reason, to a second-rate hack, Alexander Bicknell.

The five remarkable women through whose lives I will attempt to draw a portrait of this strange world span a 'long' nineteenth century, the time of the *demi-monde*'s greatest florescence in England. Harriette Wilson's *Memoirs* were published in 1824, almost exactly halfway through this period. Sophia Baddeley, the earliest of the five, first came to the public eye as a young actress in the 1770s, while the last, Catherine Walters ('Skittles'), although essentially a figure of the Victorian world, did not die until after the First World War, in 1920. What was it about this period that made it both possible and necessary? While there are many similarities between the rules of English courtesanry and those which existed elsewhere, the conditions for women in nineteenth-century England were very different from those in other countries at other times in history. Far from being rigorously repressed and cloistered, as women were in ancient Greece or sixteenth-century Italy for example, it could be argued that the nineteenth century was a time of unprecedented improvements in the status and education of women in England.

Anxieties about female freedom, perhaps for this reason, were just as acute. The 'half-world', which existed because of attempts to keep these women safely locked away from the rest of 'respectable' society, was never quite able to achieve that. Even if she was only whispered about illicitly by society ladies such as Lady Augusta Fane and her friends, the way a courtesan dressed, her clothes, her hair, her sense of personal style, frequently permeated the would-be impregnable wall between the *monde* and the *demi-monde*. Like saucy sprites, they had an inconvenient habit of leaping out of the Pandora's Box to which they had been relegated. But that was not all. Although courtesans were unequivocally morally reprehensible in the eyes of decent women, it did not take any great leap of imagination to see that the independence and sexual expression which they claimed were things of which ordinary women, for the most part, could not even dream.

While sixteenth-century Venice had its sumptuary laws and other regulations to keep courtesans safely in their place, no such limitations were available in nineteenth-century Britain. The boundaries between the two worlds were confusingly blurred. When the French courtesan and actress Sarah Bernhardt came to London in 1879 she was lionised, not only by ordinary theatre-goers – some of whom were said to have knelt at her feet as she left the theatre – but by aristocratic society as well. The Prince of Wales, who was a fervent admirer of Sarah's, made her fashionable, and it was allegedly his influence which lifted the ban on Alexandre Dumas's play about a courtesan, *La Dame aux camélias*, thus making it possible for Sarah to perform what was to become one of her most famous roles. Bernhardt found London delightful, the food excellent and the people 'charming and full of humour' (much to the irritation of her French friends). According to her memoirs, she was called on by women as well as men during her visit, and invited for dinners and rides in Rotten Row by the cream of London society. But by no means everyone condoned this acceptance of such a woman in their midst. 'London has gone mad over the principal actress of the Comédie Française, a woman of notorious, shameless character,' wrote Lady Frederick Cavendish, sister of the 7th Duke of Devonshire. 'Not only content with being run after on the stage, this woman is asked to respectable people's houses to act, and even to lunch and dinner; and all the world goes. It is an outrageous scandal!'[29] For all her extraordinary acting talent, nothing could erase the uncomfortable truth that Bernhardt, both the daughter and the niece of well-known Parisian courtesans, was herself not only a 'sinful actress' (as she was lambasted by the American journal *The Methodist*) but had also, early on in her career, frequently turned to rich, older men to keep her in the traditional way.

Even in the latter half of the nineteenth century the vast majority of people still feared not only that proximity to women of 'easy virtue' might be offensive to decent persons, but that it might influence them too. In this respect, even the lower class of prostitute was potentially a bad example. William Acton, one of the great Victorian authorities on prostitution, saw this clearly. Visiting an East End music hall in 1868, he was much struck by 'the effect produced upon married women by becoming accustomed at these reunions to witness the vicious, profligate sisterhood flaunting it gaily'. The women were freely accepting the attentions of men, and were plied with liquor; they sat in the best places, and – horrors – were dressed 'far above their station'. The conventional language of opprobrium used by English writers to describe such a lifestyle begins to seem increasingly hollow: 'with plenty of money to spend and denying themselves no amusement or enjoyment, encumbered with no domestic ties, and burdened with no children. Whatever the purport of the drama might have been,' Acton is eventually forced to admit, 'this actual superiority of a loose life could not have escaped the attention of the quick-witted sex.'[30]

A high-class courtesan, at the very top end of the scale of loose living, was an even more dangerous figure in Acton's eyes. A courtesan, he remarked, would assume 'an intense assumption of superiority over [her] less full-blown sisters' on the strength of 'an equipage, an opera box, a saddle-horse, a Brompton villa, and a visiting list'. In other words, just like the *cortegiana honesta* of sixteenth-century Venice, not only did she have all the trappings necessary 'to elbow respectability and good conduct in public places', she was indistinguishable from it. Clearly, the wages of sin did pay.

Sophia Baddeley, Elizabeth Armistead, Harriette Wilson, Cora Pearl and Catherine Walters lived extraordinary, secret lives, surviving on their woman's wits in a man's world. In their own lifetimes the choices they made – for independence, freedom, and sexual autonomy – forced them onto the margins of society. At once emulated and shunned, they were disturbing figures. To some extent they remain so: at once ancient, and yet strikingly modern. Perhaps more so than any other women in our history, their lives were their art. It is time now to describe them and their arrogant decline.

SOPHIA BADDELEY
1745–1786

The Actress Courtesan

'WE NOW BEGAN to think of the masquerade,' wrote Eliza Steele comfortably in her long and gossipy memoir of the life of Sophia Baddeley, 'and we settled it that Mrs Baddeley should go in the character of Juliet, and I in that of the Nurse. Her dress made up upon this occasion was a rich white sattin, beautifully pucker'd with a veil of fine gauze, trimmed all round with a broad rich point-lace, which had a pretty effect. Upon the whole it was so elegant, that I can venture to say, so beautiful a Juliet, was never before seen . . . Before we entered the Ball-room, I begged the favour of Mrs Baddeley not to unmask, and for some time she obliged me. Our dresses were much admired, but no sooner had she her mask off, than she attracted the attention of the whole room; even the ladies that night could not help saying many things in her praise.'

It was 1771, the same year in which Sophia Baddeley attended Samuel Foote's *The Maid of Bath* at the Little Theatre in the Haymarket, the year in which her celebrity and her fortunes were at their height. Despite her 'equivocal character' – to use an eighteenth-century euphemism – Mrs Baddeley was determined 'to go to every public place of resort, frequented by the nobility and people of fashion', and the masquerades at the Pantheon, a vast concert hall in Oxford Street which had opened in a blaze of publicity earlier that year, were then the very height of glamour.

A detailed description in the *Town and Country Magazine* of two of such masquerades, one at the Pantheon, the other at the equally fashionable Carlisle House, the home of Mrs Cornelys in Soho Square, gives some idea of the scale of these entertainments. Even though tickets were by private subscription only, two thousand guests (each of whom had paid two guineas for the privilege, the equivalent now of £120) crammed into the brilliantly lit and decorated rooms at the Pantheon. The refreshments and the supper were abundant, 'the wine was good and in great plenty'. The most striking display of all, however, was the guests themselves, whose wit and inventiveness on that night have been preserved, like tiny insects in amber, on these pages. Amongst the most striking masks and fancy dresses were:

> *Two female Conjurors, Lady N-wdigate and her sister Miss C-onyers, who supported the characters with great propriety. Pan, Mr John M-rris. A silken harlequin, the lord proprietary of Maryland. The Man in the Moon, Mr D-ere of the Temple. A group of dancers, exhibiting the bearers and attendants of a May Day Garland, Sir Watkyn Williams W-nne, and others. The dancing Stockwell clock, Mr T-lbot of Lincoln's Inn. A Sultana, with an astonishing quantity of diamonds, supposed to the value of thirty thousand pounds, lady V-llars. This lady was infinitely the most splendid figure in the room.*[1]

Famous faces from politics and the arts – the Duke of Grafton,* Stephen Fox (brother of the more famous Charles James Fox), Sir Joshua Reynolds and Dr Goldsmith – rubbed shoulders with ladies of the aristocracy. The mask of the Duchess of Richmond, 'in the character of Zobeide (dressed as Mrs Yates†)', was particularly striking; '*beauty, elegance*, and *grace*, were happily blended in her grace's figure without *affectation*'. Most striking of all to a modern reader, however, are the number of women who dressed themselves as men.

> *A great many of the ladies of rank and beauty chose to adapt the male dress in domino, and appeared as* masculine *as many of*

---

* The Duke of Grafton was the British Prime Minister from 1768 to 1770.
† A famous actress of the day.

the delicate Maccarony* *things we see swarming everywhere, to the disgrace of our* noble patient British race. *There was this difference, that they looked* lovely *and* charming, *and were justly* admired, *while every person of sense despises the ridiculous* Billy Whiffles *of the present age. The most distinguished of these belles,* clad en-homme, *were the duchess of Anc-r, lady Mel-n, lady B-n Bro-n, the Hon. Mrs John D-er, Mrs Hod-s, and Miss B-ke.*

At Mrs Cornelys's the following week the doors of Carlisle House were opened at about ten in the evening, from which time, the *Town and Country Magazine* tells us, 'an unbroken line of coaches and carriages continued advancing till broad daylight'. The file of carriages passed through crowds of 'inquisitive and impertinent idlers, who insisted on each glass of the different vehicles being let down, that they might be afforded an opportunity of fully seeing every mask; and these unwelcome spectators were not sparing of those rough and indecent observations which characterise the mobs of most free countries'.

By midnight 1200 guests – some still mysteriously masked, others now exposed to view – capered, skipped, flirted, slouched or swaggered, according to character, through Mrs Cornelys's elegantly arranged rooms. The air became sultry with candle heat and the perfume of flowers. More wine was drunk, practical jokes were played, and supper – the tables for which were arranged on an ingeniously constructed sloping false floor in the ballroom, 'beyond all description striking and splendid' – was eaten. The festivities lasted until dawn.

At seven o'clock in the morning the guard of thirty men, attending 'by the king's own permission' at Mrs Cornelys's, cleared the rooms of company. 'Festivity, mirth and licentiousness reigned as much without doors as within,' the *Town and Country* tells us, capturing that mixture of *haut ton* refinement and rowdiness which characterises late-eighteenth-century society. Several bottles of wine were thrown out of the windows to the mob still waiting below, together with 'whole pies

---

* The term 'macaroni', denoting an extravagantly foppish young man, was coined in the 1770s, and is thought to have originated from the Macaroni Club of the 1760s, whose members enjoyed all things foreign, most especially food.

and temples of pastry. And the scramble for this plunder created infinite pleasantry.'

For all her celebrity, Sophia Baddeley was by no means certain that she would be granted admission to the Pantheon. Despite their boisterousness, the exclusivity of these masquerades was part of their fashionable appeal. They were 'society' events, attended by all sections of the upper classes – and their wives. In order to preserve the propriety of their establishment, when the Pantheon first opened its owners determined that they would not admit any women 'of slight character'. Mrs Baddeley, being an actress, had been specifically singled out as 'an improper person to be admitted'.

On hearing this, an outraged group of some fifty of her most ardent admirers met together at Almack's and decided on a plan of action to enable Mrs Baddeley and her companion to attend the Pantheon on the very first night after its grand opening. It was arranged that they should be taken there by sedan chair. 'As chairs were admitted under the Portico,' wrote Mrs Steele prudently, 'it would be better in case of a riot, than to expose our carriage and horses to the insolence of a mob.'

When they reached the portico they found Mrs Baddeley's band of admirers waiting, swords at the ready. Mrs Steele got down from the chair and, unimpeded, passed the constables who were on hand to prevent undesirables from entering; but when Mrs Baddeley attempted to follow her they crossed their staves, saying that their orders were to admit no 'players'.

> At this instant every gentleman there present, the greatest part of whom were noblemen, drew their swords, and declared . . . that if they did not instantly make way, and let her pass, they would run them through. Way was immediately made, and Mrs Baddeley and I were handed in, without any intervention. But the matter ended not here for the gentlemen would not sheath their swords, nor suffer the music to play, till the managers came to beg Mrs. Baddeley's pardon, for the insult shewn her.[2]

From that day, according to Mrs Steele, not only was Sophia's admission to these fashionable establishments never opposed again, but the incident, which became something of a *cause célèbre*,* established an interesting precedent: 'So that the ladies of the Theatres, and many others, have to thank Mrs. Baddeley for their present admission.'

Sophia Baddeley's short but meteoric life was nothing if not full of drama. An actress who could not act – who, in fact, avoided the fatigue of the acting life whenever she could – she nevertheless became one of the most famous players of her day, achieving the kind of overwhelming celebrity which is rare even in our own celebrity-obsessed age. Hers was an erotic beauty which had the power to bewitch both men and women, and which exerted that kind of charisma which, unless tempered with unusual reserves of moral strength and level-headedness, can hopelessly distort lives, and even unhinge the rational mind.

Sophia Baddeley had neither moral strength nor level-headedness. She was vain, spoilt, impetuous, lazy, spendthrift, only moderately intelligent, and possessed of a great deal of sexual energy. She was also warm-hearted, affectionate, funny, mercurial, and generous to a fault. Seeing her, as we must, through the partial eyes of Mrs Steele, it is impossible not to love Sophia. It is also clear that she was much beloved by many others, not just by her aristocratic admirers – the majority of whom hunted her quite ruthlessly both for sex and for her fashionable *cachet* – but by the ordinary people who came across her: her servants, her fellow actors, the everyday public who came to hear her act and sing, and who so relished the stories of her scandalous life and loves.

Sophia Baddeley was born into a respectable family in the parish of St Margaret's, Westminster, in 1745.† She was the daughter of a theatrical musician, Valentine Snow, at one time Serjeant-Trumpeter to George II, and his wife Mary. Her paternal grandfather was Moses Snow, who had been the Royal Musician. She had at least one brother, Jonathan Snow (b.1741), who appeared as a juvenile harpsichordist at

* It was recounted in detail, for example, in a contemporary edition of the *Town and Country Magazine*.
† Her obituary notices also suggested 1744, 1749 and 1750 as the year of her birth.

the Haymarket in 1751. A certain Robert Snow, widower of Valentina Snow, who left a substantial fortune and whose will was proved on 14 December 1771, may also have been a sibling, as may a 'Miss Snow' who made her theatrical debut at Covent Garden on 10 May 1765, dancing a hornpipe.

From her early youth Sophia was trained in music by her father, who was determined that she should become a harpsichord player. Eliza Steele, who had been Sophia's friend since childhood, when they attended school together, adds that she had a 'genteel' education which afforded her 'every necessary external accomplishment of her sex'. The young Sophia was a strikingly pretty girl. There was always 'an uncommon degree of softness and delicacy in her features', Mrs Steele wrote, and this, together with her impeccable conduct, regulated always by the strictest decorum, 'ensured her general respect'.

By the time she was eighteen, however, Sophia had grown weary both of decorum and of her harpsichord lessons, which she disliked very much. A neighbour introduced her to Robert Baddeley, a player at the Drury Lane Theatre almost twice her age, and the two eloped. Their marriage, which took place in 1764, was as fleeting as their romance. Although they never divorced, in 1770 they agreed on private articles of separation (which in the eighteenth century was as close to a full divorce as ordinary folk were likely to get).*

Robert Baddeley did bequeath his wife one thing of lasting value, however, and that was her stage career. Orphaned at an early age, as a young man he is said to have been a cook for Samuel Foote, who gave him an interest in the stage (his first part was as Sir William Wealthy in Foote's comedy *The Minor*, which opened at the Haymarket on 28 June 1760). He is also said to have spent three years travelling on the Continent as valet to a travelling gentleman, during which time he acquired the smattering of foreign languages and knowledge of foreign ways which he was to draw upon when playing the character

---

* By the terms of this agreement, most of the financial bonds between them as man and wife were dissolved – for example, he would no longer be liable for her debts. They did not, of course, have the right to remarry, but both went on freely to cohabit with other partners (at least one of Robert's called herself 'Mrs Baddeley'), a common practice at the time.

parts for which he was best known. Principal among these was Moses, the German Jew in Sheridan's *School for Scandal*, which he 'created' in 1775, and was to play over two hundred times during his thirty-four-year career, only ever missing one performance. Later on in his life, Baddeley suffered from epileptic fits – it was while he was dressing for the part of Moses at Drury Lane one November evening in 1794 that the fit came on which finally killed him.

But all that was a long way in the future. In 1764, the year of the Baddeleys' elopement, Robert immediately used his influence at Drury Lane to secure Sophia her first acting engagement. The way in which Mrs Steele describes this supposed debut reveals the mixture of vitality and chaos that was the eighteenth-century theatre. Sophia was acting as an understudy in *King Lear* when the actress playing Cordelia became ill. Bizarrely, she had never even seen the play performed before she went on stage. 'When Edgar came in, as Mad Tom,' recalled Mrs Steele, 'his figure and manner gave her such an unexpected shock, that through real terror she screamed and fell down motionless, and it was some time before she recovered. The audience, to an individual, sympathised with her, and she resumed her character, encouraged by the thunder of reiterated applause from every quarter of the house.'

In fact Cordelia was probably not Sophia's first part. In the Drury Lane bills she is listed as having played Ophelia to Charles Holland's Hamlet and Mrs Pritchard's Gertrude on 27 September 1764, some nineteen months before *King Lear* was staged in April 1766.[3] Whatever the order may have been, Sophia became a regular member of the Drury Lane company, and over the next five years she played many leading parts, including Polly Peachum in *The Beggar's Opera*, Imogen in *Cymbeline*, Cecilia in *As You Like It*, and Olivia in *Twelfth Night*.

Chiefly, however, she specialised in what can perhaps best be described as 'genteel comedy'. Despite her popular appeal, there is evidence that the theatre management was not quite so enthralled by Sophia's acting abilities as her audiences were. When she returned to Drury Lane to play Cordelia once again, after a summer appearing with the company in Manchester, the prompter William Hopkins wrote disparagingly in his manuscript diary, 'very bad, all but the singing'.

But at singing Sophia truly excelled. By the end of the 1760s, in

addition to her busy stage career, she was appearing regularly as a
singer on 'high terms' at the pleasure gardens at Ranelagh, Vauxhall
and Finch's Grotto. Mrs Steele claims she was paid twelve guineas a
week for these engagements alone: the equivalent of the very highest
wage of any stage actress at that time. In the summer of 1769 she sang
in Thomas Arne's oratorio *Judith* at the great Shakespeare Jubilee at
Stratford staged by David Garrick. Her rendition of 'Sweet Willy O'
was one of the great attractions of Garrick's later stage play *The Jubilee*,
which he wrote to cash in on the huge publicity generated by his
Shakespeare extravaganza, and which was to become the longest-
running play of the eighteenth century. The song, wrote the *Town and
Country Magazine* in a rare moment of generosity, 'received extraordinary beauties from her singing'.[4]*

Life was sweet for Sophia in these days, but it was also changing
fast. A combination of her beauty and success, and the rackety life of
the theatre, had long since estranged her from her husband, who in
any case was always a man of 'great variety in his amours'. Sophia, who
was naturally passionate, liked variety too. If the *Town and Country
Magazine*, whose famous '*Tête-à-Tête*' series specialised in salacious
gossip about well-known London figures, is to be believed, her husband
not only turned a blind eye to her dalliances, but actively encouraged
them. 'Not satisfied with the emoluments of his wife's acting,' the
magazine commented, 'he resolved to turn her to every possible advantage, and profit by the first opportunity that offered to dispose of her
charms.' When a rich Jewish admirer of Sophia's, a Mr Mendez, began
to make advances to her, saying that 'such a divine woman might
command the treasures of an eastern monarch, if she could accept of
them', Baddeley pimped her with cheerful indifference, remarking that
'so valuable a friend was not to be slighted,' and advised her to behave
to Mr Mendez with 'the greatest civility'.[5]

Having 'sacrificed her person for gain', Sophia determined that next

---

* James Boswell, who attended the play, witnessed at first hand the erotic allure which
Sophia's presence on the stage had for almost all the men who saw her there: 'I rose and
went near the orchestra,' he wrote in his diary, 'and looked steadfastly at that beautiful,
insinuating creature, Mrs Baddeley of Drury Lane.' Quoted in Ian McIntyre, *Garrick*,
Allen Lane; London, 1999.

time she took a lover it would be to please herself rather than her husband. She took up first with her fellow actor Charles Holland, and when he died of smallpox she accepted the services of his physician, a Dr Hayes of Marlborough Street, with whom she lived for nine months (until Garrick, who since 1747 had been the manager of the Drury Lane Theatre, insisted she give him up). Other admirers soon followed, including Lord Grosvenor and George Garrick, David Garrick's brother.* She became a brief favourite of the Duke of York, who gave her a lock of his hair. Sir Cecil Bishop, a man of 'four score years', paid court to her, but 'finding age an obstacle' sent her £100-worth of silver plate and an invitation to tea instead – both of which Sophia nobly declined.

Other offers were less easy to resist. She became involved with William Hanger,† the son of an impoverished Irish peer, Lord Coleraine, and shortly afterwards with his brother John, whom she called 'Gaby'. Sophia fell in love with Gaby, the first and perhaps only time she ever really lost her heart to a man, and went to live with him in Dean Street, where he took a handsome lodging, hired a carriage for her, and denied her no extravagance.

These glory days did not last long, however. The handsome but feckless Gaby soon ran out of money, and Sophia found that she was using her own wages to meet their joint expenses. The lovers were plagued continually by tradesmen, and their debts rose. Before long they owed a staggering £700 (more than £40,000 today), which included the coach-master's bill for the private carriage Gaby had engaged. Faced with ruin, Gaby finally told Sophia that he was going to have to give her up. She begged him not to leave her, but he was obdurate. In a passion of grief, she took an overdose of laudanum which so prostrated her that six weeks later she was still barely able to walk. 'For the remainder of her life she was affected with a bilious complaint, that often disordered her,' wrote Mrs Steele, 'and made many of her days unhappy.'

* George Garrick fought a famous 'bloodless duel' with Robert Baddeley over Sophia. His second, curiously, was Mr Mendez.
† It was William Hanger who was the instigator of Sophia's defence at the Pantheon masquerade.

But Sophia did not remain unhappy for long. Life was too full. She was too beautiful, too successful, and too fêted. A pattern was already emerging in her life: a pattern of love affairs and unscrupulous admirers, of reckless extravagance, debt – and laudanum. Despite her little slip with Mr Mendez, she was not yet, not quite yet, a fully-fledged courtesan; but it was only a matter of time.

The first serious offer Sophia received was from Lord Molyneux, in around 1770. She was at a low ebb, still recovering from her broken love affair with 'Gaby' Hanger, and physically weakened by the laudanum overdose. She also had serious debts. It was from this period that Eliza Steele resumed her friendship with Sophia. She had apparently helped Sophia to pay some of her most pressing debts, and had taken a house for her in St James's Place, but the establishment was not yet ready, and 'his lordship made her repeated offers of a settlement in the interim, if she would consent to accept it'.

Knowing that Molyneux was a married man, Sophia refused. But knowing her circumstances, Molyneux persisted. His offer was more than generous: 'His lordship, as a preliminary, proposed to pay her debts and to settle on her £400 a year, and particularly told her that she might command instantly a thousand pounds to satisfy her creditors.' Her friends tried to persuade her to accept, telling her that the settlement was 'an object of too much consequence to be rejected; it would outlive the constancy of the donor, and be a comfortable resource when age came on'. Still Sophia refused.

At the theatre her fame as a beautiful actress and singer was growing by the day. According to Mrs Steele, her salary was raised by £6 a week (from £8 to £14). This, together with her earnings from Ranelagh Gardens, brought her total weekly wage up to £28 a week, a queenly £1500 a year (£90,000 today) – wealth beyond the dreams of most, if not all, her fellow actresses. She could now keep a private carriage and a set of servants, dress as expensively as she liked – and, most importantly, be proof against the importunities of her admirers.

Now formally separated from her husband, Sophia nonetheless

continued to play on the same stage as him, although contemporary gossip declared that they never spoke a word to one another 'except when the utterance was dramatic'. There is a story that when the two appeared in a royal command performance of George Colman and Garrick's *The Clandestine Marriage* together, Sophia acted with 'such pointed coyness' the scene in which Baddeley (as Canton) urged the actor playing Lord Obleby to make love to her (as Fanny) that a delighted George III ordered her portrait to be painted by Zoffany.[6]

With this royal seal of approval, Sophia's status, as both actress and fashionable beauty, reached its apogee. She began to receive invitations to dine amongst 'the first people of distinction' (although this would not have included their wives), and when her benefit was announced by Garrick all the boxes were engaged immediately at very high prices (Lord Paget took the first box, for which he paid £100). Noblemen of every rank swarmed to meet her, at cards, at tea, in the Park; even 'Gaby' Hanger came back, begging for forgiveness, although this, Mrs Steele remarked tartly, 'was more the effect of pride than affection: for the notice of Mrs Baddeley was at that day sufficient to give credit and *éclat* to a man of the *ton*. This was one reason among others that induced men of the first rank and character to court her company as they did.'

It was quite clear, of course, that 'credit' and '*éclat*' was not all they were after. The status of the courtesan has always been ambiguous; but that of the actress, in the eighteenth century especially, was even more complex. When women were first allowed onto the stage, after the reopening of the theatres by the newly restored Charles II in 1660, it was widely thought that their presence could only lower the moral tone of the theatres (which in any case was not high). In the seventeenth century the term 'actress' was unequivocally synonymous with prostitute.

There were only two theatre companies in those days, the Duke's Men, and the King's Men, both of which were licensed by royal patent. Despite their close association with the King and his court, it was well known that the playhouses in which they performed were the locus of a thriving street trade.* The actresses themselves, whether or not they

---

* So close was this association that a proposal, in 1670, to levy a tax on the playhouses as dens of prostitution was dismissed as an insult to the Crown.

were technically prostitutes, might just as well have been. The very nature of their work – exposing themselves to public view on a stage – was considered morally degenerate. The fact that a woman might be trying to earn her living, perhaps supporting a family through these endeavours, was not a mitigating factor, but was looked upon merely 'as an addition of new Scandal to her former Dishonour'.[7] Samuel Pepys, no stranger to the seamier side of life, was uncharacteristically squeamish in his description of a visit to his actress friend, Mrs Knepp, in the theatre:

> Met with Knepp and she took us up into the tiring rooms and to the women's shift where Nell [Gwyn] was dressing herself and was all unready, and is very pretty, prettier than I thought ... But Lord! to see how they were both painted would make a man mad and did make me loath them – and what base company of men comes along among them, and how lewdly they talk.[8]

An actress had to be exceptionally resourceful to survive in this world. Audiences were rough and quarrelsome, and women players were considered fair game by any predatory rake. Abductions and rapes were commonplace, as in the case of Aubrey de Vere, Earl of Oxford, who became so obsessed by the actress who played the part of Roxelana that he attempted first to kidnap her, and then deceived her into a false marriage. She was later compensated with an annuity of a thousand crowns.

Rough though theatrical life was, there were some advantages. The theatre provided at least some actresses with a social mobility that was unique in English history. It brought them into contact with the highest levels of society, and many of the prettiest ones were soon tempted away from the stage with offers to become kept women, with the result that there was a very rapid turnover of female players. And then of course there was always the chance of catching the eye of the King.

Charles II took two mistresses from the stage: Mary, or Moll, Davis, and Eleanor, known as Nell, Gwyn. Their background as professional women, and their close association with the court, make them arguably the first true English courtesans. A painting of Moll Davis by Sir Peter

Lely shows her, like a Venetian courtesan of the late sixteenth century, playing a double-strung guitar inlaid with a heart, a clear allusion to her position.[9] Moll had her own establishment in Suffolk Street, complete with servants, footmen and a carriage, all provided for by the King. He soon grew tired of her, however, and she was succeeded by Nell Gwyn, one of the most popular of all his mistresses.

Unlike Charles's more aristocratic lovers Barbara Villiers, later Duchess of Cleveland, and Louise de Keroualle, the Duchess of Portsmouth, Nell was never given her own apartments at Whitehall, nor was she rewarded with a title (although she was lavishly maintained by the King at her house in Pall Mall, and her two sons by him were ennobled). For all the King's affection for her, 'Pretty Witty Nell', 'the indiscreetest and wildest creature that ever was in Court', was kept firmly on the margins of royal life. Her story, nonetheless, even in her own day, had a rags-to-riches glamour about it which fascinated ordinary people. One version of her life has it that as a young girl she raked cinders for a living: 'Cinders Nell', a real-life embodiment of the fairy-tale heroine.[10] Morally disreputable as she may have been, there was always a groundswell of public sympathy for Nell which finds echoes in the story of Sophia Baddeley a hundred years later.

In the eighteenth century the social standing of the actress began, very slowly, to change. Although women still risked being disowned by their families for going on the stage, which never lost its louche associations, there was a growing sense of decorum both in the theatre world itself, and in the kinds of roles which were available for actresses. Openly lascivious and foulmouthed parts, of the type women had been expected to play after the Restoration, were largely purged from the theatre. Instead, 'She tragedies' such as those made popular by Nicholas Rowe and John Banks came into fashion, especially amongst women theatre-goers, who often became fiercely loyal to a particularly favoured actress, who was then able to command high fees as a result. Not only did these plays give female actors major roles to play, but they also portrayed them in a better light than comedies, in which women were so often exposed and ridiculed.

By associating themselves with these more refined parts, and by leading exemplary private lives, it was beginning to be possible for actresses to attain some kind of respectability.* Anne Oldfield, for example, was 'admitted with Pleasure into the company of Ladies of the First Rank for Birth, and Virtue, and seemed to take her visits as an honour done to them'.[11] Another boost to the profession came about when some actresses, not content with becoming the mistresses of their rich or aristocratic admirers, actually married them.

The first to achieve this was Lavinia Berwick, the original Polly Peachum in John Gay's hugely popular *The Beggar's Opera*, who after twenty-three faithful years married her noble lover the Duke of Bolton. Others soon followed. Elizabeth Farren, the daughter of a Cork surgeon and apothecary, became the Countess of Derby, while Harriot Mellon, the child of an illiterate Irish peasant girl, made two spectacular marriages, first to a Mr Coutts (of banking family fame), and then to the Duke of St Albans. As a young girl Harriot had been a protégée of Sarah Siddons, the greatest tragic actress of her day, and one of the first women players to achieve real respectability. 'I am told by one I know very well that this young lady for years in her father's company conducted herself with the utmost propriety,' Mrs Siddons pronounced in a queenly way in the Green Room one day. 'I therefore introduce her as my young friend.'[12]

But was respectability all it was cut out to be? Harriot, Duchess of St Albans, for one, did not find it so: 'The society in which I formerly moved was all cheerfulness, all high spirits – all fun, frolic, and vivacity,' she wrote disconsolately; 'they cared for nothing, thought of nothing, beyond the pleasures of the present house, and to those they gave themselves up with the utmost relish. Look at the circles in which I now move; can anything be more weary, stale, flat, and unprofitable, than their whole course of life? Why, we might as well be in the treadmill, as toiling in the stupid, monotonous round of what they call pleasure, but which is, in fact, very cheerless and heavy work.'[13]

The fun, frolic and vivacity of the theatre world was appealing to

* In her *Memoirs*, Perdita Robinson wrote of her mother's anxiety when she first announced her ambition to go on the stage, but 'many cited examples of females who, even in that perilous and arduous situation, preserved an unspotted fame, inclined her to listen to the suggestion'. Unfortunately, Perdita herself did not turn out to be one of them.

many more than just the performers themselves. The eighteenth century was a starstruck era. The public appetite for news, gossip and scandal about famous figures was insatiable, with the result that actors and actresses found themselves living exceptionally public lives: 'at once the focus of polite society', as the historian John Brewer describes it, 'and yet disreputably on its margins'. The situation for actresses was especially vexed. The publicity which surrounded them was in itself an almost insurmountable impropriety, and although some serious actresses – such Hannah Pritchard and Kitty Clive in the mid-century, and Sarah Siddons at its end – were able to challenge the old assumptions about an actress's virtue, after every one of them tumbled a swarm of flighty others, cheerfully flirting and sleeping their way to the top.*

If Sophia Baddeley had ever desired respectability – which is doubtful – by the time Zoffany painted her in *The Clandestine Marriage* any last, lingering hope of it was gone. Despite all Mrs Steele's remonstrances, Sophia now had another serious admirer. At twenty-one, Lord Melbourne was young, aristocratic, and very, very rich.† A contemporary portrait of him shows a tall, rather lanky individual, with a pale complexion and heavily shadowed eyes. In person he was said to be affable enough, but he was also lazy, self-indulgent and irritatingly noisy. Although recently married to 'a very aimiable woman', his 'Betsey', 'a lady of great personal and acquired accomplishment',‡ of

---

* There was also the unavoidable fact that, as in the seventeenth century, the theatres, Covent Garden and Drury Lane in particular, were at the centre of the sex trade in London.
† The Melbourne fortune was begun by Lord Melbourne's great-uncle, Peniston Lamb, an extremely successful conveyancer. He is said to have made most of his money by fleecing his loyal patrons the Cecil family of Hatfield, who were his neighbours. Melbourne's father Matthew, who was also a lawyer, inherited much of this fortune, and added to it through his work as 'perpetual solicitor' to the Post Office. He became a Member of Parliament in 1741, and considerably added to his wealth (and social standing) by his extremely advantageous marriage to Charlotte Coke, the heiress of Melbourne Hall in Derbyshire. The farms around the house alone are said to have been worth £6000 per annum. Matthew's son Peniston (Sophia's Lord Melbourne) inherited his father's fortune; he was given an Irish barony the year after his marriage, and so became Lord Melbourne in 1770.
‡ In 1769 Melbourne had married Elizabeth Milbanke, a woman of enormous beauty, intelligence and boundless social ambitions. As Lady Melbourne she was to become one of the most formidable figures of her day, a brilliant hostess and leader of Whig society.

whom he was apparently quite fond, Sophia was beautiful, sexy, and by now easily the most fashionable woman in London. Melbourne, no stranger to the gallant world, was determined to have her, and set about getting her with all the means at his disposal.

He approached her first through a friend, who brought a present of £300 (a not insubstantial £18,000) and 'an offer of a share of his fortune, in exchange for the possession of her heart'. Knowing of his recent marriage, at first Sophia refused. But Melbourne persisted. He came to call on her himself, careful at first to keep out of the disapproving way of Mrs Steele, who by now had installed herself as Sophia's companion and unofficial *duenna*. On one occasion, trying to escape from her, Melbourne 'threw up the parlour window, and precipitately leaped out', but not before he had had the presence of mind to leave a bill for a further £200 on the parlour table 'as an attonement for his intrusion'. A few days later he brought a present of another £300, declaring that 'he would spend his whole fortune if necessary to defend and protect her'. Showered with Melbourne's gold (she had now received the equivalent of nearly £50,000), Sophia finally buckled.

In the first heady rush of his success, Melbourne allowed Sophia almost total command of his purse. Despite the fact that she was already independently wealthy from her own earnings, the full force of Sophia's natural talent for spending money was now unleashed, and she began 'to launch out into expenses she had restrained before'. The massive spree which resulted was exhaustively chronicled by Mrs Steele. First came a pair of diamond earrings from Mr Tomkins the jeweller in Maiden Lane, Covent Garden. Next, ten diamond pins at £20 each, followed by nine rings valued at £920. Also, a diamond necklace valued

---

Although many found her fascinating and sympathetic – the Duchess of Devonshire was to become one of her most devoted friends and correspondents – there were many others who thought her a slightly sinister character. Lady Holland (perhaps recognising some of her own characteristics) once memorably described her as being like Madame de Merteuil in *Les Liaisons Dangereuses*. Her marriage to Peniston Melbourne – to whom she was in every conceivable way superior – was a marriage of convenience from the outset. The convenience was hers as much as his. It has always been widely believed that at least three of her five children were by her lovers, including William (born in 1779), the future Prime Minister, whose father was allegedly Lord Egremont.

at £450, which Lord Melbourne himself admired and bought for Sophia. He also bought her a cream-coloured mare for £60, so that she could 'ride out for the good of her health', at the same time presenting Mrs Steele with a fine hunter which cost £50. A few days later, after one of his visits, Melbourne left Sophia a bill for a further £200. The next morning she immediately ordered her carriage and set off shopping again. At Mr King's, the mercer in King Street, Covent Garden, she purchased silks to the tune of £120; and at Mr Price the haberdasher in Tavistock Street she paid £70 for 'ribbands, gauses, etc', and another £40 for other sundries. On another day she spent £700 in one afternoon: £200 went on cloth for a new coach lining and other 'sundry silks' at two guineas a yard from Mr Price; she also visited her milliner, and Mr Jefferson the jeweller on Charing Cross, from whom she purchased a pair of diamond earrings costing £300.*

But Sophia was generous as well as extravagant. Everyone at the theatre benefited from her good fortune. If any part of her costume was admired, she would immediately give it away. 'Mrs Hopkins of Drury Lane Theatre paid her a visit one morning whilst she was dress-ing,' recalled Mrs Steele, 'and admiring a set of silver filigree boxes that ornamented her toilet, Mrs Baddeley presented her with as many as filled her pockets.' On another occasion she gave every one of the jewels she was wearing, about £100 worth, to her friend Miss Radley. The way she dressed became increasingly extravagant, and yet however costly any garment she purchased, 'before she had worn it three or four times, she would give it to her maid-servant'.

As Sophia surrendered herself to this life of extravagance and luxury, the toils of her theatre career began to seem increasingly irksome. After Samuel Foote's compliment to her in *The Maid of Bath* (printed versions of the play differ slightly from Mrs Steele's recollection: on hearing Miss Linnet sing, Flint says: 'Enchanting! Ravishing sounds! Not the Nine Muses themselves, nor Mrs Baddeley, is equal to you'), David Garrick wrote rather peevishly to Foote to complain. Mrs Baddeley had 'considered [it] so great a compliment' that she was now applying to Garrick for another pay rise: she was demanding an extra

* A total of £3310, the equivalent today of £187,000

£3 a week, along with certain other terms and conditions regarding her roles and the timing of her benefit.[14]

The truth was that Sophia was not really interested in returning to Drury Lane. To save her from 'the fatigues of a theatre life', Lord Melbourne was offering to pay her more than three times the salary she was receiving from Garrick. She refused to 'come to her business', and when the season began again in September 1771 she did not appear as advertised as Polly Peachum on the opening night, and a Miss Wrighten had to go on in her place.

Sophia was now a courtesan, *tout court*. What did this actually mean? In many ways her life went on much as it had done before. There was one major difference, however: she had to be available to Melbourne whenever he wanted her. Melbourne was young and amiable enough, but, in Mrs Steele's rather dusty view at any rate, he was 'not the brightest man of the age'. She was fond of quoting his letters (which she may have invented) pointing out that he was 'one among many of the fashionable men of the age who are acquainted neither with good grammar or orthography':

> *My dearest Love,*
>   *This is the first moment I could get to inform you that I can't come out of doors this day, my eyes are exceedingly inflamed. I am obliged to keep them covered with parsley and cream; can scarcely look long and nuff to write this Satturday.*
>   *To Mrs Baddeley.*

Another, after Sophia had applied to him for some money to pay off her brother's debts, read:

> *My Dear Love,*
>   *I understand you at present want the enclosed sum to assist your brother with, which will be the last inconveniences you are to have for his sake. I am very hartily glad of it, because excuse me, as I have before told you, from your great goodnature, and goodness of hart, you have already been to good in frequently distresing yourself upon this account and I hope you will be prudent and nuf not to be perswaided to engage yourself further*

for his depts. I am very happey that I was informed of it,
because it always gives me the greatest happeyness to oblige
my love with every thing in my power. I hope you have got
the horsis, or will find one that will answar well, butt I beg
you will not be to ventersum as there is bad horsis, butt gett
one quite quiet. I shall long to see your dear face, which I will
as soon as possible, and will endeavour to be back, if only for
a moment, in about a fortnight. I will write to you from York.
Pray be carefull not to mention my name at Brighthelmston
[Brighton], or any where that whe may not be plagued again
by the ill-natured world.

His other letters, commented Mrs Steele, were equally ill-spelt, 'but I have taken the liberty to correct them, that they may not hurt the eye of the reader'.

Affectionate and generous, Melbourne was nonetheless dull work. He had the run of Sophia's house, and had the habit of coming in at inconvenient moments. Whatever Sophia was doing – taking tea, or playing at cards – he could interrupt her at will, and ask her to 'retire' with him. 'Lord Melbourne came again in the evening, and in unusual good humour,' Mrs Steele wrote of their life at this time, 'throwed his hat one way, his cane another, and sat himself down saying he was tired to death, with prancing about all day with his Betsy a-shopping, and wished to lay down to rest himself. Mrs Baddeley accompanied him, and I saw no more of them till ten the next morning.'

The truth was that sex with Lord Melbourne bored Sophia. She often had a headache which mysteriously disappeared as soon as he was gone. When he went away, even for a few days, it was a relief to her. 'Mrs Baddeley was not a little pleased he was going,' wrote Mrs Steele on one such occasion, 'as she called such times her holidays; and as soon as he was gone she cried, "Now the devil take the doctors. I'll not see one of them, but go and see Hampton Court and Windsor, which I have not seen for some years; and I will take as much pleasure as the week will afford."'

Pleasure was Sophia's compensation and her refuge. She was now living in grand style. Her house in Grafton Street, fashionably situated just north of Berkeley Square and within an easy carriage ride of Hyde Park, was as extravagantly furnished as good taste and money could make it. The walls of her drawing room were hung with silk curtains, drawn up in festoons in imitation of Madame du Barry's room at Versailles. She kept a staff of nine servants to wait on her, decking them out in elaborate liveries: 'superfine dark blue cloth, lined with scarlet, the edge of which just appeared; scarlet cuffs and collar, with two rows of scolloped silver lace round them; the same round the waistcoat, which was blue, with silver-laced hats'.

In addition to Sophia's home in Grafton Street, she and Mrs Steele hired a country house – complete with servants – at the newly fashionable Brighthelmstone-on-Sea. Another house in the village of Hammersmith also took Sophia's fancy, so she hired that too. She kept a carriage and four, but also took to driving a phaeton. A private box was hired for her at the opera (cost £80 per annum), and she was a frequent attender at the theatre, at masquerades, and the pleasure gardens at Vauxhall.

Sophia's wealth enabled her to make 'an appearance equal to a woman of the first rank' – a suspiciously ostentatious display for a mere actress. Nonetheless, as the celebrity of the moment she continued to enjoy the kind of public approbation that was wholly denied to ordinary courtesans, however successful. In her *Memoirs*, another famous eighteenth-century actress, Perdita Robinson, then newly arrived in London, recalled the thrill of seeing Sophia for the first time. The occasion was a concert at the Pantheon, at that time 'the most fashionable assemblage of the gay and the distinguished'.

> At this place it was customary to appear much dressed; large hoops and high feathers were universally worn ... As soon as I entered the Pantheon rotunda, I shall never forget the impression which my mind received: the splendour of the scene, the dome illuminated with variegated lamps, the music; and the beauty of the women, seemed to present a circle of enchantment. I recollect that the most lovely of fair forms met my eyes in that of Lady Almeria Carpenter ... [but] the countenance which most pleased me was that of the late Mrs Baddeley.[15]

After that first night at the Pantheon masquerade no one had attempted to bar Sophia's entry to these public entertainments. It had not only been her male admirers who had rushed to her defence on that occasion. Some of the ladies, too, had come forward to see the cause of the disturbance. The Duchess of Argyll 'was pleased to say she was much surprized at so gross an insult being offered to Mrs Baddeley, who was an ornament to any place she was seen in; and it gave her particular pleasure to see her in public at all times'. Lady Hertford had the same opinion. As a fashionable beauty, Sophia was spoken of 'with rapture' by the ladies of the nobility wherever she went: ' "There is that divine face! That beautiful creature!" others would cry out. "Here's Mrs Baddeley – what a sweet woman." '

The men were altogether more predatory. It was now widely known in the world of gallantry – as the English *demi-monde* was then called – that Sophia was the kept mistress of Lord Melbourne, but this fact, instead of keeping other admirers at bay, only served to increase their attentions. Mrs Baddeley had not so much lost her reputation, as gained one.

The morning after the masquerade at which Sophia had caused such a sensation dressed as Juliet, the door-knocker of the house in Grafton Street rapped from morning till evening. She and Mrs Steele gave orders for the servants to say they were not at home, but had the names of their callers read out. 'Among the many that called to pay their respects were, the Dukes of Northumberland, Ancaster, the Marquis of Queensberry; Lords Harrington, Lincoln, Clanbrazil, Winchilsea, Falmouth, Pigot, Mr R. Conway,* etc. And the newspapers did not omit to mention many others.' When they went to Brighton for a rest and some sea air, it was the same. They had not been in their house above an hour before visitors began to arrive to offer Sophia their congratulations: Mr William Hanger, Lord Pigot, Captain Pigot, Lord Peterborough, Captain Crawford . . . the list went on.

Sophia's admirers fell over themselves to satisfy her every whim. When at Mr Ridley's, the bookseller in St James's Street, she picked

---

* For all their grand titles, most of these men – in particular Ancaster, Queensberry (in later years known as Old Q, the Piccadilly Lecher) and Harrington – were among the most notorious rakes of their day.

out £50 worth of books, Lord Harrington, who was in the shop at the time, offered to buy them for her (but was refused). Another time, she was hesitating (the only time Mrs Steele ever knew Sophia to do so) over an exotic delicacy, a pineapple, which was on sale for the tremendous sum of one guinea, when a stray duke who just happened to be passing by bought it for her. Later, he sent her a note:

> *The unexpected pleasure of seeing Mrs B this morning gave no time for imparting a matter of some consequence to her. The pineapple will inform who writes this, and this evening he will call at nine to communicate what it is to Mrs B.*

It was in vain that Mrs Steele tried to stem the flow. When Sophia refused a request for a private interview, the more determined of her admirers sent their servants to bribe her companion instead. When the Duke of Ancaster – he of the pineapple – despatched his manservant to Mrs Steele with £200 in bank notes (£12,000 today) and a request that she might arrange for him to be allowed to call on Sophia, she reacted with fury. 'In what respect,' she asked the man, 'can [his visits] be honourable? Mrs B's situation in life does not entitle her to receive such noble visitants on *honourable* terms, and therefore they must be *dishonourable*; and I flatter myself that she is so circumstanced at present as to enable her to act with more prudence, than to suffer such insults as his Grace's visits must amount to.'

Others made no pretence at all, and were quite open in their offers to Sophia. Mr Damer offered her a settlement of £400 a year if she would break with Lord Melbourne and be kept by him. Lord Pigot's offer was better still: he would sue Mr Baddeley for divorce (an uncertain, lengthy and very expensive undertaking which in the 1770s was still possible only by private Act of Parliament), marry Sophia and make her a settlement of £600 a year. The Duke of Northumberland countered with an even more generous offer: if Sophia would accept his patronage and protection he offered to discharge all her debts, present her immediately with a thousand guineas 'as an earnest of his esteem', and settle on her an annuity of £500. Sophia refused them all. Officially, at least, she would be faithful to Melbourne. 'I have from him such favours, and his love for me is so great, that he has a claim

to my affections in return,' she explained demurely to Mr Damer.
'Distress led me to it first,' she added, not wholly truthfully, 'and his
Lordship's perseverance and generosity has continued me in it; so that
I hold myself in part to be his. How ungrateful then must I be to such
a benefactor, to listen to proposals from you or any other man.'

Sophia must have been very sure of her hold over Lord Melbourne at
this point, for her arrangement with him was – for her – a dangerously
informal one. By the eighteenth century it was a common practice for
a man to make a formal financial offer to the actress or courtesan he
wanted to keep, together with any other terms and conditions the
couple might mutually agree on.* These were legal documents, drawn
up and witnessed by lawyers. When Lord Molyneux, one of Sophia's
first admirers, had approached her, he was so anxious to expedite their
arrangement that he had actually brought his attorney – 'the dissector
of his patrimony' – and the deeds of settlement drawn up by him to
her house (although the arrangement fell through). No one amongst
the middling and upper classes would have thought of getting married
without making a similar financial settlement, so these transactions
did not perhaps seem quite so baldly mercenary as they do today.

The eighteenth century was intensely interested in details of this
kind. Although Sophia Baddeley's *Memoirs* are a particularly rich
source, they are by no means unusual in their precise chronicling of
guineas, pounds and pence. The life story of Sophia's contemporary,
the courtesan Ann Cateley, also contains a good deal of information
about the financial transactions she made during her career, including
the details of what is allegedly her marriage settlement.

Ann, or Nan, Cateley was an actress and singer of the 1760s and
seventies, who became so fêted as a leader of fashion that the term
'Cateley-fied' was coined by the ladies who copied her elegant hairstyles
and dress. According to her memoirs, which were not written by her,
a rich old man – an unnamed 'pier [sic] of the realm' – offered to

---

* Alternatively a courtesan might be pensioned off with an annuity or an allowance
when the relationship cooled or her patron decided to marry another woman. The actress
Mrs Abingdon, who was a friend of Sophia's, received a handsome settlement from the
Marquis of Landsdowne on his nuptials, and this, together with money willed to her on
the death of another of her lovers, a Mr Needham, was to guarantee her independence.

marry her. The marriage fell through when it came to light that he was in fact the father of one of Nan's young lovers (who uncharitably tells him 'what sort of a woman she is'), but not before Nan had made him sign a paper, properly drawn up by an attorney, which set out very precisely the terms and conditions designed to protect her in the (highly likely) event of her surviving him:

> 1. *That he should settle £1,000 on her, to be paid within one month of his funeral, and £100 during her natural life.*
>
> 2. *That he should settle the like annuity on every one of the children she might have by him, to be paid them also during the term of their natural life.*
>
> 3. *That previous to their marriage, he should invest a sum, or sums, sufficient to produce the aforesaid annuities in any of the public funds, or lend the same on mortgages, or lands, or houses, or on eligible securities, for payment of them.*
>
> 4. *That in the case of failure of any of the said conditions, the marriage shall be null and void, and she be at liberty to marry again.*[16]

Sophia Baddeley, however, as yet had no such settlement. She probably saw no need for one. Melbourne was lavish to the point of recklessness in his *largesse* to her. Although he probably did intend to formalise their arrangement – Mrs Steele claimed that he offered to settle £400 a year on Sophia – somehow he never got round to it. Instead, he was in the habit of dropping great wedges of banknotes – sometimes as much as £500 at a time – carelessly on the table after one of his visits. It was more than most men could afford to give her in a year; but for how long would it go on? As her friends had pointed out to Sophia before, only a settlement would 'outlive the constancy of the donor', and provide a comfortable resource on which to fall back when age came on.

It was sound advice. A courtesan had to be very astute indeed if, like Nan Cateley, she was to survive in the long term. The true measure of independence which her profession could give her depended on her shrewdness in financial matters at the time when she probably saw the least need for it. But timing was all. As the popular ditty written about

Kitty Fisher, the reigning cyprian (courtesan) of the generation before Sophia Baddeley, warned:

> Kitty, repent, a settlement procure,
> Retire, and keep the bailiffs from the door.
> Put up with wrinkles, and pray paint no more.[17]

For all the power which her beauty and desirability conferred, a courtesan, even the most fashionable one at the very height of her career, was still negotiating in a man's world. Men such as Northumberland – a duke and the possessor of vast wealth – were used to getting what they wanted, and were prepared to pay for it. They were also used to being in control, and they had an experience of business matters, of lawyers and finances, which very few women could match. The terms and conditions which a patron might think fit to impose on a courtesan, unless she was very careful, could be Draconian.

When Sophia refused the Duke of Northumberland, he came back soon after with a revised offer. He would give her his protection for life, he said, and would pay all her debts, if she had any, 'with any sum of money she might name, provided she would live with him, and see no other person whatever: that she might either live in his house, or any other she liked, on condition she admitted no other visitor than him, that he would allow her £1500 a year, and if she was faithful to him, would think of a settlement'.

Perhaps blinded by the enormous sums of money now presenting themselves, Sophia did not seem especially troubled by the extremely dubious conditions attached to them. Mrs Steele pronounced waspishly that the yearly allowance Northumberland was offering, a princely sum by anyone else's standards, would barely last Sophia three months. The importunate Duke was becoming the subject of much tension between the two friends. Bullied by Mrs Steele, Sophia again turned him down. Obsessed, Northumberland tried to compromise. 'His Grace proposed calling to see her twice a week, and that at times when he found Lord M was not with her; that on his first visit to tea, he would give her £500 ... that his Grace would discharge all her debts, and be her friend for life.'

To Mrs Steele's disgust, Sophia began to waver.

In short, she told me she gave the gentleman this answer; that she would consider his proposals, and give him her determination the next day. 'And why,' says I, 'did you not give him a positive denial then?' 'Because,' returned she, 'I wished to consult you first.' I told her she knew my sentiments on the subject, and she might assure herself, they would not alter, if the Duke had offered her his whole fortune. 'Well,' says she, 'suppose we admit him to drink tea?' 'That would only lead to further evils,' replied I, 'and I am determined he shall not come.' – 'Good God,' says she, 'I can have five hundred pounds for nothing.' – 'Certainly,' replied I, laughing at her, 'for nothing! Mankind are too fond of their money to bestow it, but in return for favours received.' 'Surely, my dear Steele,' says she, 'you are not serious; I have partly promised to receive him at tea tomorrow.' At this I lost my temper, and said, you may act as you please, but you must invite him to some other house; for he certainly shall not come here: if he does, as soon as he enters the house I will affront him, and I would do the same if he was King of England.'

Foolish Sophia did meet the Duke again, not at Grafton Street but at her house in Hammersmith – unchaperoned by Mrs Steele. There, Northumberland declared his undying love, and the next day sent her £500 (£30,000) as he had promised. 'Much against my will, he led me to my chamber,' she confessed sadly to her friend later. 'I found my resolution give way, and I did what I now repent of.'

Eliza Steele's *Memoirs of Mrs Sophia Baddeley* is unquestionably one of the great biographies of the eighteenth century. When it was first published in 1787, its literary merits were completely obscured by the fact that it was widely thought to have been written as an exercise in extortion. 'Many are the names introduced, and many the reputations that are hack'd and hew'd past all mending,' railed the *Monthly Review*.[18] It is possible that these suspicions were justified: there was a minor tradition of women of the town attempting to do this with their biographies, Constantia Phillips and Charlotte Charke, the daughter of the actor-manager and Poet Laureate Colley Cibber, to name but two (perhaps it was from them that fifty years later Harriette Wilson, who ran a famously successful blackmailing campaign, was to take the idea). What is more surprising is that Sophia's *Memoirs* should have been considered so scandalous. This is not because her life was not highly controversial (it was), but because 'Life and Loves' biographies of this kind were an extremely popular form of entertainment throughout the eighteenth century, and most of them were a good deal more scurrilous and pornographic than Mrs Steele's relatively genteel volumes.

Many of these narratives, particularly in the early part of the century, took the form of pamphlets. They tended to be highly fictionalised, often brutally satirical accounts, whose origins lay in the picaresque novel and in seventeenth-century French romances rather than in anything we would now recognise as biography. Their subjects were actresses, courtesans and now long-forgotten toasts of the town with resonant names: *Authentick Memoirs of the Life, Intrigues and Adventures of the Celebrated Sally Salisbury* (1723); *Courtezan and Posture Mistress, Eliza Mann* (1724); and *Mrs Mary Parmans, the Tall Milliner of Change Alley* (1729). Others were less savoury characters. Newgate criminals, female card sharps, pirates, murderers, smugglers and even highwaywomen were popular subjects too. One such pamphlet, issued by Captain Alexander Smith in 1714, was entitled: *The history of the lives of the most noted highway-men, foot-pads, house-breakers, shop-lifts and cheats, of both sexes, in and about London, and other places of Great Britain.*

The British, it seems, have always loved a rogue. Their stories sold, too, especially if he or she was about to be hanged (a near-guarantee of instant celebrity).* When a woman was the subject, her sex gave the story an added piquancy, as in the case of the 'celebrated' Sally Salisbury, who, we are told by the author of the truly vicious satire

---

* One of the strangest of these 'biographical' pamphlets, reprinted in 1710, must surely be *The case of John Atherton, Bishop of Waterford, in Ireland. Who was convicted of the sin of uncleanliness with a cow, and other creatures, for which he was hanged at Dublin, December 5 1640.*

which claims to be her 'life', induced an abortion whenever she found herself with child, 'but was so affectionate she always preserved the embryos in spirits'.[19]

As the century progressed, the lives of actresses, and actress-courtesans in particular, became increasingly popular. They also became lengthier and, some at least, more obviously genuine attempts at telling a life story. Certain conventions, especially descriptive ones, remained, however. Ann Cateley, whose *Narrative* is otherwise one of the more reliable ones, is described, along with scores of other women, as having 'vermillion lips', 'sparkling eyes' and a 'complexion as fair as alabaster'. Others, while trying to tell a story 'not very different from . . . life', were nonetheless principally intended to be titillating. In *The Memoirs of the Celebrated Miss Fanny Murray*, one of her admirers presses kiss after kiss upon her, whereupon 'those fair hemispheres, those orbs of more than snowy whiteness, which seemed to pant for release from irksome robes, to be still more pressed, were now discovered'.[20] Celebratory verses and 'Apologies' would often be printed in counter-attack by an actress's supporters. According to one estimate, by 1844 there were as many as 150 such volumes in existence.[21]

Mrs Steele was at once too common-sensical and too respectable (in her own eyes at least) to stoop either to cliché or to titillation. And although she does indeed spend a good deal of her memoir apologising for Sophia's behaviour, she does not try to disguise it, faithfully recording all the arguments and quarrels in their all-too-female household. When it was first published, in 1787, some of the book's earliest commentators attributed its authorship to a hack journalist, Alexander Bicknell, who had been the editor of a similar biography of an actress-courtesan, *An Apology for the Life of Mrs Ann Bellamy*, published the year before. But there is no evidence to support this view. For all its meanderings, exaggerations and uncertain chronology, the pungent odour of real life breathes from the book's every page.

The fact that the *Memoirs* were written by someone who knew Sophia intimately can be seen by what the author leaves out, quite as much as what she puts in. Nowhere, for instance, is there a physical description of Sophia, one of the most famous beauties of her day; it is as though Mrs Steele was so familiar with her looks that it simply did not occur to her to dilate upon them.[22] Instead, we learn small details about her which may well have been overlooked by a more dazzled man. In the heat of an argument Sophia blushes and grows red 'as she always did when she was vexed'; she has 'a babbling tongue' and can keep nothing secret; and is unfailingly kind to her servants, who 'flew at her command'. We learn too that she has a good memory and is very quick to learn her parts, and while not especially fond of writing, could pen a sensible letter and 'wrote a good Italian hand'.

Unreliable and partial as it may sometimes be, Mrs Steele's voluble, gossipy stream of consciousness, with its brilliant snatches of conversation, reveals the character of the two women, and their extraordinary relationship, better than any classically educated author could ever have done. We do not see into Sophia's boudoir – at intimate moments the door is always revealingly closed – but instead we see right into her private parlour: two women sitting in intimate *déshabille* over their hot chocolate, servants clattering on the stairs, papers open at the reports of the previous night's masquerade, a careless jumble of cheap trinkets and diamond pins on the table beside them, their morning caps at the ready to make themselves presentable should any gentleman visitor come knocking.

Life was not all about dukes and intrigues and masquerades. Sometimes the daily round reached such a pitch that Eliza and Sophia determined to shut out the world for a time. Mrs Steele is an eloquent and affectionate chronicler of these rare domestic moments, as if, her reader senses, it was the only time when she had Sophia to herself.

We were now at home, after a ramble of some time, and spent our evening together, talking over the occurrences of the last month, with a placid satisfaction, that no place but home, with quiet, affords. Home, however, was at present something new to us, and we determined to spend a week here, with our birds and our cats, for no one knew of our being in town. Mrs Baddeley was very fond of cats, and had one Grimalkin which she called Cuddle, and with which she would often take long journeys; and this cat was as much enquired about, by those who courted her favour, as herself. She also had a favourite canary-bird, which she brought

*all the way from Paris to Brighthelmstone, in a handkerchief, and
from thence to Grafton-street.*

Although Sophia lived extravagantly in almost every other respect –
spending as much as three guineas a day (nearly £200) on expensive
hothouse flowers such as moss roses and carnations – she was quite
modest in her housekeeping when the two women were alone together.
The elegant table, and the French and Spanish wines which they kept
for their guests, were put away, and in their place would be a simple
joint of meat, with only small beer to drink. 'As lived our servants, so
did we,' remembered Mrs Steele. 'Dinner was regularly at three, and
if we were not at home at that hour, the cloth was removed and the
joint served up below. For the many years we lived together, we never
opened a bottle of wine for ourselves, nor had we any strong beer.'

As well as her cats and her birds, Sophia loved books, especially
histories and plays, and even though she had abandoned acting, in
private she kept up her singing lessons, always from the best masters,
'and improved herself much'. Unlike the great courtesans of a later
age, whose whole life was an exercise in playing the *grande dame*, at
heart there was always something touchingly unsophisticated about
Sophia. Although she spent a fortune at her milliner on silks, ribbons
and trimmings, she always made her clothes at home. She and Mrs
Steele would cut the patterns out, and her servants would sew them.

Thanks to Eliza Steele their domestic life had, at least for a time,
some semblance of regularity. She made it her rule to settle all the
housekeeping affairs on Monday mornings, together with the coachman's bills for hay and corn. 'I never paid a shilling on Mrs Baddeley's
account without taking a receipt,' she wrote, 'and obliged her to sit
down with me once a fortnight to examine the accounts. I frequently
had trouble to persuade her to this, but I would not let her rest until
she did it.'

But Sophia's spirit was increasingly restless. Although the house in
Grafton Street was extravagantly furnished and decorated, she was
forever changing it. There were always carpenters, upholsterers and
painters in the house. 'At times she was rather whimsical,' noted Mrs
Steele; 'she would one day put up furniture in the house, and next

day pull it down, and was always changing. Nothing, either of dress or furniture pleased her long.'

Sophia's restlessness fuelled her extravagance: 'I have known her go to Mr King's, the mercer, and lay out thirty or forty guineas for a saque and coat of rich winter silk; and would purchase two or three more, at the same time; make them up, and not wear them three times before she would give them to her maid.' Of course, she had to have every new fashion: 'I have milliners receipts by me now, to the amount of two thousand pounds, spent in two and a half years; and mercers' receipts, to a much greater amount,' recalled Mrs Steele. For all Melbourne's generosity, Sophia's debts rose. Clothes were not her only extravagance. Her linen draper's bills at this time amounted to £800, and she owed various jewellers the stupendous sum of £4000 (nearly a quarter of a million pounds), 'all in diamonds'. 'In short there was no end to her expense, in dress and perfumery. It was no use to talk of economy. Every thing her fancy could suggest, she could have, if money could purchase it.'

With no work to occupy her now, other than the uncertain pleasures of Melbourne's company, Sophia threw herself into a life of pleasure. She went to the opera, where she could enjoy the luxury of drinking tea in her own box; attended yet more masquerades, ridottos and concerts. On one such occasion she came face to face with Lady Melbourne, who did not speak to her, but smiled conspiratorially. She walked or rode in the park at the fashionable hour.

London at the time was small, almost provincial, its high society arguably more fluid, and more tolerant, than it would be again for another two hundred years. The fashionable world and its seamier underbelly, the world of gallantry, were swept along in the same slipstreams, now rubbing shoulders, now merging, now separating again like the tides of the Thames.

There was no apparent shame, or immodesty, attached to knowing about London's more dubious goings-on. Cleone Knox, a young Irish heiress who spent some months in the city as part of her Grand Tour of Europe in 1764, was fascinated, but apparently not at all shocked, when she visited the famously raffish gardens at Ranelagh. 'Indeed 'tis very fine with its great amphitheatre finely gilt, painted and brilliantly illuminated,' she wrote in her diary, adding with complete *sang froid*, 'The entrance is but 12 pennies and so the place is frequented by every kind of person and you can see cheek by jowl *filles de joie* and ladies of fashion, country lawyers and beaux, in fact the mob elbows the quality and 'tis all very lively and informal, though not so *dégagé* as Vauxhall I am told.'[23]

Even when they were not elbowing one another in the parks and pleasure gardens, the town and the *ton* were kept very well informed about each other. Gossip achieved some of this;* the *Morning Post* did the rest. 'The Cyprian divinity of Berkeley Square† is said to be on her last legs. Thus the fate of the Buff and Blue extends through all their connections; famine and disgrace bring up the rear,'[24] reads a typical paragraph. Or: 'Kensington Gardens and the Park Promenades were yesterday exceedingly crowded. The latter particularly, in the evening, exhibited a very grand show of the Cyprian corps in the proper uniform.'[25]

Sophia herself, who lived in dread of being mentioned in the *Post*'s pages,‡ was never vulgar in her appearance. For all her extravagance, she always dressed immaculately, like a woman of the 'first rank'. She favoured pastel shades, which complemented her delicate colouring. At one ridotto she wore a lilac gown 'with beautiful flowers scattered down it. The sleeves were puckered gauze; worn with a veil richly trimmed with point lace, which flowed in a manner that considerably added to its beauty'. Out riding in the park she had a white habit with a pale-blue silk waistcoat, 'trimmed with silver lace, spangles, and silver frogs, as was then the fashion, with as elegant a hat as could be made'.

Many women in the late eighteenth century, ladies of fashion as well as women from the theatres and the world of gallantry, used make-up to enhance their charms.¶ They applied rouge, 'milk of roses'

---

* A breakfast attended by 'all the polite world', Cleone Knox wrote, consisted of 'Coffee, chocolate, biscuits, cream, buttered toasts, tea and Scandal'.

† A reference to Perdita Robinson, at one time the mistress of the Prince of Wales (later George IV).

‡ The *Biographical Dictionary of Actors* quotes from a letter she had published in the *Morning Post* in August 1774, protesting that the publication of a confidential correspondence between 'a beautiful actress' and 'a noble lord' had been an invasion of her privacy.

¶ Lady Coventry, one of the famously beautiful Gunning sisters (the other became the Duchess of Hamilton), is said to have died from the overuse of cosmetics, notably a lead-based whitener for the face.

and, if they could afford it, extortionately expensive pearl-powder, available from Mr Warren's shop in St James's for a guinea an ounce, to enhance their complexions.

There were other concoctions on the market that made more extravagant claims. 'Just imported, from Mademoiselle Pigout, at Paris, the veretable [sic] BLOOM of Ninon de L'Enclos,' heralded the *Morning Post*, 'which is for preserving, whitening and softening the skin . . . it removes pimples, freckles, morphews, worms etc, and gives such an amazing clearness to the skin as to entirely efface every appearance of age; it is peculiarly adapted for the hands and arms, guarding them against the severity of frost, and rendering them smooth and beautifully white'. This 'delicate composition' was quite unlike all others, the *Post* assured its readers, casting some doubt as to the quality of other eighteenth-century beauty products: 'it does not change its colour in the course of the night, or blow off upon going into the air, but continues in all its height of excellence throughout the day'.[26] Sophia, however, used none of these aids. Her beauty was still her own. '[You are] such a wonder of nature,' the Duke of Ancaster told her, 'that no man can gaze on you unwounded. You are in this respect like the Basilisk, whose eyes kill those whom they fix on.'

For a time Sophia continued to enjoy all the trappings of her celebrity. Wherever she went she was besieged by her admirers. One day her carriage was overturned, and it was 'not a little pleasant' to be surrounded by a crowd of nobility on foot, all enquiring how she was. 'Our knocker went till near two in the morning, with enquiries respecting us.'

Increasingly, however, it was a lonely, hunted kind of life. Not all the attention was desirable. Lord Harrington* called on Sophia at her box at the opera one night to declare his love, 'and it was with difficulty she could get him away'. When he was gone, Mrs Steele recalled, 'we had all the foreign ministers, one after the other, and many other noblemen'. Perhaps because they had travelled to England without their wives – who, like respectable Englishwomen, would never have

---

* William Stanhope, Earl of Harrington, was a notorious rake; he was sometimes known as 'Lord Fumble'.

consented to receive a courtesan, however fashionable, in their homes – Sophia soon came to be on dining terms with many of the diplomatic corps. Baron Diede, the Danish Ambassador, was the first to invite her.

'The dinner was splendid and elegant, and a band of soft music, in the next room, playing the whole time. When dinner was over, we retired to the music, and Mrs Baddeley sung many songs. Cards were then introduced, supper succeeded, and thus the evening closed,' wrote Mrs Steele, who had also been invited to attend. 'This meeting introduced Mrs Baddeley to all the diplomatic body, who were afterwards our visitants, and very polite to her.'

But the temporary excitement Sophia found in this new acquaintance did not last. She was soon exhausted by their attentions. 'I am so tormented with these old gentlemen,' she said in exasperation to Eliza Steele. Count Haslang, the seventy-year-old Bavarian Minister, was a particular bugbear. He always looked as if he had a stake down his back, Sophia complained; 'I hate him monstrously.' The Neapolitan Ambassador, too, became such an 'eternal plague' to her that she locked him up in a cupboard.

'Though it is pleasant to be admired and thought well of,' she complained to Mrs Steele, 'it is to the last degree irksome to be deprived of that rational conversation, which makes the company of gentlemen so agreeable, and to have one's ears filled with declarations of love, and a parcel of nonsense, that I am not in a situation to listen to. I declare to you, my dear friend, I often wish I was a hermit, and lived in a cave unnoticed by the world.'

To console herself for these vexations Sophia resorted to her usual pastime: shopping. Melbourne was still extremely generous to her, but she was so busy spending that she hardly noticed that his visits were not quite so frequent as before. A bill for £50 (£3000) would barely last her four days. When Mrs Steele once again proposed economy – Sophia could easily dress on £100 per annum, she suggested – her friend was outraged. '"Christ," exclaimed she, "that is not enough for millinery! . . . one may as well be dead as not in the fashion, and I am determined I will follow them all."'

As good as her word, on a trip to Paris Sophia bought a variety of caps, handkerchiefs, ruffles, aprons and 'trimming for a sack and coat costing £50'. From a jewellers she bought two watches and 'trinkets of several kinds with pocket books, and sundry other articles'. Several fans, some for the stage and some for her private use, were simply 'too expensive to name'. She also bought two dozen silk stockings, twelve dozen pairs of kid gloves and no fewer than twenty-four pairs of shoes.

It was not only clothes and trinkets on which Sophia spent her money. Her sprees became increasingly erratic. Once, when Mrs Steele went out of the house for the morning on her own private business, she came back to find that Sophia had bought eight white mice with red eyes, a handsome cage to keep them in, a silver collar and bell for her cat, and new cages for all her birds. 'I hated mice,' wrote Mrs Steele.

Sophia had always been extravagant, but this was something new. Increasingly she was becoming disconnected from the realities of life. The effort to curb her spending took up more and more of Mrs Steele's time and wits. In a stroke of genius, she took to sending for Sophia's hairdresser each time she had to go out alone. The elaborate coiffures of the day meant that a woman's hair could take as long as three hours to dress, which kept Sophia out of the shops for a large part of the day.* The Drury Lane hairdresser, for time-honoured reasons, was a particular favourite at Grafton Street.

> *This kind of gentry, having access to the ladies, frequently hear things in one house, which they carry to another. Ladies are too apt to converse with these fellows, and ask questions; and for every piece of intelligence they communicate, they are rewarded with news in return; so, that many women are as much diverted with their slander, as embellished by their art. This hairdresser dressed*

* This was probably a good idea for sanitary reasons, as well as from motives of thrift. On 18 June 1764, the young Irish heiress Cleone Knox, newly arrived in London, wrote in her diary: 'I spend half the day at the Hairdresser's now. My head has not been opened for over a fortnight, and this is positively the longest time I will go in this hot weather, though some Ladies keep their Heads unopened till they are Intolerable to themselves and everyone else. The dresser informed me that one lady from motives of thrift went so long a time that her head when opened was found to contain a Nest of Mice. Lord save me from that!' From *The Diary of a Young Lady of Fashion in the Year 1764–5.*

many at the theatre and used to entertain us with the scandal of the green room. Mrs Scott fell into fits because Mr Brereton took notice of Miss Hopkins ... and nothing could recover the dying nymph but the sweet odour of her Florizel's breath, and a gill glass of brandy.

The ruse did not always work. When it came to spending money, Sophia was not easily outwitted. On one occasion, when Mrs Steele left her alone for just two hours, she returned to find that in her absence Sophia had bought over £1000 worth of miscellaneous merchandise, all on credit. It included a quantity of exquisite point lace costing £200, silver flowers and trimmings worth £100, and a diamond necklace for £600.

Sophia now had debts of more than £3000 (£180,000). Although she was still besieged by her admirers, it was now obvious even to her that Melbourne's passion was cooling. To add to her problems, she found that she was pregnant – 'she was the way of many a married woman', as Mrs Steele phrased it – although she miscarried soon afterwards. Nonetheless, the frantic pursuit of pleasure continued unabated. 'Our life was such a continued scene of bustle and dissipation,' wrote Mrs Steele, 'that I wonder how she looked so well.'

Often, in summer time, have we returned from a place of amusement, at three in the morning; and, without going to rest, have changed our dress, and gone off in our phaeton, ten or twelve miles to breakfast; and, have kept this up for five or six days together without any sleep. In the morning, to an exhibition, or auction; this followed by an airing into Hyde-park; after that, to dress, then to the play; from thence, before the entertainment was over, away to Ranelagh, return perhaps at two; and, after supper and a little chat, the horses ordered, and to Epsom, or some other place again to breakfast; and, thus would she run on for many days together, and never say she was tired.

On the surface, Sophia carried on much as before; beneath, she was slowly unravelling. The arguments with Mrs Steele over her behaviour became increasingly heated. When they were invited to a grand ball at Oxford Sophia was determined to look her best, and set about getting some new clothes made up. Her diamond necklaces, she thought, could be strung together to make a beautiful band across her bosom. All that was wanted was a 'bow for her breast, and one for each sleeve' – in diamonds, of course – which she proposed to hire for the occasion from Mr Bellas, the jeweller in Pall Mall. The cost would be about £14. She said she hoped Mrs Steele would approve of her plan. Naturally, Mrs Steele did not approve at all.

I opposed it with saying that put the expence of it out of the question, the imprudence should be sufficient to prevent her; that nature had been bountiful to her; that she wanted no such additional ornaments; and that she would be as much if not more, admired with out them. I told her that vanity and extravagance was pointed at more than she thought of; that a less expensive dress would be considered as the produce of her own professional industry; but, decorated with diamonds, as she proposed, the world would only sneer at her, and cry, 'Look at Mrs Baddeley! Take notice of her diamonds! See what a quantity she has!' 'And how did she get them?' says another 'They are only the rewards of prostitution.' 'And what then?' returns she, angrily. 'I care not for any of their remarks; I will have the bows, and nothing shall prevent it. My person is my own, and I will do with it as I please.' And, growing still more enraged at the dread of a disappointment, she continued, 'Nay, I will do more than ever I have done yet; for I will not be debarred from seeing who I please, and doing with them what I please – I will have twenty times the quantity of diamonds I have.' – At this, she burst out into tears of rage, and sent her servant off for the diamonds she wanted. I let her go on uninterrupted; and, when she had finished, she ran out and bolted herself up in another room.

These passionate quarrels between the two women were always followed by equally passionate reconciliations. Sophia cried and 'hung round my neck', Mrs Steele wrote, begging her friend never to leave: 'She said it would be the study of her life to please me.' 'I looked at you often,' Sophia tells her, 'and a thousand foolish thoughts came into my head, that some reasons might in a little time take you from me; and then I should be an outcast and miserable.' Mrs Steele is 'all [that she] valued upon earth'. Mrs Steele, likewise, would have done almost anything, she tells their friend 'Mr P', if she thought it would help Mrs Baddeley. 'He said it was a strange infatuation, which he did not know how to account for; that rash as it was, he could not but commend me; as he was persuaded it must arise from affection only.'

Although Mrs Steele frequently threatened to leave Sophia if she did not mend her ways, she was never very serious about it. She really loved Sophia, for all her failings. And because she loved her, she understood her, and was generous in her understanding. 'It is an easy thing, for a woman to sit down and censure the conduct of Mrs Baddeley,' she wrote, 'but, I will venture to say, not one in ten, in her situation, could have withstood the temptations she met with.'

Money was not the only temptation in Sophia's way. She was a woman of strong appetites in every respect. While Lord Melbourne remained her official protector during this period, there was also a continual stream of unofficial lovers – mostly young officers and under-graduates, neither rich nor well connected – to whom Sophia was attracted for their own sakes. Even Mrs Steele's disapproval could not keep them away entirely. If anything, this evidence of Sophia's view of her own sexuality as a source of pleasure – rather than just as a commodity to be bartered – was the cause of even greater tension between the two women than were the scores of amorous old aristocrats laying siege to her.

Some of her intrigues were possibly quite innocent. Captain Fawkner, whom she fell for because he was 'as handsome as an angel', did nothing more sinister than flirt with her when they shared a box at the Richmond Theatre one evening. Nevertheless Mrs Steele, sitting disapprovingly behind them, was disgusted: 'In a word, no pen can describe the complexion and turn of the nonsense that fell from this gentleman's tongue,' she wrote waspishly, and when Sophia confessed that she had made 'a private arrangement' to meet him again, she was quick to scupper it.

Although no one in their household could have been in the slightest doubt as to the nature of Sophia's life at this time, Mrs Steele was always officiously anxious that she should keep up at least the semblance of propriety. She was scandalised when Sophia allowed another of her favourites, a Mr Storer, to visit her at home, and warned her gravely of the danger of 'exposing herself' in front of her servants. To this end, Mrs Steele kept up an exhausting vigil: she crept about the house, listened at keyholes. When poor Sophia – understandably desperate for privacy – finally locked the door of her chamber (she was 'conversing' with Lord Molyneux at the time), Mrs Steele remonstrated with her severely on the impropriety of her behaviour, extracted promises that she would regulate her conduct ('according to the plan I laid down for her'), and was determined that 'no one shall be admitted but such as . . . I approved'.

Sophia was forced to develop ruses in order to have her way. One day when they were engaged to dine with friends, she claimed she had a sick headache, and forced Mrs Steele to send them her apologies. 'I say *affecting to have*,' sniffed Mrs Steele, 'for Doctor Eliot, who attended her that morning, advised her, as she said, to take an airing, and I believe she pretended to be un-well, in order to keep an appointment she had made with Mr Storer the night before, at the masquerade, when I was dancing with Mr Conway; for, when we entered Hyde-Park, Mr Storer came up to the coach on foot, saying, he had been rambling in the air all morning. She asked him into the carriage, and he came in, rode once or twice round the Park with us, and on our return home, we set him down in Piccadilly.'

What was the real nature of Eliza Steele's relationship with Sophia? On a first reading of the *Memoirs*, it is clear that Mrs Steele's aim is to set herself up as the moral arbiter of Sophia's story. 'I hope it will be a lesson to some of my young readers,' she declaims in a typical aside, 'to be upon their guard against the treachery and deception of man, and learn by the fate of Mrs Baddeley . . . how much wiser and happier it is to follow the paths of virtue, and study by honest endeavours to live a reputable life, than to enjoy, as she did, for a time all the splendours and elegance of dissipation . . .' etc. etc. On another, perhaps more convincing, level, the entire six volumes can be read as a love story to her friend. 'Half the world is in love with you,' Lord

Falmouth tells Sophia, and that half surely included Mrs Steele.

In the eighteenth century there was nothing either unusual or improper about the idea of a passionately sentimental friendship between two women. The quality of Mrs Steele's devotion to her friend was very striking, however, even to contemporaries such as 'Mr P'. She would give everything for her friend, she tells him, even her life. If Sophia had written her own memoirs, would Mrs Steele have featured quite so prominently, or in quite so lustrous a light? It is impossible to tell.

Some of their contemporaries were convinced that Sophia merely provided a meal-ticket for her friend, but the relationship between Sophia and Mrs Steele was surely far more complex than that. While she certainly enjoyed the glamour and attention of being connected with Sophia, Mrs Steele claimed to have given up far more than she could ever have received: 'I had given her my little fortune, which I had for years worked for, and did not repine; that I had also forsaken my husband, neglected my family, and given her myself, and would now give up my life, if necessary, to serve her.' Theirs, she believed – or needed to believe, having sacrificed so much – was the central relationship in both their lives.

Sophia's erotic allure was such that she was quite as fascinating to many women as she was to men. Although there is no evidence that their love was ever overtly sexual, a clear erotic tension underpins much of Sophia's relationship with Eliza Steele. Mrs Steele's very bullying of Sophia, and her desire to manipulate and control her, seems part of this; her obsessive desire to keep Sophia's suitors away a form of jealousy, rather than the strict regard for propriety which she claims.

Where Sophia is pretty, flighty and volatile, Mrs Steele is brave, practical and protective. No one, we are told, drives their ungovernable horses as well as she. Although we can only guess her age (she was at school with Sophia, so must have been more or less a contemporary), or anything about her appearance, she was perhaps a little *too* fond of wearing men's clothing. When Sophia chooses a shepherdess costume for a masquerade, Mrs Steele accompanies her dressed in a domino and a man's hat. On their return from their trip to Paris, she once again dresses as a man, and is gratified when a French maidservant at the inn they stay in, mischievously egged on by Sophia, declares that she has fallen in love with her.

Indeed, as the narrative progresses, Mrs Steele's behaviour becomes noticeably more and more mannish, so much so that at one point – the most obviously exaggerated episode in the *Memoirs* – her story runs away with her and she actually begins to supersede Sophia as the main focus of the tale.

William Hanger, one of Sophia's very first lovers and the brother of Gaby, had by now inherited his father's title of Lord Coleraine, and came back in pursuit of Sophia, 'swearing like a mad-man that she should live with him, and him only'. Sophia was at this point still nominally under the protection of Lord Melbourne (when he asks Mrs Steele why she does not just keep the door of their house shut and have Coleraine denied, she expostulates: '"Denied?" cried I, "my Lord, denial was to little purpose; he would watch at the door like a dog, and whenever it was opened he would slip in and go upstairs. He offered me £1,000 to say where she was, and I was fearful he would bribe my servant to let him in at an improper time."'). Nonetheless, the two women, aided by another of Sophia's admirers, Colonel Luttrell, who has offered to give them his protection, flee to Ireland.

On this journey – which, as in a Fielding or a Richardson novel, is a sexy mixture of seduction and abduction – Mrs Steele gradually assumes centre stage. To protect Sophia, she carries a pair of pistols with her, which she is not afraid to use. In Dublin, when Lord Coleraine 'like a man crazed' finally catches up with them, Sophia is too frightened to utter, and it is Mrs Steele who both speaks and acts for her mute friend. She jumps out of the carriage behind Colonel Luttrell with her pistols drawn, and together they see off the enemy. 'As to you, Steele,' the Colonel commends her afterwards, 'you have a good spirit of your own, and had I stood in need of a second, I find I should not have wanted one.' Eliza Steele is inclined to agree with him. 'Indeed, when I considered all the different parts I played in life, and the many more I had to play,' she wrote, 'I wondered at my own abilities, resolution and spirits.'

In an era in which women were expected to be passive, modest and dependent, this is a powerful fantasy of female freedom and independence. For all their differences, Eliza Steele and Sophia Baddeley are in fact part of the same parable: Mrs Steele's actions are echoed by Sophia's vehement insistence on her own autonomy. 'My person is my own,' she rages at Mrs Steele, 'and I will do with it as I please.' Eighteenth-century readers of Mrs Baddeley's *Memoirs* may have seen this merely as further evidence of the quagmire of vice into which Sophia had sunk. But to a modern reader (and perhaps even to a few of her more free-thinking contemporaries) this plea for control over her own life is not only striking, but just. 'I will not be debarred from *seeing* who I please, and *doing* with them what I please,' she rails. Sophia's *Memoirs* show a world in which women, and women's concerns, are paramount (men, although ubiquitous, remain curiously shadowy figures); a world in which women have taken control of their own lives, at whatever the cost.

In Sophia's case, it must be said, it was a precarious kind of control. The independence offered by the life of courtesanry was always of a highly compromised and uncertain kind; and there were many other women who managed it much better than Sophia was ever able to. It is true, too, that the combination of celebrity, beauty and great riches – which she had perhaps to a greater degree than any other English courtesan has ever had – in the end came close to unhinging her. Yet she could not give her freedoms up. They may have been uncertain ones, but they were worth having nonetheless. In one of Sophia's darkest moments, Mrs Steele offered to set her up in business so that she could give up the life (she was at this point refusing even to go back on the stage), but she declined, saying that she was 'happy in her circumstances'. Nor was marriage an option that she desired. Of one of her admirers, a Mr Gill,* with whom she was briefly infatuated, Sophia declared: 'The young gentleman, I believe, loves me to adoration, but I will not be his wife notwithstanding, nor will I be the wife of any man; for I can never submit to the control of a husband, or

---

* 'Look Mrs Steele, what a beauty of a man!' Sophia whispers when she first sees Mr Gill, an Oxford undergraduate. 'He is even handsomer than Captain Fawkner.'

put it in his power to say I have been imprudent in life. I value and esteem Mr Gill, but I am resolved not to marry him.'

Although she did not yet know it, Sophia was about to pay a high price for her much-cherished independence. Not only did she now rarely see Lord Melbourne, who she had the uneasy feeling was avoiding her, but he was increasingly slow in responding to her demands for money. At a masquerade at Carlisle House she proposed to tackle him about it. Disconcertingly, when she at last discovered him in Mrs Cornelys's crowded rooms it was only to find him ensconced with Harriet Powell, another London courtesan, nearly as celebrated as Sophia herself, with whom Melbourne had lived before his marriage. Sophia, who was still masked, did not reveal herself until Harriet had left him, whereupon she at last caught hold of his arm, exclaiming, '"Ah, rebel! Have I caught thee?" – "My God!" said his Lordship, "Is it possible? What, Mrs Baddeley?" ... He then enquired how she had been entertained in her excursion [to Ireland with Colonel Luttrell], and whether she had met with the man of her heart.' Sophia made a vain attempt to explain the incident away. 'That's not a question, my Lord . . . after your neglect of me, that you have any right to ask,' she told him. 'You have not acted by me as I deserve, and I find a pleasure in telling you so.' But it was no good.

'He said it was *her* fault, not his, that he deserted her; for, had she not gone away, he should not have thought of it,' recalled Mrs Steele. 'This she denied; said, she had before made him acquainted with her situation, and that he had promised her, time after time, to relieve her, but had not kept his word; and, that being so long in the country, had it not been for the kindness of Mr P she might have been in jail; and, that that kindness had nearly ruined him. "Well," said his Lordship, "if it had, he would not be the first man, nor the last, that had ruined, or would ruin himself for a fine woman."' With these chilling words he asked her to leave him before they were both recognised.

Within hours, the news of Lord Melbourne's break with Sophia was all over town. Of course, as Mrs Steele was quick to point out, the applications to succeed him as Sophia's protector were numerous, but her debts were by now so great that they frightened off even the keenest of her suitors. To make matters worse, the many tradesmen whom Sophia had so liberally patronised, and who had never refused her credit while they were sure that she was under Melbourne's protection, now began to clamour for payment.

'I will take this opportunity to observe that persons in trade, who can have access to women in the situation Mrs Baddeley was then in are not wanting in industry to study for opportunities of laying before them a variety of pleasing and fashionable articles, and will give them credit to any amount,' observed Mrs Steele sadly. 'Mrs Baddeley . . . had what credit she pleased, but paid well in price for this indulgence; whereas, she was no sooner looked cool upon by her friends, than these tradesmen became very importunate, and even insolent.'

Who could blame them? Over the last few years Sophia had run up debts with reckless disregard for reality. Even by the desperate act of pawning her diamonds, it was all she could do to raise a few hundred pounds to keep the most pressing creditors at bay. Mrs Steele's friend, 'Mr P', had rashly agreed to take on some of Sophia's debts until she could find a way to pay him back, but when no attempt at payment was forthcoming, finally even his patience was exhausted, and he called in the loan (a bond for £1600). Sophia was arrested, but was heroically rescued from the bailiffs by Mrs Steele, dressed in drag. Within hours this scandal too was all over town.

Even the good 'Mr P''s misguided generosity would not have been enough to help Sophia now. Some idea of the scale of her debts (and a fascinating insight into the shopping habits of an eighteenth-century *fashionista*) can be seen in the bills, collected and kept by Mrs Steele, which were run up by Sophia over a three-year period.

	£.	s.	d.
Miss Brace, milliner, by ballance	£120	0	0
Mrs Bowen, ditto	£218	18	10
Mrs Titherson, ditto	£180	11	0
Mr Price, ditto, by ballance of £700	£230	0	0
Mr King, mercer, by ballance of more than £1200	£290	0	0

	£	s.	
Mr Titterson, woollen-draper	£40	10	0
Mr Burnell, silver lace man	£30	10	0
Mr Campbell, coach-maker	£200	19	0
Mr Dyford, and Mr Clark, shoe-makers	£20	14	0
Mr Rolson, hatter	£29	10	0
Mr Evans, linen draper	£140	0	0
Mr King, hoop-maker	£8	10	0
Mr Tutt, trimming-broker	£18	12	0
Mr Jefferey's, jeweller, by ballance	£180	12	0
Mrs Whitelock, mantua-maker	£10	14	0
Mrs Humphries, hosier and glover	£20	11	0
Perfumers bills	£30	19	0
Builders bills	£759	11	8
Stable rent	£18	0	0
Cornfactor, in ballance	£48	0	0
Hay and straw	£10	0	0
Farriers bills in ballance	£10	0	0
Flowerist in ditto	£18	0	0
China-man in ditto	£10	10	0
Flambeaux for one year	£20	12	0
	£2,666	4	6

This enormous sum was only 'in ballance' (i.e. still owing), as Mrs Steele puts it, on more than £8000 (nearly half a million pounds by today's reckoning) of bills run up over the period. Mostly these were for clothes, shoes, and especially hats and headpieces – a staggering £748 (£45,000) on millinery alone. They did not include any of Sophia's expenses for housekeeping, servants' wages, furniture, travelling, horses, theatres, opera, masquerade tickets or any other entertainments. Nor did they include the principal part of her outlay on jewellery.

When Sophia was forced to pawn her diamonds, Mrs Steele kept a careful record of this, too.

	£.	s.
Two diamond necklaces, which cost	£1,050	0
A pair of drop brilliant ear-rings, ditto	£350	0
Ditto rose diamond ones, ditto	£100	0

Six pins, at £20 each, ditto	£120	0
A star, ditto	£94	10
Three diamond rings, ditto	£100	0
	£1,814	10

Although they had cost nearly £2000 (just over £100,000), Sophia was barely able to scrape together £600 from the broker, less than a third of their real value. Her total debts at this time were estimated by Mrs Steele to be around £7000. Even the richest of Sophia's remaining suitors – which included Lord Cholmondley and an unnamed but extremely wealthy Jewish merchant – balked at the thought.

Sophia's decline did not happen all at once. Although now living in much reduced circumstances – she had given up her grand residence in fashionable Grafton Street, and moved to her more modest house in the riverside village of Hammersmith instead – she could still put on a good show. The diamonds may have been replaced with cheap glass beads, but as far as her public was concerned, Sophia's beauty, elegance and seductiveness were undimmed. At a benefit performance for one of her actor friends at Drury Lane she appeared resplendent in 'a rich white silk, sprigged with gold and a number of French beads, made with a train. The sleeves were covered with gauze, and decorated with point lace, with rows of beads round her arms, tied in elegant bows.' Sometime soon after, she returned to the stage.

Mrs Steele's chronology is always a little haphazard, but from the Drury Lane bills we know that Sophia appeared on 26 March 1774 as Lady Elizabeth in *The Earl of Warwick*, her first theatre engagement in over three years. She was rapturously received. The applause from all parts of the house, wrote the loyal Mrs Steele, 'was so great and so loud, that it was more than ten minutes before she could begin'.

Nonetheless, Sophia's status, in some indefinable way, had declined. Although she was still receiving an extremely handsome salary – £7 per week the following season, in which she opened as Olivia in *Twelfth Night* – it was by no means the dizzying sum she had commanded at the height of her powers. Her desertion by Melbourne had left her vulnerable in areas other than merely financial ones. Imperceptibly, that greyest of grey areas, the infinitely subtle line between a courtesan, with enough glamour and fashionable status to pick and choose her protectors, and a plain woman of the town (available to more or less anyone so long as the price was right), was slowly beginning to shift.

One day the Duke of Cumberland, one of the Prince of Wales's uncles, sent for Sophia from a well-known house of assignation called the Duke's Head Tavern, in Southampton Street, Covent Garden. Mrs Steele took up the tale: 'From this house his Royal Highness sent one day a man, whose name was Davis, with his respectful compliments to Mrs Baddeley, and requested the favour of being permitted to wait on her; or if she would indulge him by coming to him there, he would think himself obliged.' Sophia reacted with fury. 'Go and tell the Duke to send for Lady Grosvenor [Lady Grosvenor's affair with the Duke had resulted in the humiliation of a lurid and extremely public divorce for her adultery],' she retorted. 'I wonder at his impudence, in sending for me to a Tavern; and as to seeing him at my house, I am too much engaged to receive his visits.' Sophia was 'deeply affronted', added Mrs Steele somewhat unnecessarily, 'at receiving such an application'.

But the truth was that Sophia now had no choice but to consider such 'applications'. The balance of power had shifted, and there was no going back. Although Cumberland's request was really no different in substance from the offers she had received before, its peremptory tone was something entirely new. To Sophia, used to the deference of dukes, it must have sounded especially harsh. There were other, more respectful suitors, it is true: a Mr Foote, a Mr Coleman, and at one time an unnamed merchant who sent his wife in her own carriage complete with liveried servants to call on her, and then, behind her back, offered Sophia £1500 in a crude attempt at seduction. Somehow, though, it was not quite the same.

The glamour and the excitement, however superficial, of mixing in aristocratic circles had gone a long way to disguising the true nature of Sophia's profession even from herself. She must have known that she had reached her lowest ebb when she found herself seriously considering an offer from a Mr Petrie – we know nothing about him other than that he was 'a Scotch gentleman' – who was willing to settle £100 a year on her before he asked for any favours. Mrs Steele, as usual, provided all the details: an attorney drew up the settlement, properly secured on some stock in the funds, which was signed, executed and presented to Sophia, who, ever the 'changeling', at the last minute pulled out. It would be an inconvenience, she reflected, to receive the visits of a man she disliked any time he pleased.

Vulnerable and needy, Sophia had already made a much bigger mistake than any arrangement with Mr Petrie would have been. She had fallen in love. It is uncertain exactly at what point she began her liaison with Stephen Sayer, but it was probably around the same time that she returned to the theatre, in 1774. Her relationship with him marks a watershed in her life. After Melbourne, there was always hope of some sort of recovery for Sophia; after Sayer there was none.

One of the Sheriffs of the City of London, Sayer was a prominent political figure in the City; as a Wilkite* and a republican, he was also considered highly dubious by Sophia's aristocratic acquaintance. Sophia, on the other hand, was entranced. Like a storybook hero, Sayer was tall, dark and good-looking. 'Did you ever see a more elegant, handsome man in your life?' Sophia raved to her friend. 'He has a soul formed for love.' At his instigation, Sophia took a house in London again, in Cleveland Row in St James's, which she could ill afford (the cost was a cool two hundred guineas a year), and Sayer became their constant visitor.

Mrs Steele found him thoroughly unsavoury. He had 'trencher friends' and no manners, cooking messy beefsteaks for them over the dining-room fire: 'a style of living we had not been used to', she sniffed, 'and it made such a stink and dirt, that I was ready to go distracted'. Their tranquil oasis of female companionship was no more. As if this were not bad enough, Sayer mistreated Sophia too; living off her, taking her money, and ordering her about like a servant. A woman turned up, claiming to be his wife. The remainder of Sophia's old circle of friends slowly began to trickle away.

So great was her infatuation with Sayer, however, that she shut

* A follower of the radical politician John Wilkes, who despite his disreputable lifestyle (he was a member of the notorious Hellfire Club) became a champion of free speech and a self-styled 'friend of liberty'.

herself up and went nowhere, except when she was in his company. The rest of her acquaintance cut her when she appeared with him in public. Where was her much-cherished independence now? But she was in love, and pregnant, and there was no reasoning with her. Finally, when Sayer announced that he was moving in with them, even Mrs Steele decided that she had had enough.

After Mrs Steele's departure from Sophia's household, the *Memoirs* begin to peter out. Although she could no longer bear to see Sophia in the life she had now chosen, her friend did not – could not – desert her entirely. Sayer, however, soon did, leaving his mistress when she was heavily pregnant in order to marry another, richer woman. (He was later imprisoned for the treasonable offence of speaking against the royal family.)

The glimpses we have of Sophia from now on are snatched ones. After Sayer left her she fell ill, perhaps giving way to the nervous complaint which had affected her after her laudanum overdose several years previously, and was once again rescued by Mrs Steele, although they seem never to have lived together again.

Mrs Steele, who continued to see her friend throughout these troubled times, was witness to a strange little postscript in the life of Sophia Baddeley. Some years later, on one of her occasional visits to Sophia, who was lying in after the birth of her third child,* the two women were surprised by a loud rapping at the door. From the window they saw an elegant little phaeton drawn up below, with four beautifully matched ponies, and two little postboys charmingly attired in blue and silver jackets. It was Perdita Robinson – 'the person the Prince of Wales is so fond of' – who had come to pay her respects to Mrs Baddeley and to congratulate her on the birth of her son. Although the two courtesans – one royally garlanded with all the trappings of her success, the other now all but forgotten by the *beau monde* – had not met before, they proceeded to tell one another their stories.

'Mrs Baddeley gave her a particular account of the situation she was in,' remembered Mrs Steele, 'and the treatment she had experienced, from those who professed a friendship for her; which, when Mrs

* See page 79.

Robinson heard, she cried out, "Oh, the ingratitude of mankind!"'
Perhaps Perdita was remembering that night when she had first seen
Sophia at the Pantheon masquerade, her beautiful face one of the
wonders of England. Whatever thoughts were in her mind, Mrs
Robinson shed a few tears that afternoon in Sophia's little room,
although in this, Mrs Steele noticed, she was unperceived by Mrs
Baddeley, 'which induced me to conceive her to be a woman, in spite
of all her errors, possessed of the finer feelings'.

That a courtesan should end her life in a state of disease and desertion is a commonplace of almost all the stories which have been told
about them, even Mrs Steele's. But in fact, Sophia's end was rather
different from that which her friend implies. Following her desertion
by Stephen Sayer and the long illness that followed, Sophia had once
again returned to the stage, making her debut as Violante in *The
Wonder* on 27 August 1776 at Brighton. The following year, after what
had been an absence of two years, she was re-engaged by David Garrick
at Drury Lane for the extremely handsome salary of £8, with an
additional allowance of £4 to £6 for clothes, a total of £14 [£850] per
week* (considerably more than she had received on her first return
to the theatre in 1774, when she was paid just £7 a week[27]). As her
salary indicates, she was still the darling of the London audiences. She
was rapturously received – one source claims that the applause when
she attended a benefit for an actress called Miss Younge lasted ten
minutes[28] – and remained at Drury Lane for the next four seasons. At
her benefit, on 11 April 1778, she cleared £139.9s (nearly £8500). This
may not have been much compared to the immense riches she once
commanded, but for an actress of this period, using her singing and
acting talents alone, it was a huge sum.

All this evidence suggests that Sophia Baddeley, far from being
handicapped by her riotous reputation, in the end had no difficulty
in making a comeback (it seems to have been easier once she had
parted from Sayer). Although she was indeed no longer the fashion,
and was now 'unnoticed by those who once adored her', this was all

---

* The average salary, it will be remembered, for a top-ranking actress at the end of the
eighteenth century was £10 per week.

to the good for her own peace of mind at least. It was probably during this period that she began her relationship with one of her fellow actors, a man named Webster, with whom she felt happy and secure enough to have two children.

Sophia's real downfall was not the result of her career as a courtesan, but of ill-health. Her last appearance at Drury Lane is recorded on 1 December 1780, when she played the female lead in Thomas Arne's *Artaxerxes*. By 1781, however, the 'nervous disorder' she had developed earlier in her life (possibly after the end of her relationship with 'Gaby' Hanger) began to take its toll once more. It is impossible to know precisely what triggered this spell of illness, but it may have been connected with the death of her 'husband' Mr Webster.

Webster's death certainly marked another low point in Sophia's life. She had been pregnant at the time (it was after the birth of this child that Perdita Robinson visited her), and she soon turned to another man, named John, described by the disapproving Mrs Steele as Webster's favourite servant, 'a low-bred fellow, not possessed of a shilling, nor in any way to earn his bread, but as a servant'. She added with despair: 'To think that she should thus far fall . . .'

But perhaps Sophia was past thinking. Unhappiness and shock had sent her into a fatal spiral of ill-health, debt and laudanum addiction. Forced to leave London because of her creditors, she went with her young family and John – who according to Mrs Steele she had now resourcefully trained up to be a 'player' himself – to Dublin, where she appeared at the Smock Alley Theatre, and from thence, in 1783, to Edinburgh, from where the actor-manager Tate Wilkinson hired her to join his company in York.

In York, Sophia had a brief success. Her performances – which included Clarissa in *The School for Fathers*, Polly Peachum in *The Beggar's Opera* and Imogen in *Cymbeline* – were much admired, but her use of laudanum was becoming increasingly out of control. On her last night at York, so Tate Wilkinson recorded in his notebook, 'She was very lame, and to make matters worse, was so stupidly intoxicated with laudanum that it was with great difficulty she could finish her performance.'[29] The quantity of the drug she was now taking, he noted, was 'incredible', but despite this, and the fact that she ate scarcely anything, her complexion retained its beauty to the last.

Although Sophia received 'very genteel payment' from Wilkinson – he does not say how much – he was at a loss to make out what she did with it (his grim explanation was that 'Mrs Stell', her friend and companion, 'had always occasion for such sums as that unfortunate woman received'). And when Sophia returned to Edinburgh, she was 'in truth reduced to beggary, not worth a single shilling'.

Back in Scotland, however, she picked herself up sufficiently to start acting again, playing leading roles (Ophelia in *Hamlet* and Imogen among them) with the Edinburgh company, with whom she remained until the end of the 1785 season, when she 'fell into a consumption' and could act no longer.

Sophia Baddeley died on 1 July 1786, aged forty-one.* Her passing was instantly seized on as a warning to other women of the consequences of a life of vice. The poet Anthony Pasquin summed up what many of her contemporaries were still determined to think about her:

> Turn your fancy to Scotia, where rigorous snows
> Envelope her rocks, and stern Eolus blows;
> There view lovely Baddeley stretch'd on her bier,
> Whose pallid remains claim the kindred tear;
> Emaciate and squalid her body is laid,
> Her limbs lacking shelter, her muscles decay'd.
> An eminent instance of feminine terror.
> A public example to keep us from error.[30]

And yet, far from ending her days in a state of miserable penury (widely believed to be the inevitable consequence of a 'life of vice'), Sophia had in fact succeeded in supporting herself and her young family (we do not know what became of John), working as an actress continuously and mostly successfully for nearly ten years, from her return to the stage in 1776 until shortly before her death. She had done all this in the face of ill-health, drug addiction and debt (although this last, it must be remembered, was not unusual in eighteenth-century London). When she died she was surrounded by friends, the players

---

* Other obituary notices gave her age variously as thirty-seven, thirty-eight and forty-two.

of the Edinburgh company, who had loved her sufficiently to subscribe a weekly sum from their own pockets 'to afford her all the comforts a sick bed required, and a proper person to attend her'.

2

ELIZABETH ARMISTEAD

1750–1842

The Woman of Pleasure

'YOU ARE ALL TO ME. You can always make me happy in circumstances apparently unpleasant and miserable ... Indeed my dearest angel, the whole happiness of my life depends on you,'[1] wrote Charles James Fox to the courtesan Elizabeth Armistead on 7 May 1785. The tale of Charles James Fox, aristocrat, Whig grandee, and one of the most brilliant and charismatic men of his day, and Elizabeth Armistead, is one of the great love stories of the eighteenth century.

Mrs Armistead was born Elizabeth Bridget Cane on 11 July 1750.* Like almost all women of the town, even the well-known ones, her origins are obscure. One of the two '*Tête-à-Têtes*' published about her in the *Town and Country Magazine* claims that her father was a shoemaker-turned-Methodist lay preacher. Another account makes her the offspring of a market porter and a herb vendor. In neither is there any clue as to whether or not there ever was a Mr Armistead – let alone whether Fox's beloved Liz had ever married him. Some contemporaries believed that the name was only a *nom de guerre*, as it were, and that no such person as Mr Armistead ever existed. More likely is that a man called Armistead was an early protector of Elizabeth's, and that,

---

* In her excellent work *The Harlot and the Statesman*, I.M. Davis has established Mrs Armistead's real name and date of birth by the record of a land purchase made by her.

as was the frequent custom of the day, she decided to take his name.

What is certain is that by the time Fox met Mrs Armistead she was one of the richest and most celebrated courtesans of her day, the reigning toast of the town, with a string of fashionable and aristocratic lovers – including two dukes, an earl, a viscount and the Prince of Wales himself – to her name. Her success as a woman of pleasure was such that by the time she met Fox in 1783 she was already a woman of substantial independent means, having secured not one but two handsome annuities in the course of her career, and had no more worlds to conquer. 'With looks above envy, and a reputation beneath contempt, she was at peace with the world. She knew more men, and knew them better, than any woman of her day, and her final choice was Fox.'[2]

This was no Romeo and Juliet affair. Fox was thirty-four; Elizabeth was thirty-three. Yet their love, when it came, was that rare and deep passion between a man and a woman which surmounts all obstacles: social convention, politics, the vicissitudes of time and fortune, even sustained domesticity (in fact, they were to be at their happiest when living just so, with their books and their garden, at Mrs Armistead's house at St Anne's Hill).

'She is a comfort to me in every misfortune,' wrote Fox many years later to his nephew Henry Holland, 'and makes me enjoy doubly every pleasant circumstance of life; there is to me a charm and delight in her society, which time does not in the least wear off, and for real goodness of heart if she ever had an equal, she never had a superior ... The Lady of the Hill is one continual source of happiness to me.'[3]

Only death would part them.

Exactly how – or why – Mrs Armistead embarked on her career on the town (an eighteenth-century euphemism for prostitution) is not known. Unlike the story of Sophia Baddeley, there is none of the raffish glamour of the stage to disguise the baldly unsettling fact of these beginnings. Elizabeth's path was likely to have been a much harder one.

Once again, the *Town and Country Magazine*'s 'Tête-à-Têtes' give two widely divergent accounts of her initiation. In the 1776 version, Elizabeth was a very pretty girl of sixteen when she met 'a friseur [a hairdresser] of some eminence' who persuaded her to let him use her as a model. He convinced her that 'the dressing of her hair would be a great ornament to her, and that she would certainly make her fortune if she displayed herself to advantage'. This man, a Mr R–, undertook to dress her hair *gratis*, whereupon 'she very gratefully returned the obligation, by yielding to his amourous intreaties'. With this *friseur*, clearly a man of the world, Elizabeth was able to embellish not only the outside of her head, but the inside of it too, learning 'such useful ideas, as brought her forth into polite life'. But their liaison did not last.

> *After some months enjoyment the ardour of his passion subsided, and he was desirous to get rid of our heroine; he accordingly equipped her very genteely, and took a lodging for Mrs A-st-d in the polite part of the town, where, he said, she could not fail of succeeding.*[4]

The 1779 '*Tête-à-Tête*', on the other hand, makes an entirely different claim, insisting that when Elizabeth's shoemaker father decided to become a lay preacher, he simply abandoned his daughter, leaving her to shift for herself. Elizabeth was about nineteen at this time, and had no resources, other than 'the sale of her charms', to support her. Although she had none of the mesmerising erotic beauty of Sophia Baddeley, she was nonetheless an extremely striking young woman, 'tall and genteel, with a beautiful face and a most captivating eye'.[5] A portrait of her by Reynolds, painted some years later, shows her to have a luxuriant head of dark hair (so perhaps there is some truth in the story of the eminent *friseur*). It was in this 'deserted and distressed' situation that she was found by Mrs Goadby.

Elizabeth's fate was a typical one for a beautiful but unprotected young woman, for Jane Goadby was perhaps the most notorious procuress in London. Her establishment in Marlborough Street was famous because it was the first to ape the expensive and magnificently decorated Parisian bordellos which catered exclusively to the aristocracy and gentlemen of the *ton*. The establishment, the prototype for many of the luxurious 'nunneries' which sprang up in its wake, caused a sensation: 'Mrs Goadby, that celebrated Lady Abbess, having fitted up an elegant nunnery in Marlborough Street, is now laying in a choice stock of Virgins for the ensuing season. She has disposed her Nunnery in such an uncommon taste, and prepared such an extraordinary accommodation for gentlemen of all ages, sizes, tastes and caprices, as it is judged will far surpass every seminary of the kind yet known in Europe.'[6]

As a deserted and friendless female, Elizabeth's situation could have been very much worse. In his 'List of Covent Garden Ladies', also known as the 'Man of Pleasure's Kalendar', which was published in London almost every year throughout the second half of the eighteenth century, Jack Harris gives details of all the 'most celebrated Ladies now on the town or in Keeping'. As much a feature of London life as call-girls' cards in telephone boxes are today, 'Harris's List', as it was universally known, gives some idea of the immense scale of the sex trade in mid-Georgian times.

As well as a name and address, there was a physical description of each woman listed, and details of her specialities, if any. Thus, Miss B–nf-ld, at 9 Poland Street, was 'frequently mounted à la militaire, and as frequently performs the rites of the love-inspiring queen according to the equestrian order, in which style she is said to afford uncommon delight'.

Miss B-lm-t of 32 Union Street, on the other hand, while not at all pretty, compensated for her lack of looks by her mouth, which seemed 'by its largeness, prepared to swallow up whoever may have courage to approach her'.

More exotic tastes were also catered for, and could be lucrative, as Mrs L-v-b-nm of 32 George Street found when she was 'left a pretty good fortune by an old flagellant, whom she literally flogged out of the world'. (Flagellation was very popular amongst the upper classes, and high-class bordellos such as Mrs Goadby's were quick to advertise their equipment when it became available.) Miss S– specialised in a game called 'milk the cow'; while the eerily modern Mrs M– enacted scenes with herself as a schoolmistress with her 'two young beautiful tits [meaning young women, rather than breasts], one about fifteen and the other sixteen, who are always dressed in frocks like school girls'.[7]

In addition to this basic information, the List also contains a surprising amount of detail about the women themselves, their histories and, as Harris put it, 'curious anecdotes' about them. Today it makes poignant reading. The story of 'Our Sweet bewitching Miss W-ll-m' of 17 Goodge Street is typical. Miss William, who was twenty years old, was possessed of 'a most elegant figure, of a beautiful face, and has a skin so fair, that were it possible to paint its equal, would require the utmost sketch of the most fertile fancy'. A few years previously this extremely young woman had become intimate with a sea officer 'who made her his *cara sposa pro tempore*, in which state she lived happy till his official duty compelled him to go abroad, and leave his dear a prey to the precarious buffetings of fortune, who, soon after, threw her in the common road, and gave her up as public property'.

Stories of abandonment such as this were commonplace. Stories of seduction, elopement and broken promises more frequent still, as was the case with another twenty-year-old, Miss M-nt-n of 55 Berwick Street. 'A young baronet in this lady's spring of life, unrobed her of her virgin suit,' recorded Harris. 'Almost as soon as possession was granted indifference took place and desire entirely vanished, and he left his much dejected fair one to seek support in the wide field of fortune.' Miss M-nt-n had 'a good complexion . . . a lively sparkling dark eye, was of a small size, and [had] a remarkable pretty hand and arm', but she was also sadly disfigured by smallpox. 'Her demands are very moderate,' added Harris. Her experience with the baronet made her subject to great lowness of spirits, 'which in general requires three of four chearful [sic] glasses to dissipate'.

The same misfortune had befallen Mrs Alt-n, of 4 Gress Street, Rathbone Place, who as the daughter of a wealthy farmer in Berkshire might have expected an altogether kindlier path through life. When she was just fifteen this girl had eloped from her boarding school with the dancing master who 'from his wonderous adroitness and address, had then (or quickly after did) wriggle himself into her favour; she had not long been blessed with this Adonis, but satiety took place, and he left her in town to pursue the practice of heart winning immediately after his departure'.

Even in an age which was conspicuously robust in its attitude to sex, the price paid by women (particularly young unmarried women) for erotic self-expression was ruinously high. The brothels and *bagnios* of London were full of women who had committed a *faux pas*, as the saying went, and who then found themselves either disowned by their families, or too ashamed to return home. Miss Wel-ls, of 35 Newman Street, Harris tells us, was a young 'genteel' girl, the daughter of a farmer in Wales who had sent her to stay in London in the care of her aunts. 'A young gentleman ingratiated himself so far into her graces as to gain her consent to make him happy by her ruin, under a promise of marriage, but no sooner had enjoyment dampened the ardour of his love, than he abandoned her to the reproaches and calumny of a merciless world, till at length with shame and disappointment she quitted her aunts and entered on the town.'

Whatever the circumstances may have been for Mrs Armistead when she 'entered on the town' – abandonment by her family, an early seduction or elopement, or simple poverty – what is certain is that once she had embarked upon it, there was no going back. The loss of a woman's reputation, her 'character', as the eighteenth century termed it, through a perceived sexual misdemeanour (it is one of the unfairnesses of history that for a woman, 'character' depended almost exclusively on sexual conduct) was irreversible.

Although it is only the *Town and Country Magazine* that specifically mentions Mrs Goadby's establishment in connection with Elizabeth, it is very likely that it was in one of London's more exclusive brothels that she began her career. They were not hard to find. The Covent Garden area, where the principal theatres were, had been synonymous with prostitution since the time of the Restoration, but by the early 1770s, when Elizabeth was starting out, the area of St James's (conveniently close for royal customers) had come to have far greater cachet.

A hundred years previously this district had been a place of cheap brothels, and taverns with dubious reputations such as the Rose and

Crown, at which, as Pepys observed in his diary, 'cundums* could be bought'. By the mid-eighteenth century, however, the area was part of an elegant new development and boasted some of London's most exclusive attractions, as Baron Johann Wilhelm von Archenholz described on his visit to London in 1773:

> there are many noted Houses ... in St James where a great number of them are kept for People of Fashion. A little street called King's Place is inhabited by Nuns of this Order who live under the direction of several rich Abbesses. You may see them superbly clothed at Publick Places ... each of these Convents has a Carriage and Servants-at-livery for these ladies never deign to walk anywhere but in St James Park ... the price of Admission to these Temples is so exorbitant that the Mob are entirely excluded ... only a few rich people can aspire to the Favours of these Venal Divinities ... the bagnios are magnificent buildings ... the Furniture not unworthy of the Palace of a Prince. They can procure everything to enrapture the senses ... the Women are instantly brought in Sedan-chairs and only those celebrated for their Fashion, Elegance, and Charms have the honour of being admitted ... in these places more money is exhausted during one night ... than would maintain the Seven United Provinces [the Nether-lands] for six months.[8]

These high-class bordellos were little worlds all of their own. Elizabeth would have found herself living, almost cosily, *en famille* with the other girls. Mrs Goadby's fellow procuress Sarah Prendergast, for example, who operated at 3 George Court (once the house of London's most exotic madam, the former slave 'Black Harriott'), kept only three young women on her permanent staff, each of them hand-picked for her good background and perfect manners.

In these strange, hothouse environments the girls often made close friendships with one another, some of which lasted throughout their lifetimes. They had their own doctors (in an age in which venereal

---

* In English popular mythology the condom's invention was attributed to a 'Colonel Cundum': alas, he never existed. Elsewhere, the sheath had been in use for not hundreds, but thousands of years.

disease was not only rife, but frequently fatal, the women were regularly inspected to ensure that they were healthy). Discreet supplies of Mrs Phillips's 'fam'd new Engines – Implements of Safety for Gentlemen of Intrigue' were always available.* These rudimentary condoms, usually made from dried sheepgut, came in three convenient sizes. They would, of course, have protected the women as well as the men from disease (this being the principal reason that they were used in the eighteenth century), but were also undoubtedly one of the reasons why relatively few courtesans seem to have fallen pregnant during their working careers.

Thanks to the pioneering Mrs Goadby, the living quarters in all the King's Place brothels were luxurious by eighteenth-century standards. Mrs Hayes, at 5 King's Place, had special 'Elastick Beds' designed for her which provided better support and comfort for her more elderly guests (when she eventually sold up there was a mad scramble for them amongst the other 'abbesses'). As the Baron had noticed, most of these establishments also kept their own carriage, complete with liveried servants (ingeniously combining the ultimate luxury good with free advertising), in which the ladies were regularly taken for drives along the most fashionable promenades in London, resplendent in the jewellery and gold lavished on them by their grateful clientele.

Every season many of these 'families' would repair further afield, making expeditions to fashionable watering places such as Bath and Tunbridge Wells, and later to the newly 'discovered' fishing village of Brighthelmstone (Brighton). Their peregrinations were frequently recorded, in highly-coloured descriptions, in the scandal sheets and magazines of the day, which were almost as eager for gossip about the 'Cyprian Corps' as they were for stories about actresses and the stage.

---

* In the eighteenth century most of the well-known retailers of these 'machines' were women. Mrs Phillips was a keen advertiser of her wares, and she and her chief competitor, Mrs Perkins, conducted a 'handbill war' over the sale of their wares. In the *St James's Chronicle* Mrs Phillips, who operated from Moon Street in the Strand, boasted of her thirty-five years of experience 'in the business of making and selling machines, commonly called implements'. Perhaps what clinched it for most customers, however, was the catchy jingle at the end: 'To guard yourself from shame or fear,/Votaries of Venus, hasten here;/ None in my wares e'er found a flaw/Self-preservation's nature's law.'

The King's Place nunneries, as these high-class brothels were soon named, prided themselves on the elegance and 'genteel' manners of their inmates. A surprising number of them, such as Harriet Hesketh and Margaret Cuyler, both of whom were to be found at Mrs Matthews's establishment, needed no formal training in these arts.

Harriet was the daughter of Sir Robert and Lady Hesketh, a tall and elegant beauty who had run away from her dreary husband – the Rev. Mr Bone – to live with her lover, Colonel Francis Egerton, dashing son of the Earl of Bridgewater, and who later took to 'receiving' other aristocratic men. Margaret, on the other hand, had been brought up just a stone's throw from Mrs Matthews's, at St James's Palace, where her mother had been a lady-in-waiting to the queen. When she was just fifteen Margaret had also run away with a young army officer, Colonel Cornelius Cuyler, who settled £300 a year on her and provided her with a house and servants. When he was sent abroad, however, Margaret grew increasingly restless and flighty, and is said to have patronised Mrs Matthews's as a way of making extra money for her increasing extravagances, including the wild and debauched parties she was fond of giving with other well-known demi-reps such as Grace Dalrymple Eliot and Gertrude Mahon.*

A girl did not have to be well-born in order to be taken in by an exclusive brothel. A successful procuress made it her business to train up all the young women who passed through her doors, no matter what their origins may have been. Charlotte Hayes, perhaps the most famous of all the London madams in the late eighteenth century, was particularly skilful. Mrs Hayes began her career by opening a brothel near to Jane Goadby's in Marlborough Street, but in 1767 she prudently decided to move closer to the Court, and took a house at 2 King's Place. In his diaries, William Hickey describes how he often used to visit this 'experienced old matron' (Charlotte Hayes was then all of fifty) at her 'house of celebrity in King's Place'.

In later life Hickey re-encountered a girl he had known there, Emily

* Not everyone found Margaret 'genteel', despite her noble background. William Hickey thought her 'a great jack-whore' with a 'masculine vulgarity of manners'.

Warren, who turned up as the kept courtesan of one of his friends, Robert Pott. 'Bob' Pott had set her up in some style in a 'handsome, well furnished house in Cork Street', complete (of course) with a clutch of liveried servants, a dashing bright yellow carriage with the Potts' arms emblazoned on the side, and a box at the opera. 'Never did I behold so perfect a beauty,' recalled Hickey of his first sight of Emily in 1776. Mrs Hayes had then only recently acquired her, 'an unripe and awkward girl', but with features of such exquisite beauty that she was considered by her new madam to be a great prize, and one that would bring her good business.

Later, Hickey came to hear Emily's story. She had been found by Mrs Hayes on the streets of London when she was not quite twelve years of age. She was leading her father, a blind beggar, and 'soliciting charity from every person that passed'. Mrs Hayes was so struck with the 'uncommon beauty of the child's countenance' that she set her 'myrmidons' to work and, apparently without difficulty, soon got her into her clutches and set about training her up.*

'I have frequently seen the little sylph, Emily, under the tuition of the ancient dame, learning to walk,' wrote Hickey, 'a qualification Madam Hayes considered of importance, and in which her pupil certainly excelled, Emily's movements and air being grace personified, and attracting universal admiration whenever she appeared abroad. Sir Joshua Reynolds, whom all the world allowed to be a competent judge, had painted her portrait many times and in different characters. He often declared every limb of hers perfect symmetry, and altogether he had never seen so faultless and finely formed a human figure.'[9]

Emily was an apt scholar. Not only did she learn to walk and move gracefully, but she was also taught to speak and converse in a ladylike way, and although she never learned to read or write, she concealed this fact so cleverly (leaving the room whenever a note was delivered to her, for instance) that it was months before Hickey discovered it.

---

* Another ploy was to ensnare young women who came to London looking for work as servants or ladies' maids by posing as a possible employer. It was almost certainly in this way that Emma Lyon – who later became famous as Nelson's mistress, Lady Hamilton – fell into the life of courtesanry, soon becoming the kept mistress of Sir William Hamilton's nephew, Charles Greville.

Furthermore, he could never recollect hearing her make use of 'a vulgarism or a phrase that could mark her illiterateness'.*

The madams of these 'nunneries' were excellent businesswomen. As well as charging their visitors exorbitant entrance fees, they levied their young women for their board and lodging, and sold them (at doubtless thoroughly inflated prices) fine dresses, beautiful French underwear and even items of jewellery.

This combination of personal flamboyance and business acumen made many of the madams of St James's well-known figures in their own right. Charlotte Hayes was well acquainted with all the gentlemen of the *ton*. Her neighbour, Catherine Windsor at 4 King's Place, was equally so. Mrs Windsor had become famous because of her particularly strong connections with the Prince of Wales and his brother, the Duke of Clarence, both of whom were known to have been enthusiastic patrons. It has been said that almost every one of the famous courtesans of the Regency was to be found at Mrs Windsor's house at one time or another, and it may well have been there, and not Mrs Goadby's, that Elizabeth spent her first few months on the town.[10]

Charles James Fox was a regular visitor to Mrs Windsor's. A close friend of the Prince of Wales, it is said to have been Fox who first introduced the royal brothers to its delights (and indeed perhaps it was here that he first met Elizabeth, although their love affair was not to begin for at least another ten years). A contemporary caricature entitled 'King's Place, or A View of Mr Fox's Best Friends' (1784) shows two beautiful courtesans, Perdita Robinson and Elizabeth Armistead, wearing an elaborate feathered hat, talking to the Prince. Both women are known to have been intimate with him. Mrs Windsor, one of two bawds in the cartoon, is saying, 'He introduced His R– H– to my house.'

Yet another possible contender for Elizabeth's introduction to the

---

* During her time with Mrs Hayes Emily became friendly with the courtesan Harriet Powell. Harriet, who was a former mistress of Sophia Baddeley's Lord Melbourne, had also clearly benefited from the Hayes training, for she too was well known for the quality and politeness of her conversation, so much so that it was said that men paid solely for the privilege of chatting and playing cards with her. Harriet later made an extremely good marriage to the Earl of Seaforth.

life of courtesanry is Mrs Mitchell, who opened a high-class 'nunnery' in Cleveland Row in 1772 (and who later took over Charlotte Hayes's house at 5 King's Place). One of Mrs Mitchell's specialities was allegedly to find 'Studs of Quality' for bored aristocratic ladies, as well as beautiful young women to service their husbands.

What is certain is that Mrs Mitchell, like all clever madams, liked her ladies to see and be seen. Their social life, to be really useful, had to consist of much more than just a few promenades in the park. Like the women of fashion they had been trained to imitate, the King's Place courtesans openly attended fashionable events such as operas, concerts and masquerades. Although the Pantheon liked to keep up the appearance of respectable exclusivity (not always successfully, as Sophia Baddeley had proved), Mrs Cornelys at Carlisle House in Soho Square was apparently less fussy (her subscription balls, first begun in the early 1760s, were at first considered scandalous for this reason, although society soon got used to it. As Horace Walpole commented, 'they soon drew in both righteous and ungodly'). From a description of one of the masquerades given there in 1772 we learn that 'Mrs M-tchell and her three fair ladies' were among the guests, appearing in the character of a fruit-woman attended by her nosegay girls. 'Mrs K-lly [another well-known madam], with her ladies, also attended, in the more proper character of Lady Abbess and her Nuns'.

In addition to these public entertainments, the nunneries frequently held their own private entertainments, 'banquets of beauty' for which cards were formally sent out to all their regular visitors. Men would visit Mrs Hayes, or Mrs Windsor, or Mrs Kelly, as part of a whole evening's entertainment, to talk and socialise as well as to enjoy the women there. The opening of the Pantheon in 1772, however (from which they would definitely have been debarred), was considered by some of the madams to be such a serious threat to business that a counter-attack was needed. Eventually it was the ever-resourceful Charlotte Hayes who came up with an idea. She would stage an entertainment to end all entertainments, which no self-respecting gentleman of the town could possibly refuse to attend.

Thus was born the 'Tahitian Feast of Venus' at which, according to the cards sent out, '. . . twelve beautiful Nymphs, all spotless Virgins, will carry out the Feast of Venus as it is celebrated in Oteite,* under the instruction of Madam Hayes who will play the part of Queen Oberea, herself'. Some twenty-three men 'of the highest breeding' (including five Members of Parliament) turned up to take part in the festivities.

> The decor had been arranged to highlight the lewd 'Aretinian Postures' adopted by the participants. A dozen well-endowed athletic youths faced twelve 'nymphs' whose beauty could not be doubted although their virginity might be suspect. Each youth presented his nymph with a dildo-shaped object about a foot long, wreathed in flowers. The couple would then copulate with great passion and considerable dexterity since some of the Aretinian rites demanded a gymnastic suppleness which of a certainty could never be achieved by most of the onlookers. All this was accompanied by suitable music until the spectators had lashed themselves into such a state of lasciviousness that they invaded the floor, clutched the nymphs and tried to emulate the examples which had been shown.[11]

Another madam, Mrs Prendergast, arranged the famous *Bal d'Amour*, one of the principal subscribers to which was 'Lord Fumble' – Sophia Baddeley's one-time admirer Lord Harrington – who started her off with fifty guineas, and himself collected a further seven hundred guineas in subscriptions from his friends. It was advertised that 'the finest Women in all Europe would appear in puris naturalibis'. Among the guests were Isabella Wilkinson (the famous Sadlers Wells rope dancer), 'The Bird of Paradise' (the courtesan Gertrude Mahon), Lady Henrietta Grosvenor ('of moderated beauty and excessive vanity') and Lady Margaret Lucan. These last two were 'disguised as Mother Eve except that they covered their Faces with fig-leaves'. After the show, the guests danced naked, while the orchestra, to avoid embarrassing them, played facing the wall. At the end of the evening it was observed that the Ladies Grosvenor and Lucan, and 'The Bird of Paradise'

---

* Captain Cook's expedition to the South Pacific had returned in 1771, bringing with it eye-opening stories of young men and women copulating in public.

'disclaimed their Attendance Fees and the cost of the hire of Sedan-chairs, telling the Hostess to give the money to the servants'.[12]

Did Mrs Armistead ever take part in such revels? Somehow, it is hard to imagine. The most vivid picture we have of her is in later life, after she met Fox. They are very present, somehow, in those years: a devoted couple, blissful in each other's company, living in unimpeachable domestic harmony together at St Anne's Hill.

In those years we see Elizabeth largely through Fox's eyes. Many of his letters to her survive (although, disappointingly, none of hers to him), letters of heartbreaking tenderness and love. She is his Liz, 'dearest Liz', his 'dearest angel', and he cannot live without her. 'I have examined myself,' he wrote to her, 'and I know that I can better abandon friends, country, everything, than live without Liz. I could change my name and live with you in the remotest part of Europe in poverty and obscurity. I could bear that very well, but to be parted I cannot bear.'[13]

There are some women, great beauties often, who nonetheless seem somehow undeserving of the passion they inspire in men. This was not the case with Elizabeth Armistead. There seems to have been a stillness about her, a kind of luminosity, which was utterly at variance with the gaudily raucous eighteenth-century *demi-monde* from which she came. Fox – a man of prodigious, hectic energies – was to find in her the still centre which he lacked. But before him there had been many others who were equally entranced.

With her fresh good looks and her wonderful hair, Elizabeth did not last long in the brothels of King's Place, but soon acquired a succession of rich and aristocratic individual patrons. The practice of 'keeping' was a very common one in the late eighteenth century, and in most cases was a far preferable option to the brazen prostitution required by a Mrs Goadby or a Mrs Hayes, however exclusive their establishments.

While the rich and powerful had always been able to buy, or somehow acquire, high-status women as their mistresses, Harris's List suggests that by the late eighteenth century 'keeping' was common even amongst the gentry and the more affluent professional classes too. Thus we learn that the popular Miss Y–ng, of 12 Great Suffolk Street – a 'fine woman, of a middle size, fair complexion and very good teeth, inclinable to the em bon point' – had been kept by 'a country gentleman' until his marriage, whereupon he left her to provide for herself.

William Hickey refers to Emily Warren as being in 'high keeping' with his friend Bob Pott, but not all patrons could afford to be so generous – or conspicuous – and there are many references to 'kept' women moonlighting in the brothels and *bagnios* to make ends meet. Miss R–tc–ff, at 55 Berwick Street, whose 'gratuity' was a relatively paltry three guineas a week, was so closely watched by her keeper, Harris noted pointedly, 'that she [had] very few evenings, in her own possession'.

Mrs Cl–pp–o, of Gerrard Street, Soho, however, stuck with one apparently generous keeper, but was quite brazen about disposing of her spare time as she thought fit. 'This lady bears a strong resemblance to the most celebrated beauty on the town, as such it were almost superfluous to say that her person is elegant, her features regular, her eyes captivating, her teeth charming, and that her coral lips sollicit a thousand kisses,' wrote Harris. 'She is said to be in keeping by a gentleman, whose name she is known by, and who keeps the house she lives in on purpose for her, she is therefore obliged to keep pretty constantly at home, whilst he is in town, and she never receives any messages or mandates from Bagnios. In those intervals, when her friend is at his villa some distance from the capital, she shines with great splendour at all public places. Her conversation is lively and entertaining, which, added to her present situation and corporeal attractions she thinks entitles her to at least a bank note.'

'Kept' women such as 'Mrs Cl–pp–o' often changed their name to that of their patrons.* The beautiful Harriet Powell, Emily Warren's

---

* Hickey thought this strange, and could not account for it, although he had been abroad for some years at this time, and it may have been a relatively new fashion. Women could have had several reasons for changing their name: if their lover was particularly aristocratic or rich, the kudos of using his name would certainly have been a factor. I wonder, too, whether if the relationship looked set to last, the women regarded themselves as having entered into a kind of unofficial marriage.

friend from her days at Charlotte Hayes's establishment, was known as Harriet Lamb after her time as the mistress of Lord Melbourne (Lamb was the Melbourne family name), from whom, unlike Sophia Baddeley, she had also astutely secured a settlement. Emily, too, soon changed her name to Mrs Pott. It is very possibly from this custom – which may date from this time – that Elizabeth Cane had acquired the name of Mrs Armistead.

What is certain is that, like Emily Warren, Elizabeth very soon entered into 'high keeping'. According to the *Town and Country Magazine*, one of the very first of her patrons was 'the young duke of A–r' (the Duke of Ancaster, he of Sophia Baddeley's pineapple), who set her up in a house in Portman Square.* After Ancaster came the Duke of Dorset (satirised by the *Town and Country* as 'the noble cricketer'), who was soon followed by the Earl of Derby ('Lord Champêtre'). When the Duke of Dorset met Elizabeth he had only recently parted from another famous courtesan, Nancy Parsons.

In the eighteenth century, the fashionable and aristocratic world which made up 'society' was very small. Most of its members were connected in some way: either officially, by intricate patterns of kinship and marriage; or unofficially, through their more disorderly liaisons, their lovers and their mistresses. The world of high harlotry of which Elizabeth Armistead was now a part operated like a kind of parallel universe to this world, a self-contained but frequently overlapping cog within the eternally revolving and regrouping 'ronde'.†

Now, when the Duke of Dorset turned his sights upon the Earl of Derby's Countess (who when her infidelity became known was thrown out by her family and took herself off to live with the Duke), what should be more natural than that the Earl should take up with the Duke's previous mistress, Elizabeth herself. Perhaps motivated by revenge against his errant wife and her lover, the Earl's extremely

---

* The *Town and Country Magazine* 'Tête-à-Tête' for 1779 claims that during her time with Ancaster Elizabeth had an affair with another man – 'a lieutenant of a marching regiment' – by whom she had a child. I have found no other record which sheds further light on this.
† Nancy Parsons's first patron was a Mr Horton, by whose name she sometimes went. 'The Duke of Grafton's Mrs Horton, The Duke of Dorset's Mrs Horton,' Horace Walpole once wrote of her waspishly, 'everybody's Mrs Horton.'

generous terms were soon made public: 'His lordship immediately took a house for her at Hampstead,' gloated the *Town and Country Magazine*, 'allowed her his own equipage, besides two very handsome saddle horses; and as he makes no kind of secret of his amour, under his present circumstances, they may frequently be seen riding ensemble in Hyde Park, upon a fine day, and are often met upon the road to Hampstead. They seem perfectly well pleased with each other, and his lordship has had to complete a surfeit of matrimony, that this probably may be a lasting alliance.'[14]

Comfortable though it was, the alliance did not last. After Derby came Viscount Bolingbroke – known as 'Bully' to his friends – who had divorced his wife some years previously for adultery (on her subsequent marriage to her lover she was to become Lady Diana Beauclerk). Bully seems to have been aptly nicknamed. In addition to all the usual vices of the young eighteenth-century aristocrat – whoring, gambling and a serious addiction to the delights of Newmarket – he is alleged to have beaten his wife and treated her cruelly. But this does not seem to have been Elizabeth's experience of him. Part of her genius seems to have been an ability always to bring out the best in people, even the brutish Bully.* Benefiting, as a successful courtesan always did, from the greater freedom and autonomy of her position over that of a wife, she was not only introduced by Bully to all the young bloods of his acquaintance, but also to his two young sons – Frederick and George St John – who were to remain her devoted friends for the rest of her life (while one of Bully's grandsons, Henry, the 4th Viscount Bolingbroke, was to be amongst the principal mourners in Elizabeth's funeral cortège some seventy years later).

By the time her relationship with Bully came amicably to an end, Elizabeth was no longer the young King's Place *ingénue*, but a fully-fledged toast of the town. Her popularity in aristocratic circles had made her fashionable. Her next liaison, with the fabulously rich 'nabob'

---

* Bully was not all bad. He was a knowledgeable and enthusiastic collector of both china and silver, on which he spent enormous amounts of money. In the three years between 1755 and 1758 he spent 13,800 louis on his collection (in the days when one louis was a working woman's average monthly wage). See Carola Hicks's excellent *Improper Pursuits: The Scandalous Life of Lady Diana Beauclerk*.

General Richard Smith (satirised in the *Town and Country Magazine* as 'Sir Matthew Mite', the 'Nabob' in Samuel Foote's play of that name), was to make her financially independent too: the *sine qua non* of cyprian success.

'There is a fashion in intrigue, as well as other pursuits,' wrote the *Town and Country*, 'and though it must be acknowledged Mrs A-st-d is a most elegant and beautiful woman, yet if she had not been so highly rated for her charms among the Macaronies of this period, she might probably have escaped unnoticed by Sir Matthew. But as a man of taste, to establish his reputation, must have a mistress as well as a man cook, the degree of his gusto is determined by the happiness of his choice. Who then so proper to establish a man's virtu in amours as Mrs A-st-d, who can claim the conquest of two ducal coronets, a marquis, four earls and a viscount?'[15]

While this may well have been true of an *arriviste* such as Smith, fashionableness alone cannot account for Elizabeth's success. What was it about her that so charmed these men? Unlike Sophia Baddeley, whose meteoric career was fuelled by a powerful alchemy of celebrity and great physical beauty, Elizabeth's was built on something rather more subtle, something altogether quieter and more enduring.

While she was often described as 'beautiful', Elizabeth had none of Sophia's raw eroticism. Her admirers thought her looks charming, rather than classically beautiful; and her figure, although elegant, was described in the *Westminster Magazine* as 'lusty'. Although she was mistress of 'the arts of display and seduction' she was also, perhaps more importantly, that rare thing, a good and sympathetic listener. Like Fox, she had a genius for friendship. It was this charm, this kind of seductive sweetness of temperament which makes every man believe himself the centre of the universe, that was surely the secret of Elizabeth's success.

While Sophia Baddeley's reign as cyprian queen had lasted four years, from 1771 to 1774, Elizabeth maintained her position as London's most sought-after courtesan for more than ten, a very rare feat in that unforgiving world.* Only real intelligence, and a clearheaded attitude

* I.M. Davis believes that only Perdita Robinson and Grace Dalrymple Eliot – the demi-rep known as 'Dally the Tall' – could compete with Elizabeth for length of reign and splendour of clientele.

to money, could have achieved it. For all her sweetness of character, it is clear that Elizabeth knew her own worth. She played the courtesan with every card at her disposal, in the process providing us with a kind of blueprint for the progress of a fashionable woman of the town.

On the strength of the two annuities she acquired,* Elizabeth became a householder in her own right. As early as 1776 she secured the freehold of a house in Bond Street, and later a second house in Clarges Street. She set fashions – brimstone-yellow carriages, of the kind being driven by Emily Warren in 1780, are said to have been one of them – and entered into friendly rivalries with her fellow courtesans (which the newspapers, in turn, obligingly made news: if Mrs Armistead appeared one week in a phaeton drawn by four cream-coloured ponies, Mrs Robinson was reported sporting a team of exquisitely matched chestnuts the next). Her movements – to Brighton, to Bath, to the Continent – were assiduously reported. She continued her training, paying a fashionable dancing master ('the bright star Vestris') ten guineas to teach her how to make a suitable *entrée* into her box at the opera. She had an affair with the Prince of Wales.

Then, in 1783, Elizabeth fell in love with Charles James Fox.

So much has been written about Fox, yet the huge personality of the man – so brilliant and so complex, so bursting with supercharged and yet strangely childlike energies – at once begs, and beggars, description.

His physical appearance, however, is familiar to us. The cartoons and satirical drawings which were made of him – for he was much lampooned in his day – make much of his extraordinary looks: with his permanent five o'clock shadow and beetling black brows,† Fox had the hirsute air (and uncertain personal hygiene) of a dishevelled bloodhound. Nonetheless, he was a man, in Edmund Burke's phrase, who was made to be loved, a quality so potent that it transcended even his death. The poet Samuel Rogers, writing about him long afterwards,

* One of these was from General Richard Smith. It has been suggested that the other may have been from Lord George Cavendish, the brother of the Duke of Devonshire.
† Georgiana, the Duchess of Devonshire's pet name for Fox was 'the Eyebrow'.

recalled how elderly Foxites would break down sobbing when they thought of their loss, bursting into tears 'with a vehemence of grief such as I hardly ever saw exhibited by a man'.[16]

Charles James Fox was born on 24 January 1749, the second surviving son of the immensely wealthy politician Henry Fox, 1st Baron Holland, and Lady Caroline Lennox, daughter of the 2nd Duke and Duchess of Richmond.* Charles James inherited his heavy, sensual looks and his hairiness from his father. 'He is weakly, but likely to live,' wrote Henry Fox the day after Charles was born. 'His skin hangs all shrivelled about him, his eyes stare, he has a black head of hair, and 'tis incredible how like a monkey he looked before he was dressed.'[17] Nonetheless, the Hollands were besotted parents, especially Charles's father, who soon grew so immoderately fond of his son that he gave orders that he should be indulged in all things. 'Let nothing be done to break his spirit,' he used to say, 'the world will do that soon enough.' Charles was duly indulged. The anecdotes that survive of his eccentric upbringing tell of guests to Holland House watching in consternation as he burned his father's carefully prepared speeches, smashed his gold watch the better to observe how it worked, and at dinnertime splashed about unimpeded in the soup tureen.

Whereas most children would have been ruined by this shameless spoiling, Charles James thrived on it. A prodigy from his earliest years, at the age of five he was so addicted to the theatre that he read 'every play on which he could lay his tiny hands'. At Eton, and later at Oxford, he devoured books by the score – in Greek and Latin, French and Italian† as well as English – and came to love mathematics 'vastly'.‡

---

* The 1st Duke of Richmond was the illegitimate son of Charles II with his French mistress Louise de Keroualle.

† ' 'Fore God,' Fox wrote to his friend Richard Fitzpatrick, 'There is more good poetry in Italian than in all other languages I understand put together. Make haste and read all these things, that you may be fit to talk to Christians.' Quoted in Sir George Otto Trevelyan, *Early History of Charles James Fox.*

‡ This was apparently not the case with his fellow undergraduates at Hertford College, who were 'very pleasant but idle fellows'. When Fox went abroad one summer, his tutor wrote to him: 'As to trigonometry, it is a matter of entire indifference to the other geometricians of the college whether they proceed to the other branches of mathematics immediately, or wait a term or two longer. You need not, therefore, interrupt your amusements by severe studies, for it is wholly unnecessary to take a step onwards without you, and therefore we shall stop until we have the pleasure of your company.' Quoted in ibid.

It was in these early years too that he first showed signs of his formidable debating skills, developing a youthful 'schoolboy eloquence' into a mastery of the art of oratory.

These qualities, which would have made some men insufferable, made Fox a delightful companion. The Duchess of Devonshire thought that his intelligence was such that he always seemed a jump or two ahead of the rest of the company. 'He seems to have the particular talent of knowing more about what he is saying and with less pains than any one else,' she wrote to her mother in 1777, shortly after she first met him. 'His conversation is like a brilliant player at billiards, the strokes follow one another piff puff.'[18]

But there were aspects of Fox's liberal eighteenth-century education which, while considered perfectly normal by his contemporaries, shocked Fox's later biographers. 'In the spring of 1763, the devil entered into the heart of Lord Holland,' wrote Sir George Otto Trevelyan darkly in his *Early History of Charles James Fox*; 'he could think of no better diversion than to take Charles from his books, and convey him to the Continent on a round of idleness and dissipation. At Spa his amusement was to send his son every night to the gaming-table with a pocketful of gold, and (if family tradition may be trusted where it tells against family credit) the parent took not a little pains to contrive that the boy should leave France a finished rake.'[19]

He certainly came back a finished dandy, out-macaroni-ing even the most extravagant macaronis of St James's. The typical macaroni wore skin-tight breeches and a short, tight-fitting waistcoat (Fox and his brother Stephen once drove post all the way from Paris to Lyon expressly to select the latest embroidered patterns for them), embellishing this blamelessly elegant silhouette with outlandish flourishes: huge buttons and red high-heeled shoes, a scented nosegay, hair in the style à *l'aile de pigeon*, a tiny little French hat perched on the side of the head. One of Fox's specialities was his experiments with hair colours: he would appear with blue powder in his hair one day, red the next. But worse than this temporary addiction to high fashion was a far more expensive addiction: gambling.

Even in an age in which gambling was a national obsession – 'society' in those days has been described as being like a vast casino in which young men lost five, ten, fifteen thousand pounds in an evening – Charles James Fox and his brother Stephen were prodigious in their addiction. Gambling, in all its forms, was not just a game, it was a way of life. The betting book at Brooks's contains wagers of every conceivable variety, and no handwriting appears more often in it than Fox's clear, rounded hand. He laid two hundred guineas that Lord North would be First Lord of the Treasury in March 1773, and twenty guineas that he would still be First Lord in March 1776, 'bar death'; a further 150 guineas, to fifty, was laid that the Tea Act was not repealed in the winter session of 1774. Other bets were of a more frivolous nature: twenty guineas that Lord Northington did not swim one mile the next time he went into the Thames or any other river; a hundred guineas against the Duke of Devonshire having the garter within seven years. Others, tellingly, were laid about Fox himself: 'Lord Clermont has given Mr Crawfurd 10 guineas, upon the condition of receiving 500l. from him whenever Mr Charles James Fox shall be worth 100,000l. clear of debts.'[20]

Fox seemed almost wilfully determined that this should never be the case.* The wagers at Brooks's were nothing to his vast losses at the real gaming tables. Although brilliantly clever at whist, quinze and piquet – which require skilful play – he invariably chose instead games of pure chance: 'He never could resist the attractions of that table where skill could not protect him from the influence of his terrible bad luck.' In 1768, at the instigation of his father, who was always ambitious for his brilliant youngest son, Fox had become an MP for the pocket borough of Midhurst (at the precocious and, technically, ineligibly young age of nineteen), but even this seemingly sober occupation could not save him from his addiction to the gaming tables.

* Madame du Deffand, the famous Parisian salonière, found this recklessness repellent: 'I should never have believed it, if I had not seen for myself that there could be such madness . . . I declare it disgusts me; I do not know what to make of such fools,' she wrote to her correspondent Horace Walpole. She is one of the few people who was impervious to Fox's charms: 'No doubt [Fox] has plenty of spirit, and above all great talents, but I am not sure that he is right in the head . . . He seems to me to live in a sort of intoxication . . . I declare it horrifies me; his fortune seems to me frightful . . . At 24 to have lost everything, to owe more than one could ever pay and not even to care about it: nothing is more extraordinary . . . it is such a pity: he has so much intelligence, goodness and truthfulness, but that does not prevent him being detestable.'

In his journal, Horace Walpole recalled one of Fox's feverish marathons:

> *He had sat up playing hazard at Almack's, from Tuesday evening 4th, 'till five in the afternoon of Wednesday 5th. An hour before, he had recovered £12,000 that he had lost, and by dinner, which was at 5 o'clock, he had ended by losing £11,000 [£600,000]. On the Thursday he spoke in this debate;* went to dinner at past 11 at night; from thence to White's where he drank 'till 7 next morning, thence to Almack's, where he won £6,000, and between 3 and 4 in the afternoon he set out for Newmarket.*[21]

This was by no means the worst of Fox's losses. In 1772, over three consecutive nights, he and his brother Stephen lost £32,000 in one night, a fortune even by the standards of the richest families. In the end, not even his father's vast fortune could save Fox. Generous to the last, one of his father's last acts before his death in 1774 was to pay his son's gambling debts, which by this time amounted to £140,000, the equivalent today of more than £8 million.

Elizabeth Armistead and Charles James Fox had known one another for some time before they fell in love. For several years towards the end of her reign as London's most famous courtesan, Elizabeth had been closely associated with Whig society (the male section of it, that is). She and Fox were part of the same circle. Many of Fox's friends, such as Richard Fitzpatrick, were Elizabeth's friends too;† and some of those, including Lord George Cavendish, the brother of the Duke of Devonshire, Lord 'Bob' Spencer, third son of the Duke of Marlborough, Lord Cholmondley, and the Prince of Wales, had also been her lovers (although the Prince was too impoverished to last long in this company). In 1783, the same year that their affair began, Fox had

---

* The debate was about the anti-Dissenters legislation of 1688; Fox spoke against it.
† When Fitzpatrick was abroad fighting against the American rebels, Fox often enclosed letters from Elizabeth within his own missives. 'I have seen Mrs Armistead,' he wrote to his friend, 'looking very old.'

also had an affair with one of Elizabeth's friends, the courtesan and actress Perdita Robinson.* The eighteenth-century *demi-monde* was every bit as small and exclusive as the *monde* which supported it.

In outward appearances Fox had changed much in the preceding decade. He now eschewed fancy clothes and high-heeled shoes, and was instead to be seen sporting a sober frock-coat and a waistcoat in the buff and blue colours of the American rebels. Rather than a rich rake, he was now a poor one; but in essence he remained the same.

The 1780s were a time of strenuous political activity for Fox; a time when he achieved more real power than he was to do again for another twenty years. In 1782, after Cornwallis's capitulation at Yorktown, Lord North's Tory government – against which Fox had been in declared opposition for nearly ten years, principally over its American policy – fell. Under the new Whig administration, with the Marquess of Rockingham as Prime Minister, Lord Shelburne and Fox were appointed mutually hostile Secretaries of State. Fox did not last long in this position. When Rockingham died unexpectedly that same year, Shelburne was promoted to Prime Minister, and appointed the young William Pitt as Chancellor of the Exchequer. Fox resigned. But politics, as was always the case with him, was but an extension of the vastly more important business of living. He may have been one of the great political consciences of his day, and one of its greatest orators – it was once said that every one of his massive sentences 'came rolling like a wave of the Atlantic, three thousand miles long' – but he was also one of the century's greatest *bon viveurs*. There was Brooks's, Almack's, Newmarket, Perdita – and now Mrs Armistead.

The earliest surviving letters written by Fox to Mrs Armistead are much to do with politics, a distinctly unromantic, if unsurprising, subject. Although Elizabeth's letters to Fox have not survived, something of their tenor can be guessed from the replies that they elicit. There is none of the feverishness of mere infatuation in Fox's letters; nor of its anxieties either. Instead, these are warm, open, thoughtful letters addressed to a woman who has unquestionably earned his abso-

---

* There is a claim – interesting but unsubstantiated – that 'that mysterious person Mrs Armistead' had once acted as a lady's maid to Perdita. Hugh Stoker, *The Devonshire House Circle*.

lute confidence and trust. Their tone is serene. From the beginning, he writes to her as his absolute equal.

'I know I am right, and must bear the consequences,' he wrote to her at the time of the second reading of the East India Bill,* 'tho' I dislike unpopularity as much as any man. Indeed, my dearest Liz, it is no hypocrisy in me to say that the consciousness of having always acted on principle in public matters and my determination always to do so is the great comfort of my life.'

In times of crisis Elizabeth was a loving and serene friend to whom he knew he could unburden himself. 'I never did act more upon principle than at this moment when they are abusing me so,' he continued. 'If I had considered nothing but keeping my power, it was the safest way to leave things as they are . . . and I am not at all ignorant of the political danger which I run by this bold measure; but whether I succeed or no, I shall always be glad that I attempted [it] because I know I have done no more than what I was bound to do . . . with the happiness of so many millions at stake.'[22]

In matters of love, Fox had never had the confidence that he showed in his political life. He was 'foolish' about women, observed one contemporary, 'and though he takes great pains to fall in love, he cannot bring it about. Whenever he has a fancy for any woman it makes him . . . unhappy and . . . ridiculous.'[23] Women of his own class do not often seem to have held any attraction for Fox (and for all his charm and wit, they might well have been deterred by his impecuniousness, and his extremely dubious standards of personal hygiene†). But with

* Fox's East India Bill was designed to limit the power and abuses not only of the East India Company, but also, indirectly, of the Crown, by making the Company accountable to a government committee.

† A hair-raising account of Fox's appearance shortly before he met Elizabeth: 'His complexion was of the dirtiest colour and tinged with a yellowish hue; his hair was exceedingly black, uncombed, and clotted with the pomatures and small remnants of powder of the day before; his beard was unshaved, and together with his bushy eyebrows increased the natural darkness of his skin; his nightgown was old and dirty; the collar of his shirt was open and discovered a broad chest covered with hair; the knees of his breeches were unbuttoned; his stockings were ungartered and hung low upon his legs; his slippers were down at heel; his hands were dirty; his voice was hoarse like that of a hackney coachman who is much exposed to the night air. Yet under all these various disadvantages his countenance was mild and pleasing.' Quoted in Stanley Ayling, *Fox: The Life of Charles James Fox*.

Elizabeth it was different. From the start of their relationship, her intelligence and her ready sympathies made her Fox's dear confidante. He showed her a vulnerability which might have surprised his more cynical contemporaries. 'I write very gravely,' he continued in the same letter, 'because the amazing abuse which is heaping upon me makes me feel so. I have the weakness of disliking abuse, but that weakness shall never prevent me from doing what I think is right.'

Fox had always been a flamboyant public figure; and Elizabeth, as a supremely successful courtesan, was very nearly his equal in celebrity, so it was not long before their friendship was reported in the papers. There were rumours, only half-jesting, that she was speculating on his return to office. 'The terms of pacification are said to have been these: that Mr F– shall have free egress into the privy chambers of the fair one, without fee or reward, on condition that when he assumes the reins of power he shall appoint her purveyor of chickens.'[24]

And indeed it was not long before Fox was back in office. Together with his old enemy Lord North, he had formed a coalition in April 1783 which drove out the hated Lord Shelburne. Under the new Prime Minister, the Whig Duke of Portland, Fox once again was made Secretary of State (with North as his counterpart), despite King George III's bitter opposition. The rumours about Fox and Mrs Armistead continued. It was alleged that he had settled on her the fantastic sum of £1000 a quarter (implying a capital outlay of £80,000). This was untrue: Fox had lost his entire fortune on the gaming tables, and now had no money of his own; and he was always rigorously opposed to making any profit from office. Besides, his Liz was a prize beyond price.

Whenever they were apart, Fox continued to write to Elizabeth. Throughout their life together he would always snatch odd moments, any moments, at the House of Commons or at his lodgings in St James's Place, to scribble notes to her, sometimes in the middle of the night. Their affair, which had begun with no particular expectations on either side, bloomed. Mrs Armistead was becoming increasingly necessary to him; indeed, he could no longer do without her.

'I would write to you more if my mind were not entirely full of the

Veronica Franco, painted by Tintoretto. Late-sixteenth-century Venice was a golden age for courtesans, who were among the most educated and liberated women of their day. Veronica Franco (1546–91) was almost as celebrated for her artistic and poetic gifts as for her fabled eroticism. A 'public tongue' was the object of much suspicion in a woman, however. 'Thou wilt finde the Venetian Cortezan . . . a good Rhetorician and a most elegant discourser,' wrote the English traveller Thomas Coryat 'so that if shee cannot move thee with all these aforesaid delights, shee will assay thy constancy with her Rhetoricall tongue.'

Kitty Fisher painted by Nathaniel Hone (1765). The best-loved 'toast of the town' of the mid-eighteenth century, the high-spirited Kitty inspired several ditties in her honour, including the children's nursery rhyme 'Lucy Locket lost her pocket, Kitty Fisher found it'. She is said once to have eaten a hundred-guinea note between two slices of bread, perhaps inspiring her one-time patron, the Earl of Sandwich, in his invention. Such was her fame that crowds of eager sightseers flocked to watch her eat supper in her box at Vauxhall Gardens.

OPPOSITE The 'Tête-à-Tête' series, in the *Town and Country Magazine*, was one of the very earliest examples of the 'celebrity' gossip column. The late eighteenth century was a star-struck era, and there was an almost insatiable demand for accounts of the scandalous lives and loves of well-known London figures—actresses, courtesans, and their aristocratic patrons were especially popular. Sophia Baddeley is shown here with one of her early patrons, Captain Hangar (later Lord Coleraine), while Elizabeth Armistead had the rare distinction of being featured twice: 'Lord Champêtre (the Earl of Derby) and 'Sir Matthew Mite' (General Richard Smith) were two of her most prominent patrons.

N.º XIII.

N.º XIV.

The celebrated M.rs B—dl—y.

Captain H——r.

N.º VII.

N.º VIII.

M.rs A—St—d.

Lord Champêtre.

N.º XIX.

N.º XX.

M.rs A—st—d.

Sir Matthew Mite.

Sophia and Robert Baddeley in Garrison and Colman's play *The Clandestine Marriage*, painted by John Zoffany (1733–1810). Although opinions were divided as to her acting abilities, Sophia Baddeley—'that beautiful, insinuating creature' as James Boswell wrote of her— mesmerised audiences with her ravishing looks and her sexual charisma. The Marilyn Monroe of her day, Sophia's life was characterised by her many notorious amours, her vast wealth, and laudanum addiction.

OPPOSITE Grace Dalrymple Eliot by Thomas Gainsborough (1778). Although she was a con- temporary of both Sophia Baddeley and Elizabeth Armistead, the aristocratic Grace Dalrymple Eliot (1754–1823)—known as 'Dally the Tall'—came from a very different back- ground. Having committed a *faux pas*, as the eighteenth century euphemistically phrased it, and been rejected by her husband, she, and many women like her, had no choice but to embark on a career 'on the town' simply in order to survive.

Two portraits of Elizabeth Armistead, later Mrs. Charles James Fox, both by Sir Joshua Reynolds. Fox's 'beloved Liz' had maintained her position as London's most celebrated courtesan for more than ten years before she met him. Her contemporaries found her looks charming, rather than classically beautiful. 'The remaining half of my life whether it is to be happy or otherwise depends entirely on you, indeed it does,' Fox wrote to her shortly after they met. 'I have known many men and women and for many of them I have great friendship & esteem, but I never did know and never shall man or woman who deserved to be loved like Liz.'

Hon.ᵇˡᵉ Mʳˢ Fox.
by Sir J. Reynolds

Charles James Fox by Karl Anton Hickel (1793). Fox, the Whig parliamentarian and statesman and a man of prodigious, hectic energies, was the second son of the fabulously wealthy Henry, 1st Baron Holland, and his aristocratic wife Lady Caroline Lennox. He was, in Edmund Burke's phrase, 'a man born to be loved'.

BELOW A caricature of Fox as Demosthenes. Much lampooned in his day for his dark, hairy looks and his unkempt appearance, Fox was also justly famous for his powers of oratory. From very early on in their relationship he found a confidante in Elizabeth Armistead who, although not political herself, became the loving and serene friend to whom he could always unburden himself. Later, he would offer to give up his whole career rather than lose her.

'St. James Beauty'. Although her origins are obscure, it is highly likely that Elizabeth Armistead began her career in a high-class brothel like the one portrayed here. Of the many hundreds of brothels that existed in London at the time, the most expensive and luxurious were those in King's Place. Here, a fashionably dressed prostitute gazes out of the window, through which the outline of St. James's Palace can clearly be seen, a pointed reference to the many royal patrons who were known to frequent such premises. A particularly beautiful or popular 'woman of the town' might be taken into keeping by one of her clients, an important step on the ladder to true courtesanry.

one subject which occupies my whole mind,' he wrote to her in December the following year.

> *I can not have a moment's happiness or rest until I see you. I had so set my mind upon seeing you now that I can not wean myself from it, and I know I shall be so nervous and out of spirits if you are not here by the 12th that I shall disgrace myself, and be thought to be oppressed by the accidents of fortune which God knows is far from being the case. On the contrary I think things look well, and if they did not I think I have courage enough to despise them; but I cannot bear the disappointment of your not coming. Pray come even if you should think it wise to go away again, and come immediately. You may be here by the 7th or 8th. Indeed I can not doubt your affection for me, but if you do love me, you must come. Depend upon it there shall be no danger. If you do not chuse to go to your house you may come to mine. If I were to write forever it would only be to say pray come, pray come.*[25]

When Fox's duties as Secretary of State permitted, he spent as much time with Elizabeth as possible, either in London or, increasingly, at St Anne's Hill, a small house in Surrey, near the town of Chertsey, which Elizabeth had recently begun to rent. Unexpectedly, Fox, rake and man-about-town *par excellence*, loved the house, and the simple, rural life which went with it, nearly as much as she did. He brought his young nephew, Lord Holland, then a schoolboy of just nine years old, to visit her there. But Elizabeth had doubts. Now that she was with Fox – which had always been an affair of the heart – for the first time in her career she had no paying patron to foot the bills. Her lifestyle in London was expensive, as befitted a courtesan of her status; too expensive to maintain without help. She was in debt (the danger which Fox alludes to in his letter was the danger of creditors). Furthermore, Elizabeth was now thirty-three years old. At some point, in some dark moment, her experience of the world must have made her question how much longer Fox's ardour would last.

Although a surprising number of English courtesans ended their careers in a stable union, sometimes even marrying their patrons –

Kitty Fisher, Nancy Parsons and Harriet Powell, to name but three*
– many more ended in quite different circumstances, a fact which was
continually before Elizabeth. She knew that however successful she
might have been as a courtesan, it was a life which contained no
guarantees. And the fall from such heights as she had attained would
be doubly cruel, as the obituary notice of one of her contemporaries,
Mrs Elizabeth Wooley, showed only too clearly.

> *On Sunday lately ... died Mrs Elizabeth Wooley, one of the
> prettiest women to have figured in the circles of purchaseable
> beauty these many years past ... A few years since, she was the
> chief toast among those who pledge the fair frail in their cups,
> and lived in all the splendour and expense attainable by the
> artfully complying fair ... She has been on the decline for the
> past two years – and ... had moved into a very mortifying and
> humble state of prostitution. She now lies a corpse in her 25th
> year, and has left a young daughter without a shilling for her
> maintenance.*[26]

Mrs Armistead took fright. Sometime in the early autumn of 1783,
when Fox had departed London on his usual round of shooting parties,
she made up her mind. She must get out, leave London, go abroad.
She wrote to him breaking off their affair.

Fox wrote back to her at once.

> *It is impossible to conceive how miserable your letter had made
> me. No, my dearest Liz you must not go indeed you must not,
> the very thought of living without you so totally sinks my spirits
> that I am sure the reality would be more than I could bear. To
> talk of favours received from me is ridiculous, are not our
> interests one? Do I but live in you? No my dearest Angel you
> must not abandon me you must not – As to the difficulties you
> speak of they are to be sure very vexatious but not in my
> opinion at all insurmountable. Sell your house and furniture in
> town; and I by no means despair of being able to bring you*

---

* Kitty Fisher married John Norris, the Member of Parliament for Rye; Nancy Parsons
became Lady Maynard; Harriet Powell became Lady Seaforth. See page 93n.

enough from this place together with what I know I can borrow
in town and with some help from the Prince which I think we
may certainly have to pay all your debts; but pray my dearest
Life take no rash resolution. I would be with you immediately
if I did not know that my not attending the Prince to Ld.
Townshend's and Mr Coke's would be taken ill by both him
and them. I will certainly be with you the 2nd or at farthest
the third of Nov'r till when pray my dearest friend decide
nothing. Pray write to me directly and give me some comfort.
You shall not go without me wherever you go. I have examined
myself and know that I can better abandon friends, country
and everything than live without Liz. I could change my name
and live with you in the remotest part of Europe in poverty and
obscurity. I could bear that very well, but to be parted I can
not bear, but I will compose myself. Pray wait till you see me.
All my money here is so engaged that I can not send you any
at present, but in a day or two I hope to be able to send you a
little for immediate use. Adieu, my happiness depends upon you
entirely, surely you will not deliberately make me miserable –
Adieu . . .

   P.S. Pray do not think any of the expressions in this letter
the expression of passion or romantic exaggerations. I have
examined myself more than once upon this subject and know
that I cannot live without you.[27]

Against the combined forces of Fox's eloquence and his obvious distress, Elizabeth capitulated. Whatever the consequences might be, from
now on Fox, and Fox only, was to be her life.

When Elizabeth finally retired from her profession, she did so in a
way that broke all the rules. She had fallen in love with a poor man,
and given up her career for him. Neither would she be a woman of
property for much longer. The following year she not only sold both
her town houses, but, if the *Morning Post* is to be believed, her two
annuities as well (allegedly to raise money to save Fox from his creditors). St Anne's Hill, however, she would not give up. 'I wish you
would not [trade] it in a hurry,' Fox had begged her, 'and till we have

talked it over; if we find it too expensive with all my partiality we must give it up, but not for god's sake till we have some other place, for I cannot bear our having no home but London.'

St Anne's Hill was a low white house, charmingly situated on the brow of a hill, with the river Thames not far behind it, and a beautifully wooded prospect of the Surrey hills in front. It was to this haven that Elizabeth now retired.* From here she could enjoy the tranquillity of the countryside, but still be sufficiently close to London for her to visit Fox regularly during the months when Parliament was sitting, and for him to come to her whenever he could manage to escape.

The poet Samuel Rogers, who visited Fox and Elizabeth there many years later, described the house in detail. The drawing room was elegantly decorated with pink silk in panels, while a smaller morning-room contained a painting by Sir Joshua Reynolds, *Girl with the Mouse Trap*. The library, small and unadorned, was on the first floor, with the books displayed on open shelves. In the hall were yet more books and statues. Engraved portraits, principally after Joshua Reynolds, were all over the house.† His portrait of Fox's nephew, Lord Holland, was in the dining room, and alongside it a portrait of his wife Lady Holland, by Ramsey. It was the garden, however, which was the house's chief glory.

> In the garden a handsome architectural greenhouse, and a temple after a design of Lord Newburgh ... containing busts of Charles J. Fox, Lord Holland, and a son of Lord Bolingbroke, all by Nollekens. The garden laid out in open and shrubbery walks, trees breaking the prospect everywhere. The kitchen garden a square, not walled, and skirted by the walk. In the lower part is something in imitation of the Nuneham Flower-Garden. There is a terrace-

* On 8 September 1785 Elizabeth was finally able to buy St Anne's Hill, which she did with a mortgage of £2000 from the Duke of Marlborough. It is on the deeds of the house that the only existing record of her real name – Elizabeth Bridget Cane – appears.
† Rogers does not say whether any of these were of Elizabeth herself. She is said to have sat to Reynolds four times during her twenties and early thirties. See Ayling.

walk, thickly planted, to a neat farm-house; in which there is a
tea-room, the chimney-piece relieved with a fox.[28]

Fox's second term as Secretary of State in the Duke of Portland's administration had not lasted long. In December 1783 his East India Bill, which had passed through the House of Commons with a comfortable majority, reached the House of Lords, where, unbeknown to Fox, Pitt and the King had formed a plot to sabotage it. Pitt's cousin, Lord Temple, circulated an open letter to his fellow peers from the King, which stated that anyone who voted for the Bill would be regarded as the King's enemy. The Bill, not surprisingly, was resoundingly defeated. Fox and North were dismissed. Lord Temple was rewarded by his appointment as Secretary of State, while Pitt himself, at twenty-four, became the youngest Prime Minister in British history.

Although he was now out of office, politics continued to absorb Fox. As far as Elizabeth was concerned, though, they increasingly formed no more than a backdrop to the country idyll of St Anne's Hill.

Some historians have claimed that Mrs Armistead had no interest in politics, but this is not the case. It is true to say that she was herself no politician, in the way that Fox's friend and political ally the Duchess of Devonshire was, but throughout the rest of Fox's political career she was to remain his most trusted confidante. The first half of 1784, in particular, was a time of intense political activity for Fox. After the defeat of the East India Company Bill in the House of Lords, the Whigs had used the fact of the King's open interference with Parliament as proof of his despotic intentions. Debates in the House of Commons were marked by increasingly bitter battles between Fox, as champion of English constitutionalism, on the one hand, and William Pitt and the King on the other.

In January Fox and North were still able to inflict defeat after defeat on the King's administration in the Commons; but gradually Pitt gained on them, slowly whittling down their majority. By March, a motion by Fox to postpone any discussion of the Mutiny Bill until Pitt had resigned was carried by just one vote. On the twenty-fourth of that month Parliament was finally dissolved. The election which followed, during which Fox stood as one of the three Westminster candidates,* was a turbulent one for a number of reasons. It was the first time that Fox had actually had to win his votes (he had previously stood for the pocket borough of Midhurst); but, more crucially still, his election came to be seen as an almost personal duel between himself, the King, by now implacable in his hatred of Fox, and the King's servant, Pitt.

Although Fox's personal charisma was still to a large extent undimmed, his coalition had proved deeply unpopular – his determination to make the East India Company accountable to a body of commissioners, all coalition nominees, was seen as a blatant attempt to seize the Company's wealth for the Whigs themselves, rather than as the anti-corruption measure that it was intended to be. During the tense forty-day election, Fox wrote almost daily bulletins to Elizabeth, who was to remain in St Anne's Hill throughout.

On 3 April, she read:

The poll now is
Hood 2185
Wray 1973
Fox 1923

    I hope to get up my ground to-morrow, & by Tuesday night should be able to form a judgement. Plenty of bad news from all quarters, but I think (and you won't suspect me of boasting to you) that misfortunes when they come thick have the effect rather of raising my spirits than sinking them. There are few against which I can not bear up and much the greatest of those few it is in your power to prevent ever happening.[29]

On 7 April:

Worse and worse
Hood 4458
Wray 4117

---

* Westminster returned two Members to Parliament. No one doubted that Admiral Hood would win first place in the poll; the fight was between Fox and Sir Cecil Wray for the second seat.

Fox 3827

but I am afraid I must not give up tho' there is little chance indeed.

The next day, the situation was not much better:

Hood 4797
Wray 4420
Fox 4126

I must not give up tho' I wish it. I have serious thoughts, if I am beat, of not coming in to Parliament at all,* but all this I will talk with you more as soon as this business will let me go to you.

Even at the height of the election fever, Elizabeth was always at the forefront of Fox's mind. On 9 April, Good Friday, he wrote to her:

The Poll to-day was for one hour only and we had six majority
Hood 4877
Wray 4489
Fox 4201

If Sir Cecil does not beat me tomorrow which I think he will not do, I must go on tho' much against my inclination . . .
I hope you have had some hot cross buns to-day. Oh! how I do long to see my Liz.

Fox was right. Although Hood and Wray had surged ahead in the first days of the poll, by the second week in April, thanks to the extraordinary canvassing tactics of Fox's supporters, the political tide had turned. A host of aristocratic Whig ladies, dressed in the distinctive blue and buff colours of their party, with foxtails in their hats, sallied forth to tramp the cobbled streets of Westminster, canvassing energetically on Fox's behalf. Chief among these was one of Fox's dearest friends, the beautiful and celebrated Georgiana, Duchess of Devonshire, but keeping her company were many others too: Georgiana's sister,

---

* Fox had taken the precaution of also being nominated for the pocket borough of Tain Boroughs, in the far north of Scotland, which was conveniently at the disposal of the Whig-supporting Sir Thomas Dundas, so defeat in the Westminster election would not have deprived him of a seat.

Lady Duncannon, the Duchess of Portland, Lady Jersey, Lady Carlisle, Mrs Bouverie and the Waldegrave sisters.

On 27 April, Elizabeth opened her daily bulletin from Fox to learn that he was now in second place (Hood 6468, Fox 5827, Wray 5806). His first thought, as always, had been for her. 'I gained 21 today and am now as you see 21 ahead,' she read. 'I really believe we are quite sure here, but there may be a scrutiny which will be troublesome beyond measure. Adieu my dearest Liz, it is a great part indeed of my pleasure in my triumph to think my Liz will be pleased with it.'

Although it now looked certain that Fox would keep his position, Sir Cecil Wray refused to concede, and the election dragged on. It was now May, and spring had come to St Anne's Hill. Fox grew increasingly impatient to be with Elizabeth again. 'I have been quite spoiled with seeing you so much this year and begin to grow quite uneasy when I am three days without you,' he wrote. He tried to imagine how their gardens and woods were doing. 'Have you any leaves out? Or any signs of spring?'

It was in this long absence that he wrote her some of his most tender love letters.

> *Adieu my dearest Liz. It may sound ridiculous but it is true that I feel every day how much more I love you than even I know. You are all to me. You can always make me happy in circumstances apparently unpleasant and miserable . . . Indeed, my dearest angel, the whole happiness of my life depends on you. Pray, pray do not abuse your power – Adieu.*[30]

Finally, on 17 May, Hood and Fox were declared elected. Garlanded with laurels, Fox was carried in a triumphant procession by hundreds of friends and supporters to Carlton House, the Prince of Wales's residence, and then along Piccadilly to Devonshire House. Brass bands played, speeches were made, balls and dinners thrown, culminating in an extravagant banquet for six hundred guests. 'The hero of these triumphs was eager only that they should be over,' the historian I.M. Davis has written. 'As soon as he could he left for St Anne's Hill, to renew the enjoyment of the union in which he – the most loved and by many the most esteemed man of his time, the superior in rank, immeasurably the superior in talents – never saw himself as anything but a gainer.'

St Anne's Hill had been Elizabeth's home for some time now, and from May 1784 it became, increasingly, that of Fox too. Soon their life together began to assume a familiar pattern. Fox brought his books there, and it became their habit to read together, which they did on a grand scale. He shared with Elizabeth his love of the classics – during the course of one winter he was to read nine epic poems aloud to her: the *Iliad*, the *Odyssey*, Apollonius Rhodius, the *Aenead*, Tasso, Ariosto, *Paradise Lost* and *Paradise Regained*, and Spenser's *The Faerie Queene*. Elizabeth also read to him: 'Mrs Armistead,' recollected Samuel Rogers, 'when he returns fretted in the evening, takes down a volume of Don Quixote or Gil Blas, and reads him into tranquility.'[31] They gardened together (Elizabeth, especially, was to become a passionate horticulturalist), and planned improvements to their house. Fox's only fault in Elizabeth's eyes was his aversion to music. 'The utmost she could say for him was that he could read Homer, while she played and sang to herself.'[32] They became, in short, a couple.

Fox's hint to Elizabeth that he would not return to politics should he lose the Westminster election was never put to the test, but the preference which he now began to show for St Anne's Hill over all other places – including the House of Commons – was marked by many. After the election he showed no sign of returning to London, even when Parliament resumed at the end of May. 'Heard that Mr Fox had greatly offended his friends by his late absence from the House of Commons,' wrote a contemporary observer, Lady Mary Hamilton; 'they wrote to remonstrate with him on the folly and impropriety of it: he sent for answer that he was very happy and quiet at St Anne's Hill with Mrs Armistead, that he thought he should stay sometime longer, & concluded his letter by saying that Mrs A wondered that they did not come and see her.'

And friends did come. Richard Fitzpatrick (who was soon to acquire his own house at Sunning Hill, an easy seven-mile ride away), William Adam (with whom Fox had fought his one and only duel, but who was now a devoted friend), Robert Spencer, John Townshend, even, occasionally, the Prince of Wales.

A younger generation of Foxite Whigs would also make it their habit to stay at St Anne's Hill: Robert Adair, the young Duke of Bedford, and Charles Grey, future leader of the Whig party (who loved gardens quite as much as Mrs Armistead, and who once opened a political missive from Fox only to find inside it a violet, inserted there by 'Mrs A' to show him how large they were growing at St Anne's). Sometimes the older men brought their sons (but not their daughters), for Elizabeth and Fox, who were to remain childless, loved children. Henry Fox, Fox's younger brother, and his two natural children from previous liaisons, Harry Fox and Harriet Willoughby,* also came. Perhaps dearest of all was Fox's nephew Lord Holland, who often visited with his schoolfriends on their holidays from nearby Eton. Although for reasons of propriety Elizabeth was not on visiting terms with her female neighbours, they soon made friends amongst some of the men, most notably the Porter family, a Windsor brewer and his two sons, and the local apothecary, Mr Ives (Fox would one day stand as godfather to one of his sons).

In 1791 Anthony Storer wrote: 'A few days ago I made a visit to St Anne's Hill, and found our buff and blue chief lolling in the shade. Mrs Armistead was with him; a harper was playing soft music; books of botany lying about; and astronomy, in the shape of Sir Harry Englefield, assisted in the group . . . and thus, you see, like Solomon, he is to seek wisdom in the search of herbs and flowers.'[33]

But herbs and flowers, even the sweetest ones of St Anne's Hill, could not keep Fox rusticating indefinitely. When Parliament sat and he returned, with increasing reluctance, to London, Elizabeth occasionally accompanied him. William Ogilvy, the second husband of one of Fox's Lennox aunts, the Duchess of Leinster, once encountered them together taking an airing in the park. Mrs Armistead, he reported, was 'a pleasing, good-humoured-looking woman with good teeth and a bad complexion'. In public places – the park, the opera and the playhouses – Elizabeth was able to accompany Fox wherever he went. In private, however, she very frequently found herself excluded. As a courtesan,

---

* It is a strange irony that both of Fox's children were defective. Harry was congenitally deaf, and Harriet seems to have been dim-witted.

albeit a now retired one, the drawing rooms of Fox's married friends would never be open to her, nor would any society events other than a handful of the most public masquerades and balls. All-male gatherings of Fox's friends, the only ones at which her presence might have been acceptable, tended to take place in the clubs of St James's, or at Newmarket, from all of which, as a woman, she was debarred.

For all their many and complex correspondences, an impenetrable barrier divided the inner sanctums of the fashionable and aristocratic world from the denizens of the so-called world of gallantry, even in the relatively tolerant eighteenth century. Neither Elizabeth nor Fox would have been surprised or dismayed by this. It was simply the way of the world, and Elizabeth, who was a practical woman, did not repine. When Parliament sat, or when Fox was engaged on his annual autumnal round of shooting parties, she was well able to occupy herself. In the winter of 1787 she made a little holiday to Paris, where she attended the theatre, shopped for the latest fashions and, as was always her custom when she and Fox were apart, corresponded with her beloved.

On 24 January 1787, his thirty-eighth birthday, Fox wrote Elizabeth an especially long letter. Although he missed her, he was delighted to think of his Liz enjoying herself in Paris. He spoke of politics, of course, and had just come from the House of Commons, where he had spoken out 'pretty strongly against French connections and France, and Pitt made as bad a speech in answer as could be wished'. He was delighted that she had enjoyed a performance of Racine's *Andromaque* – 'I think it upon the stage is the best of all french tragedies, though Phedre, Athalie, Britannicus and Iphigenie all read as well if not better' – and was positively husbandly in his remarks on the latest French fashions: 'I dare say the dress at Paris is ridiculous enough . . . I suppose however you will grow to like it, as one does all fashions, I dare say I shall like it upon Liz, as I do every thing else.' But he was impatient to be with her again: 'Come home soon and be kind and good to old one, and it does not sig how you are drest. If you did but know the sort of longing I have to see you, you would not stay long, and the more I receive of your letters the more I long.' Writing to her must be his consolation. 'About an hour hence Liz will be drinking my good health,' he continued, in a more reflective mood.

Thirty-eight years have I lived most of them very happy and I do not know any thing at all serious that I have to reproach myself with; the remaining half of my life whether it is to be happy or otherwise depends entirely upon you, indeed it does. I never can be happy now I have known you, but with you. It is not flattery but judgement in me. I have known many men and many women and for many of them I have great friendship & esteem, but I never did know and never shall man or woman who deserved to be loved like Liz, & I am so convinced of this that having you for my Wife appears to me a full compensation for every disappointment.[34]

Elizabeth, of course, was not legally Fox's wife, but it was clear to everyone who knew them that she was the wife of his heart. The four years that they had been together, far from diminishing their love for one another, had only served to strengthen it. Fox was committed to Elizabeth for life. As his letters to her make clear, there could never be another woman for him, even if his friends did try occasionally to find him a more respectable – and richer – wife from among the heiresses of the day. Under the steadying influence of Elizabeth, Fox's gambling days were largely behind him now, but his financial affairs remained pitifully muddled. Marrying money, a completely acceptable practice in the eighteenth century, was the only way out. Mistresses, everyone knew, were dispensable. If Elizabeth ever felt the insecurity of her position, she did not show it.

Although in England Fox was always proud to be seen about with Mrs Armistead when the opportunity arose, even he realised that there were certain proprieties that had to be kept up. Abroad was another matter. Ever since she had accompanied her former patron, Lord Cholmondley, on a nine-month journey around Europe in 1781, Elizabeth had had a taste for travel, but so far she had never been away with Fox. But after the election of 1788 (at which Fox and his friend John Townshend were both returned as MPs for Westminster) they set off on a tour of the Continent together, for all the world like an old married couple.

Not everyone was so broad-minded as they had perhaps hoped.

Sometimes when they met fellow English travellers upon the road, Fox would be greeted, but the English showed no scruples in cutting Elizabeth completely. The historian Edward Gibbon, on hearing of their arrival in Lausanne, where he was then living, sent his compliments to their inn, the Lion d'Or, and was rewarded by a visit from Fox in person, who brought with him 'the fair Mrs Armistead'.

'The people gaze on him as a prodigy but he shews little inclination to converse with them: the wit and beauty of his Companion are not sufficient to excuse the scandalous impropriety of shewing her to all Europe, and you will not easily conceive how he has lost himself in the public opinion,' the strait-laced Gibbon wrote later, adding somewhat pompously, 'Will Fox never learn the importance of character.'[35]

As a man living on his own Gibbon had no objection to receiving Mrs Armistead in his house, but his perfunctory treatment of her is a clear indication of how many would have regarded her. Her status as a mistress did not earn her the courtesies which would have been extended to a wife. Gibbon was so overjoyed at the prospect of having Fox all to himself for the day that he ignored Elizabeth almost completely. 'I have eat and drunk and sat up all night with Fox in England,' he wrote, 'but it has never happened perhaps it can never happen again that I should enjoy him as I did that day, alone, (for his fair Companion was a cypher) from ten in the morning until ten at night ... Our conversation never flagged a moment.'[36]

Fortunately perhaps for Elizabeth, they soon left Switzerland for warmer climes, travelling south to Italy, where Fox enjoyed showing her his favourite paintings and works of art. At Bologna, however, their holiday was cut suddenly short. A fellow English traveller gave them the devastating news that Fox's nephew Lord Holland had died. The report turned out to be false, but no sooner had Fox and Elizabeth recovered from their shock and grief than they were greeted with another serious piece of news. King George III was seriously ill. The Duke of Portland sent an express messenger calling Fox back to London at once.

While Fox raced across Europe to the House of Commons and the Regency crisis, Elizabeth pursued a more leisurely route home, staying once again in Paris. It was not until mid-January that she was to learn that it was not only the King who was ill. On his journey home Fox had contracted a gastric complaint which so affected him that by the end of the month rumours of his imminent death were circulating freely in London.

'I never saw Fox, either previously or subsequently, exhibit so broken and shattered an aspect,' wrote a contemporary, observing him in the House of Commons. 'His body seemed to be emaciated, his countenance sallow and sickly, his eyes swollen, while his stockings hung upon his legs and he rather dragged himself along than walked up the floor to take his seat.'[37] While the King showed signs of recovery, Fox was now too ill to function in Parliament. Elizabeth took him to Bath to take the waters, and then back to St Anne's Hill.

Over the next years their quiet country life together formed a peaceful counterpoint to events in the wider world. When news came of the storming of the Bastille in July 1789, like many English radicals Fox greeted it with joy. Events in France soon took a much more serious turn, however. Four years later, in 1793, the French King, Louis XVI, was guillotined, and France declared itself at war with Britain. In the uncertain and terrifying revolutionary climate which now permeated Europe, Fox's unflinchingly liberal views on domestic and electoral reform began to seem increasingly dangerous. He had already broken with the philosopher Edmund Burke, his former friend and political ally, two years previously. Now, to Fox's dismay, the Duke of Portland and other leading Whigs seceded and joined Pitt's ministry. Fox was in the wilderness.

In the aftermath of these failures, politics began to exert less and less of a hold on him. 'I wish I could be persuaded it was right to quit public business, for I should like it to a degree that I can not express, but I can not yet think that it is not a duty to persevere,' he wrote in 1795 to his nephew Lord Holland, then just starting out on his own political career. 'I am so sure that secession is the measure a shabby fellow would take in our circumstances that I think it can scarcely be right for us.' If the choice had been a purely personal one, Fox would not have hesitated. He had everything, he told Holland, a man could possibly wish for: 'I am perfectly happy in the country, I have quite resources enough to employ my mind, and the great resource of all, literature, I am fonder of every day.'

It was Liz, however, who was the greatest and most continual source of happiness to Fox. 'You were never more right than in what you say of my happiness derived from her,' he wrote to Holland in June that year. 'I declare my affection for her increases everyday.' A sunny spring day at St Anne's Hill, with his books and Elizabeth, was for Fox a very paradise of earthly delights.

> The seventh of May
> Is the happiest day
> That ever I spent in my life.
> The sun it did shine,
> The birds sang divine,
> And I was all day with my Wife.[38]

But Elizabeth was not his wife. Everybody knew it, most especially Elizabeth herself. For all her outward composure, she had always been painfully aware that many, if not all, of Fox's friends would have considered her entirely expendable if a real contender to be his wife appeared. And now – in Elizabeth's eyes, if in no one else's – one did.

Miss Fanny Coutts was one of the three daughters of the royal banker, Thomas Coutts. The family had been friends of Fox's for some years, and he had often accepted invitations to their house (on his own, of course) when he was in London. At twenty-two, Fanny was considerably younger than Fox, and of a frail constitution, but despite these drawbacks she was her father's favourite, and her dowry would make her eventual husband very rich. What Fox really thought of Fanny is not known, but when it was indicated to him that she would like a lock of his hair as a gift, he saw no reason not to oblige her.

Fox, always so secure in himself, and so sure of his feelings for Elizabeth, could not conceive how vulnerable she might still sometimes feel. When she learned of his gift to Miss Coutts it played upon her every insecurity. In her eyes it was perfectly clear that the request for the lock of hair was only a preliminary on the part of the Coutts family. Elizabeth was nothing if not a woman of the world. While she still loved Fox, she had witnessed the fate of too many other courtesans, even those in the happiest of unions, to believe that Fox would always be hers. Now she convinced herself that the time had come for her to step aside.

No record survives of Elizabeth's letter to Fox on this occasion; and so, once again, it is his reply that speaks for her.

I have put off writing to my Liz till this hour that she may not say I write in a hurry. Indeed my dearest Liz I have considered the question as much as it is possible to consider one where everything is on one side and next to nothing on the other. I love you more than life itself indeed I do, & I can not figure to myself any possible idea of happiness without you, and being sure of this is it possible that I can think of any trifling advantage of fortune or connection as weighing a feather in the scale against the whole comfort and happiness of my Life? Even if you did not love me I could not endure the thought of belonging to any other woman, but my Liz does love me and will make me happy by living always with me, and if so & she is happy herself every wish of my heart is satisfied. Indeed my dearest Wife you are too suspicious. I assure you upon my honour that neither by word or look did I ever give the least reason to Miss C to think that I thought her pretty nor till Mr C asked me for the hair had I the least suspicion that there was any notion about me of the sort you suppose, nor indeed am I now clear about it . . . Mr Adam's conversation with Mrs C arose as I understood it in this manner. She was speaking of me very highly as she always does, and saying that it would have been better for me as a politician if I had led a different sort of life, if I had been married and led a domestic life; and this led Adam to say that I did lead as domestic a life as any man and that from what he had seen of us he was sure I considered you exactly as my Wife and that my life was in fact that of a married man though very scrupulous and straitlaced people (that was his word) might see it in a different light. That is what he told me, but my Liz what sigs what was said? I never can be happy without you and you have promised to be

*ruled in this instance by my determination. That is fixed and if
you love me I shall be happy if not I shall be miserable, but
still with my Liz, for never can I give my consent to part with
her. Do repeat to me my dearest love that you love me tenderly,
dearly and fondly for it is such a comf to me to hear it and
read it; and it is true, my dearest Liz, is it not?*

He promised that he would call at the Couttses soon and explain
that he was not going to give the lock of hair, although he confessed
that this was against his better judgement.

*I am much afraid that having been asked for it & having said
of course that I would give it, my not doing so will give Mr C
an idea that I consider his request as of more importance than
it becomes me to do, and possibly that I put an interpretation
upon it which may make him ashamed of having made it.*

But he promised nonetheless that Elizabeth's opinion would be his
guide on the matter.

*In your Sunday's letter you say that if I can be sure of always
loving Liz, & being entirely hers, you will be the happiest
woman in the World. Do pray my dear Angel repeat and
confirm that sentiment & I shall be the happiest of Men. To
think that I contribute to your happiness is a reflection so
pleasing that while I enjoy it, it gives a zest to every other
satisfaction in life, and makes me almost indifferent to every
other unpleasant event. Indeed my Liz if I were to consider for
a year I could think no otherwise than I do, & therefore pray
let me understand that every thing is fixed, for till you say so
directly an uneasy feel will hang about me, tho' it ought not as
you say you love me & leave the matter to my decision. God
bless my dearest mistress friend & wife, and make her love old
Kins,* and believe (what is true) that he is & always will be
entirely hers, yes every bit of him.*[39]

---

* One of Elizabeth's nicknames for him.

Elizabeth, always so outwardly serene, had managed to hide these innermost feelings from Fox, but now, after the Coutts affair, he could no longer be in any doubt. She had long been the wife of his heart; now he decided to make her his legal wife too.

In his encyclopedic study of prostitution in Britain, written more than a hundred years after the love affair between Elizabeth Armistead and Charles James Fox, William Acton wrote of his firm belief that 'hardly a prostitute in London has not, at some period of her career, an opportunity of marriage almost always above her original station'. Although Acton was exaggerating, and many of his views on women and their sexuality are now discredited, he was certainly right when he wrote of his conviction – a startling one at the time – that for many women prostitution was not the result of any innate 'vice', but a transitory state 'through which an untold number of British women are ever on their passage'. Although the numbers are impossible to quantify, there is no doubt that in both the eighteenth and nineteenth centuries many prostitutes married, some of them, in Acton's words, 'exceedingly well'.*

If Elizabeth married Fox, what would her new status as his legal wife bring her? How would it change her in the eyes of the world? Nineteenth-century commentators such as William Acton abominated the very notion of this kind of intermarriage; it was deeply and directly injurious to society, they believed, since women with 'tarnished bodies and polluted minds' would necessarily go on to become not only wives, but mothers too. There was far less of this kind of moral panic at the time of Elizabeth and Fox. Nonetheless, for all kinds of reasons, the transition from the world of gallantry in which Elizabeth had started her career to the aristocratic world of Fox and his friends had very rarely, if ever, been successfully made.

---

* Things have not changed so very much. I recently read an article by an aristocratic English *boulevardier* in which he recounted many of his youthful adventures, tactfully declining to name the women he had met in the high-class bordellos of London and Europe on the grounds that many of them were now respectably married to their former clients.

Marriage, however desirable it might be for its own sake, was in itself no passport out of the *demi-monde*. In Elizabeth's case this was especially so. Living as she did in an age much addicted to gossip and scandal, the legacy of her past was simply too spectacular to conceal. So much *éclat* had surrounded her during her heady days as one of London's most prominent courtesans that there was no possible hope of passing her off as anything else – a respectable widow, for example (as, for less well-known courtesans, or women who had been 'in keeping', was often successfully the case) – even if she had desired it.

Still more of a barrier than Elizabeth's loss of 'character' was the notion of class, every bit as brutal a barometer of social acceptability in Fox's day as in Acton's. As a rich and respectable widow of forty-six, the actress Harriet Mellon found this to her cost when she met her future second husband (she had first been married to one of the Coutts family), the twenty-three-year-old Duke of St Albans. Walter Scott was faced with social disaster when he invited the engaged couple to a house-party together. 'It so happened that there were already in the house several ladies, Scotch and English, of high birth and rank,' Scott was to record later, 'who felt by no means disposed to assist their host and hostess in making Mrs Coutts's visit agreeable to her.' Although Scott scolded them for their churlish treatment of his guest, the damage had been done, and the couple left the next day. As Duchess of St Albans, Harriet Mellon did finally achieve some acceptance in her husband's social sphere, but the slights she received along the way were to taint this triumph forever in her eyes, and her status in society was never completely assured.

For a former courtesan the situation was more equivocal still. Although there are plenty of examples of courtesans marrying their former protectors, the details of their lives after the fairy-tale ending – as married, and very often titled, women – are rather less well documented. The witty and high-spirited Kitty Fisher, for example, perhaps the most famous and certainly the most loved English courtesan of the mid-eighteenth century, ended her long career by marriage to John Norris, the MP for Rye. Kitty, who is alleged once to have eaten a banker's note for £100 sandwiched between two pieces of bread,* eschewed the fleshpots of London and retired into complete obscurity at her husband's estate, Hemsted Park in Kent. She died just five months later in Bath, where she was seeking a cure for a skin complaint caused by using white lead face paints, and was buried wearing her wedding dress.

A generation later Elizabeth Armistead's contemporary, the exquisitely beautiful Nancy Parsons, also married one of her protectors. Early on in her career Nancy had caused a sensation by her shamelessly public liaison with the then Prime Minister, the Duke of Grafton, for whom for a number of years she kept house and acted as official hostess. The daughter of a Bond Street tailor, Nancy was nonetheless a clever and cultured woman (one version of her life claims that she was educated in Paris), and a brilliant conversationalist. When the Duke formally separated from, and later divorced, his wife,† it was widely believed that Nancy's hold on his affections was such that he would marry her. But he did not. Their friendship ended in 1769 (Nancy was pensioned off in the time-honoured fashion, with a generous annuity – of £300, £800 or £900, depending on the source), after which she became the paramour of the Duke of Dorset, one of the most charming womanisers of his day and nearly as beautiful as Nancy herself, only to lose him soon afterwards to the more fashionable Mrs Armistead.

Perhaps on the rebound from Dorset, Nancy met and married the young Lord Maynard instead. Although she was now approaching forty and he was just twenty-five, Lord and Lady Maynard were happy together at first. Guessing correctly what the social taboo against Nancy was likely to be, even as the now irreproachably married Lady Maynard, they decided to move to the Continent, traditional repository for many of the more disorderly episodes in English aristocratic life.

---

* This is one of many charming anecdotes that survive about Kitty. Another is that when two rival suitors turned up at her house at the same time, she had the quickness of wits to hide one of them, the diminutive Lord Mountford, under the voluminous hoops of her dress. The second suitor was the Earl of Sandwich. The 'sandwich' has long been thought to have been invented by the 4th Earl, reputedly as a snack for eating at the gaming table. Perhaps it was Kitty who inspired him.
† The Duchess later married her lover, Lord Ossory, the elder brother of Fox's dearest friend, Richard Fitzpatrick.

Nancy's reception there was mixed. In Florence, the British Envoy, Sir Horace Mann, was happy to receive her, even in general company; but in Naples the social climate was not so kind. Lady Hamilton, first wife of the British Envoy Sir William Hamilton,* refused to present her at court, and she was resoundingly snubbed by all the other British residents. 'Nobody visits her,' wrote Sir William to his nephew Charles Greville. Only after a strange incident, in which Lord Maynard was able to cure the King's son, the Prince of Marino, of a fever with 'James's powders' did the tide turn in their favour.

Sadly, Nancy's acceptance came too late to save her marriage. Disillusioned by his wife's social ostracism, Maynard soon became estranged from her, eventually taking up with another actress. Although Nancy had remained a fascinating woman until well into her middle age, after her marriage she was never able to find the place in society which she had so spectacularly achieved during her courtesan days. After a brief spell back in England, she returned to live on the Continent again, dying just outside Paris, a pious old woman immersed in good works.

Was the sad fate of Nancy Parsons in Elizabeth's mind when she contemplated marriage to Charles James Fox? Something, certainly, made her hesitate. For all the personal happiness that matrimony might bring her, she was fully aware that a married courtesan was a strangely amphibious social creature: no longer fish, but not quite fowl either.

The late eighteenth century was a world in which nuances of rank and station permeated every aspect of life.† While women had always been able to marry 'above' themselves with much greater facility than men, spectacular leaps either up or down the scale were always a source of much social anxiety.[40] A courtesan, while she remained a mistress and was safely confined within the closed world of the *demi-monde*,

---

* Sir William Hamilton's more famous second wife, Emma Hamilton, was of course herself a famous courtesan. The story of her struggle to achieve social acceptability in the diplomatic and courtly circles of Naples is recounted in my book *Daughters of Britannia.*

† Sir William Hamilton was only too well aware of the implications of this when he first considered marrying Emma. Her status as the wife of the British Envoy would place her, for the purposes of etiquette, above 'every rank of nobility'. 'But,' he wrote, 'as I have experience that of all Women of the World, the English are the most difficult to deal with abroad, I fear eternal tracasseries were she to be placed above them.'

was somehow exempt from these notions. A wife would have no such luxury. She would indeed be changed in the eyes of the world. From being a queen she would, almost overnight, become a kitchen-maid again.

There were other, more disinterested, reasons for Elizabeth's reluctance to marry Fox, and it was these which weighed more with her. Marriage in Britain was easily entered into, but notoriously difficult to get out of (far more so than in any other country in Europe). What if Fox should one day repent of his decision? Would his friends think him degraded by what would be, in the eyes of the world, a scandalously unequal match? The thought haunted Elizabeth. Fox, however, would not take no for an answer. If she was uneasy at the thought of their marriage being made public, then they would do it privately. They would tell no one. They would keep their marriage a secret.

Fox went ahead and made preparations. He found a parson, John Pery, in the parish of Wyton in Huntingdonshire who not only agreed to marry them, but to comply with their wish for secrecy. He procured the necessary licence. In September, while Fox went off on his usual round of shooting parties, Elizabeth travelled north with her maid, Mary Dassonville, the only person other than the parson and his clerk who was privy to their secret, where she was to stay with Pery at the Wyton rectory in order to establish her residency in the parish.

It was there, during those solitary weeks, that she had time to reflect yet again on the consequences of marriage to Fox. On 23 September 1795 she wrote to him cancelling the wedding.

Fox's reply, so loving and so reassuring, shows just how much thought and discussion had already passed between them on the subject.

My dearest Liz, I have received your Wednesday's letters, kind as usual, but yet full of doubts, that indeed are wholly unfounded. I do assure you I have long ago given the subject all possible consideration, and I am for many reasons convinced that by following our plan we are doing for the best. In case of anything happening to me I am sure your having been my legal Wife will make your situation less uncomfortable & though this

is a case that my dear Liz can not bear to think of yet
according to the course of nature and of accidents it is a very
probable one. There are besides other reasons which you
yourself allowed to be good, after having very seriously
considered the subject and though now perhaps you do not
think so yet I am convinced the opinion you then formed was
right. On the other hand what possible reason can there be
against it? As to the possibility of my wishing it undone, I know
myself, I know my attachment to you, I know you and all those
qualities that belong to you that make me love and adore you –
more & more each day, and I will answer for it that on my
side, aye and I believe on your side too, we may go year after
year for the Flitch at Dunmow.* I can easily conceive what you
say that you had rather see me married to another, than have
to think that I repented being married to you and wished
myself free; but indeed indeed my dearest Angel you never
never shall have cause for such a thought, so on Monday
morning you must say love and obey, and be Mrs Fox.[41]

And so on a bright early autumn morning, 28 September 1795, Elizabeth
Armistead did at last submit to her beloved, and with no more demur
did indeed say love and obey, and became Mrs Fox at last.

For the next seven years the marriage of Elizabeth Armistead and
Charles James Fox remained a secret even from their family and closest
friends. While she was staying at Wyton rectory, Elizabeth had
expressed doubts about the discretion of Pery's clerk, Jeremiah Brad-
shaw, whom she described as 'a gossiping person', but her fears were
unfounded. The only person Fox considered telling at the time was
his brother Henry, but he does not appear to have done so, even
though Fox himself was far more relaxed about the consequences of
discovery than Elizabeth was. 'After all,' he wrote to her, 'if it should

---

* The Dunmow Flitch was awarded, then as now, in Dunmow, Essex, to the couple who
could prove that they had had no arguments with each other in the preceding year.

get about there is no great harm, indeed after the first talk it would be pleasanter that it should be known than not, and what sig a few additional paragraphs in the newspaper.'[42]

But it did not get about. Elizabeth continued to live happily at St Anne's Hill as Fox's mistress, claiming none of the rights or courtesies that, as Mrs Fox, might have been hers. She was as scrupulously careful as she had always been to avoid giving offence to the families of Fox's friends, waiting patiently outside in the carriage, if necessary, if she ever had occasion to accompany Fox on his calls. Even Lord Holland, Fox's nephew and the person he loved best in the world after Elizabeth, was kept in ignorance of the real state of affairs.

Holland had recently had to cope with scandal enough of his own when he became the lover, and eventually the husband, of the beautiful but domineering Lady Webster, who had become pregnant by him while she was still married to her first husband. Lady Holland, as she was to become after her divorce from Sir Geoffrey Webster, was one of the few people whom Fox actively disliked. Her bitter disapproval of Elizabeth, whom she had never met, was perhaps at the core of his feelings. Lord Holland himself, who loved Elizabeth almost as much as his uncle did, had been a free and frequent visitor to St Anne's Hill since he was a schoolboy of nine. After his marriage, however, things were very different. 'If it is not inconvenient to you Lady Holland would like to walk round St Anne's on Wednesday in her way to town,' he wrote somewhat stiffly to his uncle in 1798, 'as she is very anxious to see it particularly the seats. If I hear nothing from you I shall probably see you on the day & if it is fine Lady H will walk in the grounds.'[43] Since Lady Holland would never have consented to visit Elizabeth, the clear implication of this communication was that she should make herself scarce until the visit by her illustrious guests was over.

But for the most part, life at St Anne's went on much as it always had done. In the summer of 1797, Fox and his Whig followers had finally agreed that they could 'with honour secede from Parliament', and Fox retired, with an untroubled conscience, to the countryside and Elizabeth. 'I should not care,' he told Samuel Rogers, 'if I was condemned never to stir a mile beyond St Anne's Hill for the rest of my life.' While Elizabeth read and drew, and learned to play the harp, Fox interested himself in the farm, planned improvements to his house and garden, and wrote to his friends. They kept a journal together. Fox toyed, too, with the idea of writing an account of the reign of James II, and it was with a view to consulting French sources in the Louvre that, in the summer of 1802, the idea for the Foxes' second visit to Paris was conceived.

It was on the eve of their departure for France, nearly seven years after the event, that Fox and Elizabeth finally announced their marriage to the world. This was not so arbitrary an act as it might seem. Fox had always intended to make their marriage public (he himself had never seen the need to keep it a secret at all*), but the cosily domestic life at St Anne's that they had led up until now had simply not made it necessary. Lady Holland had not found it incumbent upon herself to repeat her visit, and everyone else they cared about (for the most part men, admittedly) came anyway, just as they always had. The principal advantage of the Foxes' trip to Paris was that they would be away from England for three months, ample time for their friends to digest this extraordinary piece of news, and for any scandal to play itself out long before they returned.

There was another immediate advantage to their announcement, of which both Fox and Elizabeth, who now for the first time took to using the name Elizabeth Fox, must have been aware. After the Treaty of Amiens, signed in March 1802, Paris was flooded with British aristocrats who had been starved of European travel, especially in France, for over a decade. On their tour of the Continent fourteen years earlier, Elizabeth had suffered the indignity of being either cut or ignored by their fellow travellers, but now, as Mrs Fox, this would be far harder for them to do. For the first time, women of the *monde* would have the chance to decide for themselves whether to accept her or not.

Most found it impossible not to like her. One of the first to express an opinion was Amelia Opie, wife of the painter John Opie, who visited

---

* Elizabeth was uncharacteristically disingenuous in one of her few surviving letters, to her stepdaughter Harriet, when, having signed herself 'E. Fox', she added the postscript: 'this . . . long has been my name but till now Mr F had reasons for not wishing it to be known but has them no longer'.

the Louvre with her. 'Mrs Fox looks like a clever woman,' she wrote approvingly, 'and I am told that she is, but I have seen too little of her to form any correct judgement of her abilities – all I know is that she is a very agreeable woman and had a very prepossessing character.' Not all were so generous. Fox's friend James Hare described in a letter to the Duchess of Devonshire how the Duchess of Gordon, Lady Charles Greville 'and some other English ladies lately arrived' were quite openly caballing against Elizabeth. Chief amongst these was Lady Holland, who as fate would have it was also in Paris.

One of the great questions among the ladies of the British aristocracy at this time was whether or not they should agree to be presented to the Bonapartes. Napoleon himself was still only First Consul, but was already giving himself noticeably royal airs. More scandal, however, and sheer upstart impropriety, was attached to his wife Josephine.* Her reputation had been somewhat sanitised by a recent decree which required that all couples living together should be married. Pasts (most especially, of course, that of Madame Bonaparte) were, by the same decree, to be forgiven and forgotten.

Although Josephine was now officially respectable, many British travellers, some of whom had known Marie Antoinette personally, still hesitated. Lady Holland, however, was not among the over-scrupulous. As a divorcee, her own 'character' was itself more than a little equivocal, and she was eager to enjoy the chance of being officially received, even if it was by the upstart Bonapartes. When she learned that the new Mrs Fox was also to be presented, however, she was furious. 'I find since Lady Holland's departure that she is not supposed to have behaved by any means kindly to Mrs Fox,' wrote Robert Adair, who also was in Paris along with Fox's other bosom friends Fitzpatrick and Lord Robert Spencer, to Lady Melbourne.

> *I am so very blind a person that I should not most probably have found it out in a thousand years, but I hear it from foreigners and women who have no sort of interest in telling*

* At a party given by one of Napoleon's ministers later that year, and attended by Lady Bessborough, Madame Bonaparte 'sat like a Queen' on a raised dais at one end of the room.

fibs about her. The grand object of jealousy, I fancy, was the
presentation to Madame B[onaparte] on the same day. This
Her Ladyship did not much like, and whether Mrs Fox's dress
really was not ready, or whether she gave the point up I cannot
tell, but it did not take place as it had been projected, Lady
Holland alone was presented. I take it, however, that she left
Paris in great dudgeon, for she fully expected that, after the
ceremonial was over, she would have been asked to the private
parties. In this she was disappointed, and perhaps Mrs F has it
all visited upon her.[44]

'Mrs F' did indeed have it all visited upon her. Fox, whose early support
for the Revolution and consistent advocacy for peace with France had
made him the object of such vilification in England, made him a
popular figure across the Channel. Receptions and public dinners were
given for him almost as soon as his foot touched French soil, and
almost as many courtesies were extended to his wife (who, it must be
said, along with Lady Holland and Madame Bonaparte herself, was
among the beneficiaries of Napoleon's recent decree). Fox, who was
personally inclined to dislike all the fuss, was delighted that his Liz
('Wife', as he now teasingly refers to her in their joint journal) was
included in it all. 'Profusion of civility to us both,' he wrote, 'which
Kins liked.'

Elizabeth's warm reception in Paris was not only the result of Fox's
fame. Her own excellent qualities (of which the exquisite good taste
which she showed in not forcing a point of etiquette with Lady Holland
is but one example), when they were seen for themselves, could not
fail to recommend her to all but the most flinty-hearted of dowagers.
(And even they found it hard to keep up such a level of disapproval
indefinitely. As one of the most rigidly moralising of them, the dowager
Lady Spencer, wrote almost despairingly to her daughter Lady Bessborough some years later: 'When one considers the frequent admission
of the Dowr Ly Jersey, Ly Holland, Ly Hamilton, Mrs Fox, your poor
cousin [Lady John Townshend], Mrs Bouvery, Mr Fawkener, and
others into all company we must acknowledge there is great merit in
the uniform steadiness that is able to exclude them all.'[45])

The Foxes returned to England in November, reaching St Anne's Hill ('dear dear home') on the seventeenth. Elizabeth had conquered Paris: all that remained now was to see what society in England would make of the new Mrs Fox. Fox's family were the first to rally. His brother Henry, now General Fox, immediately brought his daughters to visit. His niece Caroline, the daughter of his eldest brother Stephen, announced her intention of doing the same, even though both she and her aunt Marianne, the General's wife, did so at first from duty rather than preference, declaring between themselves that 'it is truly to be wished that he would have married some amiable woman whose society we could have cultivated'.

On this point, however, Elizabeth found that she had an unexpected champion. Lady Holland, for all her high-handed snobberies, had been completely won over by Elizabeth's sweetness of character (a cynical observer might have called it astuteness). 'I am truly pleased at your intention of meeting your new aunt,' she wrote to her sister-in-law Caroline Fox. 'For his sake you will like and esteem her.' Her bossy tone then softens unexpectedly:

> She is always occupied in attending to his comforts, and that absorbs a thousand little blemishes. To us the declaration will be productive of much real enjoyment, and it will bring us together without restraint. Her manners and conversation are as correct as possible. The only ridicule she has arises from his ardent love and her short memory which dispose her to forget the half-century and upward which had rolled over her head; but her temper and disposition are as good as any Fox of you all.

Other family members, most notably Fox's Lennox aunts, soon followed suit. Even though they would certainly have known the famed Mrs Armistead by sight, for these women the prospect of actually meeting a former courtesan, face to face, was rather like greeting a dangerously exotic animal out of a zoo. And it is clear from their letters and comments that, not quite knowing what to expect, they feared the worse.

When the moment came, Elizabeth's natural courtesy, her lack of vulgarity, her sheer niceness, was a source of such delight to them (and no doubt, although they do not actually say it, of relief too) that they could not help but accept her. Amongst Fox's friends there were a few who chose the Lady Spencer hard line – Thomas Coke of Holkham Hall, Fox's shooting friend, and Lord Fitzwilliam never allowed their wives to visit Elizabeth – but the vast majority, out of sheer love for Fox, accepted her, even if they were 'very angry with him at first', as Harriet Bessborough recorded. 'The odd thing is that people who were shocked at the immorality of his having a mistress are still more so at that mistress having been his wife so long.'[46]

Although both Lady Bessborough and her sister, the Duchess of Devonshire, accepted Elizabeth immediately, it was by no means a foregone conclusion. There was an unspoken assumption among many of Fox's friends that these were special, perhaps even unique, circumstances. As the Duke of Bedford wrote to William Adam: 'It is impossible to conceal from ourselves that from Mrs F's former unfortunate life, Fox's marriage to her was a severe blow to public morals, yet our affection and attachment to him induced us to overlook what nothing else ought to have suffered us to countenance, and we gave her our support and protection.'

But even those few of his friends who were still inclined to be stuffy could not help but be charmed by Fox's sheer ebullience. He was his own best advocate for marriage to Elizabeth. 'You would be perfectly astonished at the vigour of body, the energy of mind, the innocent playfulness and happiness of Fox,' wrote the diarist Thomas Creevy. 'The contrast between him and his old associates is the most marvellous thing I ever saw – they having all the air of shattered debauchees, of passing gaming, drinking & sleepless nights, whereas the old leader of the gang might really pass for the pattern and the effect of domestic good order.' Fox's political ally Charles Grey put it more succinctly still: 'Fox seems in the highest spirits & is in the best of looks,' he wrote to his wife. 'He is like a young man in the prime of life who has just married a girl of 16. Is it not a fine thing to grow young at 50?'[47]

The following summer Elizabeth's place in the Fox family was confirmed by a visit from none other than the Duchess of Leinster, Fox's aunt, who visited St Anne's Hill with one of her grandchildren in August. Any fissures in family unity which had resulted from Fox's past rakish behaviour were now behind them. 'I took him [her grandson] with me to St Anne's where he was most kindly received and you would have been pleased I am sure to see your Dr Uncle playing Cricket with him,' the Duchess wrote to her niece Caroline.

> *I passed two of the pleasantest days with him and Mrs Fox that I have known for years, the lovely weather, the Beautiful Place, their comfort in one another, their extreme kindness to me and my Dear Child all gladden'd my heart and gave feelings that I almost despaired would ever revive there again. She is a most obliging good natured woman and her conversation was particularly pleasant to me as it was all about him, giving me a sort of History of those years I had lost sight of him. You may say it required some delicacy and management to do this well, her own being so interwoven with it, & I assure you she shew'd no want of either.*[48]

On 23 February 1806, just a day before Fox's fifty-seventh birthday, the news came that William Pitt was dead. Despite having been his political adversary for so many years, Fox was devastated by the news. Some Foxites, knowing that Pitt's administration could not survive without him, rejoiced at the turn of events, but Fox himself could not share their glee. He declared that every debate in the House from now on would be 'flat and uninteresting . . . I hate going to the House,' he added. 'I think I shall pair off with Pitt.'

It was not to be. After so many years in opposition, Fox was now made Secretary of State for Foreign Affairs in Lord Grenville's new administration, the 'Ministry of All the Talents'. Working alongside him would be George Spencer as Home Secretary, Lord Fitzwilliam as Lord President of the Council, Charles Grey as First Lord of the Admiralty, Sheridan as Treasurer of the Navy, and Fitzpatrick as Secretary at War. On 3 February Elizabeth wrote in her journal: 'Lord G[renville] saw King who accepted the new Ministry which God Almighty grant may prove a fortunate one for the country and for my Angel Husband.'[49]

As Mrs Secretary Fox, Elizabeth would now truly need all the delicacy and management that were naturally hers. After more than two decades out of office, Fox threw himself into public life again with all the gusto of which he was capable. He gave himself two grand objectives: to negotiate peace with France (the Treaty of Amiens had secured only a fragile peace of fourteen months' duration) and to abolish the slave trade.

It was a punishing schedule for any man, but Fox was now fifty-seven, and his constitution was not strong. The quiet life of St Anne's Hill with its healthy country hours was a thing of the past. Instead the Duke of Bedford had lent them a house in London, Stable Yard, which now became the Foxes' official residence. It swarmed with visitors, day and night: colleagues, political place-seekers, and friends, even the Prince of Wales, who often kept them up until the early hours of the morning. On the evenings when they were alone, Fox was so swamped with official papers that he was often obliged to work on them far into the night. Elizabeth watched his health anxiously. In January he had suffered a severe head-cold, and he had another in February, but by early spring 1806 Elizabeth could observe: 'Thank God he seems nice and well and not the worse for all the fatigue he has.'

As the wife of the Secretary of State, Mrs Fox, the former courtesan, found herself with official business of her own to attend to. Some observers who had been in Paris with the Foxes the previous year had feared that her great social success there would turn her head, and that this, as Lady Bessborough reported, would 'induce her to do a thousand absurd things in England and expose herself to mortification'. But no one who really knew Elizabeth could have a moment's doubt on this score. 'He ... is so occupied so as to leave it to her to do the civil things,' wrote another of Fox's aunts, Lady Sarah Napier, incredulously. 'I believe she succeeds.'

And she did. Elizabeth's journal from this period reads for all the world like that of any other woman of fashion.

April 8th. I went out visiting a good deal. Went to the play with Lady Holland to see the '40 Thieves', a very fine show. Got home 12.30 to find Darling hard at work.

April 20th. Went with Darling to the Admiralty to see Lady Norwich and her children. She looked very thin. Took a drive in the King's Road ... made a few visits and came home.

April 22nd. Harriet [Willoughby, Fox's daughter] and I went to the Opera, Duchess of Queensborough's box.

April 26th. Made a good many visits. Dined at Lord Howick's, a very pleasant party.

May 7th. Went to Lady Stafford's Rout with Lord Henry Jellico. The house and pictures are most magnificent. They said there were 1800 people, came home before 1.

May 8th. Carl went to work early. I saw Lady Isabel Napier and 2 of her daughters, who called and stayed with me some time ... Lady Rosselyn came with her children and stayed in the garden til near dinner time.[50]

And so the days went on. Fox continued with his work. The head colds were gone, but in their place was a new, more worrying ailment. His legs had begun to swell so much that walking had become painful, and he took to using a wheelchair. Although Fox knew that his health would not hold up indefinitely under pressure of work, he was reluctant to give up just yet. Elizabeth, conscious of what was required of her as his wife, continued with her duties. She paid calls and made visits of etiquette, arranged small working dinners for Fox at Stable Yard, and continued to try to protect him as much as possible from unnecessary fatigue. She also decided to hold her own entertainment: a supper and a ball.

The date set was 19 May. The Duke of Bedford lent her Bedford House, and the Prince of Wales's upholsterers, Marsh and Tatham, were commissioned to decorate the state apartments for the occasion. The invitations were sent out, the supper menu drawn up, the flowers ordered, the musicians hired. The only question now was, who would come? Even those who had most championed Elizabeth feared that this could be one step too far. 'One can't bear to think of any mortifications to her,' wrote Lady Elizabeth Foster, 'both for her own sake and Charles Fox's.'

On the night of the eighteenth, Elizabeth hardly slept at all. The next morning she was busy inspecting the house and the gardens. After dining with her friends the Bouveries, she and Fox's daughter Harriet went home to dress at eight: 'Very tired and frightened,' Elizabeth wrote in her journal, 'for fear I should not be able to get through the fatigue of the night.' She returned to Bedford House at nine, in time to supervise the lighting of the rooms, and gradually her guests began to arrive: Fox's friends and relatives, political colleagues of all persuasions, ambassadors and ministers. They brought their sons, and their daughters too. Elizabeth, resplendent in the ball dress which she had had made up for the occasion, greeted them all at the top of the Bedford House staircase. A hundred guests arrived. Then two hundred. Then three. 'About half past 12 very full indeed,' recorded Mrs Fox with quiet pleasure in her journal. 'On the whole I fancy about 400. There were 240 sat down to supper and between forty and fifty sat down afterwards everything seemed to give satisfaction, the ballroom and gardens certainly were very beautiful.'[51]

The next day, buoyed by his wife's triumph, Fox showed no signs of having been fatigued by the party, but a week later he had developed another heavy cold. His legs became swollen again and he complained of pains in his thighs, possibly a sign of rheumatism. He worked on, and the next month achieved a still greater (but no more surprising) triumph of his own when the resolution he moved for the abolition of the slave trade was carried by 114 votes to fifteen.*

For all the headiness of this success, politics were now visibly taking their toll. When she came home one night after attending a masked ball at Landsdowne House, at which Fox was to have joined her, Elizabeth found him already in bed: 'He was kept at the House till 12,' she wrote, 'and was too tired to get to Landsdowne House.'[52]

It was not only Elizabeth who was concerned for Fox's health. His colleagues, in an attempt to find an honourable but less onerous job for him, offered him a place in the House of Lords. But still Fox clung on. 'At the mention of the Peerage he looked at [Elizabeth] significantly, with a reference to his secret but early determination

---

* This resolution became the foundation for the Act of 1807 which finally ended the slave trade.

never to be created a Peer,' recalled his nephew Lord Holland, 'and after a short pause, he said, "no, not yet, I think not yet . . . The Slave Trade and Peace are such glorious things, I can't give them up . . ."'[53]

Later that month, on 14 June, the Foxes snatched a visit, now increasingly rare, to St Anne's Hill, where they enjoyed 'a nice lounge' and drank tea at Fan Grove. Two days later they were back in London. On the nineteenth Elizabeth recorded 'Carl at House'. It was the last time she was to make such an entry. Two days later they were invited to dinner with Fitzpatrick's brother Lord Ossory, but Fox looked so ill that Elizabeth tried to persuade him not to go: 'but he said I am not well my Liz but it will be a pleasant dinner and if I were to stay at home people will think me worse than I am'. The next day he was too ill to leave his dressing room.

The painful swellings in Fox's legs, now diagnosed as dropsy, increased, as did the pain. His illness became public knowledge, and Stable Court swarmed with visitors again; not political supplicants this time, but friends and wellwishers enquiring after his health. On 29 June Lady Bessborough, still in mourning for her sister Georgiana who had died four months before, visited them, and was appalled by Fox's appearance. 'His face and hands are dreadfully drawn and emaciated,' she wrote, 'his complexion sallow beyond measure, his bosom sunk – and then, all at once, a body and legs so enormous that it looks like the things with which they dress up Falstaff.' His charm and sense of humour were undimmed, though. 'Ld Holland told him he look'd well; he smil'd and said: "I shall end with being the handsomest Man in England, for every body who comes in compliments me on my improv'd looks, and so much improvement must end in beauty."'[54]

But by now it was clear that there would be no improvement in his health. In July Elizabeth's journal entries are reduced to the most cursory bulletins.

> *6 I have thought him worse though Vaughan and Moseley [his physicians] assured me there was no danger but I thought yesterday the worst day.*
> *12 all the days so much alike that I did not think it necessary*

to say anything about them until yesterday when I thought him a great deal better indeed.

19 Some days better and some worse but very bad and low the day before yesterday but thank god pretty well yesterday and seems better still.

24 Much the same for some days passed though he had a badish night owing to the hardness of the Poultice

25 Much better

26 A good deal better

27 The same though no appetite but in good spirits and seems to get stronger

28 A good night seemed very well when he first woke but afterwards very heavy to sleep.[55]

Almost two months passed before Elizabeth opened her journal again:

Went on much the same some days better some worse (on the 7th [of August] he was tapped which he bore very well and seemed relieved by it) till about the 15 or 16 when he appeared to get much better and continued so much that we settled to go to St Anne's but the physicians were afraid it would be too far for him to go in one day and as the Duke of Devonshire had kindly offered us Chiswick we went there on the 27th.

Fox bore the move to Chiswick House well, so much so that Elizabeth briefly allowed herself to believe that he might recover, and that they might indeed reach their beloved St Anne's one last time. But it was not to be. 'Alas the dreadful disorder increased so very rapidly,' she wrote,

that on Sunday the 31st August he was obliged to be tapped again and thirteen quarts [six and a half pints] of water brought away. It lowered him very much but in a day or two he seemed to get better and recovered a little appetite went out airing on the Friday in a garden chair and on Saturday and Sunday in the carriage with me. He was very cheerful and talked a great deal to me kept my hand in his all the time we were out made me kiss him several times and admired the Thames that we saw in the road back *from Kew Bridge . . . I thought he seemed very heavy to sleep all the afternoon but in the evening and the night he had Mr Trotter [Fox's secretary] to read to him. He got some sleep in the night but not much and on Monday the 8th Septr soon after ten when Mr Trotter was reading to him Johnson's Life of Dryden the fatal symptoms came on which left no ground for reasonable hope afterwards. Oh my God and I am here to write this but I must not repine for by his great goodness to me in giving me strength to go through my last sad duty in the way I knew my angel Husband would like best which was by staying by him and giving him everything he wanted. On Tuesday Ld. Rt Spencer came to Chiswick and brought Mr J Bouverie with him he read prayers for Miss Fox* Harriet and I. He missed me out of the room and asked Dr Vaughan if I had gone to get a little rest. He had asked Dr V that afternoon what he thought of his case and his answer was that the symptoms were not as good as was expected. I saw him the moment after and could see no change in his dear countenance except that he seemed to look at me with a greater degree of tenderness. Harry Fox† came in the course of the day Wednesday and he was pleased to see him – I forgot to mention that he talked with Lord Holland after he had spoke to Dr Vaughan. He saw and shook hands with General Fitzpatrick. Mr J Bouverie read prayers by the bedside on Wednesday morn: there were in the room besides Harriet and I the General, Lord Robert Mr Trotter Miss Fox Mr Hawkins [the surgeon] Harry Fox and Conway [Fox's valet] and Dr Vaughan – he put his dear hands together and kept his eyes fixed on me. Mr Pitcairn saw him on Wednesday night and said he thought all over. On Thursday morning he seemed to be a good deal better and I could not but flatter myself with hope. He walked as far as the Drawing Room with Mr Trotter and talked to him very cheerfully of different Books. He continued pretty well all Thursday til between nine and ten when he got very restless getting out of bed every instant.*

---

* Fox's niece, Caroline.
† Fox's nephew, the son of his brother General Henry Fox.

Friday he was very weak and every moment we expected to be the last. I was so low and weak I could not as I had hitherto done hide my feelings and when he felt that I was almost in hysterics he looked up and said oh fie Liz is this your promise. We had agreed some years ago that whichever was likely to die first the other should stay by all the time and to try and look gay and cheerful but my God who could do it. I did I believe more than most people could have done and I shall never forget the goodness of the Almighty in enabling me to do it.

Fox continued to be restless throughout the next day, but was mercifully free from pain. His old friend Lord Fitzwilliam came to say goodbye to him, but Elizabeth thought it best not to mention it, for fear it would disturb him. Even speaking was now an effort.

'I had sent to St Anne's Hill for a comfortable sick chair that I knew he liked,' Elizabeth continued as bravely as she was able,

and he was much pleased with it though he did not say so but we found that he sat up longer at a time than he had before alone and he looked up at me with a sweet smile and said I like this Chair Liz – Oh Father of mercys help me to go on – Saturday morn: he seemed rather quieter. I think it was about 12 or one o clock that he bid Ld H goodbye. He had hold of my hands bid me kiss him looked at me with a heavenly smile said 'I die happy but I pity you.'

From this time his voice was less intelligible and he said something that I could not understand and when he saw that I was unhappy he made an effort and said it don't signify my dearest dearest Liz – those were his last words. He remained very quiet with his dear eyes fixed on me. I was seated on the bed and he had my hand between his two but as he grew weaker he took away his left hand and made a sign to me to leave my hand upon his right hand which I continued to do. Mr Moseley sitting on the right hand side of the bed Miss Fox Mr Trotter Mr Hawkins and Conway at the foot all out of sight except Mr Trotter. About three his dear eyes lost all motion but seemed quite fixed still on me and lay as quiet as a lamb only breathing rather hard. I still

stayed with him and till Mr Hawkins saw that last moment was
at hand had me carried out of the room.[56]

Charles James Fox died at the age of fifty-seven on 13 September 1806, the name of the woman he had loved for almost half his lifetime – 'dearest dearest Liz' – on his lips. 'Indeed,' wrote Lord Holland recalling that day, 'if one had not known it before, his last hours would have convinced us that the ruling passion of his heart was affection and tenderness for her. She had the consolation of knowing that he died with that sentiment & the comforting reflection that her society formed the happiness of his life for years & that her care prolonged it.'

Fox's 'beloved Liz' passed away peacefully on 8 July 1842 at St Anne's Hill just three days short of her ninety-second birthday, having outlived her adored husband by thirty-six years. For many years towards the end of her life she had been faithfully tended by her companion Elizabeth Marston and her servant Martha Tucker, now nearly as old as she, but she was also in touch until the last with many of Fox's old friends and family. When, in 1834, she visited Holland House, Lord Holland wrote afterwards:

> *Our old relation, Mrs Fox, has just left here after a visit of*
> *three days in which, much to her delight, she met a large*
> *portion of the Ministry and bore, I assure you a very cheerful*
> *and agreeable part in the conversation. She is, though lame and*
> *infirm in limbs, wonderfully well; and good temper and good*
> *heart seem eminently conducive to long life, or at least to the*
> *enjoyment of it if it comes.*[57]

Elizabeth's gift for friendship stayed with her until the end. Friends and relations, their children and their grandchildren, came to stay, a bemusing succession of Foxes, Hollands, Lilfords (Holland's daughter Mary had married Lord Lilford) and St Johns. One of the last entries in her journal, which she kept with the help of Miss Marston almost until the end of her life, was dated 1 March 1841: 'Mr Charles St John Lord Bolingbroke's brother [Bully's grandson] came to announce his approaching marriage.'[58]

Like her contemporary Sophia Baddeley, Elizabeth was loved by the ordinary people around her quite as much as by the Fox and Holland families and other grandees from the past. When the people of Chertsey heard of her death they sent a deputation to ask that they be allowed to pay their last respects. 'The funeral . . . however simple and unostentatious in outward circumstances,' wrote Elizabeth's niece Caroline Fox, 'will be followed by crowds of sincere mourners among the poor, & other neighbours who loved and respected her – & are not likely soon to forget her hospitality & kindness, or meet with another such benefactress.'[59]

Elizabeth was not to achieve her dearest wish, which was to be buried alongside Fox in Westminster Abbey. In 1835 she had presented a camellia from St Anne's Hill, which had grown too big to be contained within her own greenhouse, to King William IV for his collection at Kew. In return – so Caroline Fox had written to her cousin Henry* – Elizabeth had asked for nothing, but had written instead 'the simplest most unaffected and touching of letters – asking only an assurance from him that when her spirit has fled her remains may lie in Westminster Abbey entombed with those of her husband'. But Elizabeth outlived the King, and her body was laid to rest at the church at Chertsey instead.

And so it was that on 15 July 1842 Elizabeth left her beloved St Anne's Hill for the last time. With the funeral cortège were Colonel Charles Fox, Henry Fox's brother, and Lord Lilford, followed by Fox's old friend (the last survivor from the old days) Sir Robert Adair, with the rector of the parish, Henry Cotton. In the carriage behind them rode Henry St John, Bully's grandson, with Elizabeth's solicitor Mr Glazebrook, and Charles Ives, the local apothecary. The Duke of Bedford (the son of Fox's friend), who could not attend, sent instead, as a token of respect, his empty carriage to accompany her hearse. At the foot of the hill the funeral procession was joined by some forty tradesmen of Chertsey, who fell silently into place behind the line of carriages as Elizabeth's hearse made its way the half-mile to the village. Slowly the cortège passed between the shops, closed in mourning, 'through silent throngs of townspeople to the thronged and silent church . . . the unnamed many, "not quite thousands who have loved her and kept her commandment".'[60]

---

* Henry Edward Fox, Holland's son, and after his death in 1840 the 4th Lord Holland.

3

HARRIETTE WILSON
1786–1845

❦❧•❦❧•❦❧

The Demi-Rep

'I SHALL NOT SAY why and how I became, at the age of fifteen, the mistress of the Earl of Craven,' begins Harriette Wilson's notorious memoir. 'Whether it was love, or the severity of my father, the depravity of my own heart, or the winning arts of the noble Lord, which induced me to leave my paternal roof and place myself under his protection, does not now much signify: or if it does, I am not in the humour to gratify curiosity in this manner.'[1]

The year in which Harriette launched herself on the Earl of Craven – the first rung, as it were, of her extraordinary career – was 1802. In Europe an uneasy peace prevailed under the Treaty of Amiens; in the autumn of that year Charles James Fox and Elizabeth, en route to Paris, finally announced their marriage to the world. Neither of these events was of the least significance to Harriette, who was never political. Fox was to live another four years, Elizabeth another forty (Harriette outlived her by just three years), yet Harriette, emerging into the *haut ton* on the very cusp on the nineteenth century, seems to belong to an altogether different world: brasher and more brittle, with less of the extreme formality of the eighteenth century, but ultimately less of its tolerance too.

Harriette was born Harriette Dubochet in Mayfair in 1786,* one of the fifteen children of an ill-tempered Swiss watchmaker and his English wife. She was an observant and clever child; she loved her mother, but feared her father ('The very idea of a father,' she once wrote, 'put me in a tremble'), and from an early age their unhappy marriage was to reveal to her most forcibly 'the miseries of two people of contrary opinions and character, torturing each other to the end of their natural lives'. Before she was ten years old, Harriette had decided 'to live free as air from any restraint but that of my conscience'. It was an unusual decision for any woman (and quite startling in a ten-year-old), but by no means unique: no fewer than four of the Dubochet sisters were to decide on the independent life and become courtesans.

Amy, Harriette's eldest sister, was the first. 'We were all virtuous girls,' wrote Harriette, 'when Amy, one fine afternoon, left her father's house and sallied forth, like Don Quixote, in quest of adventures.' Soon Amy became the kept mistress of a Mr Trench – 'a certain, short-sighted, pedantic man' – whom she told she was running away from her father. When he put her back into school, 'from motives of virtue and economy', Amy promptly eloped with another, more exciting admirer, General Madden, with whom she was in keeping for several years.

Another sister, Fanny, a sweet-tempered girl whom many considered to be the most beautiful of all the sisters, soon followed Amy's interesting example, and was for a number of years the kept mistress of a Mr Woodcock, by whom she had three children (Harriette believed he would have married Fanny had it not been for the inconvenient fact that he already had a wife who was still living).

In later years Harriette and Fanny were joined by a 'sworn friend', Julia Johnstone, and for much of their careers the three were so close – sharing their houses, opera boxes, even their men – that many believed Julia also to be a Dubochet sister. The trio became known as the Three Graces. 'It was a pity there were only three Graces!' wrote

---

* This is the date which is usually given. But in a letter to the novelist Bulwer Lytton written in 1831, Harriette remarked that she was born 'ten minutes before eight o'clock, the 22nd February 1788', and gave her age as forty-three. If this was the case, her seduction by the Earl of Craven would have taken place in 1804.

Harriette, '– and that is the reason I suppose why my eldest sister, Amy, was cut out of this ring, and often surnamed – one of the Furies.' A fourth sister, Sophia, also became a courtesan. Seduced by Lord Deerhurst at the age of thirteen, she later married another of her protectors, Lord Berwick.

Of the five, whose society formed the centre of the Regency half-world, it was Harriette who was to become the most successful, and after the publication of her *Memoirs* in 1825, the most notorious too.

Harriette was not beautiful, but she was clever and spirited enough to make men think she was. She was also extremely good company. Even Julia Johnstone, who later broke spectacularly with her, acknowledged that Harriette had 'the knack of pleasing in a high degree'. 'She had a bewitching method of making anyone jocund against their inclination,' recalled Julia. Women as well as men fell under her spell; including Julia herself, who from the beginning was 'fascinated with [Harriette's] lovely features and arch vivacity': 'She was all animal spirits. I believe nothing could have made her grave for an hour, but the loss of her beauty.'[2]

More striking still to a modern reader is Harriette's confidence in herself. '[He] was not up to me,' she wrote matter-of-factly of one of her lovers on the eve of their parting, 'either in hand or in heart.' Her clear-sighted acceptance of the life she had chosen was matched by a cool control. 'I will be the mere instrument of pleasure to no man. He must make a friend and companion of me, or he will lose me,' she declared. This keen sense of her own worth shines though her *Memoirs*. Woe betide the foolish man, however rich or aristocratic, who presumed too far. A 'great man' she meets at Julia's house one evening (unusually, he is unnamed) calls at Harriette's house the following day and tells her servant that he desires to speak with her.

> *'Why do you not bring his name?' said I.*
>
> *'The gentleman says, it does not signify,' was my footman's answer.*
>
> *'Go and tell him that I think it does signify; and that I will not receive people who are ashamed either of me or of themselves.'*
>
> *The man hesitated.*

'Stay,' said I, 'and I will put it down for you,' and I wrote what I had said on a bit of paper.

My servant brought me back the paper, on the blank side of which was written, with a pencil, one word.

I sent it down again, with these words written underneath the word, on purpose to put him in a passion: Don't know anybody in that shire.

The servant returned once more, with one of His Lordship's printed cards, assuring me the gentleman in the parlour was walking about in a great passion.

I desired him to be showed upstairs, and, when he entered, I stood up, as though waiting to hear why he intruded on me.

'I believe, Madam,' said his Lordship, 'some apology is due to you, from me.'

'Are you going to tell me that you were tipsy, when you last did me the favour to mistake my house for an inn, or something worse?'

'No! Certainly not,' answered the peer.

'Were you quite sober?'

'Perfectly.'

'Then your late conduct admits of no apology, and you could offer none which would not humble and greatly wound my pride, to avoid which, I must take the liberty of wishing you a good morning.'

I then rang my bell and left him.

The exquisite *frisson* for Harriette's readers of seeing the arrogant pride of an English *milord* so soundly trounced is worthy of one of Jane Austen's novels. And indeed, Harriette could almost be a creation of Austen's, combining as she does the wild manners and moral insouciance of a Lydia Bennet with the sharp intelligence and limpid wits of her sister Lizzie.

This is not so outlandish an idea as it might at first sound. Harriette Wilson was a near-contemporary of Jane Austen's, whose more brazen avatar, it sometimes seems to me, she is.* As with Austen, her canvas

---

* Jane Austen was born in 1775 and died in 1817. *Pride and Prejudice*, written between October 1796 and August 1797, was published in 1813.

is small; and although urban and aristocratic rather than provincial and genteel, it is one she knows intimately. Like Austen she is a shrewdly ironic observer of the manners and morals of her fellow man and, especially, of the emotional journeys of its women. Unlike Austen, however, she can, and does, write about sexual passion with a frankness which would not be risked again by a woman writer in England for another hundred years or more.

Harriette Wilson and her sisters inhabited that nebulous, unmentionable world which is so often hinted at and alluded to in the works of Jane Austen, but which always slides just out of our curious reach; the photographic negative, as it were, of Longbourne, Mansfield Park and Hartfield. In Austen's view this is the world of unchaste women, seduced and disgraced, and then hidden away from decent folk for the rest of their lives. It is a world from which there was no coming back: Colonel Brandon's young charge Eliza in *Sense and Sensibility*, made pregnant and then abandoned by Willoughby (to her 'wretched and hopeless situation' was added 'a mind tormented by self-reproach, which must attend her through life'); Fanny Price's cousin Maria in *Mansfield Park*, divorced by her husband after her elopement with Henry Crawford (unlike Henry, who would soon find himself another pretty girl to marry, Maria 'must withdraw ... to a retirement and reproach which could allow no second spring of hope or character'). It is the world into which Lydia Bennet, had not Wickham eventually been forced to marry her, would inevitably have been thrown (and in which she would no doubt have done very well). 'She is lost forever,' cries Lizzie when she first hears of her sister's elopement.

In Austen's view that world was a Hades; in Harriette's, a place of brilliant sunshine.

Unlike Sophia Baddeley, seduced into the life of a courtesan by the promise of fabulous wealth, or Elizabeth Armistead, driven by economic necessity, Harriette Wilson came to it through her own choice. In the view of conventional morality, her seduction by (or was it of?) the Earl of Craven could only mark the end of something: a disastrous downfall for a respectable woman. In Harriette's judgement it was just the beginning: the opening of a door, and a prelude to something much better.

Harriette liked her independence, she liked having a good time, and she liked sex; as a courtesan she could have all of these things. She had no truck with the hypocrisy which made a woman's sexuality the essence of her moral character. 'Now the English Protestant ladies' virtue is chastity!' she wrote. 'There are but two classes of women among them. She is a bad woman the moment she has committed fornication; be she generous, charitable, just, clever, domestic, affectionate, and ever ready to sacrifice her own good to serve and benefit those she loves, still her rank in society is with the lowest hired prostitute. Each is indiscriminately avoided, and each is denominated the same – bad woman, while all are virtuous who are chaste.'

The loss of 'respectability' could be unexpectedly liberating. Here are Harriette, Amy, Fanny and Julia together at Harriette's house one night. They had decided to banish all men for that evening. There were no other guests, and the women passed the time gossiping together and exchanging confidences. Harriette was curious to know about her sister Amy's life with General Madden.

> 'Confess,' added I, 'how you came by all those nice-looking hundred-pound notes, which I used to see you with, when you were with poor Madden, and I was a good little girl at home.'

Amy confessed that a friend of the General's, Hart Davis, had given them to her.

> 'And all in the way of honesty?' inquired Julia
> 'Not quite,' proceeded Amy; 'he used to pat me.'
> 'How, pat you!' we eagerly and inquisitively cried out with one consent.
> 'So,' said Amy, showing me with her hand on my arm.
> 'Was that all?'
> 'Do pray send your patting men to me,' remarked Julia.
> 'That was all,' said Amy, 'I assure you. "Aamy! Aamy!" he used to say, drawing down his bushy eyebrows, and patting me

thus – "Aamy! Aamy does that feel nice?" – "No! To be sure not," I used to answer, very fiercely; but, at last, one day when he called, I wanted a hundred pounds, of all things, to hire an opera box. So when he began with his usual "Aamy, Aamy, does that feel nice?" I made a face so . . .'

'*How?' said Julia, and I, and Fanny, all at once.*

'*So . . .' repeated Amy.*

The face was too ridiculous, and yet we laughed immoderately.

'*Pray,' said I, at length, 'did that face take, with your friend Hart Davis?'*

'*Yes,' said Amy, 'I made this sort of face, and said, "Ye-s, thank you – I think it does feel ra-ther nice."*

'*This confession was always enough to secure me a hundred pounds from Hart Davis, whenever I could find it in my heart to make it, which you may conceive was only on great occasions!'*

It is a strikingly modern scene. Four unmarried young women together, without a chaperone (or at that point a protector), with their own house, keeping the company they chose and the hours they chose, with the freedom to speak as openly as they wished on whatever subject they wished. No wonder men found them fascinating. Delightfully unencumbered by most of the prevailing notions of female propriety, they had the liberty to be themselves in ways that were absolutely denied to other women.

Harriette was a woman with a libido. She liked sex, but her attitude to it was never salacious: instead she was interested by it, amused by it, and acknowledged that she needed it. 'How do you think he treated me last night?' bursts out Amy of one of her lovers.

'*God knows!' interposed Julia.*

'*He got into my bed!' continued Amy.*

'*Mercy on us!!' exclaimed Julia.*

'*Why that is the very thing you have been wanting him to do for the last six months,' returned I.*

When Harriette felt *le besoin d'aimer*, as she put it, she would go looking for a suitable object for her affections herself. Sometimes, if she had no other protector, she wrote to men to propose a meeting, as she claimed to have done with both Granville Leveson Gower* and the Prince of Wales, to see if they would suit (for different reasons, they did not). Even at fifteen she had extremely exacting standards. Her first protector, the Earl of Craven, 'never once made me laugh, nor said nor did anything to please me', she wrote; but it was her *ennui* in the bedroom (in which he always wore an ugly cotton night-cap) which really caused their relationship to flounder:

> *I resided on the Marine Parade, at Brighton, and I remember that Lord Craven used to draw cocoa trees, and his fellows, as he called them, on the best vellum paper, for my amusement. Here stood the enemy, he would say; and here, my love, are my fellows: there the cocoa trees, etc. It was, in fact, a dead bore. All these cocoa trees and fellows, at past eleven o'clock at night, could have no peculiar interest for a child like myself, so lately in the habit of retiring early to rest. One night, I recollect, I fell asleep; and, as I often dream, I said, yawning, and half awake, 'Oh, Lord! Oh, Lord! Craven has got me into the West Indies again.' In short, I soon found that I had made a bad speculation by going from my father to Lord Craven . . . we never suited nor understood one another.*

Her next admirer was Fred Lamb, the son of Sophia Baddeley's Lord Melbourne. 'Lord Melbourne was a good man,' wrote Harriette ironically. 'Not one of your stiff-laced moralising fathers, who preach chastity and forbearance to their children. Quite the contrary; he congratulated his son on the lucky circumstance of his friend Craven having such a girl with him.' At first, out of loyalty to Craven, Harriette refused Fred ('The girl must be mad!' expostulated his father, no doubt recalling his own energetically misspent youth. 'Not have my son, indeed! Six feet high! A fine, straight, handsome, noble young fellow! I wonder what she would have!'), but later, when her arrangement with Craven came to an end, she did agree briefly to his proposals.

---

* Granville Leveson Gower became Earl Granville, British Ambassador to Paris, in 1824. See *Daughters of Britannia*.

Harriette settled with Fred first in Hull, where his regiment was stationed, and then later in London. Although he set her up in a house in the village of Somerstown (now the area between London's Euston and Kings Cross stations), she soon found that Fred was not only 'a voluptuary', but a mean one, who spent all his time at balls and masquerades while an indignant Harriette, living 'in extreme poverty',* was expected to languish indoors waiting for him, and to 'pass [her] dreary evenings alone'.

Although Harriette firmly believed that Fred 'sincerely loved me, and deeply regretted that he had no fortune to invite me to share with him' (his father, of course, having spent most of it on Sophia Baddeley), it was not for this that she had left her father's house. 'I felt that I deserved better from him,' she declared. Once again taking fate into her own hands, she wrote to Fred Lamb's friend, the handsome Marquis of Lorne,† about whom she had a strong curiosity, to tell him that 'If he would walk up to Duke's Row, Somerstown, he would meet a most lovely girl.'

'If you are but half as lovely as you think yourself,' came the reply, 'you must be well worth knowing; but how is that to be managed? Not in the street! But come to No. 39 Portland Street,‡ and ask for me.'

'No!' Harriette replied. 'Our first meeting must be on the high road, in order that I may have room to run away, in case I don't like you.'

'Well, then, fair lady, tomorrow, at four, near the turnpike, look for me on horseback; and then, you know, I can gallop away.'

Harriette's meeting with Lorne was a success. They talked together for two hours. Harriette was entranced. His manner to her was soft and polished; his deep blue eyes looked at her with an expression

---

* In her *Confessions*, Julia Johnstone claimed that Fred Lamb was, on the contrary, very generous to Harriette, and supported her to the tune of £100 a year, about £5000 today.
† The Marquis of Lorne, who was in his early thirties at the time of this exchange, became the Duke of Argyll in 1806. Harriette refers to him as both Lorne and Argyll in her *Memoirs*, using the spelling Argyle. For the sake of clarity I have called him Lorne throughout. The Duke later married his mistress, Caroline, the third of the beautiful daughters of the Earl of Jersey, after she was divorced by her husband, the Marquis of Anglesey, for her adultery.
‡ This was very probably an accommodation house.

which was at once beautiful and voluptuous. She thought she had never seen a countenance so ravishing. 'I was afraid to look at it,' she wrote, 'lest a closer examination might destroy all the new and delightful sensations his first glance had inspired in my breast.' He, in turn, was quite as entranced by her. 'I never saw such a sunny, happy countenance as yours in my whole life,' he told her.

Harriette, who knew exactly why her face was so sunny, was afraid that Lorne had found her out. 'We females must not suffer love or pleasure to glow in our eyes until we are quite sure of a return,' she wrote regretfully. 'We must be dignified! Alas! I can only be and seem what I am. No doubt my sunny face of joy and happiness, which he talked to me about, was understood, and it has disgusted him. He thought me bold, and yet I am sure I never blushed so much in any man's society before.'

Lorne's passion for Harriette 'knew no bounds'. It was healthily matched by hers for him. Lorne was sexy; he was the first man who had ever really engaged her erotically. Although he frightened her sometimes with his ardour, he loved her, Harriette declared, 'just as I want to be loved'. 'The sensations which [Lorne] had inspired me with,' she wrote, 'were the warmest, nay, the first of the same nature I had ever experienced.' She was jealous of him, especially of his continuing relationship with his mistress, 'Lady W– . . . with whom the world said he had been intriguing nineteen years'. But when they quarrelled, they were quick to make it up. 'Our reconciliation was completed, in the usual way,' wrote Harriette, 'and on the spot.'

Although from Harriette's *Memoirs* it is never easy to determine a precise chronology – 'Ladies scorn dates! Dates make ladies nervous and stories dry,' was her cheerfully anarchic view – according to her it was around the time she decided to take Lorne as her lover that her official career as a courtesan began. 'I cannot, I reasoned with myself, I cannot, I fear, become what the world calls a steady, prudent, virtuous woman,' she wrote. 'That time is past, even if I was ever fit for it.' Although she scorned conventional morality, Harriette had, so she claimed, quite scrupulous standards of her own, to which she vowed always to be true. 'I must distinguish myself from those in the like unfortunate situations, by strict probity and love of truth,' she wrote. 'I

never will become vile. I will always adhere to good faith, as long as anything like kindness or honourable principle is shown towards me; and
when I am ill-used, I will leave my lover rather than deceive him.'

From being in keeping, albeit briefly, with the Earl of Craven and
then Fred Lamb, Harriette decided it was time to take a house of her
own. She moved out of her lodgings in Somerstown to a furnished
house in the more fashionable West End of London, which was better
calculated, she believed, to receive her new lover.

Launching herself into the Regency half-world was easier for Harriette
than it was for most courtesans. She had the *entrée* already through her
sisters Amy and Fanny, who were already two of London's best-known
demi-reps. Amy, Harriette's elder sister, in particular, 'a fine dark
woman', was an established hostess. Her Saturday-evening parties,
attended by half the fashionable men in town, were held at her house
in York Place after the opera, and were sufficiently *à la mode* to rival
those given by the great political hostesses of the day, such as Lady
Castlereagh or Charles James Fox's niece, Lady Holland. Guests at one
would often look in on the other on their way home. Although Harriette was never as close to Amy as she was to Fanny – indeed, she
claimed in her *Memoirs* that Amy hated her all her life – she was
always invited to Amy's parties: 'If I was present, at least half the men
were on my side of the room: if I stayed away, so did all those who
went only on my account.'

In his *Recollections* the Regency diarist Captain Rees Gronow claimed
that female society among the upper classes was 'most notoriously
neglected' at this period. 'How could it be otherwise,' he wrote, 'when
husbands spent their days in the hunting-field, or were entirely occupied with politics, and always away from home during the day.'[3] But
this was not Harriette's perception of the world. On the contrary, the
society in which she was now beginning to have such success was almost
entirely made up of men from the upper classes (indeed, Gronow might
have added the salons of the Dubochet sisters to his list of their most
favoured distractions).

The Regency half-world of the Dubochet sisters, however, was subtly different from that inhabited by either Sophia Baddeley, who came from the cheerful, gaudy, promiscuous world of the stage, or Elizabeth Armistead, from the high-class King's Place brothels of Mrs Goadby, Mrs Mitchell and Mrs Hayes. Although unusually liberated in their attitudes and mores, Harriette and her sisters very probably did not consider themselves, strictly speaking, sex professionals in the way that Elizabeth had been; while their class and education put them several cuts above the actresses, dancers and singers who, throughout the nineteenth and twentieth centuries, would continue to serve upper-class Englishmen in the traditional way.*

Amongst their contemporaries Harriette Wilson and her sisters were known as demi-reps. The term, which dates from the mid-eighteenth century and was obsolete by the beginning of the twentieth, was originally used to describe upper-class or aristocratic women who, under the guise of married respectability, were known to intrigue and take lovers.† In the same way that the term courtesan evolved in the fifteenth century, by Harriette's day the meaning of demi-rep had expanded to include sexually available women of the bourgeois classes as well.

Although the Regency demi-reps were every bit as outcast from society as the actresses and women of pleasure of the previous century, they were also closer to it than their predecessors had been. The world which they created for themselves – where they went, what they did, their houses, food and servants; all the social forms, in fact, which governed their lives – was modelled, more than ever before, on the *monde* which it mirrored.

Harriette and her sisters were not able to attend society events any more than Elizabeth or Sophia had, although they were quick to obtain

---

* Although thought to have been a stocking-mender by profession, Harriette's mother was the natural daughter of 'a country gentleman', a Mr Cheney. She had, Harriette claimed, struck Lady Frederick Campbell, aunt of the Duke of Argyll, so much with her beauty that she had been adopted by her, and brought up 'as her own child'.

† 'Demi-rep. A woman whose general reputation or, esp., chastity is in doubt. First recorded in Fielding's *Tom Jones* (1749): "Vulgarly called a demi-rep; that is . . . a woman who intrigues with every man she likes, under the name and appearance of virtue . . . in short, whom everybody knows to be what nobody calls her." Ex re*putation*.' *The Penguin Dictionary of Historical Slang.*

tickets, through their gentlemen friends, to the more public entertainments such as the famous masquerade given by Wattier's club, and attended by all the nobility of England, to mark the peace between Britain and France. They made up for their exclusion from more private events by holding their own. The Argyle Rooms were allegedly celebrated for being the scene of the annual Cyprians' Ball, given by all the 'Fashionable Impures', the demi-reps who played hostess *en masse* on this one night to their admirers and protectors.*

The immense disruption caused by the Revolution in France, closely followed by the wars against Napoleon, had seen more than merely political changes in Europe. The Regency period brought with it a complete upheaval in many aspects of life, perhaps the most obvious of which was the way people dressed. 'Women found themselves suddenly emancipated,' wrote James Laver, one of the great authorities on English fashions, 'and their first reaction was to cut their hair short and to take off most of their clothes.'[4] Eschewing the elaborate powdered wigs, the clumsy hoops and stiffened bodices of the pre-Revolutionary era, many women turned to what they imagined were the simple, democratically flowing robes of the ancient Greeks for inspiration.

The first attempts at this style of dress were radical in the extreme. The single, chilly, chemise-like garments were so flimsy that they exposed the breasts almost entirely, while clinging to the rest of the body in a most indecent way – an effect which could be artfully exaggerated by the more daring, who would dampen the muslin of their dresses to make them cling still more revealingly. In France, where the inventors of these outlandish new fashions were known as the '*Merveilleuses*', a ghoulish touch included a hairstyle known as '*à la sacrifice*', in which the hair was brushed up at the back and forward over the top of the head, in imitation of the hair of a victim decapitated

---

* Harriette herself never mentions such a thing as the 'Cyprians' Ball', although a contemporary drawing purports to show it.

by the guillotine.* In England women escaped the more outlandish of these trends, but to many of the older generation especially, used to the restraining modesty of elaborate corsetry, the effect of these modern fashions was still deeply shocking. 'Who is that very handsome, naked woman?' one dowager in her eighties, Lady Anne Barnard, was once heard to exclaim at an evening dinner party. Others were not so jovial about it, and women were hissed at in the street.

The heavy, lead-based make-up of the previous century – so lethal it was reputed to have caused the death of such society beauties as Kitty Fisher – was no longer fashionable, although other aids to beauty were just as popular as they had ever been. One recipe recommended the juice of a pineapple to remove wrinkles 'and give the complexion of youth'. If a pineapple – still a rare luxury – was not available, an onion would do just as well. Powdered parsley seed was believed to prevent baldness, and ripe elderberries to blacken the eyebrows, while a little grated horseradish mixed with sour milk was thought to remove sunburn and freckles. Another 'sovereign beautifier of the complexion' could be achieved by 'mixing 1lb of rye breadcrumbs, hot from the oven, with the whites of four eggs and a pint of white vinegar, the whole to be used as a face mask'.[5]

Scaled-down simplicity extended to fashions other than the sartorial. In rural Hyde Park, the traditional afternoon meeting place for high society (five o'clock was the fashionable hour in Harriette's time), the cumbersome carriages of the previous century were replaced by smaller, lighter and more sporty vehicles such as the two-wheeled curricle and, for women, a carriage known as a *vis-à-vis*, which held only two people, although appendages such as a powdered footman and a coachman 'who assumed all the gaiety and appearance of a wigged archbishop, were [still] indispensable'.[6] (One of the most famous courtesans of France during this period, Madame Duthé, who had lived with great splendour in Paris before the Revolution, was especially celebrated for her magnificent carriages, which were covered in gold leaf and drawn

* At the *'Bal des Victimes'*, given in Paris to commemorate parents and close relatives murdered during the Terror, all the women wore their hair in this fashion. Many of them also wore a thin red ribbon around their necks – the mark of the guillotine – 'a note of frivolity born of despair'. See Norman Hartnell's *Royal Courts of Fashion*.

by no fewer than eight perfectly matched cream-coloured horses. She emigrated to England during the Revolution, but when she finally managed to repossess her famous carriages they appeared so old-fashioned that far from being 'the admiration of all Paris' they became its laughing-stock instead.)

As far as purely sartorial fashions went, for many women there was an additional, and perhaps still greater, torment to that of being made to expose themselves in public, which was to be obliged to wear a fashion which could only ever have flattered the very young or the very, very slender. For the rest, some kind of artifice was clearly required. Although old-fashioned stays or corsets could not possibly be worn under the flimsy new garments, a kind of long knitted undergarment of silk or cotton, moulded to the figure like a modern 'body', was often used. They were horribly uncomfortable, as one rueful sufferer, Lady Morgan, remembered:

> The most uncomfortable style of dress was when they were so scanty that it was difficult to walk in them, and to make them tighter still, invisible petticoats were worn. They were woven in the stocking loom, and were like strait waist-coats ... but only drawn down over the legs instead of over the arms so that, when walking, you were obliged to take short mincing steps. I was not long in discarding mine and, of course, shocking my juvenile acquaintance by my boldness in throwing off such a fashionable restraint.[7]

After the severe winter of 1799, however, the craze for transparent dresses was over. Stays came back, reintroduced alongside a new fashion for women's drawers (it is in this period that modern under-wear originates). Originally, drawers consisted of two separate 'legs' tied together at the top with tape. Not everyone enjoyed wearing them: 'They are the ugliest things I ever saw,' wrote one Englishwoman. 'I will never put them on again. I lost one leg and did not deem it proper to pick it up again and so walked off leaving it in the street.'[8]

After the first excesses of the Directoire period, fashions soon began to modify into more wearable forms, but for a long while there was still an element of confusion. In England, waistlines and necklines rose and fell; crazes – for frills and puff sleeves, ruffles and false bosoms – came and went with bemusing rapidity ('The fashion for false bosoms has at least this utility,' wrote *The Times* acerbically, 'that it compels our fashionable fair to wear something'). Leg-of-mutton sleeves became the rage, and grew so large that they had to be kept in shape with pads stuffed with down, and the most fashionable women found it difficult to pass easily through doors. Other foreign influences, as well as the ancient Greek, were sought out, the more exotic the better. One fashion magazine described as the height of *chic* an opera dress with 'a Circassian bodice made of American velvet trimmed with Chinese cord ... to be worn with an Armenian head-dress and an Eastern mantle'.[9] Hats, too, were often elaborately decorated and trimmed, with varying degrees of success. 'I do recollect when a lady did not think it necessary to wear a bushel measure on her head ... when a face was sufficiently pretty without the foil of a coal-scuttle, or when a chimney-pot with a sweep's brush sticking out at the top of it was not thought the most graceful of all models,' wrote one fashion writer dustily about the styles current in 1815.

By dint of cutting though all this fashionable confusion, and dressing at all times with the greatest simplicity and good taste, Harriette and her sisters had perfect command of the fashion *Zeitgeist*. How fascinatingly, effortlessly modern they must have seemed (like the first mini-skirted models in the 1960s, dispensing at one swoop with all the ladylike paraphernalia of hats, gloves and stockings of the more formal 1950s). In her description of one of Amy's evening parties, Harriette gives some idea of the artistry involved, and its combined effect:

Amy's drawing room was quite full. She looked very well, and fairer, as well as less fierce, than before her confinement. Fanny appeared unusually lovely, dressed in a pale, pink, crape dress, which set off her rosy, white, delicate skin, to the greatest advantage; and with her unadorned bright auburn curls, waving carelessly around her laughing dark blue eyes and beautiful throat, she seemed the most desirable object in the room. Julia was very fair too; perhaps her skin was whiter than Fanny's and of quite as delicate a texture, but it had not that vermillion tinge, and the blue veins were less defined. Both were of the highest order of fine forms. They were also of the same height, which was that best adapted to perfect symmetry; their feet and ankles were alike models for the statuary's art, and Fanny's shoes fitted Julia as well as her own.

Although Fanny's hair was darker and more glossy than Julia's, and she had more beautiful teeth, 'there was such a decided resemblance in their *tout ensemble* that everybody mistook Julia for Fanny's elder sister'.

Harriette continued:

This evening Julia ... wore a dress of white silvered lamé, on gauze, and a Turkish turban of bright blue, fringed with gold. There was a voluptuous and purely effeminate languor about Julia's character, which was well adapted to the Eastern style of dress. The large, straight, gauze sleeve did not at all conceal the symmetry of her beautiful arm. Fanny's dimpled arms were quite uncovered, and encircled with elegant but simple bracelets, composed of plaited hair, clasped with a magnificently brilliant ruby. They were both infinitely graceful ... Amy wore a yellow satin dress, fastened round the waist, with a gold band. Her profuse raven-locks were entirely unadorned, and her neck, arms, and fingers, were covered with glittering jewels of every colour.

The most simply dressed of all, however, was Harriette herself. 'My own evening dresses were invariably composed of rich figured white French gauze, over white satin,' she wrote, 'and I never wore any ornaments in my hair, of which I was not a little proud: but my earrings were of unusual length, and consisted of diamonds, rubies and turquoise stones.'

With their good looks and their dubious reputations, and their tremendous sense of style, the sisters caused a sensation. The suppers, dances and parties which they gave were private events, attended by men and other demi-reps such as themselves. Like courtesans of the previous generations, however, they needed the oxygen of publicity, and to see and be seen at the opera and the theatres was still an essential aspect of a courtesan's life, the moment of her greatest public display.

The fashionable opera nights during the Regency were Tuesdays and Saturdays. Although the price was exorbitant – two hundred guineas (it had been £80 in Sophia Baddeley's day, just twenty-five years previously) – Harriette always took her own box, which she usually shared with Julia and Fanny, while Amy occupied the one next door. Men would come just to see them there. Amongst their younger admirers, especially, it became the height of fashion to do so, and Harriette became a kind of barometer of all that was in vogue.* 'Nothing is asked, but whether Harriette Wilson approves of this or that,' the young Duke of Leinster† told her, 'Harriette likes white waistcoats – Harriette commends silk stockings, etc. I asked my friend, the young Marquis of Worcester, why he did not curl his straight locks? Harriette considers straight hair most gentlemanlike.'

An actual introduction to Harriette, undreamed of by all but the most daring, was the very pinnacle of social success. 'On my asking him if he knew Harriette, the Marquis owned that he had never seen her, adding, "I ran up three times to the opera, on purpose; but she did not make her appearance. Will you present me to her?"' Leinster, knowing that he was the only undergraduate at Oxford who was acquainted with her, quite sensibly refused.

Harriette would have approved, but for different reasons. She was well aware of both the rules and the pitfalls of her profession. 'It is certainly, perhaps, a misfortune in many respects, for a woman to become the fashion, which was my case,' she once commented wryly, 'for what second-rate man does not like to be in the fashion? Nay, there are few, very few, who would not affect pride in the possession of what their betters have coveted in vain.'

---

* According to Harriette, this was particularly so after the disgrace and eventual exile of her contemporary and friend Beau Brummell, who in her taste for simplicity she much resembles. 'Do you know that Brummell is cut amongst us,' the Duke of Leinster tells her of his Christchurch friends, 'and who do you think sets the fashions there now?' The answer was Harriette herself.
† Augustus Frederick Fitzgerald, 3rd Duke of Leinster (1791–1874), was Charles James Fox's first cousin once removed. He was the grandson of Fox's mother's sister, Emily Leinster. He became Duke in 1804, when he was just thirteen.

The courtesan's was a strange tightrope-walk: display and entice-
ment, adroitly combined with the quelling exclusivity of the most
battle-hardened ambassadress. The Regency half-world had its own
rules of etiquette and protocol, insisted upon every bit as jealously as
those of 'respectable' society. This was an age which often lamented
the decline in good manners shown by men towards women; but in
the upper echelons of the *demi-monde* no one was in any doubt that
men were still expected to know their place. Prince Esterhazy, the
Austrian Ambassador to London in 1815, found grave disfavour because
he refused to take his hat off in Harriette's presence. Inviting Granville
Leveson Gower to walk with her in Regent's Park, Harriette was not
joking when she wrote that 'if he expected to please me, he must show
me just as much respect, and humble deference, as though I had not
ordered him up to Marylebone Fields* to be looked at'.

While Harriette could request a meeting with any man she chose,
protocol strictly forbade men from taking a similar liberty. An introduction to her, especially in a place as public as an opera box, was
not a favour to be lightly granted.† It was usually arranged in advance,
and supplicants were strictly vetted, as Harriette liked to be sure that
they were 'of the first respectability'.

Needless to say, the harder it was to get to Harriette, the greater
the lengths men went to – lobbying their friends and acquaintances,
besieging her house and bribing her servants – to accomplish it. Having
had this great favour graciously bestowed upon him, the humble
admirer was then expected to ponder his good fortune for a suitably
respectful amount of time before he could even dream of any more
substantial favours. The Marquis of Sligo committed an unforgivable
solecism when, having been presented to her only the day before, he
wrote Harriette this note:

---

* Now Regent's Park.
† To be presented to Harriette in public was, nonetheless, a favour that most respectably
married men would not risk. Most of Harriette's friends consisted either of the fashionable
young, or of older unmarried men. What happened in private was of course another
matter.

My Dear Miss Wilson,

  Will you be so condescending as to allow me to pass this evening, alone, with you, after Lady Landsdowne's party?
  Sligo.

Harriette was enraged at this impertinence.

  'Who waits?' said I, to James.
  'A servant, in livery,' was the answer.
  'Send him up to me.'
  A well-bred servant, in a cocked hat and dashing livery, entered my room with many bows.
  'Here is some mistake,' said I, presenting him the unsealed and unfolded letter of Lord Sligo's. 'This letter could not be meant for me, to whom His Lordship was only presented yesterday. Take it back, young man, and say, from me, that I request he will be careful how he misdirects his letters in future; an accident which is, no doubt, caused by his writing them after dinner.'

When could a man proposition a courtesan? In Harriette's view, never. Etiquette demanded a far subtler game, the rules of which were impossible to define, but easily transgressed. The most important of them, which the Marquis of Sligo would have done well to have heeded, was that Harriette and her sisters only ever took men on their own terms. The choosers, not the chosen, theirs was a rare privilege indeed. This inversion of the normal rules of engagement was all part of a courtesan's seductive power.

Harriette was now the most sought-after demi-rep in town. Sophia Baddeley and Elizabeth Armistead, courtesans of the previous century, had been fashionable beauties; Harriette was something else besides. She was smart, too. 'The wittiest, cleverest creature in all London,' according to one contemporary, Harriette was more than a match intellectually for any of the men who sought her company. These were not just fashionable young aristocrats like Leinster and Worcester, but some of the most celebrated wits and dandies of the day.

Not everybody had a very high opinion of this strange breed. 'How unspeakably odious ... were the dandies of forty years ago,' wrote Captain Gronow in his vivid *Recollections* of the period:

> *They were a motley crew with nothing remarkable about them but their insolence ... They were generally middle-aged, some even elderly men, had large appetites and weak digestions, gambled freely and had no luck. They hated everybody and abused everybody, and would sit in White's window weaving tremendous 'crammers' [tall stories]. They swore a great deal, never laughed, and had their own particular slang, and had most of them been patronised at one time or another by Brummell or the Regent ... Thank heaven this miserable race has long been extinct!*[10]

Harriette's friends were not on the whole from amongst these sour and spiteful types. They were rather the brilliant exceptions to the rule: men such the poet Henry Luttrell, known for his epigrammatic speech; and perhaps most *simpatico* of all, William Alvanley, of whom even Gronow approved, who was said to combine 'brilliant wit and repartee with the most perfect good nature', and who is reputed once to have enjoyed an apricot tart so enormously that he instructed his chef to have a fresh one on his sideboard every day for a year.*

George 'Beau' Brummell, one of the icons of the Regency era, whose rigorous but immaculately plain style of dressing was to influence an entire generation, was also for a time part of Harriette's intimate circle. So elaborate was Brummell's *toilette* that the proceedings took several hours, and became one of the legends of the age. The *entrée* to his dressing room to watch this piece of performance art was the height of social success, since the *sanctum sanctorum* was invariably thronged with aristocratic, and sometimes even royal, spectators, all anxious to observe how Brummell tied his stiffly starched muslin cravats.

Brummell became famous, too, for his numerous maxims on dress,†

---

* Alvanley once challenged a man to a duel for calling him, in public, a 'bloated buffoon'. Fortunately neither man was hurt, and when Alvanley tipped the hackney-cab driver who brought him home a sovereign, the man exclaimed, 'It's a great deal for only having taken your Lordship to Wimbledon,' whereupon Alvanley quipped, 'No, my good man. I give it to you not for taking me, but for bringing me back.' Gronow.

† 'No perfumes,' Brummell used to say, 'but very fine linen, plenty of it, and country washing.' 'If John Bull turns round to look after you, you are not well dressed; but either

although in Harriette's view these stemmed from 'a sort of quaint, dry humour, not amounting to anything like wit'. Harriette (in some ways a kind of female counterpart to Brummell) was too clever to have been entirely taken in by him. 'Indeed,' she went on, 'he said nothing which would bear repetition; but his affected manners and little absurdities amused for the moment. Then it became the fashion to court Brummell's society, which was enough to make many seek it who cared not for it; and many more wished to be well with him, through fear, for all knew him to be cold, heartless, and satirical.'

Being the fashion herself, for the moment Harriette had nothing to fear from Brummell or anyone else. Besides, in keeping with her status, she was now living a great deal more stylishly than she had ever done in the little house in Somerstown paid for by Fred Lamb. Her dresses may have been simplicity itself, but they did not come cheap, and she wore expensive jewels. Her domestic establishment, too, was of the first order. Both Sophia Baddeley and Elizabeth Armistead had run large households which required them to employ many servants, but Harriette now acquired several *de luxe* servants, of the kind usually kept only by the upper classes, in addition to the usual indoor staff.

These included 'a stiff, old, powdered footman' with a pigtail, called Will Halliday; Mrs Kennedy, Harriette's *femme de chambre*, or lady's maid; and a *dame de compagne*, or companion, although Harriette soon learned that these, especially, had to be chosen with care. One of them, Eliza Higgins, had the morals of her mistress, and was not above pinching Harriette's admirers for herself.

All these trappings, of course, had to be paid for. Although the Marquis of Lorne remained for some time her acknowledged lover, Harriette's relationship with him was always a fluid one, and she was never formally under his protection (he was in any case, she complained, not nearly rich enough). To make up the financial shortfall she adopted a practical solution: she did what she was good at, which was sex.

When Harriette took occasional private clients, she did so through

---

too stiff, too tight, or too fashionable.' And, curiously, 'Do not ride in ladies' gloves, particularly with leather breeches.'

the system, then current in London, of introducing houses. An introducing house was exactly what its name suggests: an establishment
through which men – often married men who desired their activities
to remain secret – could obtain an introduction to the woman of their
choice. Fifty years after Harriette Wilson wrote about her experiences,
William Acton described the introducing houses of Victorian London
with customary thoroughness. They had changed little since Harriette's
day and were still, as Acton put it, 'the leading centres of the more
select circles of prostitution', having taken over from the King's Place
models current in Mrs Armistead's day as the 'aristocracy of brothels'.
Like the establishments of Madames Mitchell and Hayes a generation
earlier, these introducing houses were extremely exclusive. It was very
hard indeed for men to gain access to them, but when they did the
women they could expect to meet – described unrepentantly by Acton
as 'first class prostitutes' – were the most beautiful, fashionable and
accomplished that were available.

The system, as described by Acton, was an admirably well-organised
one:

> The leading persons in this line of business . . . make known to
> their clients their novel and attractive wares, one might almost
> say, by circular. A finds a note at his club telling him that a
> charming arrival, de la plus grande fraicheur, is on view at
> Madame de L's. If he has no vacancy for a connexion, he may
> answer that a mutual friend, C, a very proper man, will call on
> such and such a day in – Road, or that Madame – may drive
> the object round to his rooms at such another time. All parties
> handle the affair with mock refinement.[11]

(Acton claimed to know many 'pungent anecdotes' concerning these
introducing houses, but as 'their untarnished recital here would give
my pages an air of levity quite foreign to my intention', he declared
splendidly, 'I must suppress them'.)

The leading figure in the early-nineteenth-century business of introducing houses was a well-known procuress called Mrs Porter.* Julia

---

* Later immortalised by T.S. Eliot in these lines from *The Waste Land*: 'O the moon
shone bright on Mrs Porter/And on her daughter/They wash their feet in soda water.'

Johnstone described her as a woman of about fifty, 'of an agreeable temper and conciliating manners; her face bore the remains of beauty, her figure was fine, and she was in every way calculated to wind herself into the secret recesses of the human heart'.[12] According to Julia, in her youth Mrs Porter had been under the protection of a rich duke who had left her £1000 in his will, and it was with this capital (the equivalent of £50,000 today) that she was able to start up her business. Harriette does not make it clear how often, or at what stages in her career, she accepted introductions from Mrs Porter, although we do know that her first forays into the business were very early on, while she was still in keeping with Fred Lamb in Somerstown. (It was only later, after she became fashionable, that she could afford to be more fastidious – although my conjecture is that the occasional highly paid 'one off' assignment was always a quick and convenient way of maintaining her independence.)

The clients she did take were of the very first water. It was in this way that Harriette met the man who would become the most famous of all her conquests.

'I was getting into debt, as well as my sister Amy,' she wrote, 'when it came to pass, as I have since heard say, that the – immortal!!!! No; that's common; a very outlandish distinction, fitter for a lady in a balloon. The terrific!!!! that will do better. I have seen His Grace in a cotton nightcap. Well, then, the terrific Duke of Wellington!! The wonder of the world!! Having six feet from the tail to the head and – but there is a certain technicality in the expression of the gentleman at the Exeter 'Change, when he had occasion to show off a wild beast, which it would be vanity in me to presume to imitate.'

Harriette's account of how she came to be introduced to the Duke of Wellington is very probably an embroidered one – it is always necessary to remember that the *Memoirs* were written principally with a view to blackmail – but it remains nonetheless a unique first-hand description of how the system worked. According to Harriette, the Duke went first to call on Mrs Porter at her house in Berkeley Street, and was shown immediately into her boudoir. Harriette imagined the scene:

'There is a beautiful girl just come out,' said His Grace ... 'a
very fine creature; they call her Harriette, and –'

'My Lord,' exclaimed Mrs Porter interrupting him, 'I have had
three applications this very month for the girl they call Harriette,
and I have already introduced myself to her.'

This was a fact, which happened while I was in Somerstown,
and which I have forgotten to relate.

'It was,' continued Mrs Porter, 'at the very earnest request of
General Walpole. She is the wildest creature I ever saw. She did
not affect modesty, nor appear in the least offended at my
intrusion. Her first question was, is your man handsome? I
answered frankly, that the General was more than sixty years of
age; and at which account she laughed heartily; and then, seeming
to recollect herself, she said, she really was over head and ears in
debt, and therefore must muster up courage to receive one visit
from her antiquated admirer, at my house.'

Despite her debts, Harriette claimed never actually to have gone
through with her assignment with the General, sending her old nurse
instead, heavily veiled and disguised, as a joke. Undeterred by this
prank, the Duke offered Mrs Porter a hundred guineas, and promised
the same amount to Harriette, if she would induce her to 'give [him]
the meeting'. Mrs Porter agreed to try, although she warned the Duke
(these are of course Harriette's own words) that 'I was never half so
afraid of any woman in my life. She is so wild, and appears so perfectly
independent and careless of her own interests and welfare, that I really
do not know what is likely to move her.'

Mrs Porter went to call on Harriette the next morning to tell her
of her conquest of 'a very fine, noble, most unexceptionable man'. She
dared not tell her his name, she said, but assured her that he was 'a
man of fashion and rank'.

'It will not do,' reiterated I, striking my head. 'Tell your friend
that I have no money, that I do not know how to take care of
myself, and [Lorne] takes no care of me. Tell him that nobody
wants a real steady friend more than I do; but I cannot meet a

stranger as a lover. Tell him all this, if he is really handsome . . .
and let me know what he says tomorrow.'

Mrs Porter duly reported back, saying that Harriette's terms had been agreed to, and informing her that it was none other than the Duke of Wellington who so anxiously desired to make her acquaintance, although he hoped that she would keep his name a secret. 'His Grace,' said Mrs Porter, not entirely truthfully, 'only entreats to be allowed to make your acquaintance. His situation, you know, prevents the possibility of his getting regularly introduced to you.'* She assured Harriette that he was 'a remarkably fine-looking man', and advised her, 'If you are afraid of my house, promise to receive him in your own, at any hour when he may be certain to find you alone.' With a display of reluctance, Harriette finally agreed: 'Well, thought I with a sigh, I suppose he must come. I do not understand economy, and am frightened to death at debts. [Lorne] is going to Scotland; and I shall want a steady sort of friend, of some kind, in case a bailiff should get hold of me.'

As the complexities of Harriette's introduction to the Duke of Wellington show, by the early nineteenth century secrecy was becoming increasingly a feature of a courtesan's life, and made possible a certain contradiction between her public and private personas (the one so ostentatiously scrupulous about bestowing her acquaintance, the other not quite so picky). Public attitudes towards courtesans were beginning to change. Although there was a long way to go before the full double standard of high Victorian society would be in place, men of the *haut ton* no longer seemed to take quite such open delight in parading their mistresses as they had done in the previous century. Courtesans were still fashionable figures, it is true – indeed they remained at the very cutting edge of fashion – but they were no longer the public celebrities

---

* Harriette's liaison with the Duke of Wellington actually began *before* he was created Duke (which did not occur until after the 1814 victories over Napoleon in Spain and France). He could not have known Harriette before 1805, since he was in India from 1797 until then. Harriette mentions later on in her memoir that Wellington came to take his leave of her before he went to Spain, certainly a reference to the Peninsular War, during which he assumed chief command from 1809. Wellington was married to Catherine Pakenham in 1806, and it is likely to have been this 'situation' that made it impossible for him to be 'regularly introduced' to Harriette. Their first meeting thus probably took place sometime between 1806 and 1809.

they had once been. Crowds did not turn out to watch them, as they had done for Kitty Fisher when she dined at Vauxhall Gardens, or for Sophia Baddeley when she attended one of Mrs Cornelys's masquerades. They were no longer written about in the popular newspapers – so colourful a feature of the previous century, when every detail of a glamorous courtesan's life, her dress, her carriages, even the minutiae of her financial transactions, was gleefully recounted and generally enjoyed.

Sophia Baddeley and Elizabeth Armistead had been, above all, high-status women, the equivalent of today's Ferrari or private jet; men desired to display them, as well as to have wonderful sex with them. By Harriette's day, however, more private transactions were becoming increasingly common. It is no accident that the relatively public arena of the King's Place brothel, which had acted as a kind of club in which men could meet their male friends and socialise as well as enjoy the women there, had given way to the more private, even clandestine, rendezvous made possible by the introducing house.

According to Harriette's account, her first meeting with the Duke, even though she insisted that it should be as nothing more than 'a common acquaintance', was not an unqualified success. Wellington arrived at her house, as she had requested, punctually at three o'clock. 'He bowed first,' Harriette remembered, then said

> 'How do you do?' then thanked me for having given him permission to call on me; and then wanted to take hold of my hand.
>
> 'Really,' said I, withdrawing my hand, 'for such a renowned hero you have very little to say for yourself.'
>
> 'Beautiful creature!' uttered Wellington, 'where is Lorne?'
>
> 'Good gracious,' said I, out of all patience at his stupidity – 'what come you here for, Duke?'
>
> 'Beautiful eyes, yours!' reiterated Wellington.
>
> 'Aye, man! they are greater conquerors than ever Wellington shall be; but, to be serious, I understand you came here to try to make yourself agreeable?'
>
> 'What, child! do you think that I have nothing better to do than to make speeches to please ladies?' said Wellington.

Despite this acerbic beginning, Harriette soon charmed the Duke out of his stiffness, and made him laugh. '*Après avoir dépeuplé la terre, vous devez faire tout pour la répeupler,*' she told him (Having depopulated so much of the earth, you should do all you can to repopulate it). Soon Wellington became her most frequent visitor, to the dismay of her lover Lorne (but 'What was a mere man,' she wrote smilingly, 'even though it were the handsome [Lorne] to a Wellington!!!!'). Although Harriette claimed that the Duke was not at all an amusing visitor, either conversationally or in bed (he had no merit either 'for home service, or ladies' uses', was how she put it), and that in the evenings, 'when he wore his broad red ribbon, he looked very much like a rat catcher', when Wellington announced that he was leaving England for Spain (to take up command during the Peninsular War), Harriette, convinced she might never see him again, surprised them both by bursting into tears.

The truth was that the Duke's departure left Harriette financially exposed. 'Wellington had relieved me from many duns,'* she admitted, 'which else had given me vast uneasiness.' Although Wellington paid Harriette handsomely for the *entrée* into her boudoir, a hundred guineas introductory fee – roughly the equivalent of £5000 (there is no record of what he paid her thereafter) – this was a relatively small amount compared to the vast sums which Sophia Baddeley had commanded at the peak of her career.

For all her many sophistications, Harriette was by her own admission not clever with money. She was recklessly extravagant; 'she threw away guineas as I would pence', wrote Julia Johnstone. Although she later claimed that it would have been easy for her to have secured 'no less than a dozen annuities' at the height of her popularity, the fact is that she did not. Her rackety finances – which would pursue her all her life, and ultimately precipitated her early death – were the price she paid for her independence.

As in the late eighteenth century, the alternative to the chance introductions of establishments like Mrs Porter's was to accept a formal arrangement from an admirer. Harriette's sisters eventually all took

* Debts; specifically, tradesmen asking for payment.

this more old-fashioned route. When she was still little more than a schoolgirl, thirteen-year-old Sophia, the youngest Dubochet sister, was living under the protection of the eccentric Lord Deerhurst. Deerhurst, having seduced Sophia away from her family, was eventually prevailed upon to provide her with an annuity of £300 a year, and 'two small dark parlours, near Grosvenor Place'. The settlement was formally drawn up by a man whom Harriette ringingly describes as 'a — of a lawyer', and included the proviso that should any proof of inconstancy be proved against Sophia, the annuity would be reduced to only £100.*

It was not long before Harriette's favourite sister Fanny, too, made an arrangement with one of her admirers, Colonel Parker, and although their agreement does not seem to have had the sanction of a formal financial settlement behind it, it nonetheless had all the outward trappings of a quasi-marriage. 'She shall bear my name, and I will show her all the respect a wife can require, and she shall always find me a gentleman,' the Colonel told Harriette.

Amy, too, had several offers from men who wanted to put her 'altogether under [their] protection'. One of these was Colonel Sydenham, ADC to the Marquis of Wellesley, the Duke of Wellington's elder brother, who had no money, but whom Amy liked; the other was the rich Count Palmella, the Portuguese Ambassador to London. It was a quandary. Amy drove round immediately to Harriette's house – in Count Palmella's barouche – to ask her advice. 'I like liberty best,' Amy told her sister matter-of-factly. 'If I put myself under the protection of anybody, I shall not be allowed to give parties and sit up all night, but then I have my desk full of long bills, without receipts!'

Harriette advised Amy to accept Palmella, who was 'very gentlemanlike' as well as being wealthy, and who had made a most generous offer: £200 a month,† paid in advance, and the use of his horses and carriage. In the end, however, Amy followed her own inclination.

---

* According to Harriette, Deerhurst had to be forced into this agreement after his seduction of Sophia. Sophia's family had threatened legal action against him if he did not make provision for her, but the only legal plea which could be found for a girl 'so unfortunately situated' was that her parents had lost her domestic services. It was perhaps for this reason that Sophia's settlement was a relatively paltry one.
† This was a tremendous sum – the equivalent of £120,000 a year.

Harriette met her one morning, when paying a morning call at her sister Fanny's house, and found that Amy 'had closed with Mr Sydenham's proposal, and changed her name to that of Mrs Sydenham'. (Fanny, too, had followed this custom, and was now known as 'Mrs Parker'.) Or, as Amy herself put it: 'Sydenham and I are become man and wife* and ... I have changed my name and my home for his.'

When Harriette accepted Mrs Porter's introduction to the Duke of Wellington she claimed that she too was looking for a 'steady friend', but in fact at this stage in her life she saw her sisters' liaisons, for all the security they brought, as a terrible loss of independence. 'I must never flirt, nor have any beaux again ... I must now lead a pure, virtuous, chaste and proper life,' Amy told her. 'Who had laid such an appalling embargo on you?' was Harriette's reply. (But for all that, perhaps Amy's choice of Sydenham was a good one, for Harriette tells us that as 'Mrs Sydenham' she was still allowed to give parties, 'but soberly: that is to say, Sydenham insisted on having his house quiet before three in the morning'.)

Very early on in her life, Harriette had decided 'to live free as air from any restraint but that of my conscience', but there was another reason why she preferred to maintain her semi-attached existence. For all her courtesan's ways, Harriette was a romantic. 'I was made for love,' she wrote, adding, 'Nothing but the whole heart of the man I loved could settle me.' Now, disastrously, that man appeared in her life.

John Ponsonby, later Baron Ponsonby of Imokilly, was famous among his contemporaries for being the handsomest man in England.† The Ponsonbys were a junior branch of the Bessborough family; John's father had been a Whig MP and a firm Foxite. Through these connections Ponsonby was related, both by blood and by politics, to the very cream of the British aristocracy. His marriage in 1803 to the

---

* This is a figure of speech. They were not, of course, legally married.
† Harriette was especially impressed by his wonderful teeth.

seventeen-year-old Fanny Villiers, seventh daughter of the Earl of Jersey, only cemented his impeccable lineage.*

John Ponsonby did not have only his great beauty to recommend him (although, romantically, it was this that was said to have saved him from being hanged by the mob in Paris in 1791). His looks, we are told, were matched by 'the tact and perfection' of his manners; he was also said to be 'a charming raconteur', and to have an excellent memory, attributes which were later to aid him very considerably in the success of his diplomatic career (which less charitable tongues attributed to the fact that George IV was so jealous of the notice which his mistress, Lady Conyngham, took of Ponsonby that he pressed his Foreign Secretary, George Canning, to get him out of the country. Ponsonby was made successively Envoy Extraordinary and Minister Plenipotentiary to Buenos Aires, Rio and Brussels, becoming British Ambassador to Constantinople in 1832, and to Vienna in 1846[13]).

But all this was a long way in the future. When Harriette first began to chronicle what was to become her obsessive love for Ponsonby, she had no idea at all who he was, not even his name. But – 'I have seen such a man,' she sighed to her sisters and Julia one night when they were all dining together.

> 'What manner of man have you seen?' asked Fanny.
> 'A very god!' retorted I.
> 'Who is he?' inquired Amy.
> 'I do not know,' was my answer.
> 'What is his name?'
> 'I cannot tell.'
> 'Where did you see him?'
> 'In Sloane Street, riding on horseback, and followed by a large dog.'
> 'What a simpleton you are,' observed Amy.

But Harriette was not a simpleton; she was in love. From the moment she first saw the handsome stranger with the Newfoundland dog she

---

* The Jerseys' daughters were all known for their beauty. Their third daughter, Caroline, later married one of Harriette's other lovers, the Marquis of Lorne.

could think of nothing else: 'I . . . sought for him every day,' she wrote, 'and I thought of him every hour.' He was not, she mused, the sort of man 'that generally strikes the fancy of a very young female – for he was neither young,* nor at all gaily dressed'. His appeal to her was rather 'that pale expressive beauty, which oftener steals upon us, by degrees, after having become acquainted, than strikes at first sight'.

Despite herself, Harriette's obsession grew. She haunted Sloane Street and Hyde Park in the hope of seeing him again, persuading anyone she could to accompany her on her walks. She was often joined by Beau Brummell, who at this point Harriette believed was in love with her, but she was so absorbed in her hunt for the handsome stranger that she hardly heard Brummell's 'foolish professions'.† Harriette often saw Ponsonby, and sometimes he would turn his head after she had passed him, but she could not tell whether it was to admire her, or indeed if he had noticed her at all, or whether he was merely looking back after his large dog. She was both puzzled and tormented by this. 'Better to have been merely observed by that fine noble-looking being, than adored by all the men on earth besides, thought I, being now at the very tip-top of my heroics.'

In the end it was Julia Johnstone who, at the opera one night, was finally able to identify Lord Ponsonby. Julia, who was a niece of Lord Carysfort and who had mixed in high society before an early *faux pas* had made her an outcast from it, had known Ponsonby from when she was a girl. She also knew that he was married. 'Ponsonby is, as I have always been told, very near perfection,' she told Harriette. 'But what chance can you have? He is married to the loveliest creature on earth – the youngest daughter of Lord Jersey.' A despondent Harriette agreed.

Although she now resolved to make no more attempts to become acquainted with the fascinating stranger, this noble resolution did not stop Harriette from haunting every place where she might have a glimpse of him. Julia had told her where Ponsonby lived – Curzon

---

* Harriette's affair with Ponsonby is thought to have begun in 1806, when he was twenty-six and she twenty.
† Harriette also claimed that Brummell was at one stage in love with her friend Julia Johnstone. The usual view about Brummell is that he was not at all interested in women.

Street, in Mayfair – and the very next day Harriette 'indulged [herself] in passing his house at least fifty times'. Lord Ponsonby was 'the sort of man I think I could be wicked enough to say my prayers to', she told her sisters and Julia, to their amused incredulity. 'I could live in his happiness only, without his knowing me. I could wait for hours near his house for the chance of seeing him pass, or hearing his voice.'

In the bitter and shrilly self-serving *Confessions* which Julia was later to write in revenge for Harriette's depiction of her in the *Memoirs*,* she poured particular scorn on Harriette's claims that all 'her amours were carried on for love, and that she despised money' (in fact, Harriette does not claim either of these things). No one who knew Harriette could have denied that one of her many talents was for embroidering a tale, but it is one of Julia's more dubious claims that Harriette's liaison with Lord Ponsonby was almost entirely invented.

'Mercy on me, how many lies had she made that name cover,' wrote Julia. 'I don't know whether to laugh or be serious. It is of little consequence, for of all the stories Harriette ever fabricated, this is the chief; the palladium of her *inventions* . . . Gentle readers, tender souls, when you have done sighing over fiction, listen to the words of truth. Harriette Wilson never was connected with LORD PONSONBY, and never spoke to him above twenty times in her life.'[14]

But in whatever other respects Harriette may have been tempted to embellish her affair with Ponsonby, her description of its first tremulous beginnings could only have been written by someone who had been in the grip of an obsessive love. 'I saw and examined the countenances of his footmen, and the colour of his window-curtains: even the knocker of his door escaped not my veneration, since Ponsonby must have touched it so often,' she wrote of her frequent, fruitless trips down Curzon Street. Sometimes it seemed to her as if her 'very nature' had undergone a transformation. She began to dislike society (a fact which, even while it was happening, quite horrified her). 'The fact is, I really now lived but in his sight,' she wrote, 'and I only met him once or twice in a week, to see him pass me without notice.'

* The *Confessions of Julia Johnstone* are subtitled 'In Contradiction to the Fables of Harriette Wilson'.

But gradually she began to hope that perhaps he did notice her after all, and with pleasure. Once he rode behind her all the way from Hyde Park to her front door. Not wanting to appear bold, she pretended not to see him, but immediately ran upstairs to the rooftop, in order to observe whether he had really followed her, or was simply on his way somewhere else. To her joy she saw him reach the end of her street and then turn and gallop quickly past her door, as though afraid of being seen.

> *Suppose he were to love me, thought I, and the idea caused my heart to beat wildly. I would not dwell upon it. It was ridiculous. It would only expose me to after-disappointment. What was I, that Lord Ponsonby should think about me? What could I ever be to him? Still there was no reason, which I could discover, why I might not love Lord Ponsonby. I was made for love, and looked for no return.*

Fortunately – or perhaps unfortunately – for Harriette, her love *was* returned. One evening when Fanny and Julia were dining with her, she went to open the window and saw Ponsonby riding slowly past her house, and this time 'there could be no doubt as to his blushing'. Her happiness on seeing him, she wrote, was 'of a nature too pure to be trifled with', and she said nothing to the others, keeping his appearance 'a profound secret'. That night she could not sleep at all. The next morning she was rewarded with a letter:

> *I have long been desirous to make your acquaintance: will you let me? A friend of mine has told me something about you; but I am afraid you were then only laughing at me . . . I hope, at all events, that you will write me one line, to say you forgive me, and direct it to my house in town. P*

Harriette was overjoyed. 'For the last five months, I have scarcely lived but in your sight,' she wrote back to him, 'and everything I have done or wished, or hoped, or thought about, had a reference to you and your happiness. Now tell me what you wish.'

Her joy was not in the slightest marred by the fact that, in Harriette's version of events, they were not to meet face to face for some time.

Ponsonby's father was dying, and he could not leave him, so for the next three weeks they wrote to one another instead. Her happiness while this correspondence went on was 'the purest, the most exalted, and the least allied to sensuality, of any I ever experienced in my life'.

Ponsonby was hers; that was all that mattered. When at last he did come to her she was so overwhelmed that she burst into tears. Although Ponsonby was exhausted by the long vigils at his father's bedside, they sat up the whole of that first night together talking. Harriette was ecstatic; 'yet our happiness was of that tranquil nature, which is nearer allied to melancholy than to mirth', she wrote.

The second night they were together he arrived at her house in evening dress, looking 'so much more beautiful than I had ever imagined any mortal mixture of earth's clay' that Harriette was almost unnerved. Once more they sat laughing and talking together, and he told her 'many witty things'. So many, in fact, that Harriette almost began to lose patience. When she made a move towards him, he turned from her kiss 'like a spoiled child'. '"No!" said Ponsonby, shaking his head, "I have a thousand things to tell you."' But by now, Harriette's almost religious rapture in the presence of her beloved was fading. Ponsonby's arms were around her waist, his lips nearly touching hers; Harriette was nearly expiring with expectation.

> 'I cannot listen to one of them,' said I, faintly, and our lips met in one long, long, delicious kiss! So sweet, so ardent! that it seemed to draw the life's warm current from my youthful heart, to reanimate his with all its wildest passion.
>
> And then! – yes, and then, as Sterne says –
> And then – and then – and then – and then – and then we parted.

Harriette maintained that her liaison with Lord Ponsonby lasted for three years. Although she does not seem ever to have been formally under his protection, during this time she lacked for nothing, as he looked after her and paid all her bills, although she claims – perhaps fancifully – that when she received a written offer of an annuity from him (for the relatively paltry sum of £200, the equivalent of £10,000 a year, during her lifetime) she tore it up, refusing him outright because she knew he had no money.

Harriette wrote relatively little about her time with Ponsonby. The fact that he was a married man meant that their affair had to be carried out with the utmost secrecy, and it was perhaps this fact that was to fuel Julia Johnstone's cruel assertions. What is more certain, from Harriette's own descriptions, is that her love for him never progressed beyond its early, highly romanticised, heightened state; and who knows whether this may have led her – poor Harriette – to exaggerate his for her?

She was his 'angelic Harriette', she insisted, and had he known her sooner he would never have married another woman. She, certainly, 'had neither eyes, nor ears, nor thoughts, but for Ponsonby'. Her every nerve and sinew was attuned to him: 'How I used to fancy I could feel his entrance into his wife's private box, at the opera, without seeing him, as though the air suddenly should become purer; how I have astonished Fanny, by guessing the very instant of his approach, without looking towards his side of the house.' In her drives through the Park at the fashionable hour, Harriette hardly listened to the chatter of the 'trotting beaux' who surrounded her carriage, 'because that adored, sly, beautiful face of Ponsonby's was fixed on me *à la distance*'.

They arranged to meet in Hyde Park every day after dinner; not to speak, but simply to look at each other. Sometimes a ride beside him in a hackney coach to the House of Lords was Harriette's only opportunity to be with Ponsonby. But even a humble hackney was transformed by her love into a palace of delights: 'and in that coach have I waited half the night, merely for one more kiss', she wrote, 'and the pleasure of driving with Ponsonby to his door'.

On one of her after-dinner walks through Hyde Park, Harriette was greatly struck by the beauty of a young woman driving past her in an elegant little carriage. 'It is that most lovely creature Lady Fanny Ponsonby, whom we are all sighing and dying for,' she was told by her walking companion that day, the fashionable beau Frederick Gerald Byng (nicknamed 'Poodle', apparently, because of his magnificent head of tight white curls). Owing to a violent attack of scarlet fever as a child, Lady Fanny was very deaf. 'I fancy Ponsonby sometimes wishes that his wife could be his friend and companion; but that is quite out of the question,' said Byng. 'Her Ladyship is good, and will do as she is bid; but besides her deafness, her understanding is neither bright nor lively. Lord Ponsonby shows her the sort of indulgence and tenderness which a child requires; but he must seek for a companion elsewhere.'

Not everyone agreed with Poodle Byng. Countess Granville,* one of the shrewdest observers of her day, was of the opinion that Ponsonby was always secretly in love with his wife. 'Lady Ponsonby is beautiful beyond description,' she wrote to her sister, Lady Morpeth, 'and an engaging, affectionate, gentle person, with an understanding crushed by his affected contempt and brutality, for I am convinced he is in fact desperately in love with her all the time. They have, I hear, come to an understanding ... He is to give up Miss Wilson and all that sort of thing.'[15]

From the start of their liaison, Harriette always insisted, there had been an agreement between them that if Ponsonby's wife ever discovered their intimacy they would separate forever. They were not monsters, she wrote, and would never 'indulge in selfish enjoyments at the expense of misery to any one of our fellow-creatures, much less one who depends on you for all her happiness'. Despite these noble feelings, Harriette was so besotted that she could not find it in her to believe it would ever really happen. When she received the fatal letter from Ponsonby, a mist seemed to come over her eyes, and 'a cold dew, as if from a charnel-house, overspread [her] whole frame'. Lady Fanny had indeed found them out, and Ponsonby had promised her that, after one last interview, he would neither see nor speak to Harriette again.

At first she was stunned into disbelief: 'shall Ponsonby refuse to speak to me, and even look upon me as a stranger ... Nonsense! palpable, gross absurdity! How I have been frightening myself!' When finally the truth sank in, Harriette's anguish was a terrible thing. She locked herself in her room, prostrating herself with her face on the

---

* Harriet Granville was the eldest daughter of Charles James Fox's dear friend the Duchess of Devonshire. She married Granville Leveson Gower, who was for many years the lover of her aunt, Lady Bessborough, a relative by marriage of John Ponsonby.

floor, 'and prayed fervently for near an hour, that, if I was to see Ponsonby no more, God would take me, in mercy, out of a world of such bitter suffering'. But there was to be no such consolation for her. She became ill with a fever; grew thin and pale; wrote letters, to which he did not reply. In her delirium she imagined that rats and mice were running over her head, 'which thus kept me in a frenzy, from the mere working of a disordered brain'. For two weeks she wandered the streets around Ponsonby's house like a wraith, hoping in vain for a glimpse of him, but when she did see him at last 'a bar of iron across my chest seemed to arrest my flight, and I was compelled to stand quite still for an instant'. In that instant the porter closed the door, and shut him from her sight. 'The anguish of that moment,' wrote Harriette, 'I will not attempt to describe.'

The door closing behind Ponsonby, shutting Harriette out of his life forever, is a potent image. The two worlds, *monde* and *demi-monde* – closer than ever now in so many of the externals of dress, manners and etiquette – were in all other respects moving further and further apart. Aristocratic and upper-class men of the Regency period did occasionally marry their mistresses from the half-world – one example is the Earl of Craven, Harriette's first seducer, who married the actress Louisa Brunton in 1807; and indeed, Harriette's own sister, Sophia, became Lady Berwick, but only after she had promised that she would sever all contact with her disreputable elder sisters – but the crossing places between the two worlds had, if anything, diminished over the years. The spectacular achievement of Elizabeth Armistead – one of the very few courtesans in history to have successfully stepped across from the *demi-monde* into society – remains unique: only two such extraordinarily charismatic personalities as Fox and Elizabeth, one feels, could ever have pulled it off. Harriette Wilson, by contrast, had no desire at all to become 'respectable' – indeed, the thought of being obliged to mix with so-called 'respectable' women she found quite appalling.

But confusions did occasionally arise, and were always something of a conundrum to the Dubochet sisters, who gave as much thought to how to extract themselves from these awkward situations as the other parties concerned would have done, had they realised their mistake. 'With regard to the repugnancy you say you feel, in availing yourself of the invitations from ladies who believe you to be Parker's wife,' wrote Harriette to Fanny, who had moved to Portsmouth where her 'husband's' regiment was now stationed, and was shortly expecting a child, 'I certainly, in your place, would never seek them; neither are you bound to say anything of yourself, which can prejudice society against you. You tell me that some of the ladies in your neighbourhood will take no excuses. Well, then, visit them, whenever you are in the humour, and, if they have good taste, they will be delighted with your society.'

Nonetheless, no one thought it a comfortable situation. Men, particularly married men, who were too open in their amours were no longer tolerated in quite the same way that they had once been, as Ponsonby's sudden retreat perhaps indicates. Companionate marriage, or marriage for love, so rare an occurrence in the eighteenth century, when arranged marriages were the norm in all but the very lowest levels of society, was by Harriette's day much more prevalent. Although the increased expectations of marital bliss did not necessarily make marriages any happier, women, particularly in the upper classes, were no longer treated as the mere dynastic building blocks that they had once been. Wives had feelings and sensibilities, and were beginning to take possession of a kind of moral high ground within marriage which would characterise the Victorian age.

Society looked askance at men who trampled too readily over their wives. When Berkeley Paget fell in love with Harriette's sister, Amy, cutting off his wife and all his family in order to be with her, living openly with her in her house and accompanying her to public places, he was ostracised by many of his friends. 'Everybody cried out shame,' wrote Harriette, 'and some few, some very moral men as the Duke of York, actually cut him dead, and refused to receive him at Oatlands, even on public nights; for beyond all doubt,' she added with heavy irony, 'a man ought to be of royal blood before he presumes to commit adultery.'

For women, of course, the rules and the penalties for stepping outside the sexual boundaries marked out by society were even less forgiving. 'The world is very uncharitable!' wrote Julia Johnstone in her *Confessions*; 'man may commit an hundred deviations from the path of rectitude, yet he can still return, every one invites him . . . But woman, when she makes one false step, can retrieve it no more.' The *faux pas* that Julia had committed in her early youth was a crime 'never to be forgotten'.

For Julia Johnstone, entrance into the *demi-monde* had been not so much an act of liberation (as it was in Harriette's case) or a simple career move (as it had been for Sophia Baddeley and Elizabeth Armistead) as a descent into social limbo. The history of courtesanry in Britain is full of women such as she: women of high rank whose sexual misdemeanours had made them outcasts from society, and who had no choice thereafter but to shift for themselves.* In the eighteenth century some of these – Grace Dalrymple Eliot, known as 'Dally the Tall', from an aristocratic Scots family, and Gertrude Mahon, the 'Bird of Paradise', a granddaughter of the Earl of Cavan – became among the most successful courtesans of the age, nearly as famous in their day as Sophia Baddeley and Mrs Armistead.

The aristocratic Miss Johnstone was certainly one of the leading demi-reps of the early nineteenth century. A niece of the Earl of Carysfort, her real name was Julia Storer. A portrait shows her to have been a slight but pretty woman, with languid eyes, a flawless milky skin and fashionably sloping shoulders, handsomer perhaps to our contemporary eyes than either Harriette or her sisters. Julia's mother,

---

* The historian Lawrence Stone has pointed out that it was not only sex which made these women outcasts, but often poverty too. He describes 'the small but select army of pretty young ladies of good family and good breeding . . . who lacked the money to make a respectable marriage. Their poverty combined with their gentility virtually obliged them to follow careers as mistresses to rich, titled and powerful men who had lost interest in their wives, and were seeking sexually attractive and well-bred companions and bed mates.' The most famous of these is Mrs Theresia Constantia Phillips, known as Con Phillips, whose scandalous autobiography, chronicling her five husbands and seven rich and aristocratic patrons, ran to four editions. 'I was born constitutionally with the greatest share of vivacity and spirits of any woman in the world,' she wrote, '. . . but the obligations I had to nature were perverted by my accidental poverty.' Lawrence Stone, *Uncertain Unions and Broken Lives*.

the Honourable Mrs Storer, who at one time had been a lady-in-waiting to Queen Charlotte, had educated her daughter abroad in France. When she returned she was sent to the palace of Hampton Court to stay with a family friend, Mrs Cotton, wife of Colonel Cotton of the 10th Dragoons.

Like Harriette, as a very young woman Julia had nursed rebellious feelings. The stultifying formality and pure boredom of court life was not for her, she declared. 'What a fortune is my mother's (said I), such a one will never do for me; I am for freedom and independence.'[16] According to Harriette, Julia had 'the passions of a man', one of the few facts about herself which Julia did not attempt to deny. In her *Confessions*, although otherwise presenting an improbably chaste version of her life, she speaks freely of these 'passions' which, she wrote, were 'too strong for me to keep under control without the advice of a friendly monitor – I must have been more than moral to have withstood temptation'.

True to her word, Julia did not withstand temptation for very long. At Hampton Court she proceeded to fall violently in love with Colonel Cotton. 'The first night Colonel Cotton danced with her, she was mad! In four months more she was pregnant,' wrote Harriette succinctly. 'In nine months more, having concealed her situation, she was seized with the pangs of labour.' Julia could not attempt, Harriette said later, to describe the rage and fury of her family when they discovered the truth. She was cast out immediately. Colonel Cotton hired 'a very retired cottage' near town for her and, despite the scandal, kept her on as his mistress.

When Harriette first met Julia, nine years after this event, she was still in keeping with the Colonel, with whom she now had five beautiful children. By the time she was forty ('Fat, fair and forty, even though her name did not begin with an F,' wrote naughty Harriette, who could never resist a good sharp dig at her former friend) Julia had no fewer than twelve children, her confinements occurring regularly every eleven months.

Why was it that Julia Johnstone had so many children, while Harriette, so far as we know, had none? It is a striking fact that of the five principal courtesans in this book, only one, Sophia Baddeley, had children. Women in the sex trade had always taken steps to prevent unwanted pregnancies. A wide range of contraceptives was easily available, and it is certain that Harriette and her sisters (and, in the previous century, Sophia Baddeley and Mrs Armistead, and later Cora Pearl and Catherine Walters too) would all have used them.

Since the Middle Ages many herbal preparations had been known to be menstrual promoters: calamint, cypress, agrimony, horehound, juniper, parsley, the common white saxifrage, rue and sage were all widely used,* and were sufficiently effective for generation after generation of midwives and experienced older women to recommend them. In Culpeper's *Complete Herbal*, first published in the mid-seventeenth century, there are references to eringo, or sea holly, which 'procures womens courses', and to black hellebore which, 'used as a pessary, the roots provoke the terms exceedingly', while pennyroyal also 'if boiled and drank, provokes women's courses, and expels the dead child and afterbirth'.[17]

Even more effective than these herbal remedies, or used in conjunction with them, were sponges and tampons, or pessaries, which had also been used as preventatives in England for many hundreds of years – Chaucer mentions them, as does the Marquis de Sade, and even Jeremy Bentham recommends them in his 'Situation and Relief of the Poor' in the 1800s. Francis Place, a pioneering disseminator of information about birth control in the early nineteenth century, described in detail the use of the sponge and the withdrawal methods in his pamphlets, which he first distributed anonymously in 1823. He described the sponges vividly as 'large as a green walnut or small apple', claiming comfortingly that they would not 'diminish the enjoyment of either party', and should be used 'rather damp, and when convenient a little warm'.[18]

The sponges referred to by Place sound a good deal less alarming than some of the other diaphragm-like devices which were available

---

* Bilberries did the opposite, and were believed to 'stop women's courses'.

in the eighteenth century. Casanova, a lover of Mrs Cornelys, whose fashionable entertainments at Carlisle House in Soho Square were all the rage in 1770s London, had a more unusual solution. When a guest of Voltaire's in Geneva, he made the acquaintance of the three beautiful wards of a local official, Michel Lullin de Châteauvieux. Casanova seduced all three, but, mindful of the fact that their future marriage prospects would have been ruined by an unwanted pregnancy, he first considerately took three gold coins to a local goldsmith and had them melted down into solid gold balls, which he instructed the girls to insert into their vaginas, assuring them that the chemical reaction of the gold with their natural secretions would make them temporarily infertile. Apparently it worked: although, during their more acrobatic love-making, the gold balls had a tendency to fall out, none of the women became pregnant.[19] Also effective, and rather more economical, was the use of a squeezed half-lemon, again recommended by Casanova, which like the golden balls was inserted into the body in such a way that it capped the cervix – although, perhaps understandably, it does not seem to have been adopted with any great enthusiasm.*

These rudimentary diaphragms were often accompanied by douching, which was most effective when done with a saline solution. From the beginning of the seventeenth century it was common among French prostitutes to use syringes for this purpose, a practice which would be adopted by their English counterparts about a hundred years later.

A more sophisticated version of the sponge, similar to the modern Dutch cap, appeared in the United States in the 1880s, when a Dr Edward B. Foote invented a 'womb veil', otherwise known as a *pessaire*, or female preventative. The fitting of this device, wrote Dr Foote, was 'easy and accomplished in a moment, without the aid of a light'. Radically, he added: 'It places conception entirely under the control of the wife, to whom it naturally belongs; for it is for her to say at what time and under what circumstances she will become a mother.'[20]

The most effective form of contraception, however, had an altogether

---

* Emma Dickens, author of *Immaculate Contraception*, believes that this device is still popular amongst Russian women today.

different genesis from the (to a modern mind) benign one of preventing unwanted pregnancies. The first written reference in English to the sheath appears in John Marten's *Treatise of all the Degrees and Symptoms of the Venereal Disease in Both Sexes*, published in 1704,* although the devices themselves had been in use for much longer (the remains of some thought to have been used by Royalist officers fighting in the Civil War were dug up in a privy at Dudley Castle in 1986). James Boswell, who had found the sight of Sophia Baddeley so mesmerisingly seductive, often used them when indulging in his favourite pastime. 'At the bottom of the Haymarket I picked up a strong jolly young damsel,' reads a typical entry in his diary, dated May 1763, 'and taking her under the arm conducted her to Westminster Bridge, and then in armour complete did I engage her upon this noble edifice. The whim of doing it there with the Thames rolling below us,' he added merrily, 'amused me very much.'†

'Armour' is a telling description of these early sheaths. John Marten mentions that they were made of 'Lint or Linnen rags' soaked in a special wash; rival prophylactics (one was J. Spinke's alarmingly named 'blue Apron') were made from dried sheepgut.[21] A measure of how popular the sheath really was is the fact that it was only six years after the vulcanisation process was invented by Charles Goodyear in America in 1843 that the first rubber condoms went on the market, price $5 for a dozen.‡

In the early days, however, it was not so much the sheath's discomfort as its associations with disease and vice which prevented its wider use as a contraceptive device, particularly amongst married couples. Almost all eighteenth-century references to the condom have to do with men consorting with prostitutes (such as in the penultimate plate of Hogarth's *The Harlot's Progress*, in which two limp sheaths hang on the wall of the destitute and dying Moll's sickroom). In the eighteenth century the sale of condoms was largely confined to brothels

---

* Marten's work was written nearly 150 years after Fallopio's pioneering treatise (1564) on reproduction.
† In fact Boswell did not use his 'armour' enough; his repeated infections from syphilis were to cause his early, and excruciatingly painful, death.
‡ Curiously, some connoisseurs continued to prefer sheaths made of sheepgut.

and other sleazy places, while their advertisement in the more neutral space of a newspaper was no better served by being usually placed alongside other more dubious remedies, such as the truly astonishing variety of quack cures for venereal disease.

James Boswell, who despite his use of 'armour' suffered regular venereal infections, favoured Keyser's Pills, puffed in the *Public Advertiser* on 4 February 1768 as a mild cure 'for a certain disorder, without the least trouble or confinement'; while William Hickey sought relief in 'Velnos Vegetable Syrup', which was also used for leprosy, gout, scrofula, dropsy, smallpox, consumption, tapeworm, cancer, scurvy and diarrhoea. Others included the sonorously named 'Persian Restorative Drops' – for the cool sum of half a guinea a bottle (about £25) – 'Parisian Vegetable Syrup' and, my personal favourite, 'Dr Trigg's Golden Anti-Vatican Pills'. All these potions emphasised their mild nature – deliberately so, because the only other known medicine available was mercury, the side effects of which were more devastating than the disease itself. All were equally useless.

It is possible that Julia Johnstone, being from a more aristocratic background than the Dubochet sisters, had a less earthy attitude than they to the idea of contraception. Or perhaps she was, again for reasons of her class, simply less well informed. Certainly, the number of children fathered on aristocratic women of that period by men other than their husbands would suggest, at the very least, that they were clumsy practitioners of the art.

What is more likely, however, is that a courtesan of whatever class usually only began to have children when she believed herself to be in a stable relationship. Sophia Baddeley had her first child after she had fallen in love with Stephen Sayer, while the others were the offspring of her later 'husband', the actor named Webster. Most of Julia's children were fathered by Colonel Cotton, her protector of many years' standing, while Fanny Dubochet had three children by her first protector, Mr Woodcock, with whom she lived 'a most retired steady life' for seven years before he died (and would have married, Harriette claimed without irony, had he not already been encumbered by a wife), and at least one more child after she became 'Mrs Parker'. Amy became pregnant by Harriette's former lover the Marquis of Lorne, but

Harriette believed that her sister held real hopes that Lorne would marry her (cruelly dashed when he married Fanny Ponsonby's sister, the divorced Marchioness of Anglesey).

Mistakes, of course, were always possible – Sophia, for instance, became briefly pregnant by Melbourne – whereupon the brutal but effective kitchen surgery of the backstreet abortionist was the usual option. Some courtesans may simply have been naturally infertile – although repeated abortions might also have made them so – and it is most likely for this reason that Elizabeth Armistead and Fox, who adored children, never had their own family.

In Elizabeth's day the option of an abortion was a more acceptable solution to an unwanted pregnancy than it was to become for later generations. Notices such as one in the *Morning Post and Daily Advertiser* which offered 'Advice to the Fair Sex' from a 'Mrs Miller, Midwife, of no. 4 London House Yard, the North Side of St Paul's Church Yard', were commonplace: 'through long study and experience under several of the most eminent men-midwifes, [Mrs Miller] continues to accommodate pregnant Ladies with the utmost care, attention and secrecy. All disorders incident to the female sex speedily removed.'[22]

Although advertisements such as these, with their veiled but nonetheless quite explicit claims, continued to appear throughout the nineteenth century, the consequences for women who availed themselves of such services in Harriette's day were far graver than they had been in Elizabeth's or Sophia's. Despite the widespread and ancient tradition of abortion based on folk remedies, many people – mostly men – had become increasingly hostile towards it. The private practices of the eighteenth century regarding not only abortion but all forms of birth control became, in the nineteenth, the subject of public debate. Despite the efforts of men such as Francis Place to promote information about contraception, the issue was surrounded with increasing anxiety. Inducing a miscarriage had become a statutory offence for the first time in 1803.

Abortion was regarded with particular horror in the nineteenth century, but then so too was the wholly benign practice of withdrawal (probably the most widely used method of contraception amongst married couples). Onanism – in its original literal sense of 'spilling sperm outside the womb' – was believed to lead to such a horrifying catalogue of malaises – loss of hearing, memory and eyesight, and even consumption – that it was quite surprising that men were able to survive it at all. If simple empirical proof were not enough, a wide range of medicines was available to counteract its debilitating effects. Thomas Crouch's work *Onania* advertised a 'strengthening tincture' and 'Prolific Powder', while W. Farren sold a 'Restorative Nervous Elixir', W. Brodum a 'nervous cordial and Botanical Syrup', and E. Senate some intriguing 'Steel Lozenges'. Others included James Graham's 'The Elixir of Life' and the comfortingly Biblical 'Cordial Balm of Gilead'.[23]

Despite the many advances in medical science which were made in the nineteenth century, doctors increasingly withheld information from women about their own fertility and the means available to control it, with the result that they were quite as much at the mercy of useless quack medicines – and, more dangerously, quack practitioners – as they had been in the eighteenth.*

A hundred years after Mrs Miller and her colleagues were advertising their services in the *Morning Post*, mysterious advertisements for 'female remedies' were still appearing in ladies' illustrated magazines. They included 'Ottley's Strong Pills', 'Towle's Pennyroyal and Steel Pills for Females', and the sinister 'Madame Frain's Medications'.

> *Ladies Only*
> The Lady Montrose
> – *Miraculous* –
> Female Tabules
> Are positively unequalled for all
> FEMALE AILMENTS.† The most OBSTINATE

---

* Despite this, some doctors could be found who would perform secret abortions, although they extracted a high price for this illegal practice, which was worth as much as £2000 or £3000 a year to them. See Angus Mclaren, *Birth Control in Nineteenth-Century England*.

† Did Harriette ever suffer from such a 'female ailment'? Julia Johnstone claimed that she did, insisting that Harriette had feigned pregnancy in order to ensnare the Marquis of Worcester, but later became actually pregnant by another of her lovers. There is no evidence from any other source to support this claim.

obstructions, irregularities, etc.
of the female system are removed in a few doses.[24]

Although her affair with Ponsonby had nearly broken her, Harriette was a survivor. Recalling that period in her life, she later wrote that not only was her health ruined by it, but 'the very spark of existence was nearly destroyed'.

It was an older, harder and more worldly-wise Harriette who went back on the town. Ponsonby she learned to think of as 'a wild dream', and romantic love as 'one of the most arbitrary, ungovernable passions in nature', an affliction of which she was glad to have rid herself. 'Had it pleased Heaven to have bestowed on me the husband of my choice,' she had once written to Ponsonby, 'there is nothing great, or good, or virtuous, that I had not aspired to.' But now things were different.

To the outside world, Harriette was a seasoned courtesan, still at the very height of her fashionable allure. She had had many older aristocratic patrons ('older', in Harriette's book, meant over thirty) – Craven, Lorne and Wellington; now she began to think that perhaps a younger protector might have its advantages.

It was through one of her most youthful admirers, the Duke of Leinster, that Harriette had first been made aware of the Marquis of Worcester's passion for her. Knowing how punctilious she was in the matter of introductions, Leinster had until now refused all Worcester's requests to be presented to her; but her awareness of how much he admired her had made Harriette curious about him. Worcester was then a very young man, rather pale-faced and thin; he was something of a dandy, too, which would have pleased her – 'There he is!' exclaimed the Duke of Leinster to Harriette one night at the opera. 'Do not you observe a very tall young fellow, in silk stockings . . . Upon my honour, he won't wear trousers or curl his hair, because he heard that you dislike it.'

All the same, when Worcester finally succeeded in persuading another of his acquaintances, Lord Deerhurst, to introduce him to Harriette, she was not at all amused. It was only Worcester's youth and bashfulness that saved the day.

'I do not often introduce gentlemen to ladies,' said his Lordship, 'and perhaps I am taking a liberty now; yet I hope you can have no objection to my making you known to the Marquis of Worcester.'

I bowed rather formally, because I had before desired Deerhurst not to bring people to me without my permission. However, the young Marquis blushed so deeply, and looked so humble, that it was impossible to treat him without civility ... I conversed indifferently, on common subjects, as people do who happen to meet in a stage-coach, where time present is all they have to care about. Deerhurst was lively and pleasant; the Marquis scarcely spoke; but the little he did find courage to utter was certainly said with good taste, and in a gentlemanly manner.

While Harriette was engaging Worcester in the smallest of small talk in her box at the opera, she was at the same time sizing up her conquest with a thoroughly professional eye. She saw at once that he would not 'do' for her, any more than his uncle, Granville Leveson Gower, had done when she had sent for him to walk with her in Marylebone Fields. He was not at all the kind of man she could ever love, she decided. But soon she began to think again. His person, she noticed, was very good, his air and manners distinguished. Although Worcester would clearly never have any of the 'intellectual beauty' that had so attracted Harriette in Ponsonby, his admiration for her was very flattering. 'First love is all powerful, in the head and heart of such an ardent character as Worcester's,' she observed, 'and there really was an air of truth about him which not a little affected me, for the moment.'

At first she was cautious. 'Do not mistake me,' she told Worcester when he began to look 'too happy' at her notice of him, 'for I am not one bit in love with you.' But he talked very modestly, she noticed approvingly, 'conversing on subjects unconnected with himself or his desires, apparently taking a deep interest in my health, which, I assured him, had long been very delicate'. Perhaps he would do, after all. He was also, as she must have known, heir to a dukedom, a famous house, and great riches. Without missing a beat, Harriette changed tack.

'*There is a pretty race-horse little head for you,*' *said Deerhurst,* *touching my hair.*

'*I never saw such beautiful hair,*' *Worcester remarked timidly.*

'*Put your finger into it,*' *said Deerhurst.* '*Harriette does not mind how you tumble her hair about.*'

'*I should richly deserve to be turned out of the box, were I to do anything so very impertinent,*' *interrupted His Lordship.*

'*Oh, no,*' *said I, leaning the back of my little head towards Worcester,* '*anybody may pull my hair about. I like it, and I am no prude.*'

Worcester ventured to touch my hair, in fear and trembling, and the touch seemed to affect him like electricity. Without vanity, and in very truth, let him deny it if he can, I never saw a boy, or a man, more madly, wildly and romantically in love with any daughter of Eve, in my whole life.

Harriette had come a very long way from the pert fifteen-year-old for whom the Earl of Craven, in his ugly nightcap, drew his interminable cocoa trees. She turned to Worcester again:

'*Perhaps,*' *said I, in a low, laughing voice,* '*perhaps, Lord Worcester, it may be vain and silly in me to believe that you are disposed to like me; but, as I do almost fancy so, I come to wish you a good night, and to assure you that I shall remember with gratitude those who are charitable enough to think favourably of me.*'

The London Season was over. The opera had closed. When Amy gave her last champagne supper even her usually crowded drawing rooms were half empty. It was time for a change of air. The sisters and Julia took a house in the most fashionable part of Brighton, on Marine Parade, overlooking the sea front. Brighton had been transformed from the charming fishing village it had been in Sophia Baddeley's day, and under the patronage of the Prince of Wales had become the very acme of fashionable retreats. All the *beau monde* went there, many of them as guests of the Prince, and it was here that Harriette continued her cat-and-mouse game with Worcester, playing him off deftly against her other youthful admirer, the Duke of Leinster.

Leinster's regiment, however, was soon to leave for the war in Spain, and after a while Harriette took pity on him. 'I [cannot] be tender and true to a dozen of you at a time,' she told Worcester at last, and forbade him to visit her for six weeks, until Leinster had set sail. But she was not fool enough to let Worcester go completely. 'You shall hear from me often,' she consoled him, 'and, as soon as Leinster is gone, you are welcome to try to make me in love with you. If you fail, so much the worse for us both; since I hold everything which is not love to be mere dull intervals in life.'

Everyone who knew Harriette – whose heart was now mercifully 'free as air', her fancy 'ever laughter-loving' – knew how much she loved her independence; and yet, despite herself, she needed a man, not just for money, but for her own desires too. After Leinster left England, Harriette passed a restless night. 'No women ever felt *le besoin d'aimer* with greater ardour than I,' was her frank confession. But true fulfilment, she knew, was not just about sex. 'What would I not have undertaken for the friend, the companion, the husband of my choice?' she wrote. '*En attendant*, me thought, Lord Worcester knew how to love: that was something.' Yet still she had her doubts. 'But then, where was the power of thought, the magic of the mind which alone could insure my respect and veneration?'

Perhaps against her better judgement, Harriette eventually gave in to Worcester's pleading. 'In short, I was pressed by Julia, entreated by Worcester, and inclined by gratitude, being, moreover, in a state of health which required nursing,' she later wrote of this decision; 'therefore, without being in love, I agreed to place myself under his protection.' It was the first time since the very early days of her career, with the Earl of Craven and Fred Lamb, that she had allowed herself to pass into the keeping of just one man.

Worcester was 'half wild with joy'. His regiment was stationed near Brighton, so he went there ahead of Harriette, who had returned briefly to London, to prepare a suitable establishment for her. He rented a house in Rock Gardens, and left his footman Will Haught, the 'commander-in-chief' of his servants, there to get Harriette's household ready.

'The said Mr Will Haught, was a stiff, grave, steady person of about forty,' Harriette recalled. 'He always wore the Beaufort livery, which was as stiff as himself, and used to take his hat off, and sit in the hall, on a Sunday, with a clean pocket-handkerchief tied about his head, reading the Bible, offering thus, to the reflecting mind, these two excellent maxims: Respect God, but do not catch cold.'

Haught had been a retainer in the Beaufort family since before the young Marquis was born, and although Harriette sometimes suspected that one of his functions was to watch over the morals of his young master and report back on them to his mother the Duchess, she was quick enough to see that he had settled her new establishment for her 'as though I had been the Duchess's chosen daughter-in-law'.

Everything in the household was arranged in the grand manner. On her arrival at the house Harriette found that as well as Haught, the footman, there was a coachman, a Mr Boniface, who was also an old Beaufort retainer, although he was not always as officiously polite and attentive as Haught, and had a propensity to fall asleep on the job with his cotton wig 'all awry'. There was also a groom, resplendent in Beaufort livery, waiting to take the bridle of Worcester's horse, which was then handed to an undergroom, who in turn passed it to a soldier who took it into the stable. 'What a bore it will be,' thought Harriette, feigning nonchalance, 'to have all these lazy porter-drinking men in one's house.'

Stepping through her front door for the first time, Harriette found that the household was just as well arranged inside as out. She had brought her own lady's maid with her from London, but Will Haught had also employed another female servant, carefully chosen by himself, whom he now instructed to show Harriette's woman over her mistress's new apartments. 'As to Lord Worcester,' wrote Harriette, 'he was so excessively overjoyed at finding all his fears and dread of losing me at an end, that the moment he could contrive to get rid of Will Haught, he pressed my hand first to his trembling lips, and next to his heart, and then he burst into tears! which he, however, from the very shame, dried up as soon as he possibly could, and with the genuine feelings of affection and hospitality he asked me if, after the fatigue of my little journey, I should prefer passing the night alone.'

Harriette said that she would, although she was so touched by

Worcester's extreme courtesy to her, and the 'perfect liberty' he was allowing her, that when he showed her at last to her apartment she almost regretted her decision.

'It is a nice room,' said I, 'and the fire burns cheerfully. Do you think there are any ghosts in this part of the world?'

Worcester, however, was too modest in his idolatry, and had too great a dread of giving offence to me, to take my hint.

Worcester continued to be besotted with Harriette. According to her version of events, nothing that she could desire was too much trouble for him. The next day his two grooms appeared at the door leading the 'delightfully quiet-looking lady's horse' he had selected for her. He also made her a gift of the most beautiful side-saddle Harriette had ever seen, richly embroidered with blue silk. No one, declared Worcester, was ever to use it except Harriette herself.

Soon they had established a routine. Worcester was expected at the parade ground each morning at eight o'clock, and to make sure that he was not late for his duties – he had already received a severe reprimand from his Colonel for neglecting them – Harriette accompanied him.

'Behold me now,' she wrote jauntily, 'regularly attending parade, like a young recruit, dressed in a blue riding habit, and an embroidered jacket or spencer worn over it, trimmed and finished after the fashion of our uniform, and a little grey fur stable-cap, with a gold band.'

While Worcester paraded, Harriette waited for him in his barrack room, where the ever-resourceful Will Haught made breakfast for her. As he was preparing it, Harriette would entertain herself by reviewing the troops. Worcester's Sergeant, Whitaker, teaching the sword exercise, amused her the most:

'Tik nuttiss!! the wurd dror is oney a carshun. At t'word suards, ye drors um hout, tekin a farm un positif grip o'th'hilt! sem time, throwing th'shith smartly backords thus! Dror!!' Here the men, forgetful of the caution which had just been given them, began to draw. 'Steady there!! Never a finger or a high to move i'th'hed. Dror! suards!!'

Worcester and Harriette continued to attend the parades punctually for more than a fortnight. Sometimes Harriette was invited to dine in the officers' mess (perhaps she entertained them with impersonations of Sergeant Whitaker), where as many as thirty sat down at table. Harriette, who was the only lady present, enjoyed herself vastly. At other times they dined at home, where Worcester 'did the honours of the table with infinite grace'. Harriette's sister Fanny, now the mother of a five-week-old baby girl, came to stay, and they were often joined by their youngest sister Sophia, who was still wavering in her decision as to whether or not to accept the protection of Lord Berwick (Worcester, Harriette said, used to call him 'Tweed'), who was living close by.*

Worcester continued to be an assiduous and devoted lover. He demanded that all the formalities should be observed by his friends – Harriette was not, for example, to be called by her Christian name – he considered her as his wife, he told them, and was offended by anyone who dared to treat her with anything less than the respect they would have shown the Marchioness of Worcester. He refused all invitations to events – dinner parties, balls and routs – at which Harriette could not accompany him. When she had a back tooth pulled he was 'sick with fright' on her behalf, and when the evil operation was over, took to wearing the tooth – so Harriette claimed – on a string around his neck.

He would send fur shoes and fur cloaks after me, in hot dry weather; because one could never be certain that it would not rain before my return. He took upon him all the care of the house, ordering dinner, etc, from having once happened to hear me say that I did not like to know, beforehand, what I was to eat; and always used to lace my stays himself, and get out of bed to make my toast for breakfast, with his own hands, believing I should fancy it nicer and cleaner, if the footman had not touched it.

* It was after one of Worcester and Harriette's dinners that she finally accepted him. He was to settle on her an annuity of £500, and to furnish a house for her in Montague Square in London – complete with 'a very handsome equipage' – although he was made to promise that she should be allowed to sleep alone for the first week or two.

After a while Harriette began to feel suffocated by these attentions. Although Worcester loved nothing more than to be alone with her, *tête-à-tête*, for weeks or even months on end, Harriette liked variety in society, and was unused to being so confined. She begged for leave to go to London for a week to visit Fanny and Colonel Parker, and her youngest sister Sophia, now mistress of an elegant little house in Montague Square.

Other things began to grate on her too. Despite being very seriously in debt to dubious moneylenders, Worcester was recklessly extravagant in all their household expenses. Harriette would have liked to take them over – she could have run their house for less than half the cost, she claimed – but Worcester absolutely refused to allow her to 'trouble [her] head' about them. Will Haught, Harriette knew, despite his apparent devotion to them both, helped himself to regular perks. She could not see the point of continuing to pay him a very high weekly board-wage when she was fully aware that he was also putting down in his 'pious accounts' daily provision not only for himself but for his wife too, and 'more porter than any man could drink in his sober senses'. When, at Harriette's instigation, Worcester hinted this to Haught, 'the holy man ... cried and blubbered till he was almost in hysterics', Harriette remembered, 'and I declared myself quite unable to contend with a footman of such fine nerves'.

Harriette was not the only one to be made nervous by Worcester's devotion to her. His parents, the Duke and Duchess of Beaufort, tipped off by the Duke's brother Lord Charles Somerset, were becoming increasingly alarmed about the state of affairs – one rumour had it that Harriette and Worcester had been clandestinely married. They wrote very severe letters to him on the subject which, in Harriette's version of events, only strengthened Worcester's resolve that she should be his forever. 'He deeply regretted his not being of age,' she wrote, 'that he might immediately ask me to be his wife, and then nought could separate us save death.'

Did Harriette really scheme to become the Marchioness of Worcester? The Duke and Duchess certainly believed that she did, although she herself always denied it. She was fond of Worcester, but she was not in love with him, and it is perfectly plausible that she had never had any intention of marrying him. Far from her being an unsuitable match for him, the truth was that it was he who was no match for her, either intellectually or physically (although she was never as rude about his prowess in the bedroom as she had been about some of her other patrons), and she knew she would never find the fulfilment she craved with him. Also, she was woman of the world enough to have agreed with the Duke himself, who would later observe to her that 'such unequal marriages are seldom, if ever, attended with happiness to either party'.* As her readers, we believe her when she says that she repeatedly refused Worcester's offers to marry her – 'I declare to you that I will never be your wife,' she wrote to him; and, 'I wish you too well to marry you.'

However, having nobly refused the dizzy prize of becoming a marchioness, Harriette quite reasonably thought she was entitled to a reward. She had, after all, been persuaded to put herself wholly under Worcester's protection, giving him all the rights and privileges over her that a husband would expect, including the loss of her independence; and by the unwritten rules of the half-world she deserved some recompense.

Like Sophia Baddeley before her, Harriette had all the physical and psychological talents of the successful courtesan, but she had absolutely none of the necessary business sense. Whereas Harriette's younger sister Sophia had held out against Lord Berwick until he 'came to terms' most handsomely – a London house, her own carriage, the family diamonds and an annuity of £500 (and this was in addition to the £100 which Deerhurst still paid her) – she herself had asked for nothing from Worcester, claiming that she never accepted so much as a trinket from him in her life, except for 'a small chain, and a pair of pink topaz earrings, the price of which was, altogether, under thirty guineas'. And it is probably true that Lord Worcester, who was still under-age and had not yet come into his fortune, did not have very much money.

The Beauforts' attempts to separate them, however, and their terror that Worcester would marry her, had a bracing effect upon Harriette.

* Harriette was not against socially unequal marriages when the couple were otherwise well suited to one another. She always believed that Colonel Parker should have married her sister Fanny, for example.

For all her poor business sense, she was quite clever enough to see that by remaining Worcester's mistress, she held all the cards. The Duchess's letters to her son were becoming increasingly abusive: 'This absurd attachment of yours, for this profligate woman, does but prove the total subjugation of your understanding,' she raged. His father, seeing that this approach was only strengthening Worcester's resolve, tried a different tack, and declared that 'every care and attention' would be paid to Harriette, so long as Worcester gave his solemn promise not to marry her. Eventually, persuaded by Harriette, Worcester gave his promise, although his passion for Harriette only 'became stronger with the difficulty of indulging it'.

The Duke and Duchess had hoped that after six months or so their son's puppyish infatuation would wear off of its own accord, but it did not. 'Worcester's love and passion absolutely did increase daily, although that was what I had imagined to be morally and physically impossible,' wrote Harriette, and despite his promises, he renewed his determination to make her his wife. The Duke, whose fears of a clandestine marriage were now renewed, summoned Worcester home to Badminton, from where he sent Harriette numerous 'dismal accounts' of his parents' persecution of him.

Harriette was just beginning to become 'most miserably tired of the Beaufort story' when she received a visit from the Duke's lawyer, 'a notorious swindler', she wrote contemptuously, called Mr Robinson. She had in her possession, Robinson said, numerous love letters from the Marquis in which he had made her promises of marriage: if she were to hand over each and every one of these letters, and take an oath at Westminster Hall that she had done so, 'you may make your own terms with his Grace', he promised her.

Harriette asked for a week in which to think the matter over, and in that time she took Worcester's letters, which covered the two years they had been together, both to her own lawyer, Thomas Treslove, Esq., of Lincoln's Inn, and to Henry Brougham, one of the greatest lawyers and statesmen of his day,* who were in agreement that if the

---

* Brougham had made his name by his brilliant defence of Queen Caroline at George IV's attempt in 1820 to divorce her. At some stage he was probably one of Harriette's clients; in later life he was to pay her a small annuity.

matter came to a court of law, the letters could be worth as much as £20,000 (£1 million).*

When Harriette met Robinson again she told him this, and he confessed that the Duke, realising the letters' worth, hoped that Harriette would come to terms privately with the family. Harriette declined his offer, writing instead to the Duke herself, enclosing all the letters and declaring: 'I will not sell the proofs of respect and affection which had been generously tendered to me.'

Worcester, by his father's contrivance, was now posted to Spain as the Duke of Wellington's aide-de-camp. At first Harriette considered following him there, but even though preparations were made for her, and a new maid hired for the purpose, eventually they had to abandon the plan. The army would not be stationary, and if Harriette remained in Lisbon, she reasoned, she would see no more of Worcester than if she had remained in England.

'We must then be separated for one year, since there is no remedy: but,' said Worcester, 'I shall declare to my father that, at the end of that time, we will part no more. He has implored me to make a trial of a year's absence, and I have consented; but in twelve months from the day I leave you, supposing I am not on my road to join you in England, remember, you are to come to me.'

'This I promised,' Harriette wrote, 'should the thing be practicable.'

But the thing was not really practicable. Harriette's liaison with Worcester had lasted two years, and she was fond of him – the last two weeks before his departure for Spain were spent by both of them in 'a superabundance of tears' – but neither was a steady enough character to last out a whole year's separation, as doubtless the Beauforts realised. No sooner had Worcester left the country than Harriette received another visit from Mr Robinson. The Duke wanted to buy her off. 'Why not act with common sense?' said Robinson. 'There is His Grace of Beaufort ready to provide for you, in the most comfortable manner possible, for your whole life, in short, as I told you before, you may make your own terms, conditionally, that you never speak or write to his Lordship again.'

* The implication was that Harriette could sue Worcester for breach of promise.

Harriette, whose parting promise to Worcester had been to write to him constantly (he had promised 'at least a quire of foolscap to [her] every day'), and to continue faithfully his for a year, stood firm. But inside she was already wavering. In order to keep herself from temptation she went into self-imposed retreat in the country for a year, to a village near Lyme Regis, and it was while she was rusticating there that she heard a rumour that Worcester had another woman in Spain. Harriette did not repine. She had already met the man – the 'sugar-baron' Meyler, a gentleman 'of such voluptuous beauty, that it was impossible for any woman to converse with him . . . in cold blood' – who was to become her next lover. But first she made a clumsy effort to hold Worcester's father to his promise.

Harriette had been living off a small allowance paid to her quarterly by the Duke of Beaufort, but the arrangement was not a formal one, and she had never had anything in writing, being, as she put it, 'always so perfectly independent and careless of her own interests and welfare'. These payments now mysteriously ceased, and Harriette was soon in debt. She wrote to the Duke, suggesting that she was now ready to sever her connection with Worcester, and reminded him that he had promised her an annuity of £500. The Duke replied that he had never mentioned such a tremendous sum, and offered her £300 a year instead. Harriette eventually accepted this, then retracted when she heard that the rumour about Worcester had been false. When she changed her mind again, the Duke's lawyers used this as an excuse to whittle the sum down to just £200.

The condition of Harriette's Beaufort annuity was that she should 'never once write to Lord Worcester, nor hold any kind of communication with him'. But no one stipulated that Worcester should not write to her, which he did: three or four 'very pathetic letters', first to Harriette's sister Fanny, and finally one to Harriette herself in the same style. 'He wished me happy: he knew well that he should never be allowed to see me again: he did not think I could have agreed never to write or speak to him again.' Foolishly, she wrote back.

Harriette had received only one payment of £100 from Worcester's family when one of their lawyers presented himself at her house with the request that she return the money: 'Lord Worcester has acquainted his father that you have written to him, and therefore, since you are not entitled to that £100, the Duke insists on its being returned.' Harriette was incredulous. But Beaufort, apparently, was intransigent: 'His Grace, being no longer obliged to do anything, will never give you £20 as long as he lives,' the lawyer told her.

'Not if I continue separated from Worcester?'

'Certainly not, even then. The fact is His Grace believes that his son has left you altogether.'

'What, then, is to become of me?'

'That is a matter of perfect indifference to His Grace, and also to me.'

Perhaps if the Beauforts had been more generous to Harriette, and had provided for her as she claimed they always promised they would, she would never have had cause to write her famous *Memoirs*; but if that had been the case, the world would have been deprived of one of the most sparklingly vivid documents of the early nineteenth century, and arguably its most famous case of mass blackmail.

After Harriette's betrayal by Worcester, she and Meyler became lovers, although theirs was a bitter and jealous passion which further exhausted Harriette and sapped her energies. In 1815 they drifted to Paris together, but soon parted, and it was there that Harriette was to spend a large part of the next ten years of her life. It was in Paris that she came to write the story of her life as we have it today – written 'in a sort of shorthand, the first volume in six days'[25] – which in 1825 was to explode upon London with all the force of a small atom bomb.

Not much is known about the last years of Harriette's life. Between 1821 and 1823, after her affair with Meyler, she fell into the clutches of a man named William Henry Rochfort. Rochfort – who called himself 'Colonel', although he had no claim to this rank, despite having seen some form of military service in India – was a flashy, bullying swindler about whom no one has ever had a kind word to say. Nor has anyone ever been able to explain what his hold on Harriette really was. Obviously the flashy, swindling type was attractive to her; and it has also been plausibly suggested that the 'Colonel' bore a certain physical resemblance to her adored Ponsonby. Either way, Harriette, who was now in her forties, fell for him sufficiently to go through a form of marriage – probably a so-called 'Fleet' marriage, by then of doubtful legality – after which she paid all his debts and helped to extract him from debtors' prison. From prison the 'Colonel' moved to Paris with a now impoverished Harriette, and it was from here, in a desperate attempt to support them both, that her *Memoirs* were written.

The *Memoirs of Harriette Wilson* were published in twelve paper-covered parts between January and April 1825. They caused an immediate sensation. The clubs of Pall Mall were alternately scandalised and electrified by their contents; jokes were made in the House; and barricades were erected outside the publisher Stockdale's shop in the Haymarket to hold back the besieging mobs.

At the end of each instalment was an advertisement giving the names of the people to be mentioned in the next number, thus giving them the chance to buy themselves out – if they had not already done so on receipt of one of Harriette's special blackmailing letters. A wealthy merchant and politician, Edward 'Bear' Ellice, who received one such missive, with some courage immediately communicated it to all the daily and Sunday newspapers of standing. It was published in full (complete with grammar and spelling mistakes).

> *March 8th No 111 Rue du Faubourg St Honoré, à Paris.*
>> *Sir,*
>> *People are buying themselves so fast out of my book, Memoirs of Harriette Wilson, that I have no time to attend to them should be sorry not to give each a chance, if they chuse to be out. Two noble Dukes have lately taken my word, and I have never named them, I am sure – would say you might trust me never to publish, or cause to be published, aught about you, if you like to forward £200 [£10,000] directly to me, else it will be too late, as the last volume in which you shine, will be the property of the Edetor, and in his hands . . . Do just as you like – consult only yourself. I get as much by a small book as*

you will give me for taking you out, or more. I attack no poor
men because they cannot help themselves.
  Adieu. Mind I have no time to write again as what with
writing books, and then altering them for those who pay out, I
am done up – frappé en mort.
  What do you think of my French?
  Yours,
  Harriette Rochfort late Wilson
  Don't trust to bag with your letter.[26]

If Harriette ever amused herself by wondering what effect her letters
would have on their recipients, she had no further to look – had she
been able – than Walter Scott's correspondence and diaries. A friend,
Lord Montagu, had written to Scott mentioning the *Memoirs*, and
explaining that the entire Cabinet was deeply engrossed in reading
them. George Canning had said that they were very clever. Lord Melville, on the other hand, felt they were extremely dull. Scott immediately decided that he must read them for himself. 'I am impatient to
see Harriot Wilson's biography and have sent an order for it accord-
ingly,' he replied on 18 February. 'I remember (what I trust in Provi-
dence she has forgotten) that I had some 25 years ago the honour of
supping with the fair authoress, not tête a tête however but vis-à-vis,
at one of the evening parties of Matt. Lewis where the company was
sometimes chosen in that genre. I wont give a hundred guineas however
to be struck out of the catalogue. I remember she was ugly – remarkably
witty – and society men courted her for her mental [rather] than [her]
personal accomplishments . . . It is impossible but that the work must
be a delicious scandal,' he concluded, 'and I will bet on Canning's side
without having seen a letter of it.'[27]
  On the whole, the overall authenticity of Harriette's material was
not doubted by her contemporaries. Brooks's, which held a meeting
about it, as Poodle Byng reported to Lord Granville, the British
Ambassador in Paris, decided there was nothing to be done about it
'in the way of opposition'. Lord Alvanley, when quizzed, admitted that
Harriette had been 'pretty correct' in her depiction of people and
events, and Walter Scott himself wrote in his diary after he had read

the *Memoirs*, 'there is some good retailing of conversations', and that the style of the speakers, so far as they were known to him, was 'exactly imitated'. 'After all,' he added, half-admiringly, 'H.W. beats Con Philips, Anne Bellamy,* and all former demi-reps out and out.'

Some of Harriette's victims paid up (it was widely thought that the King and his mistress Lady Conyngham were among them), and some, like the Duke of Wellington, brazened it out (although he never did say 'Publish and be damned'). Others sued. All in all, despite the numerous lawsuits for libel and damages now besieging Stockdale, Harriette and Rochfort are said 'to have fingered £10,000 [half a million pounds] of the public's money'.

What became of these great riches? Harriette had always intended to use them to procure herself the annuity she had so long hoped for, which would keep her in her old age – 'If I only can get 100£ a year no friend of mine shall ever be troubled with me again,' she wrote to her friend and erstwhile lover Henry Brougham, the lawyer and later Lord High Chancellor. But it was not to be. The likelihood is that the swindling Rochfort, who several years later deserted Harriette for another woman, squandered most of the profits.

Harriette made various attempts to make money in other ways – her two novels, *Clara Gazul* and *Paris Lions and London Tigers*, belong to this period, but her skill was at writing about what she knew at first hand, and both novels were so atrocious that they never had any chance of commercial success.

In the manuscript library of University College, London, is a slim orange folder containing some of the last letters that Harriette ever wrote. They are addressed to Brougham, whom she had at last persuaded to give her a small allowance. It was Brougham's money, and another small remuneration from Lord Tankerville, on which Harriette now depended for her survival.

The letters are written on thin, parchment-like paper; the remains of pieces of cracked sealing wax still hang off them. When I opened and read them, in Harriette's own hand, I was almost overwhelmed by the thin breath of the past, and the feeling of a life slowly guttering.

* Authors of earlier memoirs about the half-world.

At first the letters are written in a fine, strong copperplate. On 30 June 1828, Harriette informed Brougham that, for economy's sake, she was now living in Dieppe.

> *Do me the charity to send me the 20£ on the day you receive this or the next day as I am so miserably distressed, the least delay in my present very unfortunate circumstances will be severely felt . . . Lord Tankerville has had my receipt for some time. It is due the same day if you happened to see him perhaps you will tell him you have heard from me that I am much distressed and offer to forward me his 20£ . . . Pray use no delay as I am in a strange Inn without a frank [sic].*[28]

Almost entirely friendless now (her favourite sister Fanny was dead), and in increasing ill-health, Harriette tried every means she could think of to persuade Brougham to pay her the money on time, as it was the only thing between her and real destitution. He was a 'mere cold blooded calculating lawyer', she told him, but (in the same letter) the old Harriette cajoled him: 'I want to have somebody to love and like and look up to whose understanding I am not ashamed of from the moral certainty I feel that mine is superior – and there's nobody but *you*.'[29]

But Brougham, although he did continue to pay Harriette – when he remembered – seems almost wilfully not to have understood what was now a desperate situation. 'My wishes are moderate and reasonable – you eventually comply with them *all*, but *never* at *once* handsomely and as if you wished to save me uneasiness,' she wrote to him from Brighton a few years later. 'What did you gain by obliging me to sell my old favourite good piano forte (in a hurry to avoid a broker taking it for my landlord's rent) for £5 – for which I could in a little time easily have got 20£ – and then when all the mischief was done, and my fever increased by the agitation of these bailiffs in the house etc you sent me 25£ instead of the ten I required to make up the debt. I hate all suspense worse than poverty.' As her despair increases, the fine, firm copperplate turns into a thick, ugly scrawl. 'For my part the mere existence out of pain makes me as happy as I can wish to be,' she added unhappily, '– but it never lasts an hour together as does my sleep.'[30]

This letter, the very last that has survived in Harriette's own hand, seems written in a great express train rush. The lines are at first bunched narrowly together, then they separate, and seem to veer wildly off the page. The writing becomes blotched, underlined, the words frenziedly scored and underscored: '30£ – 40£ – 5£ – grateful – send me – assistance – lend me – receipt – advance – DEBTS'.

It is thought that Harriette Wilson died, aged fifty-nine, on 10 March 1845, still, by the narrowest of margins, a woman of 'independent means'.

4

CORA PEARL
1835–1886

The Parisian Courtesan

W HEN HARRIETTE WILSON first went to Paris, sometime shortly after the restoration of the Bourbons in 1815, she did so in the company of a large section of English society. Eager to put the war behind them and to savour once again the cosmopolitan delights of France, scores of English aristocrats, together with their wives and families, braved the notoriously bad roads and the ruinous cost of travelling, only to find at their journeys' end a very different Paris from the one they remembered.

The Allies who first entered the city had found one half of it a building site, the other in a state of ruinous neglect. The Arc de Triomphe was then only half-finished; the Champs Elysées consisted of a few scattered buildings; the roads and pathways running off them, even at the very heart of the city, were ankle-deep in mud; and the only street lighting was a few dim lamps strung across the road on cords.

Forty years later, however, when another British courtesan was preparing an invasion of the city all of her own, things were very different. Haussmann was already well advanced in his monumental scheme for rebuilding Paris, which now gleamed beneath the febrile sun of the

Second Empire.* For some of the old guard, such as Captain Rees Gronow, who had known the earlier metropolis, it was not only the buildings that had changed. French cookery and fashions had both become more elaborate and over-ornamented; and as for the women, they were unrecognisable. 'In former days, we old fellows may remember the French type of womanhood which was *une petite femme mignonne et brune*,' wrote Gronow – a pretty little brunette – but this was no longer the case. Instead of the grand but curiously dowdy – some even thought vulgar – great ladies of the *ancien régime*, now it was the chic young Empress, the wife of the upstart Napoleon III, who set the fashions.† It was she, for instance, who had made both pale complexions and fair hair *à la mode*, 'which with gold powder and light wigs they *do* succeed'. But this was not all. A puzzled Gronow wrote: 'One sees dozens of gigantic women every day that one goes out, perhaps even with stilts under those long sweeping petticoats. I know not how the change has been effected, but there it is.'[1]

For the younger generation of *boulevardiers*, Paris and its women had never been more bewitching. Only the French language really expresses it: '*Paris est radieux*,' wrote the Comte de Maugny ('Zed') in his delicious chronicle of the Parisian *demi-monde* of this time, subtitled *Souvenirs d'un sybarite*, '*élégant, pimpant, raffiné, animé. Paris s'amuse à tire-larigot*' (Paris is radiant, elegant, spruce, refined, animated. Paris amuses itself to its heart's content). Moneyed, sophisticated, ebulliently *nouveau*, there were few people who so perfectly reflected the spirit of the times as a young woman named Cora Pearl.

* After the abdication of Louis-Phillipe, the 'Citizen King', in 1848, France was proclaimed a republic once more. At the end of the short but bloody civil war that followed in 1851 Louis-Napoleon Bonaparte, the nephew of Napoleon I, was elected President. He was proclaimed Emperor the year after, and became Napoleon III.
† 'No one,' wrote Gronow, 'who has not arrived at my age, and lived in Paris, can form any idea of the insolence and hauteur of the higher classes of society in 1815. The glance of unutterable disdain which the painted old duchesses of the Restoration cast upon the youthful belles of the Chaussée d'Antin, or the handsome widows of Napoleon's army of heroes, defies description.'

Perhaps no English courtesan ever excited quite so much controversy as Cora Pearl. And yet despite her pre-eminence in the *demi-monde* of the Second Empire, hardly anyone who knew her seems to have been in agreement about her. Many thought her vulgar; some found her positively off-putting – 'Cora Pearl, with her clown's head, sewer of a mouth, and most comical English accent',[2] wrote the man of letters Alphonse Daudet unkindly in his diary. But even he was forced to concede that she was very sexy, and that her body was second to none. When she became old, despised by some, he defended her by pointing out what he called '*la jeunesse miraculeuse de cette chair de sorcière après 30 ans de fournaise*' (the miraculous youth of that sorceress's flesh after thirty years of blaze). '*L'inexplicable Cora Pearl,*' wrote the Comte de Maugny. 'I swear it is a success that I have never understood ... *quel philtre secret pourait-elle bien avoir?*'

What was her secret? No one could deny that Cora fascinated men. Unlike Harriette Wilson, who was essentially a good-time girl dunned into high-class prostitution as a means of paying her bills, Cora was an out-and-out professional, and she made no bones about the fact. At the height of her career, according to the Comte de Maugny's calculations, she commanded an income in excess of fifty thousand francs a month (the equivalent today of over £90,000) in addition to the jewels, the wardrobe, the horses and carriages which she acquired, '*à nul autre pareils*'.

'Cora had system, plenty of system,' wrote the Comte de Maugny. 'One day we found an extraordinary account-book at her house, divided into three columns. In one was the name of her clients, mostly well-known names and friends, in another the date of their ... *séjour*; and in the third the sum poured out for the hospitality received.' At this point a metaphorical sweat begins to break out on the Count's brow. '*Il y avait même, Dieu me pardonne, dans le fatal registre, une colonne d'observations. Pas aimables pour tout le monde, ces observations!*'[3] (There was also, God forgive me, in this terrible register, a column of observations. Not very agreeable for everyone, these observations!)

It was not only in her tidy business sense that Cora was professional; she was punctilious in every other sense, too. Cora Pearl was not an instinctive courtesan in the way that some of her fellow *demi-mondaines* undoubtedly were – the sensual Italian Giulia Beneni, known as 'La Barucci', for example, or Léonide Leblanc, who rejoiced in the sobriquet 'Madame Maximum' (although whether this was for her unique services, or her price, no one is quite clear). By her own admission, Cora had always 'preserved an instinctive mistrust of men' (the word she uses in French is *rancune*), even though she also claimed that there were many male friends and well-wishers for whom she always had a real affection. It was perhaps for this reason – a certain detachment when it came to her numerous patrons – that Cora was able to play at the role of courtesan with such brilliant success.

And play at it she did. Although, like Harriette, Cora was not conventionally beautiful, she had extraordinary physical allure, and was not afraid to use it. Marie Colombier, a fellow courtesan who knew Cora well, wrote in her memoirs that Cora personified what she called '*le style anglais de la courtisanerie*'. Hers, she said scathingly, was the '*genre écurie*' (the stable-boy type). She was above all a sportswoman, who walked bow-legged and rode like a jockey, making her riding crop whistle, and who drank '*sec et souvent*' (in other words often, and to the bottom of the glass – although Cora was in fact known to be very restrained in this respect).

Although this is somewhat spitefully put, it does give us a clue to the secret of Cora's fascination. The erotic energy and earthiness which she exuded, which some found distasteful, were almost unbearably exciting to the men who desired her. Theatrical and exhibitionist, Cora was also extremely feminine. Emile Zola, who portrayed her in his realist masterpiece *Nana* as the courtesan Lucy Stewart, after meticulous research amongst the now-ageing *boulevardiers* of Paris, wrote of her 'laughing grace of manner' and of her tremendous *chic*, which together had the effect of completely obscuring the fact that she was plain 'to the point of ugliness', and had a face like a horse. Besides, as Lucy herself says in the novel, 'Good looks were nothing . . . a good figure was all that mattered.'[4]

In real life this was certainly true. Even her fiercest detractors were agreed that Cora's body was a marvel of nature. Her waist was tiny, her shoulders shapely and fashionably sloped; but it was her breasts that were her greatest perfection. Marie Colombier, reminiscing about a dinner at the Café Anglais at which both she and Cora had been present, wrote of Cora's faultless '*poitrine de déesse*' (breasts of a goddess). Looking for some imperfection, she convinced herself that Cora must have had to colour her nipples with make-up, so perfect was the pale rose at their tips, which appeared as if '*dérobé aux pétales des églantines*' (hidden in the petals of wild roses). She retained this perfection, added Marie, even after her face had succumbed to the ravages of time.[5]

Who exactly was this charming enigma, Cora Pearl? Or rather, who was 'Cora Pearl'? – for her name, like so much else about her, was all invention. The woman who rose to become one of the dozen or so most *de luxe* courtesans of the most luxurious *demi-monde* that the world has ever known was in fact the creation of a young, lower-middle-class Englishwoman called Eliza Emma Crouch. She was born in 1835* in Plymouth in Devonshire, into a family of mildly talented but feckless musicians and musical 'artistes'. Her father, Frederick William Nicholls Crouch, was a teacher of music and the composer of a briefly famous song, 'Kathleen Mavourneen'; her mother Lydia was a singer, and at least one of her four sisters, Ciantha, also became one. Her childhood home, Cora later recalled, was so noisy that it became known as 'The Musical Box'.

In her *Memoirs*, Cora claimed that her father died when she was five, but it seems that he in fact deserted his wife and family and emigrated to America (where according to one source he went on to remarry three times, fathering no fewer than twenty-seven children[6]). Her mother remarried very rapidly, and Cora's siblings from these two marriages, so she claimed, totalled sixteen.

Cora heartily disliked her stepfather, while her brothers were hardly ever in the house. 'I cannot remember what each of them did, there were so many. There were big ones, little ones, dark ones, fair ones, to suit all tastes, in short.'[7] The young Cora was sent away to boarding school in Boulogne for eight years, where she learned to speak passable

---

* The birth certificate which she reproduced in her *Memoirs*, giving her date of birth as 1842, was also an invention. It is an obvious forgery, bearing a crude amendment which knocked a convenient seven years from Cora's actual age. The certificate was originally that of her younger sister Louisa.

French, and became sufficiently attached to her companions to regret having to return to her own country.

Back in London, Cora did not go back to her mother's house, but went to live instead with her maternal grandmother, who like so many of Cora's relations had also been a singer. Although Cora does not say so in her *Memoirs*, there is evidence to suggest that for some time during this period she worked in a milliner's shop. After her death in 1886, a friend of the Crouch family, who had been to school with the younger girls, wrote a letter to the *Daily News* claiming that she had known Cora around this time (1854–55), when she was 'about seventeen' (in fact she would have been nineteen), and was apprenticed to a milliner in Regent Street. 'From thence she disappeared,' wrote the anonymous friend, 'and was never heard of by her mother until about a year before the fall of the empire.'[8]

The story as Cora later told it is as follows. On Sundays she visited her mother, an extremely devout woman, who sent her to church with a servant to chaperone her. One day Cora came out after the service to find that the girl had gone. 'I was not used to be out alone,' she wrote. 'I found it very amusing, and set out to make my way home.' Along the way she was followed by a man of about forty years of age.

> *He accosted me.*
> *'Where are you going to, my little girl?'*
> *'To my grandmother's, sir.'*
> *'Does your grandmother live hereabouts?'*
> *'Oh, no, sir.'*
> *He then said: 'I am sure you like cakes.'*
> *I blushed a little, smiled, and did not answer.*
> *'Come with me and I will give you some.'*[9]

Cora followed the gentleman. 'How kind; what pleasant people one meets; how grandmother will laugh when I tell her my story.' She had no mistrust, she remembered. 'I knew nothing of anything, but I was a little astonished and almost as much amused.' The man took her to a large house behind Covent Garden market. On the corner she remembered seeing a ragged little urchin boy, and giving him a penny: 'it is strange how trivial incidents sometimes impress themselves on our mind'. The room they went into was very low, and filled with people laughing and drinking. The air was so thick with smoke that she was almost suffocated. Instead of offering her the cakes he had promised, the man sat down beside her, lit his pipe and asked if she would like some gin.

> The grog was not brought and he went away to seek it. I had an idea of running away, but what would the gentleman think? . . . [He] came back, carrying a glass upon a saucer. His appearance, I know not why, reminded me of an undermistress we had at school, and whom we used to call 'Quinine', because she was in charge of the infirmary. But the grog was sickening, the atmosphere reeking with smoke, the noise more and more deafening. Some one brought me the cakes, but I could not touch them, my head was so heavy. I fell asleep upon my chair.[10]

When she awoke the next morning she found herself lying in a strange bed, with the unknown gentleman beside her. 'It was one more child ruined – wickedly, bestially,' wrote Cora shortly. 'I have never pardoned men, neither this one nor the others who are not responsible for this act.'

The man gave her money – £5 – and, while he was getting dressed, offered to keep her with him, but Cora was too stupefied to answer. 'Everything appeared to me like a nightmare,' she wrote. 'I hoped for some shock that might awake me.' But none came. The man waited for a while, sitting near the table, cigarette in hand. His arms were crossed over his waistcoat, Cora remembered, 'from which hung a gold chain with huge lockets. He sat and twiddled his thumbs.' She told him bluntly that she did not wish to go with him.

Some commentators on Cora Pearl's life have been sceptical about this story, with its air of penny-novelettish melodrama, but in mid-nineteenth-century London it was only too likely to be true, for the shameful trade in children and young women on the streets of the Victorian city is well known. In her *Memoirs* Cora tells the story as if she had indeed been only a little girl of thirteen, fearful of being taken for 'a silly child' and as jealous of her dignity as 'almost a grown up girl'. If however, as seems probable, she was about nineteen when this incident took place, it is no less believable. The connection between young girls working in milliners' shops and prostitution was so marked in mid-nineteenth-century London as to be almost a cliché.

Whatever the truth of the matter, one thing was certain: it was now impossible for Cora to return home. 'Soon I realised what had happened,' she wrote, 'and that I could never more darken the doors of either my mother or my grandmother.' With characteristic resilience, she did not waste time in tears or regrets, but went instead to a lodging house which she had seen nearby, inhabited by clerks and working women, and found a room for herself. Then, with the £5 her seducer had given her she bought some clothes at a second-hand shop, 'and did everything in a practical way which astonishes me today when I think of it'.

Although the lodgings which she had acquired were very simple, consisting of a bed, a table and a little cupboard, it was not long before Cora began to enjoy herself. She did not miss her family – the bonds with them had long since been severed by her eight-year sojourn at boarding school in Boulogne. But it was her new-found independence which was the greatest revelation: 'Moreover, was it not a real satisfaction to be able to say to myself "I am at home, in a home of my own?"' she wrote. 'I could not count upon anybody but myself, I knew that. I looked the situation squarely in the face and was confident in my destiny. I have never seen again the man who played wolf to my Little Red Riding Hood. He was, it appears, a diamond merchant.'[11]

Eliza Emma Crouch was dead: long live Cora Pearl.

Cora, as she now called herself – 'from no particular reason, but purely from fancy' – soon found herself an admirer, a man who appears in her *Memoirs* as Bill Blinkwell ('Williams Bluckel' in the French edition), but who has been identified by her biographer W.H. Holden as Robert Bignell, the proprietor of the Argyle Dance Rooms.* The once high-class Argyle Rooms, where a generation previously Harriette Wilson

* In the memoirs Cora changed the name to the Albrecht Rooms.

and her fellow demi-reps were alleged to have given their annual Cyprians' Ball, had moved from its original premises to Great Windmill Street, where they had become one of the most popular nightspots in London.

Although, in his monumental study of prostitution published in 1857, William Acton was favourably impressed by the relative decorum of the Argyle Rooms, there is no doubt that this was not a place which could be frequented by any woman who valued the usual proprieties. The Rooms were the best-known of a number of casinos, or dance halls, which had recently come into existence in London, and which formed a prominent and relatively novel feature of early and mid-Victorian night life. 'The visitor, on passing the doors, finds himself in a spacious room, the fittings of which are of the most costly description, while brilliant gas illuminations, reflected by numerous mirrors, impart a fairy-like aspect to the scene,' was Acton's description.

Admission to the ground-floor dance hall cost one shilling, but an extra charge was made to those wishing to go up into the first-floor gallery, which was fitted all the way around with small alcoves with plush-covered benches, perfect for private assignations. Similar establishments included Laurent's Dancing Academy, also in Windmill Street, and the smaller and more luxurious Portland Rooms, otherwise known as Mott's, where for many years full evening dress, white tie and tails, was required of male patrons.[12]

It was the Holborn Casino, however (also known as the Casino de Venise), a 'cheerful, bouncy, sober sort of place', in which the rumbustious and newly-popular polkas and quadrilles* were danced in a huge and brilliantly lit hall, which was the Argyle Rooms' chief rival. When Acton visited it he was predictably sour in his impressions: 'the brilliant ballroom, glittering with a myriad prisms . . . was given over to a troop of dancing dervishes. The frenzy of these fanatics was stimulated not by poisonous champagne and spirits, but by the act of dancing, glasses of bitter beer, and bottles of soda water.'[13]

On the whole, though, Acton did not find much difference between

---

* The can-can (or *chahut*), which first came into vogue in Paris in the 1830s, was a form of quadrille.

the Casino and the Argyle Rooms. The women in both places, he wrote, were for the most part 'pretty and quietly, though expensively dressed, while delicate complexions, unaccompanied by the pallor of ill-health, are neither few nor far between'* – although this, he felt sure, was due to 'the artistic manner of the make-up by powder and cosmetics, on the employment of which extreme care is bestowed'.[14] They were, in his estimation, 'of course' all prostitutes.

After her violation by the diamond merchant, and her decision not to return to her grandmother's house, relatively few options were available to Cora for earning her living. Given her subsequent career, it seems reasonable to conjecture that she now turned to the most obvious of these – prostitution – to make ends meet. William Acton's vivid description of one of the most striking of the Argyle Rooms' women brings to mind, irresistibly, a picture of what Cora – with all her generosity and her genius for theatrical display – might have been like in her early English incarnation.

One woman merits a passing notice here, who had achieved a sudden notoriety, and given to the casino . . . a pre-eminence over its rival. There she holds a mimic court, attired unlike the rest of the frequenters, who come in their bonnets, in full ball dress. She is surrounded by a crowd of admirers, idlers, and would-be imitators, and gives the tone to the establishment that she patronises. It is said that the diamonds worn by this woman are worth £5000.† She is supplied daily from a florist in Covent Garden with a bouquet of the choicest flowers, amid which are interspersed specimens of the most beautifully coloured beetles, the cost being about 30s, and her habit on entering the rooms is to

---

* Acton, like many Victorians, believed that the effects of vice and general depravity were bound to show in the physiognomy of the face, and he makes frequent use of appearance as empirical evidence of 'vice'. 'I saw many an etiolated eye,' he wrote of the women who frequented the Cremorne Gardens in London, 'and blanched chaotic complexion, due to want of sun and air, and general defibrinization . . . There was, here and there, a deplorable hectic flush, distinguishable enough from carmine; and I noticed a great prevalence of sunken eyes, drawn features, and thin lips, resulting from that absorption of the cellular tissue which leaves mere threads of muscle stretched upon the skull' – the effects, he believed, not only of prostitution but of the 'dancing mania' which had recently hit London.

† Nearly a quarter of a million pounds today.

present this really splendid trifle to the female attendant at the wine bar, as a mark of her condescension and favour. On permission to visit her being requested, she would probably, like another celebrated 'fille de joie', take out her pocket-book and, after a careless glance at it, reply that she was full of engagements, but that if the petitioner would call at her house at a given hour that day week, she would, perhaps, spare him some twenty minutes of her society, for which favour she might expect the modest sum of £25.[15] [Acton was being ironic: today this would be just over £1000.]

But of course this might not have been Cora's case at all. She had been trained as a milliner, and could quite easily have found herself a perfectly respectable job (although how easy it would have been to live on a milliner's wages is another matter; it is well documented that many otherwise blamelessly employed women were forced to supplement their income through occasional prostitution).

It is beyond question that prostitution in London in the mid-nineteenth century took place on a vast scale; but just how vast has always been open to debate. In the 1860 edition of William Acton's weighty tome three separate figures are given for the total number of female prostitutes then thought to be operating in London: 9409 (estimated by the Home Office authorities in 1841); fifty thousand (estimated by a magistrate at the Thames Police Court 'sixty years ago'); and a fantastic eighty thousand (estimated by both the Bishop of Exeter and a certain Mr Talbot from the Society for the Protection of Young Females). This latter figure seems barely credible – a figment of an increasingly feverish Victorian imagination* – until it becomes clear that, by some lights, any woman who had sexual relations with a man other than her husband was considered to be in a state of prostitution.

In the volume on prostitution in his monumental work of

* The Victorians themselves were sometimes inclined to agree. A contemporary joke tells of a woman standing in the street when an ardent-looking evangelist rushes up to her with a religious tract in his hands. Thrusting it towards her, he implores her to go home and read it. 'Lor' bless you, sir,' says the woman, 'I ain't a social evil, I'm just waiting for the bus.'

documentation, *London Labour and the London Poor* (1862), Henry Mayhew saved his particular opprobrium for women whom he considered to be part-time, or 'clandestine' prostitutes, by which he meant 'sempstresses, milliners, servant girls, etc . . . who only prostitute themselves occasionally to men they are well acquainted with, for whom they must have some sort of partiality – women who do not lower themselves in the social scale for money but for their own gratification'. He believed that at least one in three of these 'female operatives' was unchaste – the 'tone of morality' among servant maids in the metropolis he believed to be particularly low – although even he admitted that this assertion could never be authenticated.

> *A thousand and one causes may lead to a woman's becoming a professional prostitute, but if a woman goes wrong without any very cogent reason for doing so, there must be something radically wrong in her composition, and inherently bad in her nature, to lead her to abandon her person to the other sex, who are at all times ready to take advantage of a woman's weakness and a woman's love.*[16]

Even a cursory look at any one of the numerous nineteenth-century works dealing with sex and the sex industry enables one to see that far from being repressed, many Victorians were completely obsessed with their own biology. (It has been suggested recently that many of these quasi-medical and sociological books, while protesting high-mindedness, might actually have been written, and were certainly read as, pornography; and it is true that there is a decidedly piquant narrative quality about both Mayhew and Acton which bears this out, and which explains why they make such riveting reading today.[17]) Rather than being either ignored or denied, the whole notion of female sexuality was the subject of hot debate throughout the nineteenth century – an important adjunct to the much wider debate about a woman's role and nature, and her political and civic place in the world, which was also gathering strength.

Perhaps as a response to women's growing articulateness and demands for reform, William Acton's views on the female libido were to become extremely influential around this time (although he always had his critics, who forcefully argued the reverse). By presenting women as sexually neutered creatures, he told many men what they wanted to hear.* Undeterred by the dominant tradition of many centuries which held that women were not merely passionate beings, but positive 'vessels of lust', Acton has the dubious distinction of having misled entire generations of historians into thinking that the ideal Victorian woman really was, or was supposed to be, as he chose to depict her: 'The majority of women (happily for them) are not very much troubled by sexual feelings of any kind,' was his view. 'What men are habitually, women are only exceptionally.' These exceptional women were 'essentially aberrant creatures, nymphomaniacs, either potential, or actual, inmates of insane asylums'.[18]†

Having successfully fetishised female purity amongst 'good' women, Acton, naturally enough, saw unbridled sexuality absolutely everywhere amongst the 'bad'. Many of his judgements about the women he describes are based on pure conjecture – the Cora figure at the Argyle Rooms, for instance, would 'probably' look at her pocket-book and charge £25 – and are coloured as much by his own anxieties about female desire and independence as by any more objective criteria. Upper-class courtesans are depicted by him as whitewashed sepulchres – 'fair to the eye, but full of inner rottenness' – who prey upon poor, weak, defenceless men; while lower-class prostitutes are often labelled as such simply because they are women living communally together (sometimes having a thoroughly good time in the process).

In one of innumerable classifications, Acton lists 'Houses in Which Prostitutes Lodge', which he describes as rooms over shops, or groups of lodging houses clustered together, probably not unlike the one

---

* Many of Acton's remarks on female sexual anaesthesia seem to have been designed not so much to squash women, as to reassure men: 'No nervous or feeble young man need . . . be deterred from marriage by an exaggerated notion of the duties required from him,' he wrote. 'The married woman has no wish to be treated on the footing of a mistress.' See Peter Gay, *The Bourgeois Experience: The Education of the Senses.*

† For all the critics who argued to the contrary, Acton's views were so satisfying to many men that he was still being echoed nearly half a century later by the influential German physician Krafft-Ebing, who in his *Psychopathia Sexualis* (1886) wrote: 'If she is normally developed mentally, and well-brought up, [a woman's] sensual desire is small. Were it not so, the whole world would be a bordello, and marriage and the family unthinkable . . . the woman who pursues sexual gratification [is] abnormal.'

in which Cora lived, cheap bedsits with shared kitchen and washing facilities.* Independent working women of all kinds – the aforementioned milliners, seamstresses and servant girls† – congregated here; but, wrote Acton darkly, in manners, habits and dress, all would inevitably be brought down to the lowest level: 'Stupid from beer, or fractious from gin, they swear and chatter brainless stuff all day, about men and millinery, their own schemes and adventures ... as a heap of rubbish will ferment, so surely will a number of virtuous women thus collected deteriorate.'[19]

Whatever Cora's early career may have been, it was not until she reached Paris, which she did sometime towards the end of the 1850s, that she really 'deteriorated', as Acton might have said. And, like everything else, she did this with the most spectacular success. 'There are women who envy our lot,' she wrote at the beginning of her *Memoirs*: 'mansions, diamonds, carriages! ... What gilded dreams!' In the course of her long career, Cora realised them all. 'If louis are made to roll, and diamonds to glitter,' she wrote jauntily, 'I cannot be reproached with having perverted from their normal uses these noble things. With the latter I glittered, the former I set rolling.' But her greatest triumph, as she recognised as she looked back on her life, lay in none of these material things: 'I have never deceived anybody, because I have never belonged to anybody. My independence was all my fortune, and I have known no other happiness; and it is still what attaches me to life.'

Cora was first taken to Paris by her lover from the Argyle Rooms, Robert Bignell, who obtained a passport for himself which stated that he was travelling with his 'wife'. He had conceived 'a very tender

---

* No doubt he had in mind the etymology of 'bordello', which comes from the French *'bord et eau'* i.e. board and water.
† Mayhew also enumerated milliners, straw bonnet makers, furriers, hat-binders, silk winders, tambour workers, shoe binders, shop women, those who work for cheap tailors or pastry cooks, or in fancy and cigar shops or bazaars, and ballet girls in his list of working women who might 'swell the ranks' of the professional whores.

feeling' for Cora, she remembered, and they would often speak in French together. Although she had no great passion for Bignell, 'he had a way of saying, "*Ma chère Cora!*" which sometimes went to my heart', she wrote. 'He loved me madly, and I was rather pleased with him.'

Leaving London filled Cora with elation: 'All the houses there appeared to me to be taverns; all the drinks narcotics; all the men diamond merchants.' In Paris they stayed at the York and Albion Hotel, and saw all the sights: the Arc de Triomphe, the vaults of the Pantheon, the Tuileries. They went to concerts, to the Bois, to the theatre, they danced at Mabille: 'In short, our sojourn in Paris was one prolonged burst of laughter.' Cora was enchanted. At the end of a month, when Bignell told her that he could no longer stay away from his family and his business concerns, she was horrified. 'He might as well have said: "We must die;" the effect could not have been more disagreeable. I replied: "Go if you want to; I remain here." ' And with that she took up the passport and threw it into the fire.

Having disposed of Bignell, Cora seems to have had no difficulty in finding other admirers. First was a sailor named d'Amenard who wanted her to be his wife, but Cora had already made up her mind that she never wished to marry ('I detested men too much ever to obey one of them,' she had told poor Bignell dampeningly). Then, altogether more profitably, there followed a man called Roubise, who was received in good society and who procured Cora numerous introductions. As a result of her rapidly widening social horizons, the ambitious Cora was introduced to Victor Massena, the Duc de Rivoli (later Prince of Essling), and it was as a result of her liaison with him that she finally 'arrived'.

Victor Massena ('Lassema' in the *Memoirs*) was 'unquestionably one of the first links in my chain of gold', Cora later wrote. 'Heir of a great name of the First Empire, rich, correct in his bearing, he was still most thoughtful, most anxious to please, most adorable, and, I should add, the man who received the least in return,' recalled Cora, who – for her posthumous reputation at any rate – was always disastrously candid in these matters. 'It is a terrible thing to have to say, but there is no regulating these matters.'

She and Massena were, nevertheless, sufficiently satisfied with one another for the relationship to last six years. Over this period Cora learned from him everything that she needed to transform herself from an unknown English dollymop into one of the most luxurious courtesans in Paris. Massena, in turn, acquired a mistress of genius. Apart from her expert sensuality, the *sine qua non* of the successful courtesan, Cora had one other great talent: she was able to turn having a good time into an art form.

The Goncourt brothers, who were at one time neighbours of one of Cora's fellow *demi-mondaines*, the courtesan Ana Deslions, recalled how in the days before they knew her, Ana used to bribe their servant, on evenings when they were having people to dine, to allow her into their apartment before they returned home so that she might walk around their table 'and sate her eyes with the sight of a little luxury'.[20] Like Ana, many courtesans worked hard to acquire the skills of their profession; skills which included the correct way to lay a table for a dinner party, quite as much as erotic technique. Cora, however, seems to have been one of those women whose knowledge of such things was almost wholly instinctive.*

In the English *demi-monde* up until this time, it will perhaps come as no surprise to know, food was never held in much esteem. Harriette Wilson's sister Amy, for example, was extremely good at supplying the drink for her famous champagne suppers, but notoriously bad at the food. In Paris, as Cora – a preternaturally fast learner – soon realised, matters were different.

One of the first things she did was to hire the best cook that Massena's money could buy. The man she chose was no mere chef, but a culinary genius who 'cultivated his art in the grand manner'. 'This artist,' Cora wrote, 'was named Salé,† a fateful name, according to Cora, because besides his functions in the kitchen, Salé himself did

---

* Another woman with a similar instinctive knowledge was Victoria Sackville, the natural daughter of the late-nineteenth-century diplomatist Lord Sackville. From a secluded Paris convent, at the age of eighteen Victoria sprang, wholly untutored in worldly matters, onto the Washington social scene, to become almost overnight one of its most celebrated hostesses. See *Daughters of Britannia*.

† Literally 'salty', but when applied to a bill it means 'steep'.

the marketing, turning in accounts of which the amounts were of the most suspiciously symmetrical roundness. 'His long additions were a dream of figures,' Cora wrote; 'the awakening came at the total.'

> I was on the point of going somewhere with [Massena] one day when I was suddenly struck with the idea that we should both go into the kitchen.
> The first thing we saw was a line of five enormous pullets, huge quarters of beef, all cooked, a perfect exhibition of cold victuals. It was like the shop of some dealer in comestibles ready prepared for the table. I can make no other comparison.
> 'Who is all this for?' I said to Salé.
> 'For Monsieur le Duc.'

Since at this point Cora never had fewer than a dozen people sitting down to dine with her in the evening, wisely she did not argue.

Perhaps no English courtesan since Sophia Baddeley knew how to spend money as freely as Cora. She was already living very much in the grand manner, a style which suited her naturally theatrical bent. Cora knew instinctively what she had to do to be noticed. When the Duke went to Baden-Baden, then one of the most fashionable watering holes in Europe, she followed him. Discretion and unobtrusiveness were never in Cora's vocabulary. 'I had a tremendous train,' she wrote, 'a baggage wagon, six horses, many servants. At first I was taken for the Princess Gargamelle! I was by no means flattered thereby.'

Not everyone was taken in. When Cora presented herself at the Casino in the evening, the commissaire forbade her to pass. 'It appeared I was the object of an exceptional measure. I asked for what motive this extraordinary step was taken; why I was not permitted to go in and lose my money like, for instance, a simple marchioness?' But Cora's pretended innocence left the commissaire stony-hearted. The rule was made by order of the Queen,* she was told. To console herself Cora went to the races, and there she was spotted by a friend who sent her over a note: 'Make haste, finish your dinner. I offer you my

---

* It is not clear who this queen is. Queen Hortense, the Emperor's mother, is mentioned in the story which follows, but it is perhaps more likely to have been the Queen of Prussia, the aunt of one of Cora's friends, the English Duke of Hamilton.

arm upon which you can enter the salon.' The note was signed by the Duc de Morny (in Cora's *Memoirs* called 'Moray'), the Emperor's half-brother, and the son of Queen Hortense.* That night Cora made her entry into the room on de Morny's arm, 'passing between two lines of people who had drawn up to gaze at me'.

Cora was quick to capitalise on her growing success and notoriety. At Vichy, another watering hole much favoured by European nobility in the mid-nineteenth century, she and Massena hired a house one season, and Cora filled it with his friends. It was no use shutting the doors, she remembered; her guests simply came in through the windows: 'If at any time in my life I was really extravagant, I can honestly say that it was at Vichy that my money flew. My friends were welcome, the friends of my friends were even more so; and it was principally this which made so big a hole into my purse,' Cora wrote. 'We danced at morn, we danced at night, in fact, at last everything danced in the house, men, women, and money.' But she never regretted it, even later in her life when she could no longer make diamonds glitter and louis roll, even though she knew that it was money spent 'foolishly ... for people who came expressly to my house to amuse themselves at my expense'.

And Cora's household expenses at this time were enormous. Her chef Salé, whom she had brought with her to Vichy, continued to excel himself ('My table – the sight of it was enough – and my cook – he surpassed Vatel himself'), but at a price. 'One day I met my faithful Salé with half a sheep across his shoulder,' Cora remembered.

> '*What have you got there, Salé?*'
> '*Half a sheep, madam.*'
> '*Why half a sheep?*'
> '*Because, madam, they won't sell less.*'

Not only Salé, but all the tradespeople of Vichy profited from Cora. In just two weeks her household expenses topped thirty thousand

---

* Hortense de Beauharnais, Napoleon's stepdaughter. A great favourite of Napoleon's, she later married his brother Louis, King of Holland. The youngest of their three children became Napoleon III. The Duc de Morny was Queen Hortense's son by her lover Count Charles de Flahaut. He was later adopted by the Comte de Morny.

francs (£56,000). But it was her own extravagance, her extraordinary byzantine taste for luxurious display, that was the most crippling. In the winter months she had fruit brought to the table embedded not in moss, as was the fashion at that time, but in Parma violets, which had cost her a ruinous 1500 francs (nearly £3000). It was not merely empty extravagance which guided Cora; her instincts were the finest ones of the born hostess. Once one of her guests broke a liqueur glass, one of an extremely expensive set of which Cora was particularly proud, whereupon his hostess 'accidentally' broke another four, simply to put him at his ease.

In other respects, however, life with Massena was anything but refined. Tricks and noisy practical jokes – the throwing of firecrackers was a particular favourite – were all the rage at this time, and Cora was an enthusiastic participant. The house at Vichy had a charming garden, and in this space, which her friends laughingly called her '*parc*', Cora arranged firework displays, bonfires and illuminations, until one night one of the outhouses nearly caught fire. After that Cora confined the pyrotechnical displays to firecrackers ('*bombes*') at the table, and bowls of flaming punch.

After dinner, the men – 'all more or less vinously excited' – liked to go to the gaming rooms, which they would invade 'like an avalanche, scattering toy explosives over the floor, making a most terrible row, and shrieking at the top of their voices', wrote one of Cora's *bande* at this time, the Englishman William Osgood Field. On one particularly enthusiastic evening, according to Osgood Field, the croupiers were so frightened by the sound of the firecrackers going off that they jumped on the tables and 'sprawled over the money to protect it'.

I was in the room with two school-boy friends, and Caro Hamilton, in fun lurched me over onto a pile of the explosives, and the result was naturally an increase of noise and tumult. This battalion of Bacchanalians was now followed by a contingent of the leading Paphian priestesses; and the arrival of these be-diamonded women did not of course tend to bring peace and calm. While the croupiers were lying on their stomachs over the gold and notes on the tables, trembling with terror . . . the can-can was danced; and Prince

Hohenlohe and Prince Thurn and Taxis [brother-in-law of the Emperor of Austria] joined hands like little children and gambolled round Cora Pearl singing at the top of their voices:

> *Nous donnerons tout, même l'Allemagne,*
> *Pour aller ce soir boire du champagne*
> *Avec Madame Cora,*
> *Tra la la![21]**

Cora, with all her chameleon skills of transformation, was able not only to fit herself effortlessly into Massena's boisterous circle, but soon found that she could beat them at their own game. 'My desire to please my guests sometimes led me into eccentricities more or less amusing,' she recalled. This is doubtless the period in her life that gave rise to the legends that so richly survived her death. Even then, stories of her voluptuously extravagant tricks swelled and grew. When an admirer sent her £1000 worth of orchids, so it was said, she strewed them all over the floor of her drawing room and danced a hornpipe (another source says it was the can-can) on top of them. On another occasion she is alleged to have filled her bath with the very best vintage champagne and invited her guests to watch her in her ablutions. The most famous story about Cora, however, is the one in which at dinner one night four footmen, resplendent in her livery, came staggering into the dining room carrying a long silver dish which they placed in the centre of the table. On taking off the cover, there lay Cora herself, completely naked.† Are these stories true? On one level it does not really matter. Cora had achieved her aim: in a remarkably short space of time she had become both a spectacle and a legend.

* 'We would give everything, even Germany itself, to drink champagne this evening with Madame Cora.'

† As one commentator has remarked, the story of the eminent courtesan being dished up *au naturel* is as persistent as that of the Indian rope trick. La Belle Otero claims to have served herself like this at a banquet in St Petersburg, and Marie Duplessis, 'La Dame aux Camelias', is also rumoured to have done the same thing.

Back in Paris, the general tenor of life was a little more refined. Here, the Germanic and Anglo-Saxon influences of Baden-Baden and Vichy would not altogether do. And besides, in Paris there was stiff competition from Cora's fellow *demi-mondaines*.

In his paean of praise to these incomparable women, Zed bears witness to their great elegance and good taste. Perhaps more than any of their predecessors, the courtesans of the Second Empire cultivated a grand style that made them indistinguishable from the aristocratic *mondaines* on the other side of the social fence.

'*Et, chose remarkable,*' wrote Zed, '*ces irrégulières apportaient, en général, dans leur parure une sobriété de bon goût, une affectation de simplicité qui, tout en laissant une marge énorme aux ornements luxueux et aux fantaisies coûteuses, ne leur imprimait pas moins, dans l'ensemble, un air de distinction et de tenue à tromper le plus physionomiste sur leur position sociale.*' (And, remarkably, these 'irregulars' showed, in their style of dressing, a sobriety and a good taste, an affectation of simplicity which, while leaving an enormous margin for luxurious ornaments and costly fantasies, did not in any way lessen, overall, an air of distinction and a bearing which would have tricked even the most able physiognomist as to their social position.)

Although Cora was very far indeed from being the jumped-up trollop she has sometimes been portrayed as, the grand aristocratic manner was not something that could be acquired overnight (and, more to the point, was never quite her style). She needed something, some distinguishing mark or feature, which would set her apart from everyone else.

She soon found it. Although for the last six years Massena had been her *amant en titre*, or official lover, Cora never accepted that this gave him exclusive rights over her (that he possessed a season ticket would perhaps have been a more accurate description of his status). During that time she had many other admirers, including, simultaneously, a father and son, Prince Joachim Murat and his son Prince Achille, who burned for her 'with all the ardour of seventeen'. Between them the Murats made Cora many gifts, of money, silver plate, and once, a solid gold watch engraved with her monogram. It was Prince Achille who gave Cora the one present she would never forget: her first horse.

When Marie Colombier wrote bitchily that Cora was in the *genre écurie* of courtesans, she meant it quite literally. Cora was a natural horsewoman, and although she always claimed that she never had a riding lesson in her life, another of her many self-creations was the role of the consummate horsewoman, unsurpassed in skill and style.

Cora's equestrian prowess is well attested by those who knew her. Nestor Roqueplan, the director of the Opéra and the Châtelet theatres who also wrote for *Le Figaro*, described her glowingly as 'a centauress and the originator of the amazon'. 'She rides with peerless distinction and skill,' he exclaimed rapturously, 'and the most refined people have taken her carriages as models of line and colour.' It was not only her knowledge and good taste that impressed the French; it was her outrageous and apparently insouciant extravagance which really left them breathless. After Prince Achille's present to her, Cora's collection of horses grew vastly. She was now living at 61, rue de Ponthieu, and at one time – so it is said – she kept as many as thirty horses in the stables there. Some estimates have it that between 1863 and 1868 she bought more than sixty fine saddle and carriage horses, and that over a three-year period she spent ninety thousand francs (£170,000 today) with one horse dealer alone.[22] 'A visit to her stables makes one understand how she calmly spends insane sums on this one item in a fantastic budget,' Roqueplan wrote. 'It is a rational form of insanity.'[23]

Once again, by capitalising on her Englishness, Cora had beaten the French at their own game. Although her skills as a horsewoman were best displayed on the hunting field, it was to the afternoon carriage rides in the Bois de Boulogne – in social terms, the equivalent of Hyde Park – that her equestrian energies were mostly directed. For, as Nestor Roqueplan indicated, second only to the beauty of Cora's horses was the elegance and splendour of the carriages she owned, which were soon famous throughout Paris. She would employ none but English grooms – subtly emphasising the superiority of all things English in equine matters – whom she brought over to France especially. It was not long before they too, who were known throughout the metropolis as 'the men who never smile', became incorporated into the Cora myth.

Although the Empress and the ladies of her court had long been in

Emily Warren as Thaïs, by Joshua Reynolds. Emily Warren's career also began in a King's Place brothel. At the age of twelve she was found begging on the streets by one of London's most notorious madams, Charlotte Hayes, who was so struck by the child's 'uncommon beauty' that she set about training her up, giving her lessons in how to speak and converse in a ladylike way, and to walk and move gracefully. Reynolds, who painted her many times, is alleged to have declared that he had never seen 'so faultless and finely formed a human figure.'

Lord Ponsonby, by Henry Pierce Bone, after Thomas Lawrence. Widely regarded as the handsomest man in England, John Ponsonby (later Baron Ponsonby of Imokilly) was the love of Harriette Wilson's life. Her attraction to him was intellectual as well as physical, a fact of which she was acutely aware. 'Had it pleased Heaven to have bestowed on me the husband of my choice,' she once wrote to him, 'there is nothing great, or good, or virtuous, that I had not aspired to.'

1812 Lord Ponsonby for after Lawrence

'The Cyprian's Ball' at the Argyle Rooms'. Engraving by Robert Cruikshank (c.1825). Although they could frequent public places such as the opera and the theatres, courtesans were debarred from all private Society events. Their own social life, however, was designed to mimic aristocratic entertainments as closely as possible. Cruikshank's engraving shows a ball given by Harriette Wilson and her three sisters — the leading lights of the English *demi-monde* at this time — for their patrons. Harriette herself is shown standing, fourth from the right. Her sister Amy is sitting at the extreme right.

'King's Place, or a View of Mr. Fox's Best Friends' (1784). It was widely believed that it was Charles James Fox who first introduced his friend the Prince of Wales (later George IV) to the pleasures of the exclusive King's Place brothels. Here the Prince is shown with two of his mistresses, Perdita Robinson (first left) and Elizabeth Armistead (third left, in a feathered hat). With them are three of London's most notorious madams. Mrs. Windsor, who was known to be a personal friend of the Prince's, is shown second from the right.

'Employment!' Although Harriette Wilson was always jealous of her independence, she was for a time the kept mistress of the young Marquis of Worcester, who set up a house for her in Brighton.

'Cupid Conducting the Three Graces to the Temple of Love'. The 'three Graces' were Harriette's patrons, from left to right, the Reverend Lord Frederick Beauclerk, the Duke of Wellington, and the Marquis of Lorne (who later became the Duke of Argyll).

'La Côterie Débouché' (1825). Harriette Wilson's *Memoirs*, first published in instalments in 1825, caused a sensation and barricades were erected outside the publisher Stockdale's shop in the Haymarket to hold back the besieging mobs. Harriette's former patrons, shown here (the Duke of Wellington, in military uniform, is in the foreground), were invited to buy themselves out for £200, the equivalent today of £10,000. At one time the entire Cabinet were said to be engrossed in reading the book.

Detail from *Derby Day*, by William Frith (1858). By the second half of the nineteenth century, courtesans ceased to have the kind of public celebrity that for the past hundred years had been theirs, although their existence was still widely known. 'A great deal of mystery was made about these ladies of the half-world,' wrote Lady Augusta Fane. 'In conversation they were only mentioned in private and in a whisper…It was an unheard-of thing for any respectable dame to acknowledge that she knew such ladies…existed.' Frith shows a fashionable courtesan, seated in her carriage to the far right of the painting, at once at the center of a large crowd, and yet both physically and spiritually separate from it.

Perhaps no courtesan has ever created as much controversy as Cora Pearl. In Paris, where she lived all her adult life, many thought her vulgar, even ugly; but to the men she chose as her patrons she was a mistress of genius. Her talents made her an extremely rich woman. Cora's several houses, her jewels, her wardrobe, and her immaculate stables were, according to one commentator, '*à nul autre pareils*' (second to none). Her pearls alone, some of which she wears in this photograph, were worth a fortune.

Portrait of Laura Bell by Ernest Girard (1873–97). Laura Bell, the daughter of a Belfast shopkeeper, was one of the few courtesans of the mid-nineteenth century who could rival the success of her contemporary Catherine Walters. The Nepalese Prince Jung Bahadoor once allegedly paid her £250,000 to spend a single night with him.

Along with all the other wealthy women in Paris, Cora was quick to adopt the exquisitely cut and ruinously expensive dresses made by the English couturier Charles Worth. She is shown here, c.1863, wearing one of the extravagant crinolines which he popularised. Her *toilettes de boudoir* were, if possible, even more expensive: one bill from her Parisian lingerie supplier came to more than £18,000, a fact which was reported by a scandalised British press.

An early photograph of Catherine Walters, or 'Skittles' as she was popularly known, possibly taken when she was still the kept mistress of 'Harty Tarty', the Marquis of Hartington (later the 8th Duke of Devonshire), whom she met on the hunting fields of Leicestershire. So many crowds came to watch her drive her famous phaeton in London's Hyde Park that letters were written about it to *The Times*.

The English poet, diplomat and traveller Wilfred Scawen Blunt (1840–1922) fell in love with Catherine when he met her in France in 1863, when he was just twenty-three and she twenty-four. He vividly described his passion for Catherine, his 'phoenix of creation', in his secret diaries, and their remarkable correspondence lasted nearly sixty years.

One of several previously unpublished photographs of Catherine Walters which Wilfred Scawen Blunt kept secretly, amongst her letters to him, until his death in 1922. This portrait was taken in Paris, probably in or around 1863, the year when Catherine, then 'in the full glory of her *demi-mondaine* beauty,' and Blunt first met.

Catherine's classical beauty, and her great elegance and good taste, made her as successful in Paris, where she lived for a short time, as in England. Her great gift for friendship with men meant that many of her lovers became lifelong friends. Among the most prominent of them was the Prince of Wales (later Edward VII), who looked after her even when she was an old woman, when he paid for her to have her bedroom redecorated in sumptuous blue silk.

Another previously unpublished photograph from Blunt's collection. Catherine, who was a famous horse-breaker and huntswoman in her day, was equally renowned for the perfect fit of her 'Princess' riding habit, into which she had to be sewn. When she appeared in it in Hyde Park, aristocratic women rushed to copy its design, while their husbands wondered whether she could possibly be wearing any undergarments beneath its skin-tight folds.

the habit of taking their daily constitutional with a carriage ride in the Bois de Boulogne, it is Cora Pearl who has been credited with starting the fashion amongst the most *racé* of the Parisian courtesans. No one knew better than she the sheer theatre and erotic power of these displays. In his essay *La Vie Parisienne* Sacheverell Sitwell gives a vivid picture of the peculiar romance, as he described it, which attached to these promenades, imagining the moment when the lady of one of the huge new mansions near the Bois comes out of the house in her immense crinoline and makes her way to her carriage – a *calèche* or a *brischka* – waiting below.

> *A footman holds the door open and the groom stands by the horses. The lady has to hold up her crinoline with both hands in order to descend the steps; and then like a cloud, she climbs into this boat or skiff and seats herself. The groom has his box seat at the back of the calèche. He holds the reins high above her head, and the calèche goes forward as easily as a gondola and much more swiftly.*[24]

The *calèche* was the lightest and quickest of all the carriages then in fashion, and was designed for one person only. An open landau for summer use, a barouche, a berlin, or the Empress's favourite, a daumont, on the other hand, all had room inside for two. According to Sitwell, there were strict rules of etiquette governing the correct procedures for driving out to the Bois at this time. To be alone in a *calèche*, 'the swiftest and most skiff-like of carriages', was not considered indelicate, but 'to the sensibility of the time, there was something decidedly indecorous in sitting, alone, in a carriage where there is room for two'. The slower pace of these bigger and more cumbersome vehicles only emphasised the impropriety. Perhaps oddly, given these extremely delicate sensibilities, it was considered perfectly respectable for a woman to drive herself: the crucial point was that she should drive fast enough.

For all this, the daily procession down the Champs Elysées and into the Bois was generally a decorous one, with very little passing or overtaking: 'On its way, other carriages join in from every direction until the wide avenue, striped with the shadows of the trees, becomes no more than a stream of traffic. It ends on the banks of the lake.'

To those who were acutely tuned to the subtleties of these parades, there were other clues and *caveats* too. Even the way a woman sat in her carriage, and how she arranged the folds of her dress, might speak volumes about her. 'The implications of this dumb language may be lost on us, now,' Sitwell wrote, half regretfully.

> But, indeed, the crinoline might have been specially designed for the display of its folds and billows in an open carriage. Driving in a light pony chaise the crinoline would fill the whole body of the carriage. Were this the summer . . . an open landau with two ladies seated in it, in bonnets and with open parasols, comes past us and the billows of their crinolines, like waves upon the shore, beat high up against the coachman's box. Not only does the landau glide past us like a caïque or a gondola, but the billowing of their crinolines is as though the ladies, who lazily recline in it, were marine bodies allowed their convention in this covering of foam.

By these most delicate of nuances it was perfectly possible for actresses and *demi-mondaines* to advertise their charms only too clearly on their afternoon carriage rides.

The vision of Cora and her friends riding in the Bois de Boulogne in their smart new carriages, each with its own distinctive livery, became one of the sights of Paris. The *monde* and the *demi-monde*, which up until now had been separated, as Zed put it, '*toujours et partout, par une muraille infranchissable*' (always and everywhere, by an unbreachable wall), now met head on. Society was scandalised, but there was nothing to be done. Other conventions, equally subtle, sprang up to accommodate the clash.* A 'clubman', if he was on his own,

---

* French society, which had always had the knack of combining extreme public formality with great private latitude, was no stranger to this kind of sidestepping. Captain Gronow tells a charming story of the celebrated statesman 'Comte G–', who was seen at a party 'saluting in the most respectful and distant manner, and with all the formal politeness of *la vieille cour*, the Comtesse de C–, with whom it was supposed that he had long been on terms of more than friendly intimacy, and whom he had probably left but a few hours before. The lady, without even extending the "shake hands" now so much in vogue, returned the salutation by an equally reserved and dignified courtsey; and a minute after this formal greeting, Lady G– overheard the elderly minister, in a voice full of enthusiastic admiration, address the middle-aged lady thus, "Pauline, tu as 15 ans!"'

was free to signal his greeting, but discreetly so. If he was in the company of a courtesan, however, it was considered the height of impropriety for him to acknowledge any other woman of his acquaintance, however well he knew her, even if their carriages were side by side. A Danish diplomat who one day found himself abreast of the Empress Eugenie herself when he was riding in the Bois with his mistress, the courtesan Adèle Courtois, in his confusion committed the unforgivable solecism of bowing to her. The next day the Empress complained formally to his embassy of 'this grave infraction of all the common laws of decency. The diplomat was severely taken to task in high quarters and suspended for an unlimited period.'[25]

Although women who had been 'born', as the splendid French expression goes, were scandalised, they were also secretly intrigued by these women, by whom, if Zed is to be believed, they were consistently and effortlessly outclassed. 'I have had much money, many jewels, some magnificent *parures*,' Cora wrote in her *Memoirs*, and went on to give an account of how the Marquise de Kaiserlick had once profited by a visit Cora made to Fontainebleau in order to come and see her dresses, 'and to make the acquaintance of my modiste and my dressmaker'. She was not exaggerating. Parisian society women employed many ruses such as this for just a glimpse into that forbidden world. Sometimes they even had the opportunity kindly provided for them, such as on the occasion that Esther Guimond, as a joke, put it about that the house of a certain fellow courtesan, Antonia Sari, was up for sale. 'The women of society were glad to be appraised of such an interesting fact,' smiled the writer Frédéric Loliée, 'for they could now visit this abode of sin on the plea of purchasing some art trifle.'[26]

Very occasionally, a particularly daring woman might make an open raid right into the enemy's lair. One such occasion is recounted by the Comtesse Louise de Mercy-Argenteau in her memoir of society life during the Second Empire. She wrote of the 'morbid curiosity' which a certain type of Parisian woman had for all things relating to the forbidden world of the *demi-monde*: 'They were dressed by the same dressmakers, their carriages rivalled one another in elegance and style, and their jewels were very often paid for by the same generous hand.' When the Countess heard that Cora Pearl, the 'celebrated beauty of the moment', was giving a masked fancy-dress ball, this curiosity finally overcame her:

> We knew some friends of the house, and the Princess Metternich, the Duchess de Cadore, and I were allowed to go there after much begging. We were quite excited at the idea of approaching those dreadful and fascinating persons, and were probably eager to learn by what contrivance they could so easily win over our fathers, brothers, and husbands. Pauline [Metternich], who laughed aloud and could not repress her mordant sallies, was mistaken, to her great delight, for Caroline Letessier,* to whom she had some resemblance.[27]

For all this, the visit was not a success. Cora's apartment, which they inspected throughout 'with precautions a burglar might have taken', was a disappointment to them, 'even the *cabinet de toilette*, of which we were expecting so much'. 'I found these women repulsive, silly, and dirty,' wrote the Countess petulantly (although it is worth noting that she has hardly a good thing to say about anyone – even her own friends† – in her memoir, a work of such breathtakingly venal snobbery that Cora's own reminiscences appear positively chaste by comparison).

The truth was that the real contrivance by which a courtesan of Cora's *marque* could win over all the brothers, fathers and husbands in Paris, should she so choose, was not something that could be gauged merely by the contents of any apartment. Cora now had all the packaging – the master chef, the superb stables, the brilliantly masterminded aura of extravagance and fantasy. But it was sex that sold.

By her own admission Cora never had what she called 'a preferred lover'. Unlike Harriette Wilson, who was almost destroyed by her love for Ponsonby, Cora was always able to preserve the deepest part of herself intact. It was to prove an essential component of her business success. 'As regards what is conventionally termed blind passion and fatal attraction, no!' she wrote at the end of her life. 'Luckily for my

---

* Another notoriously celebrated 'beauty'.
† Elsewhere, for example, she refers to Princess Metternich as '*la Reine Peste*'.

peace of mind and happiness, I have never known either.' Never at
risk of being attracted to any one person in particular, she could give
herself more easily to many. Her philosophy, for which she has been
much criticised, was – in courtesans' terms – a sound, even an honest
one: 'A handsome, young and amiable man who has loyally offered
me his arm, his love, and his money, had every right to think and to
call himself my "favourite lover",' she wrote; 'my lover for an hour, my
escort for a month, and my friend for ever. That is how I understand the
business.'

Cora's strange psychology in regard to men in general – her 'instinctive horror of the stronger sex', characterised by what she herself called
her 'coldness and utter contempt' – did not extend to everyone.

> *I have often made an exception in favour of the individual! A
> select few – enough for me – know well that I speak the truth,
> and that having now disappeared from the stage – considering it
> is a stage like any other – I cherish within me an ineradicable
> tenderness for him who, in a transient connection, was able to
> inspire me with that charm that never dies: delicacy of good
> breeding.*

And, crucially, although she was never inclined to 'immoderate ardour',
Cora liked sex. She was, she wrote modestly, 'as sensitive as any other
woman'. Paradoxical as these elements in her sexual make-up may
seem, for a courtesan it was a very nearly perfect psychology.

For the patrons fortunate enough to have been able to afford her,
Cora was not only 'the last word in luxury', but 'the acme of sensual
delights'. In one important sense these two attributes were really the
same thing. Sex, for all its greatest practitioners, was not just a physical
act, but also a state of mind. Among the many things that Cora learned
from her fellow *demi-mondaines* in Paris was the art of eroticising not
only her behaviour in the bedroom, but her whole way of life. Everything about a courtesan, from the way in which her apartment and
her carriages were appointed to the smallest detail of the way she
walked and dressed, was given over to the idea of pleasing men. And
it was from this, ultimately, that her power came.

It was no less effective for being, very often, highly artificial. Arsène

Houssaye, who knew Cora in her early days, remembered his first sight of her: 'I met the lady at Ems, walking gracefully like a doe. She was soon enough undressed,' he added unchivalrously, 'but Good Lord, what labour in the morning to put on her make-up.'[28] It was, he wrote, 'art hiding nature'. For Cora, although she was not beautiful, nonetheless had the mysterious gift of being able to inspire the 'idea of beauty', as Houssaye put it, through her skills.*

This artifice was in itself something that many men found fascinating. The interior of a courtesan's house, for example, always had a '*très grand air*', wrote the indefatigable Zed:

> *Tout y était large, à profusion, gaspillé; en même temps que, dans les détails les plus intimes, les plus imperceptibles, le raffinement, la coquetterie et la luxure débordaient. Tout y semblait arrangé et preparé en vue des hommes, à la fois superlativement aristocratiques et démesurément épicurieurs . . .* (Everything there was large, in profusion, and extravagant; while at the same time, all the most intimate and most imperceptible details overflowed with refinement, coquetry and luxury. Everything there seemed to have been arranged and prepared with a view to [pleasing] men, at once superlatively aristocratic, and immeasurably epicurean.)[29]

The ultimate packaging lay with the woman herself, and the courtesans of the Second Empire were nothing less than masters of this art. It is perhaps hard for us, in an age which is so accepting of nudity, to appreciate the immense erotic charge of the '*toilettes de boudoir*' (somehow the baldly English 'dressing-gown' does not have quite the same ring) which were '*l'apanage exclusif de ces demoiselles*' (these ladies' exclusive preserve). For Cora and her fellow *demi-mondaines* knew only too well what we tend to forget: that what is mysteriously

---

* I wonder if Cora ever followed the laborious beauty regime recounted by one society lady to the Goncourt brothers: 'Out of bed by six thirty in the morning, at the window until eight o'clock in order that her complexion may have an hour and a half's bath of fresh air. Then, an hour in the tub. After breakfast, a period of rest taken in a pose such that nothing comes into contact with the skin of the face.' They called it 'the torture of beauty'.

and enticingly half-wrapped is far more alluring than the clinically bare.

It is worth repeating, I think, and in the almost untranslatably beautiful original French, Zed's delirious description of these wonderful garments, on which so much time and imagination were lavished: '*Les toilettes de boudoir, les déshabillés galants, les dessous émoustillants, les fouillis de dentelles, de soie et de batiste, le luxe de linge et d'accessoires,*' he wrote, '*à vous donner la chair de poule . . . Je rénonce à les decrire.*' (The toilettes for the boudoir, the romantic negligées and tantalising undergarments, the tangles of silks and muslin, the sheer luxury of lingerie and other accessories would give you goose pimples . . . I cannot even begin to describe them.)

The eagle-eyed Goncourt brothers, too, bore witness to the extraordinary importance given to these special toilettes by their neighbour Ana Deslions, writing in their journal:

> We saw in the porter's lodge the toilette that our neighbour, Deslions, sends by her maid to the house of the man to whom she has given a night. It seems that she has a different outfit for each of her lovers in the colour that he prefers. It consists of a dressing gown of padded and ticked satin, with gold embroidered slippers of the same colour; a nightgown of batiste trimmed with Valenciennes lace and embroidered insertions which come to five or six hundred francs; and a petticoat trimmed with three flounces of lace each of which costs three or four hundred francs. In sum, these accessories of gallantry come to 2,500–3,000 francs [more than five and a half thousand pounds] a set and are sent off to any house whose master can afford the lady.[30]

Naturally Cora too spent fabulous sums on her underwear; so much so that in February 1864 she is recorded as having taken her *lingère* to court. Her latest bill, which was for the sum of 9500 francs (nearly £18,000) for 'part of the year', even Cora, no stranger to the art of conspicuous consumption, found excessive. In court, some of the trimmings and exquisite lace work were produced as evidence, causing such a stir that the case was reported back in London by the *Daily Telegraph*, which sniffed disapprovingly over the 'extravagances of modern Paris'. The defendant was Madame Roux des Florins, and the bill included 'a tea-gown with Zouave braid, 125 francs; a laced muslin dressing gown, 200 francs; a nainsook tea gown, 135 francs; 6 pairs of laced linen knickers, 270 francs; 6 cambric chemises, the tops and arms trimmed with lace, and embroidered with monograms, 840 francs'.[31] In the end, Cora won her case, and a thousand francs was knocked off the bill.

All this exquisitely expensive 'artillery', as Zed called it, all these delicious seasonings, were an essential part of the courtesan's *mise en scène*. It was this kind of erotic theatre that made her at once 'so precious, so desirable, and so charming'; and of which, according to Zed, women of society never had anything but the vaguest and most distant notion.

And it was for this – this mystery and this promise – that men were prepared to pay.

Cora's liaison with Victor Massena, the Duc de Rivoli – the first link in her golden chain, as she put it – had lasted a very respectable six years. During that time she had had many other admirers, all of whom had added generously to her coffers, but now it was time to find another *amant en titre*. For a while this honour belonged to the Prince of Orange, the heir to the throne of the Netherlands, who once gave Cora 'five blue notes' (that is, five notes of a thousand francs each*) for a single assignation. 'Duke Citron', as Cora refers to him in her memoir, with whom she remained for some time, was always very generous to her – it was he who gave her the magnificent necklace of black pearls 'of phenomenal price' which were to become her signature, and in which she was so often photographed – but it was another man, the Duc de Morny ('Moray' in her *Memoirs*), who was the next really significant link in Cora's golden chain.

'It was in the Bois de Boulogne,' she would later recall, 'in December, when the thermometer was four degrees below zero, that I made the

---

* £9500.

acquaintance of Moray whilst skating. I was enveloped in furs. Moray came to speak to me.

> *'Cora upon the ice!' said he. 'What an antithesis!'*
> *'Well,' said I, 'since the ice is now broken, won't you offer me something warming to drink?'*
> *'C'est tout mon désir,' said he.* [It is my heart's desire.]

Later in her life Cora had lovers even richer and more imperial, but she never had one more fascinating, more powerful or, it must be said, more worthy of her. The Duc de Morny was the illegitimate son of Queen Hortense* of Holland and her lover the Comte de Flahaut. Born in Paris in 1811, he was later adopted by the Comte de Morny, and was made Duke in 1862. A man of prodigious energies and intelligence, he had a varied career as a soldier, financier and diplomatist. In 1842 he was chosen as a deputy, and he is credited with having engineered the *coup d'état* of 1851, which made his half-brother, Louis Napoleon, Prince-President, and later Emperor Napoleon III. Under the new regime he at first held the post of Minister of the Interior, but at the time Cora knew him until his early death in 1865, he was the President of the *corps législatif*, and one of the most powerful men in France.†

Arsène Houssaye once wrote that Cora's 'great appeal to a gentleman lay not so much in having her as in showing that he could afford her',[32] but the Duc de Morny, a man of both refined tastes and strong sexual appetites,‡ was not the kind who would ever have been interested in mere display. Two days after their fiery meeting upon the ice Cora consented to visit him at his residence. She was deeply impressed:

---

* Hortense de Beauharnais was Napoleon Bonaparte's stepdaughter. She married his brother Louis Bonaparte, the King of Holland, in 1802.

† On his death a report in the *Gentleman's Magazine* stated: 'There were hardly any important speculations . . . with which his name was not mixed up – railroad companies, mines, credit societies, and so forth, and the possession of a refined taste was evidenced in his splendid gallery of paintings.'

‡ Among his many mistresses were both Sarah Bernhardt's mother and her aunt, the courtesans Rosine and Youle Bernard. De Morny has been credited with using his influence to have Sarah accepted at the Comédie Française, thus giving her her first break as an actress.

'he had a residence indeed that was worth seeing', she wrote. But it was not only the size of his immense double-fronted house which amazed her, or even the secret staircase which she was instructed to use, but the sight of the multitudes who came there each day 'to wait upon the all-powerful man'. 'I found persons [there] assembled who represented more or less happily every type of France,' she wrote. 'Padded figures, mutton-chop whiskers, waxed moustaches ... and also the infirm of every type among the old guests, the lame, the gouty, the deaf, in short a very *cour de miracles*.' From the secret entranceway with which she was soon familiar, Cora could contemplate at her ease 'a scene more remarkable than the Bourse during its busiest hours'.

It was not just this first aphrodisiac encounter with power that drew Cora to the Duke. He was also good-looking, very generous, and 'a perfect gentleman',* attributes which, when combined, made for the ideal patron. She enjoyed de Morny's gifts, to be sure – soon after they met he gave her a present of an exquisite white Arab which was to become one of her favourite horses – but she enjoyed the man himself, with all his subtleties and charm, even more. 'No one could turn a compliment better than he,' she wrote, 'but his compliments were never overdrawn. He had a horror of stupidity. He knew how to speak with taste even when he was reproachful; it was a pleasure to be scolded by him. He was one of those who never grow old.'

With de Morny Cora was no longer required to play childish tricks, or pranks with *pétards*. Instead they discussed poetry and the theatre. The Duke was a great admirer of de Musset, and he himself had been known to write a comedy in the brief interval between a diplomatic reception and an official speech.† 'My greatest delight when I was with him was to listen to his delicate irony and his fine criticism,' Cora wrote. She enjoyed hearing him play the piano, too, which he did charmingly, wearing a violet velvet suit. 'He played with much feeling,'

---

* It was de Morny who had chivalrously offered Cora his arm so that she could gain admittance to the Casino in Baden-Baden.

† This was a one-act opéra bouffe, *Monsieur Choufleury restera chez lui*, and was written in collaboration with Offenbach. It had some success, apparently, at the Théâtre des Bouffes-Parisiens.

she wrote (although she never liked him to become too carried away by his feelings), 'and sang with exquisite taste.'

It is clear that from the very beginning of their relationship de Morny and Cora understood one another very well. Cora, of course, was perfectly aware that he had not invited her to use his secret staircase, his *escalier dérobé*, merely so he could play her tunes upon his piano (delightful though this preliminary may have been). And she knew that if she did not please de Morny, there were plenty of others who would.

But de Morny had chosen Cora, and that a man of his gifts and sensibilities had done so reveals more about her real nature than anything her detractors could later throw at her. With all her laughing grace, her wit and her tremendous intelligence, Cora was more than a match for him (as her contemporary Esther Guimond once remarked, 'it is strange that we courtesans should alone be worthy and able to converse with philosophers'). But we can imagine, too, how he must have enjoyed her in other ways. Cora was an exciting person to be with: you never quite knew what she was going to do next. She who was always so physically at ease, with her very un-French exhibitionism and her taste for 'voluptuous eccentricities', so unabashed and sparkling with erotic energy, whether skating on the ice or displaying her beautiful body for him, with her perfect breasts, her tiny waist no bigger than the span of a man's hands, and her 'almost superhuman knowledge of the arts of love'.

Through the works of, among others, Zed and Frédéric Loliée, the courtesans of the Second Empire are uniquely well documented. By the time Cora came to know the Duc de Morny her position as one of *la bande*, a small, extremely select group of pre-eminent Parisian *demi-mondaines* – the aristocracy, as it were, of French courtesanry – was assured. As with the English courtesans of the eighteenth and early nineteenth centuries, theirs was a completely self-contained society, a separate but parallel world which intersected, at certain crucial points, with 'the *crème de la crème* of aristocratic and intellectual men about town'. Of these there were about a hundred, all told – men of exquisite politeness and incomparable elegance, with whom the members of *la bande* had usually made their debut, with whom they 'frolicked', and from whom, Zed informs us, in some measure their cachet was derived. Cora, of course, knew them all.

One of Cora's most treasured possessions, which remained with her until it was auctioned amongst her other effects after her death, was a watercolour of the Nile at sunset which had been painted for her by the actress-courtesan Blanche d'Antigny (on whom, famously, Zola was to base the character of Nana) gracefully inscribed with the words 'Ma Perle Chérie'. With some of her fellow members of la bande, such as Caroline Hassé who lived for a time in the same apartment block as Cora in the rue Ponthieu, and who was alleged always to sleep upon black sheets so as to enhance the perfect creamy whiteness of her skin, Cora had her quarrels; but for the most part – and contrary to what has often been said about her – she was loyal and generous to her women friends. A manuscript letter survives in Cora's own clear and confident hand in which she invites one of her fellow courtesans, Adèle Remy, to join her one evening at a soirée at the rue Ponthieu.

> Paris, '61
> Rue Ponthieu
> Dear Adèle,
>
> If you are not leaving before Sunday, will you not do me the pleasure to come and dine on your return from the races? You will thus have an opportunity of meeting the Baron again. He found you charming yesterday as hostess. Pray do not fail, for I wish to prove to you within all the measure of my means that I am extremely grateful for all the kindness you have invariably shown me. There will be only three ladies present, including ourselves, and three or four gentlemen – not more than eight people –; a homely little meal as we are accustomed to have in my country.
>
> Yours ever,
> Cora Pearl[33]

Like Cora, Adèle Remy was a paradigm of the Parisian courtesan. She had a mass of heavy blonde hair which, when loosened, fell to her feet and completely covered her. In addition to this marvel, she was 'bien faite, douce, rieuse, caline, intelligente comme un singe, originale et amus-

ante' (shapely, sweet, laughing, loving, as intelligent as a monkey, original and amusing). And, best of all, beneath her '*tenue d'ambassa-drice*', the bearing of an ambassadress (it is quite strange how often this comparison arises) and her '*ton irréprochable*' lay a temperament of fire. '*Une imagination absolument dévergondée*', breathed Zed. An absolutely shameless imagination. There was always a sense with Adèle, he wrote, that she would give free reign to her ideas, even the most depraved, without the least scruple, a trait which he, among others, found completely bewitching. When you had known and loved her, he wrote, '*quand on avait mordu à la pomme*' (when you had taken a bite of the apple), '*c'était fini: on ne pouvait plus la quitter*' (that was it: it was impossible ever to leave her).

The ability to give free reign to natural sensuousness was the hall-mark of the great courtesan. Another of the most prominent of *la bande* among Cora's contemporaries was the actress Léonide Leblanc, who, despite preserving a look of 'childish innocence' even into her middle age, managed to combine 'voluptuousness in flesh and blood, with the style of an eighteenth-century marquise', as Zed wrote of her; while William Osgood Field likened her to a modern Ninon de L'Enclos: 'witty, very *intrigante*, very ambitious, very good-natured, and very amusing and *bonne fille*. She was not beautiful, indeed hardly pretty, but she had a clever and pleasing face.'[34] And, like Cora, she was renowned for having brought *la galanterie* up to the level of a fine art.

The Italian Giulia Beneni, 'La Barucci', was – again, like Cora – one of the very few non-French women to reach the heights of the Parisian *demi-monde*. She too was a woman whose sexuality oozed from every pore. With her luxuriant black hair, golden Italian skin and air of languid sensuality, she was, in Zed's estimation, the personification of the '*grande cocotte*' of her generation. (She would have agreed with him: '*Je souis* [sic] *le Venus de Milo. Je souis la première putaine de Paris*,' she was fond of boasting in her heavily accented French.) '*Et quelle puissante organisation! quel tempérament d'acier! quelle prodigi-euse activité*' (And what bold organisation, what a temperament of steel, what prodigious activity). The rest he could only leave to his readers' imagination. One thing, however, was sure: La Barucci's 'activities' soon brought her one of the most magnificent collections of jewels in Paris (said to be worth a million francs in all, one necklace alone, a *'collier historique'* which she wore every night *'comme une armure de combat'*, was valued at 200,000 francs – nearly £400,000), the gifts of her grateful clientele.

La Barucci's apartment at 124, avenue des Champs Elysées was known, in one way or another, to all of fashionable Paris – she was even rumoured to lend it to society ladies for their most secret assignations – for she knew everyone. The Goncourt brothers, who were invited to dine with her one evening by her latest lover, the wit and journalist Aurelien Scholl, were amazed when Scholl took a mountain of visiting cards out of a Chinese bowl which La Barucci kept by her fireplace, and from it read out nearly every name in high society: there were gold-embossed cards from the court, crested ones from the Imperial family, from the fashionable *faubourgs*, and from almost the entire diplomatic corps of Europe.

It was not surprising then that when the young Prince of Wales went on a visit to Paris it was La Barucci whom one of his friends, the Duc de Grammont-Caderousse, himself a well-known *noceur*, chose to invite to dine with them at the Maison d'Or. The Duke instructed her carefully beforehand on the proper etiquette that would be required when meeting the future King of England and, most especially, of the need for the strictest punctuality. When the appointed hour came the Duke and the Prince waited as ten, and then twenty minutes went by. After half an hour the Prince's mood of heightened expectancy had turned to restlessness, and then downright irritation. Finally, three quarters of an hour late, La Barucci swept in, unrepentant, regal, and ablaze with diamonds. 'Your Royal Highness,' said Grammont-Caderousse, 'may I present to you the most unpunctual woman in France?' At which point La Barucci turned gracefully around, and with one sudden movement lifted up the skirts of her dress, then bent over to reveal to the startled Prince (as one source charmingly puts it) 'the white rotundities of her callipygian charms'.[35]* 'Did you not tell me

---

* This story has been told many times. In one version of it she is supposed to have wriggled out of layers of diaphanous chiffon in order to bare her bottom. Since the crinoline was then in fashion this seems unlikely, however. The English translator and

to behave properly to His Royal Highness?' she is said to have defended herself when the Duke upbraided her for this behaviour later. 'I showed him the best I have – and it was free.'[36]

Unfettered by the ordinary requirements of respectability and etiquette, these queens of the *demi-monde* – Adèle, Léonide, La Barucci, and Cora chief among them – were the Cleopatras of their day, outrageous, eccentric, infinitely various. But of all the great personalities of the Second Empire, there was one woman who almost equals Cora in reputation. She was La Païva, and her story is worth telling in full.

La Païva was born Thérèse Lachmann in the Moscow ghetto in 1819, the daughter, quipped one of her acquaintances, of a witch and a broomstick handle. After an early marriage she abandoned her husband and young son and made her way to Ems, the fashionable Prussian watering-hole, where she made the acquaintance of the French composer and pianist Henri Herz, who was Jewish like herself. Thérèse, by all accounts, was not beautiful, but with her dark, almost blue-black hair and eyes, and her powerful personality, she had a kind of exotic charisma which was very striking. Herz soon took her as his mistress, teaching her music, buying her jewels and clothes, and, most importantly of all, taking her with him to Paris.

In Paris Thérèse began to acquire something of the extravagance that would so characterise her later career, to the extent that when Herz went on tour to America his family, in despair at the recklessness of her spending, threw her out of the house. Luckily for Thérèse she had two powerful friends to whom she now turned. One was the writer Théophile Gautier, the other the courtesan Esther Guimond. While Gautier advised her on strategy, Esther introduced her to her milliner, Camille, and Thérèse's career as a courtesan was launched.

She decided first of all to try her luck in London. Gautier saw her the day before she left, trying on her spectacular new dresses 'as a

---

adaptor of Loliée, in which the story also appears, excised the anecdote altogether. 'Prudence and a sense of duty prevent us, however, from giving a free reign to our pen,' he wrote in 1909.

soldier might try his weapons before a battle ... "Not badly equipped, am I?" she said. "But you can never be too sure ... I might misfire ... and then *finita la commedia.*" [37] She then asked him to procure her a supply of chloroform, which she intended to take should she not succeed. Gautier duly did so.

Thérèse did not need the chloroform. Her mission was a complete success. In London she almost immediately ensnared Lord Stanley, and after him a succession of rich and aristocratic lovers, but none of them was enough for Thérèse's insatiable ambition. She desired respectability and a name, and she soon found at least one of these in the form of the Portuguese Marquis de Païva, who became so besotted with her that he offered her his hand in marriage.

'The morning after the marriage,' wrote the historian Viel-Castro, 'when the new husband and wife awoke, Madame de Païva addressed her satisfied lover more or less as follows:

> You wanted to sleep with me, and you've done so, by making me
> your wife. You have given me your name, I acquitted myself last
> night. I have behaved like an honest woman, I wanted a position,
> and I've got it, but all you have is a prostitute for a wife. You
> can't take me anywhere, and you can't introduce me to anyone.
> We must therefore separate. You go back to Portugal. I shall stay
> here with your name and remain a whore. [38]

Could this story be true? The history of La Païva, as from then on she would always be known, is more spun through with myth and surmise than that of any other courtesan in the Second Empire, even Cora herself. No doubt it suited Thérèse that way; although the facts about her which are verifiable are every bit as sinister. What is certain is that she did not stay long with the Marquis (although she remained formally married to him for twenty years*), but had soon acquired a young and equally besotted new protector, the fabulously wealthy Prussian Count Guido Henckel von Donnersmarck, eleven years her junior. It was many years later, at her *hôtel* in the avenue des Champs Elysées,† that the Goncourt Brothers met La Païva for the first time.

---

* He shot himself in 1872.
† This building still exists, and is now the premises of the Travellers' Club in Paris.

For once their fastidious distaste for almost everything in 'modern Paris' does not seem overdone. 'Théophile Gautier, who is at the moment *maestro di casa*, introduced us to La Païva and her legendary town house on the Champs-Elysées,' they wrote on 24 May 1867, adding dismissively: 'An old courtezan, painted and plastered, with a smile as false as her hair and the general air of a provincial actress.' They were given tea in the dining room, which, for all its opulence, fared no better beneath their gimlet gaze.

> *Despite all its luxury and the excess of its Renaissance decoration in the worst taste, and despite the ridiculous sums spent on its marbles, its wainscoting, its paintings, its enamels, and the work- manship of its candelabra of solid silver from the mines owned by the Prussian protector who was also present, this room remains the luxurious cabinet of a public restaurant, a hideaway for millionaires.*[39]

Having acquired a noble title and access to what was, almost literally, the bottomless wealth of von Donnersmark's silver mines, Madame de Païva now set out to create the most glittering intellectual salon in Paris. She almost succeeded. All the famous men of letters of the day attended – the editor of *La Presse*, Emile de Girardin, Théophile Gau- tier, Arsène Houssaye, the critic Saint-Beuve, the Goncourt brothers themselves – although La Païva herself was always the only woman present, since (perhaps with the exception of the intellectual Esther Guimond) she thought herself above the rest of *la bande*, while any 'respectable' women 'would have blushed and veiled their faces' at the mere thought of entering her house. But somehow, if the Goncourts are to be believed, it never quite worked. Even La Païva's old friend Gautier, that master conversationalist, the Goncourts wrote, 'could not put himself quite at ease in this house'.

La Païva spent fabulous sums entertaining her guests, holding open court five days a week, while Fridays and Sundays were reserved for just a handful of specially selected guests. 'The rarest dishes and the costliest first fruits were always served,' wrote Frédéric Loliée, 'for she had the magic power of always being in advance of the times in everything . . . Her hothouses provided her with fresh and ripe fruit all the year round, and her guests were almost tired of eating enormous strawberries in the depths of winter.'

One day, thinking that his hostess was not within hearing, one of her guests estimated that the Marquise must now be worth between eight and ten million francs. 'You must be mad,' chimed in Madame de Païva, who was hidden in an arbour. 'Ten millions! Why, that would barely yield an income of 500,000 francs [around £1 million]. Do you think I could give you peaches and ripe grapes in January on 500,000 francs a year? Why, my table alone costs me more than that!'[40]

But for all the riches lavished upon her palace, the Goncourts always maintained that it was the most uncomfortable house in Paris. La Païva, they shrewdly surmised, was really a businesswoman, and, unlike Cora and most other courtesans, she was not a natural hostess at all. Her mind, they felt sure, was never really on her guests, 'but on the two little strongboxes in her chamber where she keeps her jewels'. The place was always cold. And, with a strangely Faustian irony, it was impossible to get a drink of water. The water pitchers – 'cathedrals made of crystal which it would take a water carrier to lift' – were simply too heavy to pick up.

Nonetheless, the Goncourts continued to attend La Païva's salons. It gave them the chance to study their extraordinary hostess more closely:

I kept my eyes on the mistress of the house, and studied her a bit. White skin, good arms, beautiful shoulders, bare behind down to the hips, the reddish hair under her arms showing each time that she adjusted her shoulder straps; large round eyes; a pear-shaped nose with heavy wings and the tip thick and flattened, like a Kalmuck's nose; the mouth a straight line cutting across a face all white with rice powder. Wrinkles which, under the light, look black in the white face; and down from each side of the mouth a crease in the shape of a horseshoe meeting beneath the chin and cutting across it in a great fold bespeaking age. On the surface, the face is that of a courtezan who will not be too old for her profession when she is a hundred years old; but underneath,

*another face is visible from time to time, the terrible face of a
painted corpse.*[41]

Of course, not everyone agreed with the Goncourts. Arsène Houssaye,
another regular at La Païva's salon, thought that the conversations
there were always lively and original: 'I think that that sumptuous
table ... stimulated wit quite as much as the frugal table of Madame
de Maintenon.' And Théophile Gautier agreed: 'The conversation was
always sparkling, original, rich in unheard-of ideas and expressions.'[42]
But neither man had all that much to say about their hostess herself,
and somehow it is the Goncourts' descriptions, exaggerated though
they may be, which ring true.

The 'terrifying luxury' of the house, as Delacroix, who was an
occasional reluctant guest, put it, and the uneasy presence of La Païva's
consort, a handsome but mute shade hovering uneasily in the background, added to the general sense of disquiet. La Païva herself clearly
enjoyed these effects; perhaps she even worked to achieve them.

'She came into her drawing room dripping with emeralds all over
the flesh of her shoulders and arms,' the Goncourts recorded after
another particularly chilly evening. '"I am still a little blue with cold.
My maid has just done my hair with the window wide open," she
said. Out of doors it was snowing, and the night was so cold that,
coming here, we shivered for the ill-clad poor of Paris. This woman
is not built like the rest of humanity. She lives in icy air and water,
like a kind of boreal dragon in a Scandinavian myth.'[43]

Over the years La Païva became, like Cora, one of the legends of
Paris. Her pearls alone, it was said, were worth half a million francs;
in the winter her carriage was lined with the finest sable, while she
herself was swathed in blue fox furs 'of inestimable price'. The besotted
Henckel von Donnersmarck, who had spent ten years and countless
millions creating the Païva palace in the avenue des Champs Elysées,
also bought her a castle, the sixteenth-century Château de Pontchartrain, on the road from Paris to Rambouillet. And here the whispers
grew more sinister still. There was a man at Pontchartrain, the story
went, whose sole job was to open and shut the castle's 150 windows;
this task took him every day from six o'clock in the morning until

midnight, until one day he dropped dead from exhaustion. The gardeners at the château were fined fifty centimes for every leaf found on the ground (who counted them, I wonder?), and Madame de Païva herself collected the fines at dawn. She had a horror, it was said, of animals and children, and when one of her horses threw her when she was out riding, she took a gun and shot it.

Stories accumulated around her like autumn leaves. One admirer, Adolphe Gaiffe, who was not a rich man, was so importunate in his pleas for her favours that eventually she gave in to him, instructing him to bring her ten thousand francs in small-denomination notes. When her would-be lover arrived with not ten but twelve thousand francs – a ruinous sum for him – she took the money and promptly set fire to the first note. 'I will be yours,' she told him, 'but only for as long as it takes for this money to burn.'*

As the years passed and Thérèse grew older there were many men who were still hypnotised by her dangerously exotic appeal – one of them, Loliée recounts, used to rave about her whenever she appeared in a particular shooting costume cut like a man's – but to most she had become a kind of Carabosse figure. Despite an increasingly frantic beauty regime – she was said to take a succession of daily baths, the first in milk, the second in lime-blossoms, and the third in scented water, to counteract the acidity of her blood – age was catching up on her at last. She took to blackening her eyelids and to powdering her black hair blonde, and in this strange guise the journalist Emile Bergerat (Théophile Gautier's son-in-law) gave a chilling description of the sight she presented as she made her entrance at a Wagner concert one night:

> She was coming forward between the chairs like an automaton, as if she was worked by a spiral spring, without gesture, without expression . . . Behind her, as a trainbearer, a magnificent human stallion shortened his giant strides to keep pace with this rolling puppet from a danse macabre . . . He had married her with his eyes open, out of love, and officially, if you please. Don't talk to me about your Ninon de L'Enclos, the nineteenth century can

---

* Gaiffe apparently had the last laugh, however, for the notes were all forged. See Loliée.

*offer you something better. At the age of sixty-five La Païva still
'made' a Hohenzollern.*

'I don't even dare tell you all my thoughts on the subject,' continued
Bergerat. 'You either believe in vampires or you don't, I believed in
them at that concert.'[44]

After the outbreak of the Franco–Prussian War in 1870, La Païva,
who was known always to have had Prussian sympathies, went to live
at her husband's château at Neudeck, in the wilds of Silesia. Neither
she nor the Count had ever been popular in Paris – their house was
rumoured to have been a hotbed of espionage, and von Donnersmarck
himself, a personal friend of the Kaiser's, later became the Prussian
governor of the conquered territories of Alsace-Lorraine.

After more than twenty years La Païva managed to acquire an annul-
ment to her marriage to the Marquis, and in October 1871 finally
married the still-faithful von Donnersmarck, who as a wedding gift
gave her a necklace which had once belonged to the Empress Eugenie,
three rows of faultless diamonds. Despite this, the fall of the Empire
somehow marked the end for La Païva. Although she and the Count
returned to Paris after the war, where they continued to hold their
receptions, she was hissed at by audiences in theatres, and her husband
was publicly horsewhipped in the Champs Elysées one day.

La Païva died at her husband's castle at Neudeck on 21 January
1884. She was sixty-five. Bergerat claimed that no one ever knew what
happened to her body; that she had no tomb, and that she never lay
in consecrated ground. But he also gives a macabre postscript to the
prodigious existence of this adventuress of love, as the Goncourts called
her. Von Donnersmarck's second wife, young, well-born and beautiful,
was exploring the upper rooms of her husband's castle one day when,
stumbling into a chamber in one of the top towers that before had
always been carefully locked, she came across the corpse of La Païva,
perfectly preserved in alcohol. Who knows, it might even be true.
'Even in death,' wrote the historian Joanna Richardson, 'von
Donnersmarck had not been able to leave her.'[45]

What was the hold that La Païva had over Guido Henckel von
Donnersmarck? That the Count really loved his mistress of so many

years seems beyond question, but it also seems reasonable to hazard the guess that she had some hold over him which went beyond the bounds of any ordinary relationship. Almost all the descriptions of La Païva – both contemporary and posthumous – are of a cold, cruel, domineering woman, possessed of an almost superhumanly implacable will (all her desires, she once boasted, had been brought to heel like whipped spaniels). She was, in short, a textbook dominatrix.

If it were true – as seems highly probable – that the Count had unusual psychosexual tastes, La Païva was not the only courtesan who made it her business to cater to them. One of the most unusual set-ups in Paris at this time belonged to the Drake sisters. One sister was fair, the other dark, and their patrons, Loliée claimed, were expected to pay homage to both on their visits (and no doubt delighted in so doing). Their apartment was 'a model of refinement', a maze of secret passageways· which betrayed 'an ingenious and scientific mastery of the purposes for which it was used'.

> It was devised like the scenery of a fairyland spectacle, and divided, like the premises of a dentist, into a number of independent closets or studies, hidden under draperies. It was impossible for a stranger to find his way in this maze. Three or four visitors might meet face to face. The labyrinth was guarded by a clever maid, who was perfectly trained in the art of hiding one visitor from another. She was known to the habitués of the establishment as the Pointsman, for it was she who prevented collisions.[46]

Most courtesans, however, had a more straightforward approach to business. Although Cora always seems to have had one principal patron (a 'lit de parade', as a French courtesan of the previous generation, Madame Duthé, had once quipped*), one man alone, however wealthy, was simply not enough to keep her extremely expensive establishment going. Zed gives an extraordinary description of how the system worked. A courtesan did not on the whole have 'les associations en syndicat'; instead, in addition to her 'lit de parade' – a man like Massena

---

* Madame Duthé is said at one time to have had two lovers, the Lee brothers. One she called her 'lit de parade', her state bed, the other her 'lit de repos', her bed for relaxing on.

or de Morny, chosen for his fashionable status and breeding as much as for his money – she would usually acquire another protector (and there was almost always a tidy queue of these, he adds, which stretched right around the block) to help make ends meet.

These subsidiary patrons, if one could call them that, though extremely rich, usually came from a slightly less elevated social class than the *noceurs* with whom Cora and Léonide, Blanche and La Barucci usually socialised. They had their fixed hours and rights; they were treated with discretion and even a certain deference by the women themselves; but their principal pleasure, other than the purely sexual one, was the satisfaction of knowing that they too now possessed the mistress of this or that *grand seigneur*. In all other respects they were kept firmly at arm's length. It was considered neither elegant nor necessary to mix with them socially. The courtesans themselves did their work gallantly (*'faisaient crânement . . . la part du devoir'*), and then got on with enjoying themselves. *'On s'amouse au moins avec vous,'* La Barucci once confided to Zed.

It was in this way, wrote Zed, that they organised themselves (La Païva, with her one protector, was an exception). And in this way, too, that they secured their independence: an independence, he noted, that they clung to with astonishing tenacity, and which enabled them, like so many grand duchesses, to put firmly in their place anyone who overstepped the mark.

Cora herself refers to her independence, and its importance to her, many times in her memoir. 'Being the mistress of my own free will, I have kept my independence towards and against all. It was the only way to make men who were worth my while love me,' she wrote with typical candour, 'and to keep myself from being the prey of scamps.'

Not all men, of course, were as happy with this arrangement as they might have been. When the Duc de Morny, brilliant, bald, and irresistible to women, died prematurely in 1865, Cora was in need of another *lit de parade*, and it was with no difficulty that she found one. She had been hunting at Meudon with her friend and admirer Achille Murat, and when the day's sport was over she saw 'a bald gentleman' wagging his head from left to right, 'and apparently delivering an animated monologue'.

'Where can I find her?'

'Won't you tell me whom you are looking for first?'

'In vain I range the woods . . .'

'What for?'

'Ah, she must hide herself in the centre of the earth! This Cora Pearl is invisible. Oh! pardon me, I did not see you.'

The man was the secretary of the person Cora refers to throughout her memoir as 'Duke Jean', and had been sent by him to ask Cora to come up to his château. 'If I accepted,' Cora wrote, 'some one would meet me in one of the walks of the garden.' Of course, she agreed to the assignation, and there, sure enough, 'the Duke awaited me, walking up and down with his hands behind him'. He asked Cora if she liked milk. ' "That," said I, "depends on the circumstances. At present I am thirsty." ' And so it was, over an innocent glass of milk, that Cora's relationship with Prince Napoleon began.

Christened Napoleon Joseph Charles Paul Bonaparte, but known familiarly either as Jérôme or 'Plon Plon', the Prince was the son of Napoleon I's brother, old Prince Jérôme, the ex-King of Westphalia, and therefore the Emperor's cousin. Although he had neither the brilliance nor the charm of his predecessor and half-cousin the Duc de Morny, he was to become the longest-lasting of all the links in Cora's golden chain, and she had a genuine fondness for him.

To a modern eye Prince Napoleon was anything but prepossessing. A photograph of him taken round about the time he first met Cora shows a thick-set, heavy-chinned man of middling years, stout before his time, with the typically beetling brows, wary gaze and thin, rather greasy-looking black hair of the Bonaparte clan. He was forty-two, although he appears much older, and was famous only for the aggressive plainness of his wife, the Princess Clothilde (a daughter of King Victor Emmanuel of Italy), and for his many highly-publicised affairs with other women.

But Cora, who was intimate with the Prince for more than nine years, and who could claim, with some justice, to know him better than anybody, always saw the best in him. Like her he loved horses and dogs and country pursuits, and was always bored by the 'mummeries' and etiquette of the Tuileries. 'My first impression concerning the Duke has never been modified. This man was an angel to those who pleased him,' Cora wrote loyally. 'His voice was agreeable, his laugh frank, his conversation witty, even playful when necessary.' But he was an angel, she cautioned, only to those who pleased him; he could be 'a demon, roué, madman, unhesitating insulter' to those who did not.

And at the beginning of their liaison there were certain things about Cora which did not please the Prince at all. She had other friends, for example, whom she liked to entertain, and did not see any reason why she should give them up. The principal one of these, and her favoured lover of that moment (the word she uses is the euphemistic 'ami'), was a man whom she names 'de Rouvray', while the second was the Prince of Wales's friend, the playboy Duc de Grammont-Caderousse.*

Two, and on some occasions all three of these ill-assorted bedfellows would sometimes accidentally meet at her house, which gave even the normally phlegmatic Cora an uneasy twinge: 'kindness was by no means the sentiment they cherished one towards the other'. But instead of turning into 'an unhesitating insulter', as she evidently feared that he would, the Prince instead put pen to paper, and wrote Cora a series of grumbling letters. 'I have heard all that took place at the last dinner you gave (on Saturday, I believe), about your friends . . . and the disgraceful scene which occurred,' he wrote in one epistle (tantalisingly, he does not give any clues as to what this was). And in another:

> I adore you, you know it . . . but your conduct, my darling Pearl, is fatal. You will never understand in what a state I have been during the last few hours. To see you only to lose you is too hard, and things will come to a crisis. You wish to come, and then to leave me again in an hour, and thus to put us in an impossible position.[47]

Having whipped the Prince into a thoroughly satisfactory fever of desire for her, Cora now had to deal with his jealous rages. 'I said that I had many visitors,' she told him bluntly when he complained about

---

* In her memoir, Cora wittily gave the Duke the name of Barberousse, 'for the sake of euphony'.

de Rouvray, 'and kept much company,' but the Prince was not having any of it. He did not want to share her with anyone.* He replied that 'formerly that was all very well; but since our relations had become fixed, above all when they had become known, that – in short, I must choose between my own door and my visits to the Palace back-stairs'.

Cora, like the great courtesan she was, knew exactly how to handle such a situation. 'I promised all he asked,' she wrote, adding slyly: 'One must be polite. To my friends I gave it to be understood that they must allow me a little time to satisfy the whims of a new and sole protector. My assurances, coupled with my prudent reserve, restored the Duke to good temper. I dined with him tête-à-tête,' she added. 'The Duchess was absent.'

Cora knew very well what she was doing. The Prince had an annual salary from the civil list which, according to one source, was a million francs a year (nearly £2 million).[48] He was quite prepared to share them with Cora. Soon he was keeping her to the tune of twelve thousand francs (£23,000) a month. 'I am not a bad fellow,' he told her, 'and I want you to be always satisfied when you leave here, so that you may be always in a good temper when you come again. If you were a little more orderly in your affairs, you would not be the worse for it. Too many people are after your money.'

The Prince was generous in other ways, too. In addition to her monthly allowance he gave Cora a magnificent house, a mansion at 101, rue de Chaillôt, conveniently close to his own residence at the Palais-Royal, to which she was also given a key which let her into the Prince's apartments by a side street.

There was still the question of de Rouvray, however. Although it was no longer possible for Cora to keep on the same terms with him, she found it rather awkward to break off their relations so very suddenly. She strained at the unaccustomed leash. In order to explain 'a rather long interruption in my visits' to the Prince, she pretended that she had twisted her ankle. 'To speak the truth, it was my faithfulness to [him] that had been rather lame,' she admitted. The Prince was

---

* It is worth noting that he himself harboured no such inhibitions, and felt quite free to share himself out amongst many women even while he was with Cora.

still very jealous; he spied on her, she complained, and quizzed her servants. He had one hold over her, however, that was far worse than any of these things.

> He found nothing better and more to the point than to threaten me with the prospect of an expulsion [from France] if I ceased going to the Palace. I thought expulsion was the most disagreeable trump he kept against me in his hand. I confess that I felt within myself some revolt against such autocratic proceedings. I had to submit, or else I must go, it was clear. I was under the reign of 'his kindness'. Indeed, I did not like it. My freedom, of which I was so jealous, and so proud!

But it was in her interests, Cora decided, to submit – for the time being at least. She went to the Prince to sign peace. Moved by her repentance he proved to be, as Cora put it, 'a good bone-setter', giving her as a present, in addition to the mansion in the rue de Chaillôt, another *hôtel* in the rue des Bassins, valued at 425,000 francs (£800,000), of which he immediately put down the first 200,000 francs.

For all his bullying and overbearing behaviour towards her, the Prince's patronage had made Cora one of the wealthiest women in France. She was now a considerable property owner. In addition to her two splendid residences in Paris she was also the châtelaine of her own castle, the Château de Beauséjour, on the banks of the Loire near Orléans, where her guests might admire her magnificent bronze bath (perhaps with Cora herself in it), which had been specially cast for her in Paris and was engraved with her personal monogram, three 'C's intertwined.

During the second half of the 1860s Cora's career was at its zenith. She was better known, as one observer quipped, than the marshals of France, and her exploits were regularly reported in the papers in both Paris and London. In 1866, when she attended a fancy-dress party at the Restaurant des Trois Frères Provençeaux dressed as Eve, an English journalist wrote in *Baily's Magazine* that Cora 'looked very well, [although] her form and figure were not concealed by any more garments than were worn by the original apple-eater'.[49] Naturally theatrical, she even tried her hand at acting, appearing for a short stint in

January 1867 as Cupid in Offenbach's comic opera *Orphée aux enfers* at the Théâtre des Bouffes-Parisiens. Her entrance upon the stage caused a gasp of astonishment, for the costume she wore, held together by enormous diamonds, was almost as scanty as her apparel as Eve.* 'That evening the Jockey Club, in its entirety, graced the theatre,' wrote Philibert Audebrand of her first night; 'All the names which are blazoned in the Golden Book of the French nobility were there, complete with white gloves and ivory lorgnettes.'[50] But despite the support of her friends – almost all of *la bande* were there, too – Cora was only a moderate success on the stage, and after just twelve nights she retired.

There were other kinds of theatre, however, at which she would always excel. Despite the Prince's jealous rages and his efforts to control her, Cora continued to be a hostess of dazzling originality, giving banquets, masked balls and intimate suppers for her friends just as she always had done, and spending fabulous sums (although the Prince gave her twelve thousand francs a month, she invariably spent twenty-five).

The fashions of the day – over-ornamented, almost baroque in their heavy sensuousness – suited Cora's tastes exactly. Rooms were headily scented with patchouli and vetiver. There was a craze for Asiatic and tropical flowers, for artificial flowers that looked real, and real flowers that looked artificial. The petunia, the gloxinia and the calceolaria became wildly fashionable, and every season saw new varieties, 'speckled, mottled, dappled, all shrill and violent in hue'. The humble geranium was bred into its 'shrillest and most blatant tones', while the equally unassuming ivy was trained over rustic boxes, into pyramids, draped over firescreens and pianos. The fashionable florist Constantin specialised in fabulously expensive flowers from Mexico and Africa – the oppoponax and the mesembryanthemum – which had to be grown in steam heat, and whose Latin names, wrote Sacheverell Sitwell, 'might have been the name of a scent invented by a perfumer, or, more

---

* One of the most striking features of Cora's costume, remembered William Osgood Field, was that the soles of her boots were completely encrusted with diamonds. The buttons on them too were said to have been 'diamonds of the purest water'. An unnamed count later offered fifty thousand francs for them.

simply, the name given to any one of those crinolined women under the glittering chandeliers'.[51]

Although no first-hand account exists of Cora's hospitality during these later years, a detailed description of a dinner given by her friend Blanche d'Antigny at this time gives an idea of the scale of entertaining in the Parisian *demi-monde*.

> *Blinis and caviar gave the guests a thirst, quenched by St Emilion, Volnay accompanied the foie gras, while Chablis and Château d'Yquem came with the lobster. There was peacock in aspic, partridge with champagne . . . Château Lafite came with the asparagus and sauce aurore, and the chicken in aspic with Parisian salads. On to the deserts: strawberries in Kirsch, a bavarois of fruits and mille feuilles Pompadour flavoured in marsala, malmsey wine and sherry. The liqueurs were then passed around and everyone toasted the glorious Diva.*[52]

The biggest surprise was kept till last, however, when Blanche's famous silver chamberpot was brought in, alight with punch. 'When some hesitated, fearing that the pot had already been in use, [one of the guests], showing great spirit took the pot and drank out of it.'

Cora's legendary extravagance inspired acts of equal lavishness in her admirers. One sent her a parcel in which were four *marrons glacés*, each wrapped in a thousand-franc note; another gave her a book in which each of the pages was also a thousand-franc note; a third sent her a massive silver horse which he had filled with jewels and gold. 'If the Frères Provençaux served diamond omelettes,' the Duc de Grammont-Caderousse once remarked, 'Cora would go and dine there every evening.'

Cora's jewels, it was said, were worth as much as a million francs at this point, but she is likely to have spent just as much on her wardrobe. The Second Empire was an age of such conspicuous consumption, both within the *demi-monde* and without, that women could be seen wearing 'whole estates upon their backs'. 'What a society!' wrote the Goncourt brothers in their journal. 'Everybody is determined to bankrupt himself. Never have appearances been so despotic, so imperious, and so demoralising. The Field of the Cloth of Gold, so to speak, is outdone by the luxury in which women live.'[53] Even respectable women spent so vastly beyond their means that some shops opened special accounts for their clientele, who paid only the interest on their debts. Every winter thousands of women's riding habits were pledged at the government pawnshops.

When the artist Felicien Rops arrived in France from Belgium and had his first sight of the 'almost fantastic rig of the Parisian women', he told the Goncourts that they seemed to him like beings from another planet. The styles then in fashion – which included, between 1856 and 1868, the crinoline – were not to everyone's taste. A journalist from the periodical *La Vie Parisienne* who met Cora Pearl at the house of a friend in 1866 was so scathing about her get-up that he said she was fit only to be put 'with the curiosities of the Barnum Museum':

> *A pink satin dress, with a kind of mauve gauze flounce on the hem of the skirt, over which was some blond-lace sprinkled with white bugles. A gathered, décolleté bodice, with two little mauve flounces all round it. A loose belt, with four mauve streamers, sewn with pearls.*[54]

What is more likely – and may perhaps account for the journalist's scathing tone – is that Cora was in fact at the cutting edge of fashion. Unlike many of the other courtesans of the day, who were known for the sobriety of their dress, Cora had always been flamboyant in her tastes (*Le Figaro* once described her dresses as '*saisissantes*', or very striking). She dyed her hair, which was at one time red,* at another blonde; and once even dyed her dog blue to match one of her outfits (unfortunately the dog died). She was extremely skilled in the use of make-up, and is credited with having introduced the modern forms of it into France. And, like all the richest women of her day, when it came to her wardrobe, Cora was dressed by no less a personage than the world's first *haut couturier*, Charles Worth.

Worth had come to France from his native England in 1845 at the age

---

* Henri Rochefort wrote in *Le Figaro* on 27 September 1864 that the latest craze amongst Parisian women was for bright red hair, which they obtained by applying a mixture of ammoniac and powdered brick-dust. 'The celebrated Cora Pearl, who is dark, was the first to unfurl this scarlet flag.' See W.H. Holden, *The Pearl from Plymouth*.

of just nineteen. Having trained as a boy at the London haberdashers' emporium Swan & Edgar's, he soon found a job in one of Paris's most fashionable shops, the silk mercers Gagelin et Opigez. At that time there were very few ready-made clothes available for women to buy. In terms of dressmaking, things had not changed much since Sophia Baddeley's day: most women still either made their own clothes at home or took their material to a local milliner, of which there were thousands in London alone, to have it made up for them. A few of the most talented of these milliners made a name for themselves amongst the aristocratic and the very rich – in Paris, Marie-Antoinette's Rose Bertin had been one, Esther Guimond's Camille another – and all of them, without exception, were women.

The 1840s have been described as one of the most static decades, in fashion terms, in the whole of the nineteenth century, but with the return of the Bonapartist aristocracy after the *coup d'état* of 1851, the mood changed. The Emperor Napoleon III, who was determined to bring both energy and glamour to his newly-minted Imperial court, married the Spanish Eugenie de Montijo, who was young, beautiful, and very stylish. The ambitious Worth, who had been looking for ways to branch out of the haberdashery business, realised that this was his moment. For some time he had been using his French wife, Marie Augustine Vernet, as a *'demoiselle de magasin'*, or shop model. His department specialised in accessories such as wraps and mantles, and Worth had designed a perfectly simple white muslin dress for her to wear when modelling them. The pattern of this dress was so exquisite, the fit so good and the line so elegant, that many customers had commented on it.

Emboldened by this success, Worth suggested to Monsieur Gagelin himself that they should open a new department selling ready-made women's dresses. Gagelin was horrified. Dressmaking, as everyone knew, was lowly women's work, and he wanted nothing to do with it. Eventually, however, the demand for Worth's dresses became so great that Gagelin was forced to relent. A sop to his injured pride was perhaps provided by the new term which came to be used to describe the exquisite craftsmanship and unparalleled skill of his employee's cut: 'It was not dressmaking; it was *haute couture*.'[55]

By 1858 Worth's success was such that he had opened his own business, Worth et Bobergh (the Swedish Otto Bobergh was his partner). They had no premises of their own, and their first customers were received by Worth and his wife in their bedroom. Paris was outraged. The idea of a 'man-milliner' (or a 'bearded milliner', as Charles Dickens wrote disparagingly) had been shocking enough even when it had the sanction of a famous institution like Gagelin's. But the idea of a man actually fitting a woman for a dress, watching her robe and disrobe, perhaps even touching her while she was in a state of *déshabille*, was indecent in the extreme. Rumours were put about that Worth et Bobergh was a brothel, a centre for the most outrageous immorality.

The women for whom Worth made his dresses, however, felt well able to make this sacrifice. Worth's designs were quite different from anything they had ever known. Unlike the heavy, dowdy drapery of the previous decade, the confections produced by Worth were simple, elegant and, above all, light as air. If the loss of a little modesty was the only price, these rebels thought, then they would grin and bear it.

Although Worth did not himself invent the crinoline, he was by far its most gifted exponent. In his hands this most bizarrely cumbersome of fashions was elevated into nothing short of an art form. Throughout the 1840s women's dresses had become increasingly bulky and cumbersome. As more and more petticoats were needed to achieve the desired width in the skirts, some were stiffened with whalebone, others with buckram or split sugar canes, while the most unwieldy of all were padded out with horsehair ('*crin*' in French*), until women could hardly move beneath the sheer weight of fabric. By 1856, however, special petticoats held out by light steel bands had been introduced which were originally known as 'cage-crinolines' – the crinoline as we have come to think of it today.

Just two years later there were factories which made nothing but crinoline steel, but when it first appeared the 'cage-crinoline' – which today has become the familiar shorthand, along with frilled coverings

---

* In the 1840s a 'crinoline' meant a horsehair petticoat.

for piano legs,* for all the worst excesses of Victorian prudery – was regarded with shocked incredulity. The steel hoops held out the skirts so effectively that there was no longer any need to wear multiple layers of petticoats. Thus, not only was a woman who wore a crinoline almost indecently naked beneath her skirt (by the standards of the 1850s), but when she moved the 'cage' had the disconcerting property of swaying provocatively from side to side and, horror on horror's head, showing her ankles.†

In England meetings were held for the express purpose of trying to abolish the crinoline, but to no avail. *Demi-mondaines* everywhere rushed to purchase this interesting new garment, and 'respectable' women were almost as quick to adopt it (and were no doubt just as aware of its erotic possibilities: in England, old Lady Jersey, George IV's former lover, aged eighty but looking fifty, gamely began to wear Worth's creations straight away). 'The girls of our time like to show their legs,' wrote William Hardman‡ mildly to his friend Holroyd. 'I don't see why they should be interfered with; it pleases them, and does no harm to us.' Although it may seem paradoxical to a modern eye, the crinoline, for all its magnificent bulk, gave women a freedom of movement they had not enjoyed for decades.¶

---

* The historian Peter Gay attributes the origin of this to Captain Marryat, the English naval officer and novelist, who wrote of a prudish headmistress of a ladies' seminary in Massachuestts who concealed the 'limbs' of a pianoforte in frilled 'modest little trousers'. It has enjoyed, he points out, a quite unwarranted posthumous fame. See Gay's *The Education of the Senses*.

† A joke, apparently rejected by *Punch* about this time, went as follows: 'Why may the crinoline be justly rewarded as a social invention?' 'Because it enables us to see more of our friends than we used to.'

‡ A diarist and letter-writer of the period. His memoir, *A Mid-Victorian Pepys*, was published in 1923.

¶ In 1862, as a young girl of twelve, the novelist who became known as 'Gyp' was taken to the races at Longchamps by her uncle. She later wrote an account of women's fashions there. In order to see better, many women had taken to standing on their chairs: 'When the race was nearing a finish all the women suddenly leaned forward, and the pressure of the cages against the backs of the chairs made them shoot up behind like a lot of fans. And then I could see everyone's underwear right up to the waist, and found that now I had plenty of variety before me. Some of the interiors were frothy, a foam of lace and muslin, some were cold and severe, others had a casual air or were frankly ludicrous. The weather was extremely hot, and most of the women had not put on a *petit jupon*, that is to say a skirt between their knickers and the cage, and I noticed to my surprise a thing I had not seen before, small ends of material which hung down here and there.'

Princess Pauline Metternich, the wife of the Austrian Ambassador to France, daringly adopted some of Worth's creations, and his great moment came when the Empress Eugenie herself followed suit. His career was made, and soon he dominated the fashion scene – as it could now perhaps be called – to the exclusion of everyone else. At court entertainments a gown by Worth became almost *de rigueur*. Before long Worth et Bobergh were employing 1200 seamstresses, and at the height of his career Worth was producing a thousand new ballgowns, four times a season, all of which had to be ready on the same night, and each one different. The fascinated women who patronised him gave little thought to the dizzying logistical demands of such an exercise. The Comtesse de Mercy-Argenteau vividly described the experience of a visit to his *atelier*.

> Worth was very amusing, and his vogue came quite as much from his personality as from his talent as a dressmaker. When I wanted an important toilette for a Court ball or some reception at the Tuileries, I had to call several times. He would first look at me for a long while without speaking: then in an inspired and faraway voice: 'Light gauze ... pearl grey ... roses and leaves ... a trail of lace ...' and he would disappear. Then I had to go; the Master was building his new masterpiece and would let me know when I could try it on. If he decided that I was to wear blue or green I had to do as I was told. He was a tyrant, but we all adored him.[56]

Although the basic form of the crinoline was to remain high fashion for another ten years, Worth's creative instincts were such that he was constantly making small innovations. When crinolines finally became so impossibly big that they interfered with almost all normal daily pursuits, it was he who took the matter in hand and invented the more practical flat-fronted crinoline, adopted by the entire French court in 1864. The year previously he had designed an ankle-length

---

Her uncle told her, casually but knowledgeably, that these were chemises. See Norman Hartnell, *Royal Courts of Fashion*.

skirt for the Empress to wear when skating and indulging in other outdoor pursuits. But although Worth began to think of himself not as a 'man milliner' at all, but as an artist – even adopting the flowing coat and velvet beret, modelled after Rembrandt, which were the accepted dress of an artist at this time – his creative genius was always combined with a shrewd business head.

No one was refused a fitting by him – so long as they could afford his prices. The expense of acquiring a dress by Worth was immense. Even the simplest day costume cost 1600 francs (£3000), while the evening gowns in which he specialised were 2500 francs (£5000). In 1863, when the American Mrs Charles Moulon was invited by the Empress to one of her intimate Monday-night parties for just four hundred guests (usually there were several thousand present), she estimated that the combined value of all the Worth dresses there was $200,000. The cost of her own wardrobe for a visit to the Imperial country retreat at Compiègne, for which all twenty-one of her day and afternoon costumes and evening gowns had been made by Worth, was so astronomical that when she was invited for a repeat visit her multi-millionaire father-in-law protested that it would bankrupt him.[57] Nonetheless, between ten and twelve in the morning, and three and five in the afternoon, the sight of the massed carriages of *grandes dames* outside Worth's premises in the rue de la Paix continued to be one of the sights of Paris.

Cora's carriage, naturally, was amongst them. All the most chic courtesans, it was well known, like other ladies of fashion, were dressed by Worth. Although *demi-mondaines* had no use for court dresses, Worth's masterpieces, even the very grandest ones, were perfectly suited to their extravagant lifestyle, which was as yet unaffected by the political situation in Europe. In 1866 there had been clashes between Prussia and Austria, and a nervous France had ordered the return of her troops from Mexico, then briefly under French control, where they had been bolstering the unpopular puppet-king, the Emperor's cousin Maximilian. But when, in 1867, news came that the unprotected Maximilian had been tried and shot in Mexico, a sea-change came over Paris. The court went into mourning, and Cora, like everyone else, was quick to adopt the new, severer fashions which were now introduced.* In 1868, after a reign of a dozen years, the crinoline was finally dead. Just two years later the Second Empire itself followed suit.

In 1870 came the Franco–Prussian War. Although Cora's first thought was for her horses – she managed to get eight of them out of Paris, on the pretext of 'exercise', before the siege of the city began – she, like many of her fellow courtesans, turned her *hôtel* at 101, rue de Chaillôt into a small hospital, paying all the expenses for its upkeep herself. But while the war was short-lived – the Emperor and his troops surrendered in September – for Cora the world would never be the same again.

Like the rest of the Imperial family, Prince Napoleon went immediately into exile. First he went to his wife's family in Italy, from where he wrote to Cora regularly. The following year he suggested that he and Cora should try to meet, albeit briefly, in London (a place that the Prince detested). His letters to her from this time are solicitous and loving. 'My fondness for *la P[earl]* is still lively,' he wrote to her in December 1871. 'I love her, think of her, and will see her in a few weeks' time ... Believe me, there is no coolness on my part ... my own dearest P–.'[58] It was to be Cora's first visit to England for more than twenty years. When she arrived she booked a suite of rooms for them at the Grosvenor Hotel, but she was recognised and thrown out. It was not an auspicious homecoming.

Although she had been born in England, Cora always had the heart and soul of a Frenchwoman. As soon as she could, she returned to Paris. She no longer had the Prince as her protector, and debts of more than 200,000 francs had forced her out of at least one of her houses – the mansion in the rue des Bassins – but it was not long before she managed to pick up a semblance of her old life. She must have written many letters during this time to Prince Napoleon, for his to her are still affectionate, full of references to the fêtes and parties she was attending, and anxious advice to her not to give too many of her dinners. 'You are still pretty, are you not?' he wrote to her solici-

---

* With dresses pulled smoothly over the hips and stomach, and gathered generously into a bustle at the back, the female form was now shown again as it had not been for more than a decade. Forgetting how scandalous the crinoline had been when it first appeared, many commentators were now equally shocked by its absence.

tously from London in 1874. 'Do not drink too much bouillon; it is too fattening, and your pretty waist would suffer.'[59]

It was in 1872 that Cora first met the man who was to be her nemesis: Alexandre Duval. Cora was now thirty-seven years old, Duval was ten years her junior. He was the son of Pierre Duval, an immensely wealthy man who had made a fortune through a chain of cheap restaurants known as the Bouillons Duval.* When Pierre Duval died Alexandre inherited a fortune of more than ten million francs. He became besotted with Cora, and although he was far from being one of the aristocratic playboys from whom she had always been used to pick her patrons, for a while his money was enough to keep things running smoothly between them.

He bought her jewels and horses, some of which came from the ex-Emperor's stables, and it was largely thanks to him that she was able to keep up her mansion at 101, rue de Chaillôt and her château near Orléans. But when he was unable, or unwilling, to go on paying, Cora refused to see him. Beside himself with fury, on the evening of 17 December 1872 Duval tried to force his way into her house, but Cora's servants, under her strict instructions, shut the door on him.

Since Cora herself has left no account of the events that followed, it has only ever been possible to piece together what happened through the subsequent, predictably lurid, newspaper accounts of it. Two days later, still in a desperate state, Alexandre once again went to Cora's house, and this time managed to force his way in. During the terrible scene that followed he took a pistol from his pocket, which went off, wounding him so badly that he was lucky to escape with his life. One account claims that he deliberately put the pistol to his side – the bullet entered below his lung and lodged in his back – but another maintains that it was Cora he intended to kill.

The scandal that became known as 'the Duval incident' destroyed Cora completely. 'The pig might at least have done it in the ante-room,' she is alleged to have said afterwards; 'then he would not have stained my carpet.' Even if she had not in fact said this (and it seems highly

---

* Perhaps the Prince's reference to Cora not ruining herself with too much *bouillon* was meant as a coded joke. If so, given what happened next, it was a macabre one.

unlikely that she did), she was no match for the young Duval – handsome, apparently dying, and ruined by her extravagance – in the public sympathy stakes. The whole of France, it seemed, was up in arms against her. 'Two days after that man was wounded,' Cora wrote, 'a police officer visited me notifying, with the utmost politeness, the order to leave French territory immediately. I obeyed, and departed from my friends. Though I was not responsible for the folly of that young man, I had to pay, in that way, for his madness! And pay dear!' Exiled from France, Cora's worst nightmare had come true.

The death of Cora Pearl has continued to puzzle her biographers almost as much as her extraordinary life. In the immediate aftermath of the 'Duval affair' and her exile from France, she was given refuge by her friend the courtesan Caroline Letessier, who was at that time being kept by the Prince of Monaco's son. But eventually, having drifted through Europe – Monte Carlo, Nice, the Italian Riviera – for several years, Cora did manage to return to her beloved Paris again, where, although no longer fashionable, she seems at least to have been tolerated. Her glorious mansion at 101, rue de Chaillôt had been sold to Blanche d'Antigny, but she still owned property both in Paris and at Maisons-Laffitte. And although she is on record as having auctioned off much of her silver at Drouot's in 1877 – there were 232 items in the catalogue – her estate at Olivet, which included the Château de Beauséjour, although heavily mortgaged, was not sold until 1885, just a year before her death.

Cora had parted company from Prince Napoleon in 1874, although for some years she continued to have other protectors. 'Faced with my duty,' the Prince had written to her with real feeling, 'I can have no choice. I have decided against you, against myself, in favour of what must be done. I have a life of work before me, it must not degenerate through dissipation . . . I shall not see you for some time, but one day I shall clasp your hand and kiss you with great joy, my dear Cora.'[60]

Accounts of Cora at this time are as varied as they always were. Some claimed that she became a pathetic, over-painted figure, haunting the scenes of her former glories and shunned by most of her old acquaintance. The French political journalist Henri Rochford was annoyed by what he unkindly called 'that ugly old wreck with her negress lips, grey eyes, and dripping nose', who would accost him in the Bois de Boulogne and ask for racing tips. Arsène Houssaye, although never a particular fan of Cora's, gives a more spirited description of her at this time in his *Confessions*.

> *I had known Miss Cora Pearl in her ascendancy. I wanted to see her again in her decline . . . She was living then near the hôtel Païva, two doors further down, in an entresol full of odds and ends, over a carriage shop. One day I went and knocked on her door. 'Good afternoon, Cora!' She threw her arms round my neck, she was so glad to meet a friend from her good days again. 'Yes, Cora,' she said, 'but Cora without the pearls.' 'You're still pretty!' I answered, without conviction. 'No, I'm not. Look, my cheeks are furrowed with tears. Don't say that in the papers. Paris doesn't like women who weep.'* [61]

But the description which, for me at least, rings truest is the one recounted to Cora's biographer W.H. Holden by an eighty-seven-year-old American gentleman, Mr Walker, who in October 1947 was living in Paris, and who remembered how numerous members of the Jockey Club used to subscribe to a special fund, which one of their number delivered to Cora each month.[62] Mr Walker also remembered seeing her arrive at the races in her *barouche*, around the year 1878 (when he would have been eighteen). 'She was immediately surrounded by fashionable men; and he says that although not pretty, she was very animated, there was much talking and laughing, and the men evidently enjoyed her company.'[63]

Cora Pearl died on 8 July 1886, from cancer of the stomach. She was fifty-one.

5

CATHERINE WALTERS
1839–1920

The Courtesan's Courtesan

A LL HER LIFE Cora Pearl had played upon her essential difference from the other great courtesans of *la bande*. Her originality and inventiveness (some would call it eccentricity), her flamboyance (some would call it brashness), her love of the outdoors and her physical daring – her Englishness, in short – had always set her apart.* It had been the source of her great *cachet*, but it was also ultimately her downfall.

As Cora's immediate exile from France in the wake of the Duval affair shows, the French were every bit as xenophobic with regard to the English as traditionally the English had always been towards them. And in Paris under the Second Empire only one other English court-esan was ever to come close to having Cora's success: Catherine Walters, known to her contemporaries as 'Skittles'.

Unlike her countrywoman, from the very beginning Catherine was the paradigm of everything it was believed a courtesan should be. Whereas Cora always remained deeply puzzling to those whom she did not immediately captivate, no one in France could fail to appreciate the classical loveliness of 'Skittels' (Zed's Gallic spelling of her name). While Cora was psychologically complex, sometimes even challenging

---

* If she were operating today, Cora would surely favour Versace and Vivienne Westwood over, say, Yves St Laurent and Chanel.

to her lovers (Arsène Houssaye had once remarked that she treated her horses better than she did her protectors), Catherine was – or appeared to be – sweet, yielding, and delicate as a flower. If Cora's gift was to fascinate men and to hold them sexually in thrall, Catherine had the kind of beauty that inspired hopeless romantic passion. The English poet and adventurer Wilfrid Scawen Blunt, who fell in love with her when he was a young man of twenty-three, called her a 'phoenix of creation'. Some of his most ardent poetry was inspired by her, and when their affair was finally over, so it was later said, he was never really able to love a woman fully again.

If Catherine Walters is not usually included in the annals of the *grandes horizontales* of the Second Empire, it is only because the time she spent in Paris was relatively short. When she arrived there in 1862 she had already taken London by storm. Now she proceeded to conquer Paris with the same apparent effortlessness with which she drove her famous phaetons or rode her horses.

For Zed it was almost enough that Catherine was as unlike Cora as it was possible to be: 'An English girl like Cora Pearl, beautiful, but distinguished, and a good horsewoman, which Cora was not.' According to him, Catherine had blonde hair, dark blue eyes, clear skin, and a pure complexion. Photographs of her taken at this time show a young woman of ravishing natural beauty. Her waist is the requisite handspan, her neck long and graceful, her profile pure; she is dressed with a sobriety which borders on the austere. Although both Zed and Blunt remembered her as blonde, all the photographs show her as being dark-haired, and in later years she described herself as auburn.

It was not only Catherine's great beauty which impressed the French; it was also her naturally aristocratic air, and her almost patrician way with horses. Hers was the kind of exoticism that Parisians could really understand. 'This was something special, very select,' wrote Zed approvingly, 'and reminiscent of London and Hyde Park.' Cora Pearl had always prided herself on the quality and extravagance of her stables – had made them, indeed, the talk of Paris – but when it came to pure horsemanship, Catherine had no rivals. The sight of her riding sidesaddle in her famous 'princess habit', cut so perfectly to the contours of her body that it was rumoured she was completely naked beneath it, was a rapturously erotic experience for the appreciative *boulevardiers* of Paris.* 'And how smart, how elegant, what a horse-woman, what an air of originality and honesty in the presentation of her carriages!' wrote Zed in his portrait of her. 'When she appeared on the avenue de l'Impératrice driving herself with two beautiful sparkling pure-blooded horses, followed by two grooms on horseback in splendid and elegant uniform . . . every head turned, and all eyes were on her.'[1] For the short time that she was to stay in Paris, he recalled, the whole world was at Catherine's feet.

Catherine Walters was very far from being the aristocratic *ingénue* that she at first appeared. She was born in Liverpool on 13 June 1839, the daughter of a sea-captain and his Irish wife, and was baptised a Catholic. There are several variations of the story of her early life, but the most reliable of them is that which was written down by Wilfrid Scawen Blunt in his secret diaries exactly as it had been told to him by Catherine herself. According to Blunt, Catherine's mother died when she was four, and she was sent to a convent school in Cheshire, from which she later ran away after a fight with the Mother Superior. Catherine always had a passion for horses, and soon she was employed by the owner of a livery stable to display his animals on the hunting field (she rode chiefly with the Cheshire Hunt), apparently receiving a percentage of the sales. Her nickname 'Skittles' was acquired around this time, from her skill in a Cheshire skittles alley.

When she was sixteen Catherine became the mistress of George, Lord Fitzwilliam, a hunting man and master of the Fitzwilliam Hounds. She separated from him a few years later (receiving a very generous settlement of £300 a year and a further £2000 lump sum in the bank[2]),

---

* For daring and style Catherine's only rival on the hunting field was Empress Elizabeth of Austria, who often hunted with the Grafton in England, and was also renowned for the tightness of her riding habit. A room at the house where the meet was held was always set aside especially for her, and the Empress's dresser would arrive there before her with a footman to carry her hunting clothes and other accoutrements (which always included her own private chamberpot, made of gold and bearing the Imperial arms). The dresser would then stitch the riding habit onto the Empress, starting with a special chamois undergarment, a process which took hours. The result was a garment so perfectly fitting – buttoned down and strapped in every direction, for these were the days before the safety habit – that she could barely walk. If she suffered a fall it was impossible for her to stand up without the buttons and straps being unfastened first.

and transferred her affections to Spencer Compton Cavendish, Marquis of Hartington and the son and heir of the Duke of Devonshire.

'Harty-Tarty', as he was sometimes called, was to become a major figure in Liberal politics, and was considered by many as Gladstone's natural successor (although he refused the premiership three times). He was, however, not Catherine's most exciting patron: 'He stood by himself and could have come from no country in the world but England,' wrote Margot Asquith of the future 8th Duke of Devonshire. 'He had the figure and appearance of an artisan, with the brevity of a peasant, the courtesy of a king, and the noisy sense of humour of a Falstaff. He gave a great wheezy guffaw at all the right things, and was possessed of infinite wisdom.'[3]

Before the opening of the Blunt archive in 1973 it had always been thought that the *liaison* of Hartington and Catherine had lasted only a few months; but Blunt's papers contained a packet of some two hundred letters from Hartington to Catherine, which had been kept by her until her death in 1920 and were then given to Blunt for safekeeping. This correspondence, which took place at least once, sometimes two or three times, a week, covers a period of four years, and clearly shows that the relationship was a deeply affectionate one on both sides.

Catherine was just nineteen when she first met Hartington; he was twenty-six. A shy and somewhat immature man, when he wrote to her his rather blunt letters are nonetheless charged with real feeling. 'My darling little Skitsy', he begins, 'My little darling', and – when things were not quite right between them – 'my poor little darling child'. He signed his letters 'H', and she called him 'Cav' (short for Cavendish), which was his family's pet name for him. Some of the Devonshire House slang current in the previous century during the lifetime of his great-great-aunt Georgiana, the celebrated 5th Duchess of Devonshire, still survives in his letters: 'Cav loves oo and nobody else.'[4]

The great passion that Hartington and Catherine shared, and the only one they were able to indulge in publicly together, was that of hunting. It was on the hunting field that they probably met, and many of their letters make references to their continued enjoyment of the sport. 'Take care of yourself,' he cautions her in one letter, 'and don't break your neck.' And in February 1862 he had to watch her 'go home all by yourself on a lame horse ... I hope you didn't cry as you went home, poor little child.'

Catherine's horsemanship, for which she was passionately admired by her contemporaries, meant that she found an acceptance on the hunting field that was denied to her in every other social situation. Stories about her daring, both on the field and off, abound. She once cleared the eighteen-foot water jump at the National Hunt Steeplechase at Market Harborough for a £100 bet with ease, after three other riders had tried and failed.

These skills brought with them other benefits. Englishmen, perhaps even more so than their *confrères* over the Channel, found the sight of a pretty woman on horseback a powerful aphrodisiac. 'I remember very well one day in the early 'sixties riding home from hunting with my father by the side of Stouton Wood,' wrote one hunting devotee, Sir Willoughby Maycock, in his *Annals of the Billesdon Hunt*.

> *Suddenly we heard the sound of horses galloping behind us; two people passed us by and were over the fence and in front of us in the twinkling of an eye ... One was a man in black; the other a woman ... [she] wore a habit that fitted like a glove, and a bit of cherry ribbon round her neck. In short, she was a perfect dream. She made a remark to her pilot as she passed by which we both heard distinctly ... I am afraid I cannot give it word for word, but it was to the effect that she felt convinced that when she reached home a certain portion of her anatomy would probably be of much the same hue as the tie she wore round her neck. I noticed my dear old father biting his lips to suppress his merriment, and trying to look as if he hadn't heard it. I asked him if he knew who they were. 'Yes,' he replied, 'the man is Jem Mason,* and the woman Skittles.'*[5]

Despite the unusual licence of the hunting field, not everyone was always so tolerant. Hartington once wrote advising Catherine not to

---

* A famous steeplechase rider.

accept an invitation to hunt at Loughborough, 'for I think some of them are snobs'. There is a story, too – one of many legends which grew up around her, and of which there are several versions – of a dispute which once arose while she was riding with the Quorn in Leicestershire, which was, and remains, one of the smartest and most select of all hunts.

The Master of the Quorn was the Earl of Stamford, who had married a gamekeeper's daughter. His Countess, despite having been (depending on which version of the story you prefer) either a bareback rider at Astley's Circus* or a performer at the Cremorne Gardens, took such exception to Catherine's presence on the hunting field that she asked one of the whips to get rid of her. Catherine left with good grace, but not before she had called out, as her parting remark, 'Why does Lady Stamford give herself such airs? *She's* not the Queen of our profession, I am.'⁶† That this story has some basis in fact is borne out by one of Hartington's letters to her, which sympathises with her after 'the stupid people in Leicestershire' had tried to ostracise her.⁷

It is not known exactly when Catherine first came to London, but it is likely to have been sometime at the end of the 1850s. Hartington's first surviving letter to her, dated July 1859, indicates that by then she was already well-established as his mistress, and she had probably followed him there for the London Season. Although he had been elected to Parliament in 1857, at this stage Hartington was not yet especially involved in politics, although there are some references to the inconvenient timings of debates in the House. He would come round to her, he once wrote, 'if [the debate] is not very late indeed: but don't expect me after two o'clock'. To fill her days, and sometimes her nights, Catherine took lessons with a governess. She was very quick to learn, and Hartington was full of praise for her letters to him, 'without any mistakes in spelling or grammar. You are getting quite a learned little Skits,' he wrote.⁸

---

* This is a favourite old chestnut, and there are many courtesans, including Blanche d'Antigny and Catherine herself, who have been alleged to have begun their careers in this way.

† In another version of the story she is reputed to have said: '*She's* not the Queen of our profession, Lady Cardigan is.' See page 313.

Years later, when Catherine confided to Scawen Blunt the story of her early life, she claimed that Hartington had intended to marry her, if only he could obtain the consent of his father, the 7th Duke of Devonshire. Did she really believe that this would ever happen? To his credit, Hartington seems to have been a true aristocrat, in that he was unimpressed by most of the forms and 'mummeries of etiquette' of his time; but all the same, even he must have been aware of the inconvenience (at the very least) of having a wife whose reception in polite society would have been so doubtful.

As a protector, however, he was generous to a fault. For all his great expectations, by the standards of the day Hartington was not personally very rich, and was obliged to survive on an allowance from his father. Despite this he paid Catherine a generous allowance of her own, and in his letters there are references to additional gifts of £100, £150 and even £250. He also provided her with the horses and hunters that were to become so much her signature, and a house, 34 Park Street in Mayfair. 'My little Skits is rather expensive,' he wrote to her in a husbandly way.[9]

Out of Season he was able to see even less of her than when they were in London together. He wrote to her from Chatsworth – 'more black and dirty and beastly and dull than ever' – and tried to reassure her that he had not forgotten her.

In the late summer of 1860, when Hartington was engaged in the usual round of aristocratic shooting parties, Catherine took herself on a holiday abroad to France and Italy. Hartington wrote to her jestingly that she was not to 'make eyes at the Pope or Garibaldi', but in fact he was the least jealous of men. 'It is very nice of you to say that you are so fond of me, but you know there is somebody you like better,' he wrote to her disarmingly once. 'Have you seen him lately?'

In fact it was Catherine who was the jealous one, as Hartington's letters to her make clear. 'There are a lot of people here,' he wrote to her from one of his house parties, 'but I don't look at them because Skits says I mustn't.' Yet increasingly, as they both must have known, their relationship was becoming untenable.

If Hartington had hoped for a sweet, docile mistress who would wait patiently for him at home, he was not to find her in Catherine.

Catherine's house was conveniently close to Hyde Park, and she took full advantage of it. It was not unusual for livery stables in London at this time to employ young women to advertise their horses by riding them in the park, and by the mid-century these 'pretty horsebreakers', as they were known, had become a common sight in Hyde Park during the fashionable promenading hours of five to seven. It has always been thought that it was through one of these livery stables that Catherine first came to prominence in the Park, although given that she was by this stage already Hartington's mistress, with an establishment and a fine stable of her own, this seems unlikely. Instead she joined that even more well-known group – which in the eyes of the moralists was, in any case, indistinguishable from the dubiously self-advertising parades of the 'horsebreakers' – the fashionable Victorian courtesans.

Although there had been many well-known *grandes horizontales* in England in the early Victorian era – some of whom, such as Laura Bell, Agnes Willoughby and Mabel Grey, were household names in their time – none was to be more celebrated than Catherine.* During her first few years in London she kept away from the more popular areas of the Park. According to a notorious article in *The Times* which was later written about her, up until the early 1860s she was 'a shy damsel', who avoided the crowds and kept instead to the more unfrequented roads, where she could more freely exercise her ponies, and talk to her numerous male acquaintances 'with becoming privacy'.[10]

But her attempts – whether real or carefully orchestrated – to keep to herself failed. Catherine, as she must have known, was too striking, and too good a horsewoman, not to attract attention. In 'The Season', a satirical poem published in 1861 by the future poet laureate Alfred Austin, 'Skittles' is already a notorious feature of London life:

With slackened rein swift Skittles rules the Row.

Austin imagines how the 'scowling matrons' and the 'unmarketable maidens of the mart', with their 'plumpness gone' and their

---

* In her own lifetime no fewer than four 'biographies' of Catherine, Holywell chap-books of uncertain authenticity, were published by George Vickers, the same publisher who published the translation of Cora Pearl's *Memoirs*.

... propped-up bosoms bare
To catch some boyish buyer unaware

might view her:

Answer me, all! Belle, heiress, flirt and prue!
Who has our notice? Skittles more or you;
'The nasty wretch! Regard her saucy leer'
Well, own her conquest, and I'll own it queer.

In a footnote to the poem, Austin explained to any readers he might have 'who reside wholly in the Provinces' that Skittles was currently the cynosure of every eye in the Park, and that all the young ladies of society speculated endlessly on 'her origin, abode and doings'.[11]

By the following Season of '62, however, the fame of Catherine's beauty and her equipage had become so great that privacy was now impossible for her. The anonymous article which appeared in *The Times* gives some idea of the impact she had on London society in the early 1860s:

The fashionable world eagerly migrated in search of her from the Ladies Mile to Kensington Road [Rotten Row]. The highest ladies in the land enlisted themselves as her disciples. Driving became the rage. Three, four, five, six hundred guineas were given for a pair of ponies on the condition they should be as handsome as Anonyma's, that they should step as high as Anonyma's. If she wore a pork pie hat, they wore pork pie hats; if her paletot was made by Poole, their paletots were made by Poole. If she reverted to more feminine attire, they reverted to it also. Where she drove, they followed, and I must confess that, as yet, Anonyma has fairly distanced her fair competitors. They can none of them sit, dress, drive, or look as well as she does; nor can any of them procure for money such ponies as Anonyma contrives to get — for love.[12]

As Lady Augusta Fane was to remark in her memoirs, it was unheard of for any respectable woman of society to acknowledge that she even knew such women existed, yet here was 'Skittles' quite openly discussed in no less a newspaper than *The Times*. Not to be outdone, The *Daily*

Telegraph soon came thundering into the debate. On 4 July one of its leaders fulminated against its rival's attempt to convert Catherine into a heroine of the moment. The 'preposterous alias', as the *Telegraph* put it, had fooled no one.

> *The plain truth of the matter is that Hyde Park, like every other place of public resort, has been for a lengthened period infested by a number of lewd women, who, being well paid by wealthy profligates for selling their miserable bodies for the purpose of debauchery, are enabled to dress splendidly, and drive handsome equipages. Many of these shameful creatures are the daughters of stablemen and rough riders in the country, and elsewhere; and are dexterous enough in using the whips, which, in the old Bridewell days, would have been laid about their own shoulders ... Their principal pre-occupation is to interchange salutes with Lord Dundreary,* and to stare modest women out of countenance ... Is* The Times *newspaper powerful enough to persuade its readers that any good can accrue from petting and patting on the back, and simpering over the splendid shame of these impudent wenches? We think not ... For 'Anonyma' in her pony carriage we have not one grain of pity or sympathy. She is a worthless and shameful jade, and it is a scandal to have mentioned her.*[13]

Unwittingly, and at least in some measure thanks to the *Daily Telegraph*'s self-serving cries of 'scandal' (always a good way to sell newspapers), the 'shameful jade' now found herself in a glare of publicity the like of which no English courtesan had enjoyed since the days of Sophia Baddeley. Like Sophia before her, Catherine had become that rare but unmistakable thing, a star: followed, imitated, stared at, surrounded by fascinated multitudes whenever she stopped to speak to one of her acquaintances in the Park.

If Hartington minded he did not say so, but there was no mention of marriage now. In fact, for the past year, far from seeking his father's consent to marry Catherine, Hartington had been hinting, in the

---

* A foolish fop in Tom Taylor's famous contemporary comedy *Our American Cousin*. 'Dundrearies' became the term for long whiskers cut sideways from the chin, as sported by the original character in the play.

gentlest and most roundabout way, of his desire to extricate himself from their arrangement. On his way to Scotland in September 1861 he had written to her of the impossibility of coming to visit her before his departure:

> I wish I could come and see my little darling first but I don't know how to manage it. I have got no good excuse for going up to London now; and I don't want my people here to know anything about you Skitsy if I can help it . . . Poor child I am of no use to you am I?'

He added hopefully: 'You want some one to look after you more than I can, don't you?'

In November the same year he wrote to her again, this time with even greater clarity:

> Sometimes I think that it would be better for you if you could forget me . . . Because you are too good to be left in the world all alone so much, and some day, you ought to find some one who will take care of you for the rest of your life . . . which I am afraid I shall never be able to do.[14]

Whether Catherine had courted celebrity as a way of luring Hartington back to her it is impossible to know; but what is certain is that if she had ever really craved respectability as Hartington's Duchess, then this alone – the vulgar glare of publicity, quite as improper in the nineteenth century as it had been in Sophia Baddeley's day – was fatal to her cause. In the autumn of 1862 Hartington at last told Catherine that their affair must end.

It was understandable, if not especially brave, that he chose to make the break by letter, from as far away from Park Street as possible. In August that year he had set off for a six-month tour of North America. 'My poor little child,' he wrote to Catherine in September, 'I trust you are better now, and that even if you have thought me very hard-hearted . . . you will begin to see that it must have been done some day and that putting it off only made it harder to both of us every day.'[15]

But Catherine was not to be discarded so easily. Despite her frail constitution and her delicate looks, she was much tougher and more enterprising than even Hartington realised. From Ems, the German spa town in which she had been staying to drink the waters, she set off immediately to join him in New York, pursued by a besotted Aubrey de Vere Beauclerk, who had deserted his wife for her and who in turn, for all the world like a real-life bedroom farce, was pursued across the Atlantic by his irate father-in-law and uncle.*

One of Hartington's letters suggests that under intense pressure from Catherine the two were briefly reconciled in New York – 'I gave way, though I knew it was wrong,' he wrote to her, 'because I could not bear to see you suffering' – but there was no going back. 'You ask me in your last letter to come back to you as I was before ... but you must think darling whether that can ever be possible now. Can either of us forget what has happened now?'

Although there was to be no really clean break, and the relationship floundered on in unhappy fits and starts for almost another year, Catherine knew that Hartington would not be swayed. In December she decided to move to Paris, and to the delight of the London gossip-mongers, her house in Park Street was sold. The 'scowling matrons' of London were every bit as keen to see inside the house of this fascinatingly infamous woman as their Parisian sisters across the Channel had been to inspect the living quarters of their own most notorious courtesans. 'Her luxuriously decorated house is in the hands of the auctioneer, her horses and carriages are sold,' wrote Sir William Hardman in one of his long gossipy letters, 'fair patricians, eager with curiosity to know how such a one lived, and, if possible to learn the secret of her attractions to the young men of their acquaintance, throng to the deserted halls of "Skittles" and admire *le cabinet* with its seat padded with swansdown.'[16]

Had Catherine truly believed that Hartington would one day marry her? Perhaps 'the girl with the swansdown seat', as a later biography of her was titled, really had loved her 'Cav', for the break made her genuinely unhappy. However unlikely such a match might seem today, there were quite as many precedents for it in Victorian England as

---

* Beauclerk, of Ardglass Castle in County Down, Northern Ireland, was described by Sir William Hardman in his account of this elopement as 'a married man of good family'.

there had been in the days of Mrs Baddeley and Mrs Armistead.*

Catherine would have known about at least two of these, both of which, although for very different reasons, were celebrated cases. She may have personally known one, Agnes Willoughby, an exact contemporary of Catherine's who had been one of her fellow 'horsebreakers' in Hyde Park in the early days of her career. She was the mistress of a high-class brothel keeper, a Mr Roberts, who is said to have kept her to the tune of £2000 a year in an establishment in St John's Wood.†
Through Roberts, Agnes met a wealthy young Etonian, William Frederick Windham, fittingly nicknamed 'Mad Windham', and in 1861, just three weeks after he attained his majority, they were married.

Windham, a true British eccentric who once ate seventeen eggs for breakfast and liked to dance on top of billiard tables, remained true to his sobriquet and proceeded to lavish jewels and money upon Agnes, including promising her an annuity, in perpetuity, of £1500. At the news of this his scandalised relatives attempted to ask for a Commission in Lunacy to declare Windham insane. The case, which was gratifyingly of 'a very disgusting character' according to *The Times*, became one of the great *causes célèbres* of the day, *The Times* alone devoting some 170,000 words to it. After a thirty-four-day inquiry Windham was declared sound in mind, for as *The Times* put it, 'society cannot undertake to protect men against the consequences of their own vices'.[17]

The story of Laura Bell was an altogether more edifying one. In the decade before Catherine and Agnes Willoughby had 'ruled the Row', Laura was the most celebrated of all the popular 'beauties' of her day. Born in 1829 in County Antrim on the estates of the notorious Marquess of Hertford, she started her career as a shopgirl in Belfast. When she was twenty she left for London, where she found employment at Jay's General Mourning House in Regent Street. In common

---

* The 7th Duke of Devonshire, when he was apprised of the facts about his son's liaison on Hartington's return to England in March 1863, gave Catherine's uncertain health as one of the main reasons for his objection to their marriage – which implies that he did not dismiss the idea out of hand. Wilfrid Scawen Blunt learned this after Catherine's death, when he was able to read the Hartington–Walters correspondence, noting that the Duke had meant 'the epileptic fits she was subject to, which were such a puzzle to me in those first days'.

† St John's Wood was by the mid-century the favoured location for these establishments.

with many working girls of the time, Laura was soon supplementing her income in the traditional way. She was pretty, blonde and doll-like, and quickly made her way up the ranks to the world of high court-esanry. Before long she had all the trappings of her profession, including a smart little phaeton which she drove daily in the Park, accompanied by a liveried 'tiger'. She had many conquests, but the greatest of them by far was Prince Jung Bahadoor, the brother of the Maharaja of Nepal, who had come to London as Nepalese Envoy to the Court of St James. Jung Bahadoor set Laura up in a house in Wilton Crescent in Belgravia, and proceeded to lavish an estimated £250,000 of his fortune on her. This fact alone caused a sensation. Laura's name, as well as her fortune, was made. Amongst her admirers was a young army officer, Captain Augustus Frederick Thistlethwayte, a relative of the Earl of Bathurst, and in 1852 he and Laura were married.

Mr and Mrs Thistlethwayte set up house together at 15 Grosvenor Square, although the marriage does not seem to have been an especially happy one. Perhaps repenting of her former existence of loose living and debauchery, Laura underwent a religious conversion and embarked upon a second career as a passionate revivalist preacher.

In her *Memories of Fifty Years*, the society hostess Lady St Helier recalled the sensational appearance of Mr and Mrs Thistlethwayte in Ross-shire, in Scotland, where they had taken a house on Loch Luichart in a deer forest belonging to Lady St Helier's aunt and uncle, Lord and Lady Ashburton.

> At first the country looked askance at the new arrivals, and she was not visited. Rumours which reached my grandmother's ears of her extreme repentance and great spiritual gifts, backed up by an entreaty from my aunt, Lady Ashburton, that she would recognise her tenant, produced a great sensation in our family; and after many consultations and heartburnings, my grand-mother consented, in order to please my aunt, to receive Mrs Thistlethwayte. We children were all sent out of the house the day when she paid her first visit, and only gathered from the mysterious whisperings of the maidservants that someone who

ought not to have come to the house had been there, and that we had been sent out of the way to avoid meeting her.[18]

Later, however, Lady St Helier did have a chance to view this notorious personage, when Mrs Thistlethwayte announced her intention of conducting a revivalist service at the little Free Church building just outside the grounds of Loch Luichart. Even though she was now past her prime, Laura still bore the remains of her great beauty.

> *She was a very striking-looking woman, and the large black mantilla which covered her masses of golden hair, the magnificent jewels she wore around her neck, and the flashing rings on the hands with which she gesticulated, added to the soft tones of her very beautiful voice, made a great impression on those who listened to her.*[19]

Largely thanks to her pious works and preaching, which she continued vigorously until her death in 1894, Laura Bell achieved a measure of grudging acceptance. But the truth was that hardly any other woman with her ambiguous background was likely to have the social champions – in practice, other women – necessary to pull it off.

Lady St Helier tells the story of another famous *demi-mondaine*, Mrs Trelawney, who visited the Highlands shortly before the arrival of Mrs Thistlethwayte. Despite the 'vigilant curiosity' of the ladies in the area, nothing could be discovered about their mysterious new neighbour other than that, although past her first youth, she was still 'a very beautiful woman, and magnificently dressed', and that she and her husband, a keen sportsman, had come to the Highlands for the shooting.

'We had so few neighbours that a new-comer was always welcome,' wrote Lady St Helier, 'and a certain number of people called upon her.' To their surprise and disgust, however, none of these calls were returned, and although Mrs Trelawney remained in the county for several years no one ever saw her, except when she went out driving. She might have passed quietly out of their lives altogether if it had not been for the fact that Mr Trelawney was one day taken ill, and the local doctor had to be called in.

'Then a thunderbolt fell on the community,' wrote Lady St Helier, 'when the news spread that Mrs Trelawney was no other than Madame de Beauregard, for many years the mistress of the Emperor Napoleon. Had there been any suspicion of her past, the fact that she was French,* combined with the hue of her magnificent *chevelure* [dark red, the Emperor's favourite colour], might have put more sophisticated people than ourselves on the *qui vive*.'

As it was, there was great difficulty in getting the doctor to continue his attendance, and even the local tradesmen began to wonder whether they should continue to supply somebody 'with so stormy a past'. In the event Mrs Trelawney disappeared 'as mysteriously as she came, and was another problem added to those which puzzled us as children'.[20]

Unlike Laura Bell and Mrs Trelawney, Catherine Walters was never to discover whether or not she would find acceptance as the 8th Duchess of Devonshire.† If she had married Hartington, the chances are that hers would have been a very hollow victory. While aristocratic circles were still discreetly tolerant of a man's irregular liaisons, just as they always had been, the mid-nineteenth century was no more accepting of any attempts to give them official sanction than the eighteenth had been.

The truth was that Catherine was better off without Hartington. She had received a generous pay-off from him – according to Blunt the relieved Devonshire family had settled £500 a year on her,‡ an annuity which was continued by the Devonshire estate after Hartington's death in 1908 until hers in 1920¶ – and now she was free.

---

* In fact she was English, and had been known as Elizabeth Howard before the Emperor created her Comtesse de Beauregard.
† After a long affair, Hartington was eventually to marry Louisa, Duchess of Manchester, who was once privately described by Bernard Holland, Hartington's official biographer, as 'rather a Skittles in higher life'. See Anita Lesley, *Edwardians in Love*.
‡ Hartington had always said that he 'meant to do something' for Catherine, and in one of his later letters he mentions a down-payment of £2500 on a house and an allowance of £400 a year.
¶ A few months after her death, Bernard Holland wrote of her to a friend: 'She survived the late D of D who always made her an allowance. On his death the question arose whether the present Duke should continue it. The Duchess did not like this proposal – however, I believe that it was done. She had entangled Hartington, in a sleepy mood, into a promise of marriage. This was, of course, before he knew Louisa . . . to whom he was pretty faithful.' See Lesley, *Edwardians in Love*.

It was in the autumn of 1863, in the immediate aftermath of her break from Hartington (his last known letter to her is dated 31 July of that year) that Catherine met Wilfrid Scawen Blunt for the first time. She was now twenty-four years old; Blunt was just twenty-three, sensitive, highly emotional, and a young man of extraordinary physical beauty. Although he was a member of the diplomatic service, serving at this time as Attaché to the British Embassy in Madrid, he was – fatally – about as far from the conventional nineteenth-century diplomatist as it was possible to be. In Bordeaux, where they met, Blunt, with his ragged Bohemian clothes still stained with summer dust, must have appeared every bit the Byronic hero that he imagined himself to be.

Blunt's meeting with Catherine occurred as he was heading back to Spain after a summer break. She was on her way south to the fashionable seaside resort of Biarritz. 'All that was most extravagant in French fashion was assembled there,' Blunt later wrote. All etiquette was suspended there, and even the Emperor and Empress themselves, then at the 'zenith of [their] renown', seemed to return to their 'pleasant old Bohemian life' unrestrained by convention.

Under this carnival dispensation, the *monde* and the *demi-monde* mingled with unprecedented freedom. It soon became clear to Blunt not only that Catherine was well known to the Imperial circle, including the Emperor himself, 'who had paid her his addresses at one time in secret', but also to the Empress, who although she of course did not acknowledge her, 'regarded her for her notoriety with a certain protective interest'. Catherine was the undisputed queen of the moment. But as yet Blunt knew none of this.

He was never to forget his first meeting with Catherine. It was the day, he wrote, when 'my fate without a sign or warning overtook me'. Half a lifetime later he recorded in his secret diary that it was '32 years today since I first met Miss Walters . . . though she has forgotten it'.[21]*
At the time he devoted two entire sonnet sequences, 'Esther' and

---

* In fact it was forty-two years – the diary entry is for 20 September 1905.

'Manon', to his description of the events which followed their meeting. Blunt always maintained that the poem 'Esther' – the name by which he often referred to Catherine – was a true representation of 'the fair woman at whose knees I worshipped . . . The tale as there narrated is at least too near the truth to be easily re-told,' he explained, 'and I prefer to leave it in the half light of the romance where it has stood so long without unveiling it further or relating its every circumstance.'[22]

According to 'Esther', in Bordeaux* Blunt had turned into a wayside show advertised as 'The Booth of Beauty'. But inside there were in fact two female 'monsters', one a girl 'marked like a leopard with pied arms and face', the other a giantess, seven feet high. The only thing of real beauty in the booth was 'a little woman dressed in black' who clutched at his hand every time the monsters sent a shiver of excited fear through the crowd.

Later, outside a theatre where he had stopped to examine a handbill advertising 'Mademoiselle Esther, Muse of Melancholy' who was to play in the well-known *'drame' Manon Lescaut*, from a side door out stepped into the moonlight none other than 'my little woman of the Fair', Mademoiselle 'Esther' herself. Blunt's fate was sealed. Soon he was walking through the streets with her, hand in hand, listening to her talking 'like a running stream', hearing her barter with shop assistants and stallholders, until in a kind of mad dream she took him back with her to an apartment.

In this apartment, which 'Esther' tells him is that of her dressmaker, Madame Blanche, but which clearly doubled as a house of assignation, Catherine seduced him. Sending the other women away, she

> Undid her jacket and anon her dress
> With the jet buttons of it one by one
> And stood but clothed the more in loveliness,
> A sight sublime, a dream, a miracle,
> A little goddess from some luminous field
> Brought down unconscious on our Earth to dwell.
> And in an age of innocence revealed,
> Naked but not ashamed . . .[23]

---

* In the poem Blunt calls Bordeaux 'Lyon'.

He claimed that he would not 'tell the secrets of that place', but when Madame Blanche returned it was to find a trembling Blunt kneeling at 'Esther's' feet and being comforted by her. It was the dawn of their love, and 'joy had triumphed'.

Later, in Biarritz, the lovers gave themselves up entirely to the holiday spirit. It was not hard to do. Catherine paraded Blunt proudly as her 'youthful lover' and favourite.

> *My appearance publicly with her . . . in manifest enjoyment of her supreme favours, a stranger to them all, clothed in my rags with my 'John the Baptist face' (for so she called it), sunburned and untamed, was of necessity an event attracting every Parisian eye. It would have been a scandal in any place less tolerant than was the Biarritz of that day, or at any other Court. As it was, we were regarded with a favouring eye, and when we met, as we did, each morning on the place, the slow-footed Emperor, with an old man's gait on the arm of his Chamberlain Tacher de la Pagerie, both smiled protectingly, and more kindly still the Empress with her laughing escort of young Basques . . . good-looking youths who bathed with her daily.*[24]

So great was the favour in which Blunt found himself, in fact, that he was even invited to the Empress's Imperial entertainments at the Pavilion. Urged by 'Esther', who was not herself on the Court list of guests, he attended and 'was amiably received'. 'I have the card still,' he wrote many years later, 'it is dated 28th September, eight days only after our arrival at Biarritz.'

So besotted was Blunt that he could not imagine that their love would ever come to an end. Although the incident in Bordeaux had not been his first sexual experience, it was the first time that he had found himself in the grip of erotic obsession – an altogether new adventure for him. 'What a debauch it was of passion and vain glory,' he wrote of their time together in Biarritz, 'the two most potent influences in my youth. What a wonder that it overset my reason! That I deemed that I had discovered the secret of all life, that I imagined myself to have stolen into Paradise, and made conquest of the Tree of Knowledge and become as a God for ever!'

In his 'insanity' Blunt even wrote to his brother Francis back in England, telling him of this astonishing turn of events, and assuring him that his whole life was now bound up, 'without possibility of change', with this 'phoenix of creation'. That Catherine was the most beautiful of women was an undisputed fact, and it seemed to him indisputable, too, that she loved him. 'The suddenness of her fancy seemed to prove it, and the publicity of her passion paraded as it was each day before the world and to me without reserve each night.'

And perhaps Catherine really did love him.

Although her settlement from Hartington had made her comfortably independent, Catherine clearly had no intention of giving up the life of courtesanry just yet. £500 a year would have seemed a princely sum to most of her contemporaries, but it was not enough to live on in the grand manner she desired. Besides, the life of the courtesan was one that suited her. She was naturally passionate – her impulsive seduction of Blunt, who only too clearly was without means, had been done entirely for pleasure – and she had more than a taste for the high life, with all its trappings, to which her liaison with Hartington had introduced her. For the time being, however, Catherine renounced all other callers. 'She closed her doors to everyone but me,' wrote Blunt, 'even to her friends in the Imperial entourage, making them I know not what excuse for her withdrawal.' In fact she needed no excuse other than the conventional one of 'caprice de jolie femme': a pretty woman's right to an occasional folly. As such, Blunt believed, her behaviour would have been both understood and respected by everyone.

It was not until the third week of this 'astonishing experience' that his own doubts began to intrude upon their happiness. Blunt both knew, and did not know, the circumstances of Catherine's life before she met him. That is, she had always been honest with him about her past having been, as he would call it, 'a notorious one of folly', but he had chosen not to believe it. At twenty-three, Blunt was not without experience of the world. Before Madrid he had already had three other foreign postings, in Athens, Constantinople and Frankfurt; and in Madrid he had even kept a mistress for a time. Where Catherine was concerned, however, he was a passionately naïve young man. In one of those 'efforts of absurd fake logic' of the very young when they are in love, Blunt now chose to believe in a kind of 'miraculous virginity' for Catherine. His beloved, he insisted,

> had never till she met me found the actual lover of her perfect choice, the man to whom she had surrendered all as she had surrendered it to me, and so had given me the right to call her mine, a miraculous virginity which entailed on me a corresponding duty of perpetual love service not less binding than that sanctified by marriage vows.[25]

What was more, Blunt allowed himself to believe that Catherine thought this too, and that she accepted 'the offering' of his love as one that effectively bound her to him. Nothing could have been further from the truth.

Catherine was indeed a phoenix; beautiful, exotic and rare. She was no longer the pretty little *ingénue* of the Cheshire hunting fields, herself the afternoon sport of aristocratic men. She was a woman of some experience now, a woman 'in the full glory of her *demi-mondaine* beauty', confident, vibrantly sexual, and unashamed to explore her own nature. 'She was,' Blunt wrote with uncharacteristic harshness, 'far too convinced of the supreme value of her own incomparable beauty of body to pretend a chastity which in her view of things could hardly add to its attractions.'[26]

If Blunt had been just a little older, if he had been French and worldly, perhaps, instead of English and romantic, he might have experienced their love affair differently, and been able to see the great and generous-spirited gift that Catherine was giving him for what it was. Later, when as an old man he came to revise his secret memoirs, he saw what he described as his own 'supernatural innocence' in the matter very clearly.

> I was too penniless to be a temptation for her in that way, and she too wise to spoil her holiday love with more than it could give us both of wayside pleasure. I was her shepherd boy with whose John the Baptist face she was in love, and that must be enough ... She had acted with a queen's munificence throughout and as

a queen I must regard her, content with the happiness she had given me and asking no impossibilities – and yet I clung to my illusions.[27]

The result, of course, was to make Blunt as passionately unhappy as he had been joyful. He had not been looking for a *cinq à sept*, however exhilarating, he had been looking for his one true love, and the disillusion, when it came, was terribly painful.

The first 'sting of jealousy' came when Catherine received a bundle of letters from Paris. They turned out to be love letters from a Russian prince, written 'from somewhere beyond Moscow in which he described himself as travelling with galloping post horses in a carriage towards the Ural mountains with her portrait on the seat opposite to him, the icon of his adoration'.

Later that same afternoon, Blunt had his first taste of a very different Catherine from the one he thought he knew. They had been romping for possession of a cushion that Blunt, the stronger of the two, had held onto for just a second too long for her liking when, to his amazement, he saw a look of anger in her eyes, 'a flash of passionate resentment, almost of hatred, as when playing with a panther it should turn without warning and strike one with an unsheathed claw. "You would dare," she exclaimed, "try strengths with me!"' There was a note of such scorn in her voice that it almost frightened him. He dropped the cushion instantly. Although the incident only lasted a fraction of a second, 'I seemed to see an abyss of possible disaster opened at my feet,' wrote Blunt, 'and I was giddy at the thought.'

Although there is, regrettably, no record of Catherine's own account of her affair with Blunt, his own recollection of what happened next is a speaking one: 'Her eyes, which used to be constantly seeking mine, were now turned elsewhere.' The truth was that Catherine had become restless and bored. Blunt's possessiveness was starting to irritate her. The Season was over now, and so, as far as she was concerned, was their romance. She told him that she must go back to Paris, and that he must return to Madrid. Blunt was devastated: 'Her readiness that we should go separate ways was a new pain, it filled me with amazement.'

But Catherine was not, and never had been, his to keep. In this she had never tried to deceive him. 'Knowing the world as I know it now,' he wrote, 'I see that the fault lay wholly in my own childish folly which attributed to her a virtue she laid no claim to . . . She herself had told me enough of her past life to make it clear what that life had been, and if there had been any doubt,' he added unchivalrously, 'the facility with which she had given herself to me should have been enough to enlighten me.'

The worldly tone of this pronouncement was of course a later addition to the story. 'I should have kissed my goddess's fair hands,' wrote the older and wiser Blunt, '. . . and gone my way with benedictions on her head and thanks to Heaven for a pleasure harvested.' But, alas, this was not to be. Instead, the distraught and weeping young man clung to Catherine's skirts, literally, 'as a child clings, passionately, unreasoningly, to the last moment of its doom'.

Worn down by these scenes, Catherine allowed Blunt to accompany her to Paris after all. It was a mistake on both their parts. Paris was only ever to be 'of bitter memory' to Blunt, for Catherine's life there was very different from what he had known with her in Biarritz, where they had enjoyed 'an intimacy shut off from all the world'. In Paris Catherine positively encouraged visits from her admirers.

One particular group, a quire of noisy young attachés from the Russian and British Legations was very much part of her social circle. These young men had a sophistication which Blunt, with his 'vagabond attire', simply could not emulate. In their presence he became gauche and silent. Catherine was alternately protective of him, and exasperated. She sent him off to Cumberland, the English tailor, to be fitted up with new and respectable clothes, but somehow he still did not fit the part. For a time she shielded him from the jokes and comments at his expense, but after a while she too joined in the fun. 'What else was there for her to do?' wrote Blunt forlornly. It seemed to him as if she had deserted him.

> I could bear it no longer and bursting into tears upbraided her with inconstancy. It was a fatal madness and set the seal on my disgrace. Esther was not a woman to be dealt with in such a fashion. My reproaches only angered her, and in a few plain words

she told me the fool I was and the childishness of my displeasure.
She would not be made ridiculous by my stupidities. I had better
go back to my friends in Spain – here I was an embarrassment
to her and had best be off. She would not listen to another word
. . . I turned away still weeping like a child and made my prep-
arations for departure in my own room, the key of her door being
ruthlessly turned on me.[28]

Blunt's affair with Catherine was a shattering experience for him. His biographers have speculated a great deal as to how it affected his later relationships with women (he was to become a tireless Lothario), but he himself never blamed her for the anguish he suffered. Nonetheless, the indulgence of this first 'passionate debauch', as he called it, 'so publicly paraded and with so little respect for any convention of decorum . . . perverted and disturbed me'. Their affair, as Blunt's best biographer, Elizabeth Longford, has written, 'changed the landscape of his mind' forever.*

Catherine, with her fragile looks and almost childlike air, had beneath this charming exterior a 'potent' personality. She had made a man of Wilfrid, but had at the same time somehow unmanned him too; she 'dominated me to a degree for which I have long learned to be ashamed'. This was not only a moral and physical domination, but an intellectual one too. Although Catherine was later to become the subject of what Blunt considered to be his best poetry, this was not so during their actual connection. On the contrary, not only did he not write her a line of verse, he 'kept carefully concealed from her the fact that I had even written or even thought seriously on any subject until the moment of our meeting'. During their affair, it was only the vanities and trifles that preoccupied her which allured him. 'These at times still [after some forty years] affect me.'

---

* Longford has an interesting theory that Catherine was making Wilfrid act out her own suffering at the hands of Hartington. She quotes one of Catherine's letters to him after their break – 'I pity you my poor little child from the bottom of my heart . . . We are so very different . . . now darling please try to be a good and sensible child you know I am not so thoroughly without a heart as the world makes me out . . .' – which almost exactly imitates the tone and language of Hartington's to her during their protracted split. See Longford, *A Pilgrimage of Passion*.

Blunt's self-abasement was not over yet, for in August 1864 he was posted to Paris. He had not forgotten Catherine but, busy in his new duties, he did not seek her out either, so it was not until Christmas that he met her again. A letter arrived for him, written by Catherine's maid Julie, calling him back to that world which still seemed to him 'the only one of romance, the only one of full life and reality'. The bitter memories Blunt still had meant that his feelings were 'by no means all of pleasure'; but they were at the same time so alive that 'all things else [seemed] mere shadows to its substance'.

When Blunt finally saw Catherine he found her in circumstances that were decidedly less splendid than the ones in which he had left her. She was living in a single room on the second floor of a small hotel just off the Champs Elysées. She was still beautiful, but 'pale, almost ill-dressed, almost untidy'. Catherine did not give Blunt a very coherent story of her misfortunes, saying only that she was unhappy and did not wish to see her friends. 'But she wanted me because I had really loved her and we had been happy together . . . and now we would be happy again.' Ecstatic at finding himself in her arms once more, Wilfrid did not ask any questions. 'Indeed, I loved her infinitely better thus forlorn than in her regal moods, and when she talked of renewing our life together as it had been in those first days at Biarritz I returned rapt [illegible] at once into the heaven I had lost and asked no more.'[29]

Together again, they made their plans. They would spend two days in Paris before Catherine returned to England briefly to attend to some business matters, and on her return they would set up house together. They would find a small apartment somewhere – she was tired of luxury and expense, she said – and Julie, who loved Catherine, Blunt wrote, 'with canine devotion', would be their *bonne à tout faire* (maid of all work). The improbability of Catherine's fantasy of the quiet, bohemian life they would lead – they would buy a simple roast fowl every day from the *rôtisseur* around the corner, and Julie would make up their coffee for them – might have put Blunt on his guard, but it did not. Instead, he wept for joy. All else was forgotten. 'Once more,' he wrote, 'I was a prince of fairy land inhabiting a dream castle in the clouds.'

While Catherine was away Blunt and Julie scoured the Champs Elysées for 'the house of love desired', and eventually found an apartment that seemed to answer perfectly. Julie agreed that although it was not what Madame was accustomed to, the four small rooms were 'good sound stuff', and Blunt took them.

But alas, wrote Blunt, all their plans were to prove 'dreams only'. Once in England, Catherine showed no signs of returning. A week went past, then another, and another, and still there was no sign of her, 'only excuses for delay, letters hinting at some other plan'. And when at last she did come, 'in what a different mood from that of her departure! She was no more of the woebegone pale face which had moved me so profoundly ... She was once more in the full glory of her wonderful beauty, gay, talkative and well-dressed.' In addition to this worrying ebullience was an even more disturbing fact. Blunt found that Catherine was now mysteriously set up in an apartment of her own at 123, avenue des Champs Elysées.* They were not going to live together after all.

Julie tried to comfort a devastated Blunt. Madame had arranged to live in the new apartment, she told him, because she had brought her young sister Evelyne,† who was then aged sixteen and had just recently left her convent school in England, back to live with her. He was to keep the four rooms, and Julie was to keep house for him just as they had planned, as Madame had her own set of servants now. Blunt would go to and fro daily between the two houses, and would spend as much time as he liked with Catherine.

What he saw when he first went to visit Catherine and her sister in the avenue des Champs Elysées would have made any other man immediately suspicious. The apartment consisted of a suite of 'much begilded rooms', a riot of satin upholstery, and many gold mirrors. But Blunt, still supernaturally innocent despite his six months in Paris, did not suspect anything. Catherine's sister Evelyne turned out to be 'a pale girl' with a pretty figure but no very great beauty, with whom Blunt soon made friends, noting how silent and unassertive she was,

* La Barucci, whose apartment was at 124, avenue des Champs Elysées, was now her neighbour.
† This must be Blunt's code name for her. Her real name was Caroline.

'in extreme contrast to Esther', and how content to merge into the background. Although he could not hide his disappointment from her, Blunt found Catherine in a kind mood 'and for a while', he wrote, 'I was happy. There was as yet no visible serpent in my Eden.'

Although Blunt saw Catherine every day, he found that his time with her was rationed rather more strictly than Julie had seemed to promise. Before long a daily pattern emerged in this new dispensation. 'She was an early riser,' remembered Blunt, 'and it was my habit to be with her almost as soon as it was light and to take my early breakfast with her and her sister, the *café au lait* and crescent rolls with which all Paris is accustomed to begin its day, and then go out with them for a ride towards the Bois.'[30]

Sometimes they would ride together before the rest of 'the gay world' was up at all, and there would be time for him to spend another idle hour or two with her before he left for his Chancery work at the Embassy. Although he did not generally see her again for the rest of the day, he learned to think of these mornings as his 'special privilege, shared with none other'.

Besides, in the afternoon Catherine was a different woman altogether from the one he knew and so passionately loved. 'Dressed up and glorified for the world, beset by a crowd of wondering fools' as she drove her ponies, making the *tour du lac* with the rest of fashionable Paris, this was a Catherine who was forever out of the reach of a humble Embassy attaché such as Blunt. Sometimes he would go to the Bois just to watch her there, 'but always from a distance', he recalled, 'and with a savage eye'.

Although it was a fact that – even now – Blunt seems scarcely to have comprehended, Catherine was at the very height of her career as a courtesan, admired and fêted by London and Paris alike. There were very few people, on the other hand, who would ever know the private Catherine as Blunt did at this time in her life. Where did she go to after the afternoon's promenade, the anonymous author of the letter to *The Times* in 1862 had wondered; what unknown world did she inhabit, and to whom did she really belong? This element of mystery was not displeasing to Catherine, in fact she astutely cultivated it; so much so that it became, Blunt was later to claim, indelibly part of her great *cachet*. She had two golden rules, she told him: never to sell herself to the first comer, and never to have a woman friend.

Blunt, on the other hand, was her friend as well as her lover. There were times when Catherine would come back from one of her promenades, or from an evening party, and discarding all her finery, dress herself in plain black clothes and wrap her head in a woollen veil. Disguised in this way against any chance encounters with her acquaintances, she would go out into the streets with Wilfrid. In the back alleyways of Paris Catherine's favourite amusement after dark was to search the *bric-à-brac* shops, 'mystifying the owner with pretence of buying'. Then, with their cache of treasures, they would go home, stopping on the way at the *rôtisseurs* that Catherine had talked of before, and carrying their dinner, 'smoking hot', back to Blunt's rooms for Julie to serve up, buying chestnuts at the next-door stall to complete the feast. 'These were evenings of pure delight for me,' wrote Blunt, 'compensating for much that was an annoying puzzle in her way of life, and the cause of no few pangs for my too jealous heart – I did not dare enquire too closely,' he added, 'how she spent her time away from me.'

Blunt's fool's paradise was not destined to go on much longer. The day came at last when he could no longer hide from himself the fact that Catherine had a lover, the very one 'who provided for her extravagances and in whose rooms she lived'. He arrived one afternoon to find her protector, having returned unexpectedly from abroad, ensconced proprietorially in the white and gold apartment.

The existence of the other man – an Englishman whom Catherine said she had known from childhood (there is unfortunately no other clue to his identity) – was like poison in an open wound to Blunt. Nothing that Catherine could say was of any comfort to him, although she did try. He must not mind, she told him, for the man made no claims on her other than the appearance of affection. Clearly, she had learned the lessons of the Parisian *demi-monde* only too well.

He was, in fact, though she did not use the word, her amant en
titre, *content to be supposed her lover without enjoying a full
lover's rights. Nor was the explanation quite beside the truth. He
was one of those many foreigners who in the days of the Empire
sought for themselves a position in society at Paris by their expen-
diture in ostentatious ways, and how more scandalously than by
maintaining one like Esther whom all Paris knew ... it was
enough for him that she should lend him the prestige of her living
[with him] ... for the few weeks he should be there. Her love for
me would be no less for it. Why should I mind?*[31]

Of course Blunt minded passionately. Catherine had been generous to
him, he could not deny it. She had spared his 'young man's slender
purse' and had always been 'a giver, rather than a receiver' in their
relationship. Now she was offering him the honour of being her official
amant de coeur ('as such things are accepted by the half-world code
of immorality'). There was no conventional disgrace in this, rather the
opposite in fact, but Blunt could not help himself. 'I loved her and it
was repugnant to me.'

When challenged, Catherine wrote him a letter which was at once
exasperated and tender.

May 1865 123, L'Avenue Champs-Élysées
My darling child,
*I answer you at once you old darling to tell you I pity you
from the bottom of my heart though you do drive me mad and
to distraction at times darling. We are so very different in
nature. However, darling, I will say no more. Poor boy, you
seem to suffer enough without my giving you more. Now
darling, please try and be a great and sensibal [sic] child.*
*You know I am not so thoroughly without heart as the world
makes me out to be and I do indeed wish to be honest towards
you if you will only see it dearest. Now darling what do you
really mean by saying I deceived you? I have nothing I want to
deceive you in, and if I want to do anything dearest I do it. If
you were to ask me I would tell you straightforwardly.*[32]

For the time being Blunt was grudgingly forced to accept the 'hateful ménage'. Now, more than ever, as he struggled to reconcile his feelings of love and shame, he felt that he was in complete surrender to Catherine's will. 'In these disputes,' he wrote, 'my daily pleasure vanished and all comfort in my love.' Even their evening rambles ceased.

The end came one night when Wilfrid, passing Catherine's house, looked up and saw her in the window with Lord Dunmore, a young man-about-town whom he knew a little from his days at the Athens Legation. They were laughing together, and Dunmore had his arm around Catherine's waist. In a passion, Blunt sent her 'a wild letter of reproaches', but this time Catherine refused all explanations, and forbade him from meddling. 'It brought me, as Esther's anger always did, to my knees.' Despite his repentance he could get no further word from her. Even the devoted Julie, deputed as a go-between, failed to gain a response from Catherine, and was reduced to comforting and scolding Blunt by turns in her 'good Breton patois'.

This was a dark time for Blunt, who even contemplated throwing himself beneath the wheels of Catherine's carriage: 'It would be my expiation,' he wrote. But on the day in question her carriage was not with the rest in the Bois, and he 'was cheated of my thought'.

After four days of torturing himself in this way, a saner mind returned to him. He decided that the only thing to do was to leave Paris, which had become a place of infinite pain to him. When he did leave, however, it was not through his own choice, but at the desire of his outraged Ambassador, Lord Cowley, who had come to hear that Wilfrid's name had been linked with Catherine's, and was now quite as anxious to have him dismissed from Paris as he was to go.

From being the source of a poetically personal anguish, Blunt's affair with Catherine had blown up into a public scandal of such proportions that it could not be covered up. And the Cowleys, to his infinite shame, were at the centre of it. For, all the time that he had been sighing in vain over his 'Esther', Blunt had also been 'making love' – in the Victorian sense – to the Cowleys' daughter Feodorowna, known to her family as Feodore.

Catherine had once remarked on how very different she and Blunt were in character, but in one crucial sense they were actually rather alike. Both had the ability, so far as their private lives were concerned, to compartmentalise to an extraordinary degree. For a courtesan, of course, this had always been a necessary skill, and Catherine found no contradiction in having an *amant de coeur* and an *amant en titre*; Blunt, unbeknownst to anyone, including Catherine, had found no apparent difficulty in doing the same thing.

It is a measure, perhaps, of the profound imaginative and emotional gulf between the two worlds that, even for a man so clearly besotted as Blunt, the *demi-monde* should entirely vanish from sight the moment the *monde* made its appearance, and vice versa. The truth was that Blunt had been intimate with Feodore Wellesley from the moment he had first arrived in Paris. She was his own age, and had ease, gaiety and 'laughing blue eyes'. As an attaché to her father, the Ambassador, he had of course gone everywhere with the Cowleys, but the friendship between the young people looked sufficiently promising – Blunt, although not rich, was sufficiently eligible – for the romance to be encouraged by Feodore's parents. Besides, Blunt's Chancery duties were much more pleasant when there was someone to flirt with nearby. Within a very short space of time he found himself treated like one of the family. He received, and accepted, invitations not just as a family friend, but as Feodore's unofficial fiancé.

It was against this background that Wilfrid had found himself once again in love with Catherine. Throughout the winter of 1865, when he was tormenting himself with Catherine's elusive behaviour, he himself was happily returning to the imposing mansion in the Faubourg Saint-Honoré – which had been bought for Britain after the Napoleonic wars by Lord Cowley's uncle, the Duke of Wellington – to continue his dalliance with an unsuspecting Feodore.

Unluckily for Blunt, the crisis with Catherine occurred almost at the same time as the crisis with Feodore. After a year of playing the patient chaperone, Lady Cowley was understandably anxious that Blunt should make his engagement to her daughter official. There was at this point no doubt in anyone's mind what his intentions were towards her. In the summer Lady Cowley announced that she was taking her daughter home to England to pass what remained of the Season there. Blunt knew what was expected of him. After dinner one warm evening he and Feodore wandered out into the garden. There, sitting on a bench between lilac bushes, and screened from the house, 'I had it more than once upon my tongue to talk of marriage', Wilfrid wrote. But he did not. Each time, 'the image of Esther arose to "forbid the banns"'. As Blunt's biographer Elizabeth Longford believed: 'Up to this moment he had felt scarcely affected in his relations with Feodore by his love for Esther, the two being on so different a footing. Now he knew the truth.'[33]

The two made their way back into the house, 'to the enquiring glances of the Wellesleys', and shortly afterwards, an embarrassed Blunt remembered, 'I took my leave and so passed out from among them, never, as it was fated, to find myself with them again.'*

In many ways Blunt's behaviour was not at all unusual for a man of his class and his times. The ability to separate what he himself would call 'practical romance' from either idealised romance or sexual conquests was a perfectly acceptable way for a man to conduct his affairs, so long as he was discreet; and Blunt, who later quite consciously made the decision to marry for money, saw no shame in it. His case is especially interesting, however, not only because he was a man of particularly strong emotional as well as sexual drives (although he was to go on to become a serial philanderer, it must be said in his defence that he genuinely liked women, and always imagined himself in love with the women he seduced), but also because the double standard he reveals is uniquely well documented, as he himself was aware. Of the secret memoir, 'Alms to Oblivion', which he wrote but never published, he commented: 'I am surprised to find how well it is written. Indeed I doubt if any English memoir (I do not say French) was ever better than it is so far, for it is absolutely truthful and at the same

---

* Luckily, Feodore was clearly a woman of some spirit. Six years after this débâcle she married Frank Bertie, who as Sir Francis Bertie later became British Ambassador to Paris. Lady Bertie was to go down in the affectionate annals of British Ambassadresses to Paris because of her unsuitable fondness for playing poker.

time decent, though treating of the least decent period of my life.'[34]*

It goes without saying that when women tried to emulate this masculine behaviour it became an 'immorality' for which society could not forgive them. The only women who were in some measure outside these constraints were courtesans. The penalties meted out by society could not touch the *demi-monde* (although some would say that being a part of this shadowland *was* the penalty), and as a social group they were thus almost uniquely free.

It was not just sexual chastity that was the issue here, but also, by extension, a woman's whole autonomy. Blunt, who was in many ways a forward thinker about women, never really blamed Catherine for her promiscuity, or even for the fact that she accepted money for it (although he did not like it). His blame was for something altogether more subtle, something that he himself could barely articulate: the fact that she could accept him as her lover, but still desire to keep her independence from him. This was the really tormenting fact for him about their liaison. And it was this which, in his eyes, made her 'unvirtuous'.

Catherine was not unusual, however. All the other great courtesans of the eighteenth and nineteenth centuries treasured their autonomy and guarded it jealously, an impropriety which marked them off, more than almost anything else, from their 'respectable' sisters. This was so even though the position of women – particularly married women – in the mid-nineteenth century was better than it had ever been. It is hard to imagine, at the beginning of the twenty-first century, the profoundly radical changes to the position of women brought about by the Divorce Act of 1857, and the Married Women's Property Act of 1882. Before the latter a married woman could own no property

---

* It is interesting to speculate what would have happened if Blunt had ever published this memoir. The great English critic and essayist William Hazlitt, who in 1823 had published his account of unrequited love in the ill-fated *Liber Amoris*, was ruined by the scandal. See A.C. Grayling, *The Quarrel of the Age*.

(although, amongst the very rich, pre-nuptial settlements often circumvented this*), nor even control any earnings she might have (this was changed by separate legislation in 1878), and she had the legal status of a minor, on a par with children, criminals and the insane. Although prior to 1857 she could be divorced by her husband, she herself was debarred from bringing a divorce suit – or any other kind of legal action – against him, regardless of his treatment of her.† Most critical of all was the fact that a husband had complete control over his children, who, like his wife, were his legal property.‡ A woman had no redress. In the case of her adultery, for instance, a husband could – and invariably did – simply take her children away from her for good.

The Acts of 1857 and 1882 changed all this. As well as divorce and other law reforms, the nineteenth century saw many other campaigns by women to improve their circumstances – the campaigns for the vote, for the expansion of job opportunities¶ and for better educational rights all belong to this period. And yet despite these groundbreaking steps towards full legal and civil emancipation, the social proprieties which had governed the behaviour of women during the late eighteenth and early nineteenth centuries remained largely intact. In fact, if anything they now became more pronounced; the limits of what was considered good 'womanly' behaviour were narrower than they had ever been.

'What I remonstrate against is the negative forms of employment,' wrote Margaretta Grey, the sister of the campaigning reformer

---

* Some of the worst recorded cases of both physical and mental cruelty by husbands towards their wives resulted from efforts to try to force the woman to give up her 'pin money' and other property. See Lawrence Stone, *Uncertain Unions and Broken Lives*.
† It had, of course, been very rare for a husband to divorce his wife before 1857, since it required a ruinously expensive Act of Parliament to do so. After 1857 the double standard was effectively enshrined in the legal system. It was enough for a husband to prove adultery against his wife; but for a wife to divorce her husband, adultery alone was not sufficient grounds. She had to provide other evidence, such as cruelty or desertion, as well.
‡ The 'crim con' ('criminal conversation') cases so prevalent in the Regency period were civil law suits brought against a woman's lover by her husband, who was essentially claiming damages to his property.
¶ When Elizabeth Garrett Anderson (1836–1917) became qualified to practise medicine in England by passing the apothecaries' examination (the old Guild regulations of which did not explicitly exclude women), the members changed the regulations.

Josephine Butler, in her private diary; 'the wasting of energy, the crippling of talent under false ideas of station, propriety, and refinement, that seems to shut up a large portion of the women of our generations from proper spheres of occupation and adequate exercise of power.'[35]

These words are echoed by the opening lines of Florence Nightingale's 1852 work *Cassandra*, an impassioned indictment of the confinement of privileged women: 'Why have women passion, intellect, moral activity – these three – and a place in society where not one of the three can be exercised?'[36]

Ever since the late eighteenth century, women had been bombarded as never before with literature – pamphlets, sermons, manuals and homilies – about their rightful place in society: they were born to obey men, belonged in the home, and any activity which might lure them away from it was not only inappropriate, but actually degrading. Great intellectual talent could never be anything other than a misfortune in a woman, wrote Sarah Jane Ellis, the writer of a number of best-selling manuals for women in the mid-nineteenth century: 'a jewel which cannot with *propriety* be worn'. ('The crimsoning blush of modesty,' added the High Tory clergyman Richard Polwhele, 'will always be more attractive than the sparkle of confident intelligence.'[37])

The gulf between the relative independence and freedom of a courtesan, and the highly circumscribed existence which was the lot of all other women, had never been greater. In one sense, though, the tremendous emphasis that was given to the need to exclude women from public life (which included university education, and training for jobs such as doctors, nurses and teachers, quite as much as the Holy Grail of the vote) was necessary precisely because the boundaries between the two spheres were becoming increasingly unstable.

But although the largest and best-known women's rights movement of the era was arising in England at this time, the vast majority of women did not choose this kind of overt rebellion, but something altogether more subtle, something which they did not think of as rebellion at all. For women confined to the domestic sphere, the way to gain a degree of freedom and power was to place an increased emphasis on their moral authority, and it was this which was to become the main source of all the positive changes which, much later, came about in the status of women.

Florence Nightingale had been wrong about at least one thing. Although the full exercise of woman's passion and intellect would not be possible for at least another hundred years, her moral authority – which since Rousseau's immensely influential and dazzlingly successful work *Emile* (1762), which argued forcefully for separate spheres for men and women, had become enshrined in European psychology* – was, increasingly, a force to be reckoned with.

Even the outwardly conservative works of the above-mentioned Mrs Sarah Ellis – which included the hugely popular *The Wives of England* and *The Women of England* – struggled to reconcile these shifting perceptions. In an enlightening chapter on 'Behaviour to Husbands' she manages to link, without apparent contradiction, a long lecture on the innate superiority of all men to women, and the 'dangerous heritage' of an intellect in a wife, to the conclusion that 'nothing, however, can be more delicate and more trying than the situation of such a woman, and especially when her husband is inferior to herself; but if he should be absolutely silly', she finished with a sigh, 'it would require more skill than the writer of these pages can boast, to know what mode of treating him to recommend'.[38]

In the late nineteenth century, quite as much as in the late eighteenth, marriage and the joys of domestic life were, amongst the middle and upper classes, overwhelmingly considered to be the only proper vehicle for a woman's energies. Those who questioned this were still few. What had changed was the perception of what marriage was. Sarah Ellis, a natural successor to Rousseau, saw it as a morally active state. Despite her claim that a truly good man had 'a power and a sublimity ... nearly approaching what we believe to be the nature and capacity of angels', she was also careful to stress her belief that 'morally and spiritually there is perfect equality between men and women'. In fact, her claims for women, especially wives, were greater still. So much of the moral and religious character of a household depended on the

---

* 'Even if she possesses genuine talents,' Rousseau wrote, 'any pretension on her part would degrade them. Her dignity depends on remaining unknown; her glory lies in her husband's esteem, her greatest pleasure in the happiness of her family.'

wife, she believed, that her influence – and power – was profound indeed. 'I know not what love is, if it seeks not the moral and intellectual perfection of its object,' she wrote in *The Wives of England*, and in marriage 'no opportunity may be lost, and no means neglected, of raising the tone of a husband's character to the highest scale which man is capable of attaining'.[39]

There was, of course, still a long way to go. By the standards of the rest of Europe, English women had always had unparalleled licence to choose their own husbands (we never, for example, had marriage brokers in the way that was customary in France); but they made mistakes. With the cult of domesticity at its relentless height, an unhappy marriage, once entered into, was in most cases a sentence for life. Divorce, although technically possible, was still an extremely rare and scandalous enterprise (as it would remain within our living memory). The vast majority of women, even those who were unhappily married, did not risk extramarital affairs. Despite the fact that a certain licence had always been given to women of the aristocracy and the upper classes, the boundaries of what was permissible remained, in all cases, a perilously grey area, often only visible once it had been irretrievably crossed.

And to cross that line had consequences that were, for the women involved, nothing short of catastrophic. As far as marriage was concerned, it was men who still held all the cards. In her *Recollections*, the Countess of Cardigan – that improbable but magnificently English figure glimpsed in the Hyde Park promenades of the 1880s in her golden wig, three-cornered hat and Louis XVI coat, with a leopard skin flung over one shoulder – told the sad story of one of her greatest childhood friends, Lady Constance de Burgh. Although it was now rare for a woman in England to have no influence over the choice of her own husband, Constance – a pretty, charming girl, but of a somewhat colourless character – was one of the exceptions. Lord Ward, 'who had always been considered a great *parti* by mothers with marriageable daughters', proposed to her, and though Constance was not in love with him, her parents told her she must accept. 'Marriage frequently means disillusion,' wrote Lady Cardigan, 'and the Ward marriage was not a success.'

Although William Ward seemed to be a pleasant man to those who knew him, he had, according to Lady Cardigan, 'extraordinary ideas' of how to treat a wife, 'ideas which could only be tolerated by a tactful woman who could laugh at them, and forget all the unpleasantness they entailed'. But alas, poor Constance was 'not tactful, and not accommodating'. 'Her husband worshipped the beautiful; he had selected his wife partly on account of her beauty, and he treated her like some lovely slave he had bought,' Lady Cardigan wrote.

He had a strange, almost barbaric passion for precious stones, and he bought quantities of them and lavished them on his wife, who appeared at great entertainments literally ablaze with diamonds.

What pleased Lord Ward more than anything was to make Constance put on all her jewels for his special benefit when they were alone. He would admire her thus for hours, delighting in her lovely unclothed figure, and contrasting the sheen of her ropes of pearls with her delicate skin, as she sat on a black satin-covered couch.

At first the sexually inexperienced Constance was terrified by these 'strange proceedings', a terror which soon turned to disgust. While any courtesan would have understood Ward's predilection and known how to play the part he required, Constance had been respectably – which is to say ignorantly – raised. She appealed to her father for help, but her parents decided that her husband's peculiarities 'came within the meaning of the marriage vows', and she was told that there was nothing for it but to submit to them. It was then that she met Lord Dupplin, 'with the result that the tragedy began'.

After a fancy-dress ball given by Lady Londonderry at Holderness House, Lord Ward returned home much later than his wife, in the early hours of the morning, only to notice a man leaving by his own front door. Their eyes met, and he saw that it was Lord Dupplin, who turned and ran for his life down the street.

Lord Ward entered and startled the sleepy footman by telling him to rouse the servants and bid them assemble in the hall. He then

*went upstairs to his wife's bedroom ... [where he went] to her
bedside and accused her of committing adultery with Lord
Dupplin. 'Get up, madame,' he continued, 'my house is yours no
longer; arrangements shall be made for your future, but henceforth
you are no wife of mine.'*

Constance's tears and protests were in vain. Although she was pregnant
at the time, her husband forced her to dress and then, leading her past
the scandalised servants who by now were assembled downstairs in
the hall, he turned her out of doors.

Constance managed to reach her parents' house in Grosvenor
Crescent, and implored them to take her in, but they were as heartless
as her husband. Eventually, 'more dead than alive', she found shelter
with her old singing master, who allowed her to remain with him until
the next day, when she took a boat to Ostend. From there she travelled
to Schwalback, where her child was born prematurely, 'and the
unhappy young mother died'.[40]

A courtesan's life was emphatically different from all this. Outside the
vigilance of society – and free from the dictatorship, benign or otherwise, of parents, brothers and husbands – she was free to choose her
own way through life. Although she had forfeited some of the protection afforded by society, she was free from some of its more arbitrary
cruelties, too. Catherine Walters did not stay long in Paris after her
last explosive parting from Blunt, but returned to London, where she
resumed her old life and with it her old ways. She set herself up in a
pretty house in Chesterfield Street, and it was from there, in 1882, that
her correspondence with Blunt began again, which, with only one
short gap, she was to continue for nearly forty years.*

---

* Catherine was in touch with Blunt throughout the 1870s, but none of her letters from
this period have survived. Elizabeth Longford tells an intriguing story of how Catherine
used her influence with the Prince of Wales to prevent Blunt being publicly named as a
co-respondent in the divorce of Lady Zouche in 1876.

6 *Chesterfield Street Mayfair*
My darling Winny,
I saw the Prince yesterday and he told me he made your
acquaintance on Sunday in Ebury Street. I had no idea you
were back in England. Look in and see me when you have a
mere moment to spare. The afternoon between 5 and 6 is the
best time to find me. How are you old darling? I hope well and
happy. I am very unwell with lungs which give me much
trouble. I have lots to tell you . . .[41]

In the 1880s Catherine was as much a feature of Mayfair life as she had been as a pretty young horsebreaker in the 1860s. Now in her early forties, and in indifferent health, she had nonetheless lost none of her beauty or her grace of figure. And, as her letter to Blunt shows, she was as seductive as ever.

Who, and how many, her protectors were during this period it is impossible to know. The Prince of Wales, whom she had met in the early days through Hartington,* was almost certainly one of them. Like Blunt, he became a lifelong friend and confidant of Catherine's, looking after her with great kindness in her later years and corresponding with her until his death in 1910. Shortly before her own death, on one of Wilfrid's last visits to her, she showed him an entire drawerful of the Prince's letters to her, 'very interesting ones . . . which ought not to fall into the wrong hands', and which she had meant to be returned to him one day. Alas, they have never been recovered. Another was the immensely rich Jewish financier Achille Fould, who had been one of Catherine's patrons in Paris, and whose name Blunt had been horrified to see inked in mirror image on some blotting paper at Catherine's house the first time he visited her after the Paris débâcle.†

---

* The Prince is alleged to have teased Hartington about his fondness for playing skittles.
† Elizabeth Longford believed that this may have been the source of Blunt's later anti-Semitism, which went beyond the 'normal upper-class aberrations of his era'. Blunt had travelled to London in September 1865 from Lisbon, where he was posted after Paris, in response to a pleading letter from Catherine. She had asked him to give her £2000 – the first time she had ever asked him for money – in order to free her from some debts. Blunt's discovery of her 'friendship' with Fould had been the final curtain call of their affair. 'What baser could there be than to share her with this Jew on the self-same terms of money payments?', Blunt wrote of the episode later. 'It was the worst that could befall.'

Catherine continued to ride and to hunt, passions which never left her, and on equestrian matters was knowledgeable enough to advise not only the Prince, but the Princess of Wales as well, whom she knew personally, and who often asked her to try out new horses. For the most part, however, she remained the *demi-mondaine* that she had always been.

Maturity, the death-knell of so many courtesans before her, in Catherine's case simply brought with it additional rewards. From the 'Fair of Vanity', which when Blunt had known her as a very young woman in France had been the sum of all her interest in the world, she had developed a fascination with politics. It was a very different Catherine who wrote to Blunt from her new house at 15 South Street on 21 April 1884:

> *When do you get back home I wonder. I have read all your letters in The Times with great interest. How right you were in saying what you did to me two years back about all the trouble we should have out in Egypt [General Gordon had recently marched into Khartoum] . . . How it will all end God alone knows. That vile man Gladstone will be the ruin of us all ere long.*[42]

This new awareness, combined with her gift for conversation and companionship with men, made Catherine – or Katie, or Kitty, or even Kittsy, as she now often signed herself – the perfect *salonnière*.

At the beginning of the 1880s the French custom of being 'at home' on a certain day was largely unknown in private houses in England. The salons which had been so much a feature of late-eighteenth-century London, with their intellectual and, in the eyes of the world, morally ambiguous hostesses, had not suited the more sober nineteenth century (by which time cleverness and goodness, in women, were only too often seen in moral opposition). The society hostess Mary Jeune, later Lady St Helier, who was one of the very first to re-adopt the practice, described her first experiments to introduce it at her house in Harley Street in 1881.

At first only a very few people came. The informality of the arrangement alone was one that was still very novel. Previous to this there had been dinners (usually very long-drawn-out affairs) and, during the short London Season there had been balls (which started very late, at ten or eleven o'clock), but other forms of evening parties and receptions were rare, and were only attended by older people;* restaurants, of course, were almost unknown. Besides, society in London in the first few years of the 1860s, after the death of Prince Albert, was 'not very brilliant', largely because of the Queen's retirement from social life. It was not until the marriage of the Prince and Princess of Wales in 1863 that new impetus was given to society, and there was a great revival in hospitality. Now, at least in part thanks to the markedly European tastes of the Prince, society at this point also became far more fluid and cosmopolitan than it had ever been.

Until now the great society hostesses of the early Victorian era – Lady Palmerston, Lady Waldegrave, Lady Margaret Beaumont, to name but the leading few – were all highly political in their social outlook and influence, and it was the Liberal Party which in the 1860s possessed the monopoly 'for social purposes' of nearly all the large houses in London. Although differences in political allegiance did not preclude friendships between families,† as sometimes happened on the Continent, small and select 'party' dinners were still the norm in households such as that of the Dowager Lady Cowper, who was a strong Whig, and whose house in St James's Square always seemed to Lady St Helier 'to represent the true embodiment of refinement and beauty, without any of the luxury and display which are so often associated now with great riches'.

But even while she was lamenting the passing of the simplicity and economy which had characterised her young days, Lady St Helier remembered also 'the extreme dulness and narrowness of English life' at this time. The London Season began after Easter and lasted until the end of July; and there was then no winter Season, so before April

---

* According to Lady St Helier, even these dinner parties were hardly ever attended by young unmarried women, who were usually put to bed at eight o'clock to sleep until 9.30, when, 'refreshed and beautified', they rose to dress themselves for the ball.
† An exception to this was during the debates in the 1890s over Home Rule, which sharply divided society, supporters of the Home Rule party being virtually ostracised by their friends.

London was 'empty' of everyone except lawyers and other professional men, who were not generally considered to be part of 'society' anyway. Besides political barriers, there were still just as many social restrictions as there had ever been, the two main debarred professions being drama and medicine. (In Lady St Helier's youth there was only one doctor, the eminent surgeon Sir Henry Thompson, 'who wandered beyond the social boundaries of his own professional brethren'.)

It was not until her own days as a hostess, some fifteen or twenty years later, that society 'of a sudden, as it were' opened up, conventional rules were thrown away, 'and those who had the courage and appreciation to open their houses to everyone who was interesting and distinguished found an ideally delightful society waiting for its new entertainers'.* Disraeli's 1867 Reform Bill, while bitterly debated and opposed at the time, had not only democratised politics, but had forced the leaders of 'society' to recognise that the boundaries of their hitherto exclusive world must change too. (The first of the political hostesses to welcome this new order of things had been Lady Waldegrave, generally recognised as the natural successor to Lady Palmerston after the latter's death, who was able to bring into contact for the first time both 'representatives of the old order' and those who stood for 'the new conditions of society'.)

After their slow start, Lady St Helier's 'At Homes' were more radical still. It took some courage at first, for there were still many traditionalists who viewed all such innovations with suspicion, but eventually she carried the day, mixing not only statesmen and politicians (her husband was a Tory) but men of letters, intellectuals, scientists, painters, famous generals and naval officers, medical men, lawyers and even women of distinction in her drawing room, which was soon recognised as an English counterpart to the brightest of the French salons. Most shocking of all, however, was her welcoming of actors, both men and women, into her home, a move which even in the most

---

* It is from this period that the formal etiquette current in 'good society' began to evolve, too. Lady St Helier was once terribly scolded by the Dowager Duchess of Cleveland because she shook hands with, rather than curtseying to, one of her guests when he was presented to her. The fact that the man was a friend of her husband's made no difference.

tolerant later decades of the eighteenth century had only ever very rarely been sanctioned.

'Whether [society] realized the intellectual superiority and the infinite gifts of the new recruits is difficult to say,' recalled Lady St Helier, 'but it showed no hesitation in acknowledging that it had gained everything by the new movement. The *moment psychologique* had arrived, and the admission to society of these cosmopolitan elements was the distinctive characteristic of the Victorian era.'[43]

No one was to be more of a beneficiary of this *moment psychologique* than Catherine Walters. Although society was not yet quite ready to welcome courtesans, Catherine could see no reason why she should not welcome society. The women would not come, but she knew that the men undoubtedly would. With this in mind, Catherine decided that her 'At Homes' should be given on Sunday afternoons. In the days before the 'weekend' had been invented, Sunday was the only day on which busy men were able to pay visits. Better still, Sunday was the one day of the week on which women were *not* expected to do so, however well they knew one another. 'It was always understood that the husbands went,' wrote Lady St Helier, 'and their wives stayed at home.'

Catherine's Sunday-afternoon tea-parties at her elegant little house in South Street were soon a Mayfair institution. The Prince of Wales was a regular visitor, and so too was her old friend Blunt. Although Catherine's circle consisted mostly of Establishment gentlemen, some women, mostly singers and actresses, or writers such as the popular novelist Marie Corelli, also attended. Like all good hostesses Catherine took particular pride in bringing her friends together. In September 1884 she wrote to Wilfrid from South Street:

> *My dearest Winny,*
>   *Last night the Prince was here and we had a talk about you as I told him you had been so kind coming to see me etc. He said of course he would be kind to you and ought to be for we were once something very dear to each other. I said yes but people are so cruel and change so. He said I like Blunt although I may not agree with him on certain things. He said he would*

*like to meet you here next month if you would come and take a
little dinner such as I could give, a chicken and so on. I make
no fuss with him as I am a child of nature always to Prince or
commoner just the same. I said you were going to Paris and
was afraid you might be away. Well he said when he returns
let us make a meeting so that I may know him better. He also
said something else I will tell you only in person . . .*

God bless you kindest darling old friend.[44]

If Catherine had the gift of converting her old lovers into friends, she
had not lost the knack of making new friends either. Although her
letters are impeccable in the proprieties they observe, in person her
conversation was salty and free. She knew everyone's secrets, and was
always generous with gossip ('I know that man [Lord Clanricarde] *too*
well,' she wrote in indignation after his brutal eviction of his tenants
in Ireland (a cause which was particularly dear to Blunt's heart), 'too
well in some things, and if you come to see me I will tell you a few
of the cruel and vile things he did even to his own mother.'[45]) The
following year Blunt recorded with amusement how he had been summoned to dinner with Catherine ('Lady C' in his published diaries) to
hear an account of how she had 'captivated no less a personage than
the G.O.M. the Grand Old Man [Gladstone] himself!'

Clearly Catherine had chosen to forget her sentiments of the previous
year. Although the Prime Minister chose to visit her on a Saturday,
rather than on one of Catherine's regular Sundays ('Saturdays and
Sundays are his evenings out,' she explained), 'nothing improper',
wrote Blunt, 'seems to have happened, except that the old man kissed
her hand saying in a rather formal manner "If it is permitted for an
old man." On the contrary she seems to have forced the conversation
into politics and attacked him on his wickedness in killing the Arabs
. . . But he took it all in good part.'[46]

A few days later Catherine sent Blunt an ebullient note:

*Mr. W. Gladstone has sent me a cargo of the best Russian tea by
Sir A. Clark* today sending me also a charming message to say*

---

* Sir Arthur Clark, the Prince of Wales's personal physician.

he will come to tea on Saturday next so you see he likes coming. Clark tells me that he was so much struck with all my go and charming ways. In fact he says Mr Wig [sic] never had anyone before who dared shout out in the way I did to him. He says he likes being taken like a bull by the horns, it is something new and most amusing for the old boy to be rubbed up in a different form so out of the way of the rest of the world. I shall have some good reports to tell you when we meet.[47]

The following Sunday Blunt went to South Street to hear all about Gladstone's second visit. The Prime Minister had arrived alone, bringing Catherine a bunch of narcissi. He had not come to talk politics, he said firmly, but had remarked instead on the smallness of her waist, she told Blunt, and went on to test its size 'by manual measurement'. 'If she wrote to him, as Gladstone hoped she would, she should mark the envelope private, followed by a little cross thus, "Private X".' Catherine looked forward to bearding him rather more about politics *'next time'* – even the Prince of Wales had warned her not to trouble him to much about them at first – 'but when he has got into the habit of coming', she told Blunt triumphantly, 'then I mean to let him have it'.[48]

Over the next few years Catherine continued to entertain her friends at South Street, and maintained her interest in politics. Many of the great men in Parliament at this time were either her friends, such as Gladstone and Disraeli,* or her former lovers, such as Hartington, now a leading figure in the Liberal Party; although Blunt himself – a radical anti-imperialist – was never to win a seat. In December 1885 Catherine wrote to console him about his defeat in the seat of Camberwell North in the election. 'Have courage and you see your next chance will come off. It's a hundred to one on it,' she wrote bracingly. 'Now do not dispair [sic] darling above all things. Into the house you must get and it will not be long before you will have another try when you will understand matters better. The Prince was so sorry . . .'[49]

---

* She preferred 'old bully Gladstone' to Disraeli, who was 'a kind old fellow but very dull'.

Although Catherine's views, perhaps influenced by Blunt ('A charming person,' Gladstone had confided to her, 'but on politics mad'), were radical ones, there was always a highly personal flavour to her political commentaries. 'I suppose you heard Hartington's speech and all the rest of them,'* she wrote to Blunt in December the following year. 'What do you think of it? I hope that that beast Clanricarde will be knocked on the head and that the poor people of his estate will not pay the brute one penny. He's such a real hard heart ... I think you ought to go over to Ireland to see for yourself what is the real state of affairs there. Do come back *dear soon*. I long so to see you.'[50]

But the truth was that Catherine was not well. She had always been delicate in her constitution, and her lungs had begun to trouble her increasingly. 'I nearly died dear since you left,' she wrote to Blunt on his return from one of his long trips abroad, 'and have been two months in bed on my back with inflammation of the lungs and bronchitis and no end of other things ... I had to have ... Sir A. Clark and a doctor here for a week sleeping in the house. My recovery is a wonder to all. I have H.R.H. coming to see me *ce soir*. He has been most kind.'[51]

Her doctors advised warmth and sea air, and Catherine began to spend increasing amounts of time abroad. In March 1889 she wrote to Blunt from the south of France to tell him that she would not be back in London again until May – 'my doctor will not allow it' – but she was having a high old time visiting friends. She had not made the planned journey to Egypt after all, but had stayed in the south of France, and in a few weeks' time was going back to Paris again for a couple of weeks. 'I must tell you Hartington was out at Cannes and we became great friends again,' she told Blunt with evident pleasure. The Prince of Wales, too, had been there for a month, 'and was so good and kind to me, as he always is, and he introduced me to no end of nice people and a lot of Russians'.

---

* The debate was on Home Rule, which was the principal issue of the day. Catherine had known the Earl of Clanricarde in Paris, where, as Hubert de Burgh, he was an Attaché at the Embassy. His brutal evictions had made him one of the most hated landlords in Ireland.

'What a lovely climate it is out here,' she wrote happily, 'and how much it does for me, all my cough gone, no asthma, no bronchitis, the only drawback is the burning sun here plays the very deuce with ones eyes and skin. It dries and burns one . . . I shall come home wrinkled like an old fossel [sic], but well in body, so one must not mind about looks I suppose.'[52]

But this new state of health was not to last. In August that year her doctors sent her abroad again, this time to the spa town of Homburg, where she had been advised to take the waters. There was none of the social ease or the benign climate of the south of France here. 'I do not like it at all,' she grumbled to Blunt.

> I hate the place and the people . . . all the old painted and got up old girls and men, vulgar slang Americans and all the German Jewesses and Jews, I keep out of the way of them all. The dear old Prince is the only one I see and he looks in most evenings and stops for an hour or so. His sister the Empress Frederick* is stopping at the red castle here. I hope to be home the first week in October.[53]

When Blunt wrote to cheer her up, Catherine replied affectionately:

> My dearest kind Winny,
> How glad I was to get your letter. Poor dear boy. So sweet and dear of you to say the kind things you do of me, it quite touched my heart and my eyes filled with tears of joy and pleasure . . . You are not the least changed to me, only perhaps kinder and dearer in some ways. I cannot write more now as I have the Prince coming here to tea at 3 today to say goodbye he leaves for London tonight . . .
> p.s. Write a long letter in a day or so.[54]

Catherine's friendship and correspondence with Blunt continued in this vein until the 1890s, when, inexplicably, he ceased to reply to her letters. 'It has so pained me never to have heard from you though I

---

* Queen Victoria's eldest daughter, Victoria, the Princess Royal, married the German Emperor Frederick III (he succeeded in 1888).

have written 2 or 3 times,' she wrote to him reproachfully in 1897, in the letter in which she signed herself for the first time as 'Kitty Baillie'.

It is unlikely that Catherine ever formally married Alec Baillie – in her will, which was dated only a few months before her death more than twenty years later, she is unequivocally still 'Catherine Walters ... Spinster' – but from this period, in what is perhaps an echo of a bygone age when courtesans often took the name of a favoured patron, she certainly took to using his name. Catherine's biographer Henry Blyth identified her friend as a Scotsman, Alexander Horatio Baillie, but nothing more is known about him other than that he was allegedly a friend of the Prince of Wales.

Although as early as 1879 Baillie and Catherine had visited Blunt at his famous Sussex stud, Crabbet, he remains a shadowy figure in her life. At the time of the Crabbet visit the mysterious Mr Baillie was already described as Catherine's 'husband', but by the 1890s his exact relationship to her can only be surmised. He does not ever seem to have lived with her at South Street, nor did their liaison bring her any particularly rich financial rewards, for in 1905 she made one last desperate attempt to get into contact which Blunt again.

> September 2nd, 1905
> My Dear old friend Wilfrid,
> May this reach you safely. I do not know where you are nor have I even heard from you for some years. As I am now quite bedridden for more than two years – I had to go under more severe and dangerous operations,* as now there is no hope of my ever getting better I should so like to see you and say goodbye before I go into a Home. I also am in the greatest state of poverty, and must now get out of 15 South Street. I want to know if you could see your way to help me with the lease ...
> you said when we last met that as you were too poor to present me with the £300 you ought to see your way to doing so later as a present. It would be a God's blessing to me in my present state dear old friend as I want to try to sell the lease ... to

---

* According to Elizabeth Longford, she had also had radium treatment for cancer.

*help me to go into a private Home where I could at least be
kept out of my suffering to a certain extent.*[55]

Catherine was now in her mid-sixties, and ill-health dominated her
life completely. She had to have daily sulphur injections, she told
Blunt, to help keep down the pain, and for this was obliged to keep
a fully-trained hospital nurse with her at all times – 'a fearful expense'.
'You know poor old Alex Baillie has not one sou, in fact he is a pauper
like myself,' she went on. 'He would do everything for me if he could,
but he is kept by his brother and tired out. He is trying to find
something to do to help to earn a living, but he is too old like the
rest of us.' If she did not think it a wicked thing to do, she would end
her life at once. 'It is so sad to feel how everyone deserts one when
ill,' she wrote. She had often wondered about Blunt, 'as you always
said you would be a loyal old friend to me in my old days. I do hope
from the bottom of my heart that you will come and say goodbye to
me before I die, for I can't last for long now. Goodbye and God Bless
you, dear old friend,' she concluded the letter, 'May this find you well
and happy.' She signed it 'Kitty Baillie'.[56]

If Catherine's request for money had been the source of their breach
in 1897, Blunt never made any allusion to it. 'It is 32 years today since
I first met Miss Walters, and ten days ago I had a letter from her, the
first for more than ten years,'* he wrote in his secret diary on 20
September. While a more cynical man might have detected a certain
artifice behind her composition, Blunt, who knew Catherine perhaps
better than anyone, did not. 'She writes in great distress of health and
saying that she is leaving her house in South Street for a nursing home
in which to die – poor woman – and poor all of us,' he recorded
simply. Blunt had himself been ill, and was recuperating in Brighton.
'A second letter from Miss Walters has just come precisely on this
anniversary, though she has forgotten it.' So it was as an anniversary
present, although she never knew it, that 'Esther' received one last
tribute: the lease of 15 South Street.

The letter Blunt received in reply from Catherine was jubilant. 'God

---

* Blunt was rather vague with his figures. He had in fact met Catherine forty-two years
previously, and they had not corresponded for eight.

bless you 100 times dear old friend Winny for your noble generosity to me with regard to the lease of South Street,' she wrote, much of her old vim suddenly restored. 'If your kind and tender heart only knew how much it means to me ... How happy it has made me to hear from your Hospital Nurse you are so much better also ... yes, you will get well now somehow I feel you will and that your good and dear and precious life will be saved.'[57]

The following spring, when the weather was clement, Blunt made one last visit to his old love. On Easter Day 1906 he was wheeled through Hyde Park in his 'perambulator', down Rotten Row – once the scene of Skittles's greatest triumphs, but now frequented only by 'working men and shopkeepers' – to South Street. 'It must be a dozen years since I saw her last and I found her just as I left her in her house in S. Street only that the house has been much smartened up and with servants strange to me,' he wrote in his diary. 'She herself, poor woman, has for years [been] more or less bedridden with some internal malady, which brings her from time to time to death's door.'

With the help of these servants, the invalid Blunt was carried up the stairs to Catherine's bedroom and laid out on the sofa by her bed. Although she was now 'an old woman' – 'she will be 67 on 13 of next' (for once Blunt had his dates right) – in his eyes she was almost miraculously unchanged, 'and her talk was just as vivacious as of old'. Catherine talked on 'in uninterrupted flow' for two hours, while Blunt patiently listened. 'She told me first of course of her maladies, and from then went on to the King's. According to her H.M. is thoroughly unsound, having a cancerous throat, varicose veins, and his bones turning to chalk.'

Frail and old, and debilitated by ill-health though she was, Catherine's gift for friendship remained with her until the last. As did one of her other principal talents: gossip. King Edward VII, as 'the Prince' now was, had like Blunt remained a loyal friend to Skittles. He had been very good to her, Catherine confided to Blunt, 'or you would not find me here in this house still'. When she was ill it was always his personal physicians, Sir William Broadbent and Sir Francis Laking, 'by command of the King', who attended her. The King himself still visited her sometimes, despite his own ill-health, and wrote often (it was on this occasion that she showed Blunt the drawerful of the King's letters). Blunt was amused to note that Catherine's bedroom, with its Louis Seize bed, had recently been redecorated in sumptuous blue satin, a last graceful tribute to an ageing but still beautiful courtesan from the monarch who had once surely been her lover.

As of old, Catherine knew all the scandal. The King and Queen argued; he was tired of his mistress Mrs Keppel, and was using Sir Ernest Cassell to try to pension off her husband; the Queen swore at her servants. The previous year, when everyone had thought Catherine was dying, the Queen herself, who remembered her from her horse-breaking and hunting days, had sent her a message promising that she was going to come and visit, but Catherine had felt so very ill that she had asked to be excused. 'I used to try horses for her,' she told Blunt, 'and got her one she has had for fifteen years and is very fond of.'[58]

Although Catherine and Blunt were to see one another again only a very few times, they now revived the correspondence that they had first begun in 1863. From passionate young lovers they had become friends; a friendship which now, nearly half a century later, was trans-muted once again into something very like love. They discussed their ailments ('I have been so ill with dreadful influenza and the after effects of it all,' wrote Catherine. 'I am very weak and lost nearly two stone in weight, and the bad air and filth and dirt of this city is enough to kill anyone'), their doctors, their mutual friends, many of whom were now either dead or dying ('Poor old Lord Rosebery is gravely ill, doesn't look as if he will recover. Do you see Lord Hardinge . . . ?').

There were some new friends, too. Although Catherine, to the end, would continue to sign her letters 'Kitty Baillie', her principal com-panion at this time was the Honourable Gerald du Saumarez, a man some twenty years younger than she whom she had first met when he was an Eton schoolboy of fifteen*. She also introduced Blunt to her niece Daisy, the daughter of her sister Caroline, now Viscountess du Manoir, with whom Catherine was now reconciled.

'Daisy du Manoir is so delighted she is allowed to lunch with you

---

* In her will, Catherine left almost everything, except her Louis Seize bed and her furs, but including her house, 15 South Street, to du Saumarez. The gross value of her estate was £2764.19s.6d, about £55,000 today.

tomorrow . . . She is only just nineteen years old and she sees everything *couleur de rose* but she is just delicate . . . I have never known or seen such a sweet girl,' Catherine wrote, adding cautiously, 'Be careful dear you say nothing of me to her, for the poor child knows so little of worldly things.'[58](Blunt, of course, was charmed by Daisy: 'I don't know whether I did wrong in kissing her,' he reflected in his diary after their lunch, 'but she seemed to like it . . .')

Some of Catherine's old vanity remained. 'I am much better and fatter,' she wrote to Blunt soon after their meeting at South Street. 'I was a skeleton now I am plump. My face has always kept its shape and you will be surprised to see how bonny I look for my age, for I am an old lady now and I am not ashamed to say so . . . I have heaps of hair and . . . [throughout my] illness kept a pretty complexion.' But increasingly, ill-health prevailed.

In the spring of 1918 Gerald du Saumarez took her down to Newbuildings Place, Blunt's Sussex country house. Although Catherine was by now half deaf and nearly blind, she was, according to Blunt, 'unconquered in talk, and gave us all the gossip of the hour, though it is too piecemeal for reproduction'.[60] Any kind of outing, however, was becoming increasingly rare. From her bed in South Street she dreamed of returning to Newbuildings one day. 'I have been boxed up for over three years,' she wrote to Blunt sadly in September that year. 'I have not seen a green field or a flower growing since I paid my visit to you with G.S.'

Her letters, now written in pencil instead of ink, become harder to read, an old lady scrawl which slides off the page; but her mind is still sharp. Since she could not visit the country, Blunt sent the country to her: rabbits and pheasants from his fields, a basket of butter and eggs, and sometimes flowers – a bunch of early primroses. In December 1919 Catherine sent him 'a pretty drawing I had done 25 years ago when I was young' as a Christmas present. 'I am sending you all my best and dearest wishes for Xmas and the New Year,' she ended the letter, adding longingly, 'How I would love just to see you again, and if it were the summer I would go.'

It was not to be. The following summer, on 15 July 1920, Catherine wrote a last short note to her 'dear and kindest Wilfrid'. Although she had been very ill that spring, she was better now and proposed coming to see him at last. The ever-devoted Gerald du Saumarez would bring her down by train, she wrote, adding anxiously, 'I do hope dear dear old friend you are better.'

They were her last words to him. Three weeks later, on 5 August 1920, Catherine suffered a fatal stroke at her house in South Street. The last great Victorian courtesan was gone, bringing to a quiet end a life which had dazzled all who came within its orbit with its beauty, sensuality and grace.

CONCLUSION

THE DEATH OF CATHERINE WALTERS in 1920 brought to an end the golden age of British courtesanry.

There would be others after her, of course (and I have no doubt that they still exist today), just as there were courtesans before the glory days of Sophia Baddeley; but it is beyond dispute that it was during the 'long nineteenth century', the 150-year period which lies between Sophia and Catherine, that the English half-world – that parallel universe, at once glittering and ghostly – found its greatest expression, and its five greatest exponents.

In telling the stories of Sophia Baddeley, Elizabeth Armistead, Harriette Wilson, Cora Pearl and Catherine Walters, I have been constantly aware of the things that we can never know about them. Hidden away and denied a voice for so long now, there are times when they still seem to run just out of reach, slipping like saucy ghosts in and out of the uncertain shadows of history and time. These are not intended to be definitive biographies; and, in any case, perhaps no such thing is possible. The memoirs of Cora Pearl and Harriette Wilson are, as memoirs will always be, both partial and idiosyncratic; as is Eliza Steele's remarkable biography of her friend Sophia Baddeley. But then, so too, perhaps more so, are the cries of their detractors, those who wished to deny them the right to any voice at all.

These women wrote about life as they experienced it, and as such the records they have left are of immeasurable value to us. But they are unlikely to be the whole story. What, I still wonder, did they leave out? Cora Pearl always claimed that she never had a 'preferred lover', but other sources believe she had a long affair with the artist Gustave Doré, and may even have contemplated marriage to him.[1] (On her death, a set of books with illustrations by Doré was found amongst Cora's effects, while a photograph of her belonging to Doré, and signed by her 'Remember. C.P.', was exhibited in Paris in 1948.) There is no clue, either, to the identity of the mysterious 'Cécile Emmeline' to whom Cora referred in an undated letter which was published in the *Echo de Paris* on 3 March 1886, just a few months before her death:

> *Ah, my poor friend, I was so happy to have your letter. Although you now live in retirement, you have heard that I have lost Emmeline.*
>
> *Emmeline, that other half of myself. Yes, my dear Cécile Emmeline is dead . . . to have lived side by side, to have been tied so intimately one to another, to have partaken of the same joys, drunk of the same cup of pleasures, wept over the same disappointments, we the inseparables!**

The survival of other source material, such as unpublished letters and journals, is an equally capricious one, and may appear to give a bias which, in real life, was perhaps not quite so pronounced. That Wilfrid Scawen Blunt was a lifelong friend to Catherine Walters is beyond question, but how would her story have been changed if that drawerful of letters from the Prince of Wales (or from Alec Baillie, or Gerald du Saumarez) had survived – as who knows, perhaps they have – in some forgotten attic somewhere?

What is certain is that these women are unique in our history. It may seem inappropriate to use the word 'feminist' to describe a group of women whose success depended on their skill in pleasuring men, but they were ahead of their times in so many things. Although rarely intentionally political, a courtesan was nonetheless a powerful symbol of a woman's potential for autonomy, for sexual and emotional self-expression; and a sweet-throated counterblast to the stultifying tyranny of female 'propriety'. No wonder she was kept out of sight.

It occurs to me, too, that it is difficult to think of a group of women whose personalities are so wholly different as those of Sophia, Elizabeth, Harriette, Cora and Catherine. There is no single 'type' – no blueprint, as it were – of the successful courtesan, yet certain aspects of the way

---

*· Cora's biographer W.H. Holden believed this letter to be genuine, and the Mademoiselle L—— to whom it was addressed to be Cora's friend Caroline Letessier.

they lived their lives will always unite them. As single women, all of whom originated in relative obscurity (mostly from the *petit bourgeoisie*, the lower and lower-middle class), they rose to create a lifestyle for themselves that was on a par with that of the aristocracy – in itself a startling achievement.

But it was not merely financial and material independence, vital though that was, that they held so dear. Their moral and spiritual autonomy – the freedom to think and speak for themselves, even when their conclusions were deeply uncomfortable to the society around them – was every bit as precious. It is worth listening, I think, to those proud voices just one more time:

> *'The young gentleman, I believe, loves me to adoration but I will not be his wife notwithstanding, nor will I be the wife of any man; for I can never submit to the control of a husband, or put it in his power to say I have been imprudent in life.' (Sophia Baddeley)*

> *'I will be the mere instrument of pleasure to no man.' (Harriette Wilson)*

> *'My independence was all my fortune, and I have known no other happiness; and it is still what attaches me to life.' (Cora Pearl)*

> *'Now darling what do you really mean by saying I deceived you? I have nothing I want to deceive you in and if I want to do anything dearest I do it . . .' (Catherine Walters)*

Shunned in their own day for being moral degenerates, courtesans were, quite to the contrary, some of the most quick-sighted and astute observers of the moral issues at the heart of women's lot. Harriette

Wilson, who once declared that she valued her liberty 'more than my life', spoke for all her sisters in the half-world when she wrote this excoriating indictment of public morality:

> Now the English Protestant ladies' virtue is chastity! There are but two classes of women among them. She is a bad woman the moment she has committed fornication; be she generous, charitable, just, clever, domestic, affectionate, and ever ready to sacrifice her own good to serve and benefit those she loves, still her rank in society is with the lowest hired prostitute. Each is indiscriminately avoided, and each is denominated the same – bad woman, while all are virtuous who are chaste.

Although the Cinderella glamour of their 'rags to riches' stories made many courtesans the folk heroines of their day, their relationship with 'society' continued to be an ambiguous one throughout the nineteenth century. A paradox remains: high-class courtesans were at once famous figures, and yet also belonged to a culture – an entire world, indeed – that was essentially covert, and socially inadmissible. This suggests that they were in fact just the tip of an iceberg: an iceberg that it was in men's interests to conceal as much as possible (which explains why so few of them wrote about it, and why even the more emancipated women of the late nineteenth century continued to see courtesans as a social evil). It suggests that they were the most visible and victorious pennant waving from the top of an informal system of concubinage vastly greater than anyone has realised.

In the past, the life stories of courtesans have often been used as morality tales. Perhaps as an enforced atonement for having so brazenly jumped out of the box allotted to them by a grudging society, their biographers delighted in giving them the most grisly possible end. Even Sophia Baddeley's devoted friend Mrs Steele could not resist the temptation to make an example out of her: 'Let the fate of Mrs Baddeley be a lesson to all young minds not to stray from the paths of virtue,' she wrote; 'for with all the beauty she possessed, with all the splendour she enjoyed, and all the admiration she met with, she fell at last a sacrifice and lived to be unnoticed by those who once adored her. In short, let them learn from the heroine of these memoirs, to be wary and circumspect, and stand upon their guard against the seduction of men.'[2]

It is true that Sophia, as we have seen, found it hard to live up to her much-cherished ideals (which of us does not?). But although all the evidence suggests that she did indeed die in much reduced circumstances, as we have seen, her end was very far from being the one of complete destitution that Mrs Steele implies.

Just as there is no single blueprint of the successful courtesan, so it is impossible to generalise about their demise. Like Sophia, Harriette too died in less than glorious surroundings, but Elizabeth and Catherine, both of whom lived to be very old women, died in the same houses – in the very same beds – that had been theirs for most of their lives, still nurtured by the love and companionship of their friends.

Perhaps the most ambiguous death of all is that of Cora Pearl. At the time it was widely claimed that she had died in the greatest poverty and distress, but these accounts were surely exaggerated. The flat where she died, on the third floor of 8, rue de Bassano, still exists, just a street away from her beautiful *hôtel* in the rue Chaillôt (which does not). It is an austerely handsome grey-brick Parisian house, not luxurious, but comfortable enough, even by a courtesan's exacting standards.

When Cora told Arsène Houssaye that she was 'Cora without the pearls' she was speaking figuratively only. After her death, in September 1886, a sale was held of her effects. Spread over two days, the auction included a pearl necklace which was sold for a handsome twenty thousand francs (it was bought, according to the English newspaper *The Truth*, appropriately enough by 'an old gentleman' for a 'charming young lady'). Other items included many silver cruet stands, fish trowels, asparagus tongs, sugar basins, cream ewers, napkin rings and dish warmers 'such as one sees at a fashionable wedding'. There was also 'an exquisite silver tea service for two persons' which had been presented to Cora by Prince Bonaparte. Some of the silver vessels had carved on them, in imitation of the cipher of Henri II's mistress Diane de Poitiers, 'three interlaced crescents, which served for capital C's'.

Amongst the most popular items were the remains of her household and body linen, of which there was a great deal, all of 'extraordinary fineness': 'The "linen" embraced a quantity of underclothing of foulard silk, very fine, very strong, very supple, and got up as only Paris *lingères* know how to get up such garments. Some of them were of the natural shade of the cocoon, others light blue, and others black.'[3]

Like a cabinet of curiosities of Cora's life, the sale went on: the watercolour drawing of the Nile at sunset, inscribed *'Ma Perle Chérie'*, which had been given to her by her old friend Blanche d'Antigny; the bow and arrows which she had carried as part of her costume in *Orphée aux enfers* nearly twenty years before; her bed, upholstered in satin with silk trimmings; several hairpieces ('very long ... and the colour of mahogany of a poor quality'); a whip; a riding habit; numerous fans; books illustrated by her one-time lover Gustave Doré; a plaster cast of her beautiful breasts.

Last of all were the paintings. Written off as 'wretched daubs' that were only bought for the sake of their expensive frames, one of them, in light pastels, was a portrait of Cora herself. 'The legend was,' reported *The Truth*, 'that a millionaire, who had no perception of fine art, had the portrait done in order to place a single pearl worth 9,000 francs in a kind of reliquary in the front of the frame, and that he sent the whole as a birthday gift.'[4] Beneath it ran the inscription *'Avant d'y retrouver une perle aussi chère'*.

For the men who adored and desired them, these great courtesans were indeed pearls without price, richly worth the fortunes that were spent on them, and more. For all their follies and extravagance, as personalities they surely rank among the most outstanding women of all time: magnificently, ruinously – but wholly – themselves.

NOTES

PROLOGUE

1 Mrs Elizabeth Steele, *The Memoirs of Mrs Sophia Baddeley, Late of Drury Lane Theatre*. London, 1787.

INTRODUCTION

1 Sacheverell Sitwell, *Selected Works*. Robert Hale Ltd; London, 1955.

2 Lady Augusta Fane, *Chit Chat*. Thornton Butterworth; London, 1926.

3 Marie Colombier, *Memoires. Vol. 1: Fin d'Empire*. Ernest Flammarion; Paris, 1898.

4 Honoré de Balzac, *Cousin Bette*. Oxford University Press; Oxford, 1992.

5 Quoted in Frederick Brown, *Zola: A Life*. Macmillan; London, 1996.

6 Quoted in Sandra Richards, *The Rise of the English Actress*. Macmillan; London, 1993.

7 Quoted in Hannah Barker and Elaine Charlus (eds), *Gender in Eighteenth-Century England: Roles, Representations and Responsibilities*. Longman; London, 1997.

8 Julia Johnstone, *Confessions of Julia Johnstone, written by herself in contradiction to the fables of Harriette Wilson*. Benbow; London, 1925.

9 *Letter to The Times*, 3 July 1862.

10 Quoted in Georgina Masson, *Courtesans of the Italian Renaissance*.

11 Ibid.

12 Cathy Santore, 'Julia Lombardo, "*Somtuosa Meretrize*": A Portrait by Property'. *Renaissance Quarterly*, vol. 41, issue 1 (spring 1988).

13 'Zed' (the Comte de Maugny), *Le Demi-Monde sous le Second Empire: Souvenirs d'un sybarite*. Ernest Kolb; Paris, 1892.

14 *Gazette des Etrangers*, 10 September 1868. Quoted in Guy Vauzat, *Blanche d'Antigny (Actrice et Demi-Mondaine) 1840–1874*. Charles Bosse; Paris, 1933.

15 James Davidson, *Courtesans and Fishcakes: The Consuming Passions of Classical Athens*. HarperCollins; London, 1997.

16 Quoted in ibid.

17 Quoted in Margaret F. Rosenthal, *The Honest Courtesan: Veronica Franco, Citizen and Writer in Sixteenth-Century Venice*. University of Chicago Press; Chicago, 1992.

18 Fynes Moryson, *Itinearary Containing his Ten Yeeres Travell*. London, 1617.

19 Quoted in Masson, op. cit.

20 Quoted in Rosenthal, op. cit.

21 Ibid.

22 Ibid.

23 Ibid.

24 Quoted in Irving Wallace, *The Nympho and Other Maniacs*. Cassell & Co.; London, 1971.

25 Ibid.

26 Colette, *My Apprenticeships and Music Hall Sidelights*. Secker & Warburg; London, 1957.

27 *The Times*, 3 July 1862.

28 The Journal of Mrs Arbuthnot, 1820–1832. Quoted in Christopher Hibbert, *Wellington: A Personal History*. HarperCollins; London, 1997.

29 Quoted in Arthur Gold and Robert Fizdale, *The Divine Sarah: A Life of Sarah Bernhardt*. HarperCollins; London, 1992.

30 William Acton, *Prostitution, Considered in its Moral, Social, & Sanitary Aspects in London and other Large Cities and Garrison Towns ...* John Churchill & Sons; London, 1870.

1 · SOPHIA BADDELEY

1 *Town and Country Magazine*, May 1772.
2 All quotations from Mrs Steele's *Memoirs* are from Steele, Mrs Elizabeth. *The Memoirs of Mrs Sophia Baddeley, Late of Drury Lane Theatre.* London, 1787.
3 *A Biographical Dictionary of Actors, Actresses, Musicians, Dancers, Managers, and other Stage Personnel in London 1660–1800.* 3 vols, Southern Illinois Press 1973–76.
4 *Town and Country Magazine*, May 1772.
5 'Tête-à-Tête', ibid.
6 *A Biographical Dictionary of Actors...*, op. cit.
7 Sandra Richards, *The Rise of the English Actress.* Macmillan; London, 1993.
8 John Brewer, *The Pleasures of the Imagination: English Culture in the Eighteenth Century.* HarperCollins; London, 1997.
9 Catherine Macleod and Julia Alexander, *Painted Ladies: Women at the Court of Charles II.* National Portrait Gallery Publications; London, 2001.
10 Ibid.
11 Richards, op. cit.
12 Ibid.
13 Ibid.
14 *A Biographical Dictionary of Actors...*, op. cit.
15 Mary Robinson, *Memoirs of Mary Robinson 'Perdita', from the Edition Edited by her Daughter with Introduction and Notes by J. Fitzgerald Molloy.* J.B. Lippincott Co.; Philadelphia, 1894.
16 *A Brief Narrative of the Life of the Celebrated Miss Cateley, Containing the Adventures of the Lady, in her Public Character as a Singer, and Private one of a Courtesan.* London, 1780.
17 Horace Bleackley, *Ladies Fair and Frail: Sketches of the Demi-Monde During the Eighteenth Century.* John Lane, The Bodley Head; London, 1909.
18 *Monthly Review*, vol. 77, 1787.
19 Captain Charles Walker, *Authentick Memoirs of the Life, Intrigues and Adventures of the Celebrated Sally Salisbury, with True Characters of her Most Considerable Gallants.* London, 1723.
20 *Memoirs of the Celebrated Miss Fanny Murray.* London, 1759.
21 Richards, op. cit.
22 Donald A. Stauffer, *The Art of Biography in Eighteenth-Century England.* Princeton University Press; Princeton, 1941.
23 Cleone Knox, *The Diary of a Young Lady of Fashion in the Year 1764–5.* Thornton Butterworth Ltd; London, 1925.
24 *Morning Post*, 13 July 1784.
25 *Morning Post*, 2 July 1784.
26 *Morning Post*, 24 December 1784.
27 For this and for all following dates and prices see *A Biographical Dictionary of Actors...*, op. cit.
28 John Fyvie, *Comedy Queens of the Georgian Era.* Archibald Constable & Company; London, 1906.
29 Ibid.
30 Anthony Pasquin, 'The Children of Thespis', 1787.

2 · ELIZABETH ARMISTEAD

1 Holland House Add Ms 47,570, CJF to EA, 7 May 1785.
2 Christopher Hobhouse, *Fox.* Houghton Mifflin; New York, 1935.
3 CJF to HH. Quoted in David Powell, *Charles James Fox: Man of the People.* Hutchinson; London, 1989.
4 *Town and Country Magazine*, July 1776.

5 Ibid., March 1779.
6 Quoted in I.M. Davis, *The Harlot and the Statesman: The Story of Elizabeth Armistead and Charles James Fox*. The Kensal Press; Bucks, 1986.
7 'Harris's List of Covent Garden Ladies or Man of Pleasure's Kalendar', for the years 1789 and 1793.
8 Baron Johann von Archenholz, *A Picture of England*. Byrne; Dublin, 1791.
9 William Hickey (ed. Peter Quennell), *The Prodigal Rake: Memoirs of William Hickey*. E.P. Dutton & Co. Ltd; New York, 1962.
10 E.J. Burford, *Royal St James's: Being a Story of Kings, Clubmen and Courtesans*. Robert Hale Ltd; London, 1988.
11 Ibid.
12 Ibid.
13 Holland House Add Mss 47,570, CJF to EA, undated.
14 *Town and Country Magazine*, March 1779.
15 Ibid., July 1776.
16 Quoted in L.G. Mitchell, *Charles James Fox*. Oxford University Press; Oxford, 1992.
17 Quoted in Stella Tillyard, *Aristocrats: Caroline, Emily, Sarah and Louisa Lennox 1740–1832*. Chatto & Windus; London, 1994.
18 Quoted in Amanda Foreman, *Georgiana, Duchess of Devonshire*. HarperCollins; London, 1998.
19 Sir George Otto Trevelyan, *Early History of Charles James Fox*. Thomas Nelson & Sons; London, 1861.
20 Ibid.
21 Quoted in Stanley Ayling, *Fox: The Life of Charles James Fox*. John Murray; London, 1991.
22 Holland House Add Mss 47,570, CJF to EA, undated.
23 Quoted in Ayling, op. cit.
24 Davis, op. cit.
25 Holland House Add Mss 47,570, CJF to EA, 30 December 1784.
26 Quoted in Davis, op. cit.
27 Holland House Add Mss 47,570, CJF to EA, undated.
28 Samuel Rogers, *Recollections*. Longman, Green, Longman & Roberts; London, 1859.
29 This and the following four election letters quoted in Davis, op. cit.
30 Holland House Add Mss 47,570, CJF to EA, 7 May 1784.
31 Rogers, op. cit.
32 Ibid.
33 Davis, op. cit.
34 Holland House Add Mss 47,570, CJF to EA, 27 January 1787.
35 Davis, op. cit.
36 Ibid.
37 Nathaniel Wraxall, *Historical and Posthumous Memoirs*. London, 1884.
38 Davis, op. cit.
39 Holland House Add Mss 47,570, CJF to EA, dated 'Wednesday'. '1795' added in another hand.
40 For a discussion of this fascinating topic, see F.M.L. Thompson, *The Rise of Respectable Society 1830–1900*. Fontana; London, 1988.
41 Holland House Add Ms 47,570, CJF to EA, 25 September 1795.
42 Ibid.
43 Quoted in Davis, op. cit.
44 Ibid.
45 Lady Bessborough (ed. The Earl of Bessborough, GCMG, in collaboration with A. Aspinall), *Lady Bessborough and her Family Circle*. John Murray; London, 1940.
46 Foreman, op. cit.
47 This and above quoted in Ayling.
48 Davis, op. cit.
49 Holland House Add Ms 51,476, Mrs Fox's Notebook.
50 Ibid.
51 Ibid., 19 and 20 May 1806.
52 Ibid.
53 Henry Holland, *Memoirs of the Whig Party*. London, 1852–54.
54 Davis, op. cit.
55 Mrs Fox's Notebook.
56 Ibid.
57 Davis, op. cit.
58 Ibid.

59 Holland House Add Ms 52,054, Miss Fox to H.E. Fox, 12 July 1842.
60 Davis, op. cit.

3 · HARRIETTE WILSON

1 For this and all other quotations from Harriette's *Memoirs*, first published in 1825 in four volumes by John Joseph Stockdale, I have used *Harriette Wilson's Memoirs*, Selected and Edited with an Introduction by Lesley Blanch. Century Publishing; London, 1985.
2 Johnstone, *Confessions*, op. cit.
3 Rees Howell Gronow, Formerly of the First Foot Guards, *The Last Recollections of Captain Gronow*. Selwyn & Blount Ltd; London, 1934.
4 James Laver, *English Costume of the Eighteenth Century*. A. & C. Black; London, 1945.
5 Venetia Murray, *High Society: A Social History of the Regency Period, 1788–1830*. Viking; London, 1998.
6 Captain Gronow (ed. Christopher Hibbert), *Captain Gronow: His Reminiscences of Regency and Victorian Life 1810–1860*. Based on the original four volumes published 1862, 1863, 1865 and 1866. Kyle Cathie; London, 1991.
7 Murray, op. cit.
8 Norman Hartnell, *Royal Courts of Fashion*. Cassell; London, 1971.
9 Murray, op. cit.
10 Gronow, *The Last Recollections of Captain Gronow*, op. cit.
11 Acton, op. cit.
12 Johnstone, *Confessions*, op. cit.
13 *Cockayne's Complete Peerage*. St Catherine Press; London, 1910.
14 Johnstone, *Confessions*, op. cit.
15 Quoted in Valerie Grosvenor Meyer, *Harriette Wilson: Lady of Pleasure*. Fern House; Ely, 1999.
16 Johnstone, *Confessions*, op. cit.
17 *Culpeper's Complete Herbal*. W. Foulsham & Co.; London, 1975.
18 Emma Dickens, *Immaculate Contraception: The Extraordinary Story of Birth Control From the First Fumblings to the Present Day*. Robson Books; London, 2000.
19 Derek Parker, *Casanova*. Sutton Publishing; Stroud, 2002.
20 Dickens, op. cit.
21 Angus Mclaren, *Birth Control in Nineteenth-Century England*. Croom Helm Ltd; London, 1978.
22 *Morning Post and Daily Advertiser*, Tuesday, 13 July 1784.
23 Mclaren, op. cit.
24 Angus Mclaren, 'Abortion in England, 1890–1914'. *Victorian Studies*, vol. 20.
25 Letter to Bulwer Lytton, 1831. Quoted in The Earl of Lytton, *The Life of Edward Bulwer, First Lord Lytton*. Macmillan & Co.; London, 1913.
26 Angela Thirkell, *The Fortunes of Harriette: The Surprising Career of Harriette Wilson*. Hamish Hamilton; London, 1936.
27 Ibid.
28 UCL Manuscript Library. H. Wilson to H. Brougham, 30 June 1828.
29 Ibid.
30 Ibid.

4 · CORA PEARL

1 Gronow, *Last Recollections*, op. cit.
2 W.H. Holden, *The Pearl from Plymouth*. British Technical and General Press; London, 1950.
3 'Zed', op. cit.
4 Emile Zola, *Nana*. Penguin; London, 1972.
5 Colombier, op. cit.
6 See appendix in Holden, op. cit.
7 All quotations in English are from E.E. Crouch, *The Memoirs of Cora Pearl, the English Beauty of the French Empire*. George Vickers; London, 1886. Quotations in French are from *Memoires de Cora Pearl*. Jules Levy; Paris, 1886.
8 Holden, op. cit.
9 Pearl, *Memoirs*, op. cit.
10 Ibid.
11 Ibid.

12 See Kellow Chesney, *The Victorian Underworld*. Penguin; London, 1970.

13 Cyril Pearl, *The Girl with the Swansdown Seat*. Frederick Muller; London, 1955.

14 William Acton, *Prostitution – Considered in its Moral, Social, & Sanitary Aspects in London and other Large Cities and Garrison Towns, with Proposals for the Control and Prevention of its Attendant Evils*. John Churchill & Son; London, 1870.

15 Ibid.

16 Henry Mayhew (with J. Binny, B. Hemyng and A. Halliday), *London Labour and the London Poor. Vol IV*. London, 1862.

17 See Roy Porter and Mikulas Teich (eds), *Sexual Knowledge, Sexual Science: The History of Attitudes to Sexuality*. Cambridge University Press; Cambridge, 1994.

18 Quoted in Peter Gay, *The Bourgeois Experience: From Victoria to Freud. Volume I: The Education of the Senses*. Oxford University Press; Oxford, 1985.

19 Acton, op. cit.

20 Edmond and Jules de Goncourt (ed. Lewis Glanatière), *The Goncourt Journals 1851–1870*. Cassell & Co.; London, 1937.

21 William Osgood Field, *Things I Shouldn't Tell*. Eveleigh Nash & Grayson Ltd; London, 1924.

22 See Holden, op. cit.

23 Quoted in ibid.

24 Sitwell, *La Vie Parisienne. From Selected Works*, op. cit.

25 Frédéric Loliée (adapted by Bryan O'Donnell), *The Gilded Beauties of the Second Empire*. John Long Ltd; London, 1909.

26 Ibid.

27 Comtesse Louise de Mercy-Argenteau, *Last Love of an Emperor*. The Iris Publishing Company; London, 1916.

28 Arsène Houssaye (trans. and ed. Henry Knepler), *Man About Paris: The Confessions of Arsène Houssaye*. Victor Gollancz; London, 1972.

29 'Zed', op. cit.

30 Goncourt, op. cit.

31 Quoted in Holden, op. cit.

32 Houssaye, op. cit.

33 A facsimile of this letter appears in Loliée, op. cit.

34 William Osgood Field, *Uncensored Recollections*. Evelyn Nash & Grayson Ltd; London, 1924.

35 Quoted in Michael Harrison, *Fanfare of Strumpets*. R. & R. Clark; Edinburgh, 1971.

36 Quoted in Joanna Richardson, *The Courtesans: The Demi-Monde in Nineteenth-Century France*. Phoenix Press; London, 2000.

37 Goncourt, quoted in ibid.

38 Ibid.

39 Goncourt, op. cit.

40 Loliée, op. cit.

41 Goncourt, op. cit.

42 Quoted in Richardson, op. cit.

43 Goncourt, op. cit.

44 Emile Bergerat, *Souvenirs d'un enfant de Paris. Tome II: La Phase critique de la critique*. Charpentier; Paris, 1912.

45 Richardson, op. cit.

46 Loliée, op. cit.

47 Quoted in Pearl, *Memoirs*, op. cit.

48 See Holden, op. cit.

49 Quoted in ibid.

50 Philibert Audebrand, *Petite memoires d'une stalle d'orchestre*. Jules Levy; Paris, 1885.

51 Sitwell, op. cit.

52 Guy Vauzat, *Blanche d'Antigny: Actrice et Demi-Mondaine 1840–1874*. Charles Bosse; Paris, 1933.

53 Goncourt, op. cit.

54 *La Vie Parisienne*, quoted in Richardson, op. cit.

55 Diana de Marly, *Worth: Father of Haute Couture*. Elm Tree Books; London, 1980.

56 Mercy-Argenteau, op. cit.

57 Ibid.

58 Quoted in Pearl, *Memoirs*, op. cit.

59 Ibid.

60 Ibid.

61 Houssaye, op. cit.

62 This is corroborated by William Osgood Field in his *Uncensored Recollections*, op. cit.
63 Holden, op. cit.

5 · CATHERINE WALTERS

1 'Zed', op. cit.
2 See Elizabeth Longford, *A Pilgrimage of Passion: The Life of Wilfrid Scawen Blunt*. Weidenfeld & Nicolson; London, 1979.
3 Anita Leslie, *Edwardians in Love*. Hutchinson; London, 1972.
4 See Patrick Jackson, 'Skittles and the Marquis: A Victorian Love Affair'. *History Today*, December, 1995.
5 Quoted in Sir William Hardman (ed. S.M. Ellis), *A Mid-Victorian Pepys: The Letters and Memoirs of Sir William Hardman, MA, FRGS*. Cecil Palmer; London, 1923.
6 See Cyril Pearl, op. cit.
7 Jackson, op. cit.
8 Ibid.
9 See Longford, op. cit.
10 *The Times*, 3 July 1862.
11 Henry Blyth, *Skittles: The Last Victorian Courtesan. The Life and Times of Catherine Walters*. Rupert Hart-Davis; London, 1970.
12 *The Times*, 3 July 1862.
13 *Daily Telegraph*, 4 July, 1862.
14 Jackson, op. cit.
15 Ibid.
16 Hardman, op. cit.
17 Cyril Pearl, op. cit.
18 Lady St Helier, *Memories of Fifty Years*. Edward Arnold; London, 1909.
19 Ibid.
20 ibid.
21 Fitzwilliam Museum. Wilfrid Scawen Blunt Diaries. 385/1975.
22 'Alms to Oblivion'. Fitzwilliam Museum Ms 295/1975.
23 Wilfrid Scawen Blunt, *The Poetical Works of Wilfrid Scawen Blunt. Vol. 1*. Macmillan & Co; London, 1914.
24 'Alms to Oblivion', op. cit., Chapter 1.
25 Ibid.
26 Ibid.
27 Ibid.
28 Ibid.
29 Ibid, Chapter 2.
30 Ibid.
31 Ibid.
32 Fitzwilliam Museum. Wilfrid Scawen Blunt Collection. 633/1976. C. Walters to WSB, May 1965.
33 Longford, op. cit.
34 Ibid.
35 Jane Jordan, *Josephine Butler*. John Murray; London, 2001.
36 Quoted in Bonnie S. Anderson and Judith P. Zinsser, *A History of their Own: Women in Europe from Prehistory to the Present. Volume II*. Penguin; Harmondsworth, 1988.
37 Quoted in Linda Colley, *Britons: Forging the Nation, 1707–1837*. Vintage; London, 1996.
38 Mrs Sarah Ellis, *The Wives of England: Their Relative Duties, Domestic Influence and Social Obligations*. Fisher, Son & Co.; London, 1843.
39 Ibid.
40 Countess of Cardigan and Lancastre, *My Recollections*. Eveline Nash; London, 1909.
41 Fitzwilliam Museum. Blunt Collection. 634/1976 C. Walters to WSB, 1882.
42 Ibid. 635/1776 C. Walters to WSB, 21 April 1884.
43 St Helier, op. cit.
44 Fitzwilliam Museum. Blunt Collection. 636/1976. C. Walters to WSB, 10 September 1884.
45 Ibid. 640/1976. C. Walters to WSB, 3 November 1887.
46 Longford, op. cit.
47 Fitzwilliam Museum. Blunt Collection. 486/1975. C. Walters to WSB, 14 May 1885.
48 Longford, op. cit.
49 Fitzwilliam Museum. Blunt Collection. 251/1975. C. Walters to WSB, 8 December 1885.

50 Ibid. 639/1976. C. Walters to WSB, 14 December 1886.
51 Ibid.
52 Ibid. 646/1976. C. Walters to WSB, 25 March 1889.
53 Ibid. 644/1976. C. Walters to WSB, 26 August 1889.
54 Ibid. 645/1976. C. Walters to WSB, 6 September 1889.
55 Ibid. 672/1976. C. Walters to WSB. 2 September 1905.
56 Ibid.
57 Ibid. 673/1976. C. Walters to WSB, undated, 1905.

58 Ibid. 385/1975. WSB Diaries. 385/1975. July 1905-April 1906.
59 Ibid. 666/1976. C. Walters to WSB, 20 April 1906.
60 Blyth, op. cit.

CONCLUSION

1 See Joanna Richardson, *Gustave Doré: A Biography*. Cassell; London, 1980.
2 Steele, op. cit.
3 'Notes from Paris', *The Truth*, 14 October 1886.
4 Ibid.

SELECT BIBLIOGRAPHY

1. MANUSCRIPT SOURCES

British Library

Holland House and Fox Mss. Add Mss 47,570, 47,569, 51,476

Fitzwilliam Museum

Blunt Mss. Papers and Correspondence of Wilfrid Scawen Blunt, including letters written by Catherine Walters to Wilfrid Scawen Blunt

University College London

Harriette Wilson Mss. Letters written by Harriette Wilson to Henry Brougham, Lord High Chancellor

2. PRINTED SOURCES

Books

Acton, William. *Prostitution, Considered in its Moral, Social and Sanitary Aspects, in London and other large Cities and Garrison Towns.* John Churchill & Sons; London, 1870

Anderson, Bonnie S. and Zinsser, Judith P. *A History of Their Own: Women in Europe from Prehistory to the Present.* Vol. II. Penguin; Harmondsworth, 1990

Aretz, Gertrude. *The Elegant Woman.* George G. Harrap & Co.; London, 1932

Arnold, Julian B. *Giants in Dressing Gowns.* Macdonald & Co.; London, 1940

Ayling, Stanley. *Fox.* John Murray; London, 1991

Balzac, Honoré de. *La Cousine Bette.* Oxford University Press; Oxford, 1992

Banks, J.A. *Prosperity and Parenthood: A Study of Family Planning*

Among the Victorian Middle Classes. Routledge & Kegan Paul; London, 1954

Barker, Hannah and Charlus, Elaine (eds). *Gender in Eighteenth Century England: Roles, Representations and Responsibilities.* Longman; London, 1997

Bessborough, Earl of (ed.). *Lady Bessborough and Her Family Circle.* John Murray; London, 1940

Blanche, Lesley. *The Game of Hearts: Harriette Wilson and her Memoirs.* Gryphon Books; London, 1957

Bleakley, Horace. *Ladies Fair and Frail: Sketches of the Demi-Monde during the Eighteenth Century.* John Lane/The Bodley Head; London, 1909

Blunt, Wilfrid Scawen. *The Poetical Works of Wilfrid Scawen Blunt: A Complete Edition.* Vol. 1. Macmillan & Co.; London, 1914

Blyth, Henry. *Skittles: The Last Victorian Courtesan.* Rupert Hart-Davis; London, 1970

Bourne, Kenneth (ed.). *The Blackmailing of the Chancellor: Some intimate and hitherto unpublished letters from Harriette Wilson to her friend, Lord Brougham, Lord High Chancellor of England.* Lemon Tree Press; London, 1975

Brewer, John. *The Pleasures of the Imagination: English Culture in the Eighteenth Century.* HarperCollins; London, 1997

Briggs, Asa. *Victorian Things.* Penguin; Harmondsworth, 1990

Brown, Frederick. *Zola: A Life.* Macmillan; London, 1996

Buford, E.J. *Royal St James's: Being a Story of Kings, Clubmen, and Courtesans.* Robert Hale; London, 1988

Cannadine, David, *The Pleasures of the Past.* Penguin; Harmondsworth, 1997

Cannadine, David, *History in Our Time.* Penguin; Harmondsworth, 2000

Cardigan and Lancastre, Countess of. *My Recollections.* Eveleigh Nash; London, 1909

Castle, Charles. *La Belle Otero: The Last Great Courtesan.* Michael Joseph; London, 1981

Cateley, Miss Ann. *A Brief Narrative of the Life of the Celebrated Miss Cateley. Containing the adventures of that Lady in her Public character as a singer, and Private one of a Courtezan.* London, 1780

Chesney, Kellow. *The Victorian Underworld: A Fascinating Re-creation.* Pelican Books; Harmondsworth, 1972

Claudin, Gustave. *Mes Souvenirs: Les boulevards de 1840–1870.* Michel Lévy Frères; Paris, 1884

Colette. *My Apprenticeships and Music Hall Sidelights.* Secker & Warburg; London, 1957

Colley, Linda. *Britons: Forging the Nation 1707–1837.* Vintage; London, 1996

Colombier, Marie. *Mémoires.* Pres L'Odeon; Paris, 1889

Colombier, Marie. *Mémoires. Vol. I: Fin d'empire.* Ernest Flammarion; Paris, 1898

Davidson, James. *Courtesans and Fishcakes: The Consuming Passions of Classical Athens.* HarperCollins; London, 1997

Davis, I.M. *The Harlot and the Statesman: The Story of Elizabeth Armistead and Charles James Fox.* The Kensal Press; Bourne End, 1986

Deacon, Richard. *The Private Life of Mr Gladstone.* Frederick Muller Ltd; London, 1965

Dickens, Emma. *Immaculate Contraception: The Extraordinary Story of Birth Control from the First Fumblings to the Present Day.* Robson Books; London, 2000

Diguet, Charles. *Les jolies femmes de Paris.* Librairie Internationale; Paris, 1870

Ellis, Mrs Sarah. *The Wives of England.* Fisher, Son & Co.; London, 1843

Fane, Lady Augusta. *Chit Chat.* Thornton Butterworth; London, 1926

Foreman, Amanda. *Georgiana, Duchess of Devonshire.* HarperCollins; London, 1998

Fyvie, John. *Comedy Queens of Georgian England.* Archibald Constable's Company; London, 1906

Gay, Peter. *The Bourgeois Experience: Vol. 1. The Education of the Senses.* Oxford University Press; Oxford, 1984

Goncourt, Edmond et Jules de. *The Goncourt Journals, edited and translated from the journals of E. and J. de Goncourt with an introduction and notes and a biographical repertory by Lewis Galantière.* Cassell & Co. Ltd; London, 1937

Gronow, Captain Rees Howell. *The Last Recollections of Captain Gronow, Formerly of the First Foot Guards.* Selwyn & Blount Ltd; London, 1934

Gronow, Captain Rees Howell. *Captain Gronow, His Reminiscences of*

Regency and Victorian Life 1810–60 (ed. Christopher Hibbert). Kyle Cathie; London, 1991

Hardman, Sir William. *A Mid-Victorian Pepys: The Letters and Memoirs of Sir William Hardman* (ed. S.M. Ellis). Cecil Palmer; London, 1923

'Harris's List of Covent Garden Ladies or Man of Pleasure's Kalendar'. London, 1789 and 1793

Hartnell, Norman. *Royal Courts of Fashion*. Cassell & Co.; London, 1971

Hibbert, Christopher, *The Grand Tour*. Weidenfeld & Nicolson; London, 1969

Hibbert, Christopher, *Wellington: A Personal History*. HarperCollins; London, 1997

Hicks, Carola. *Improper Pursuits: The Scandalous Life of Lady Di Beauclerk*. Macmillan; London, 2001

Hobhouse, Christopher. *Fox*. Houghton Mifflin; New York, 1935

Holden, W.H. *The Pearl from Plymouth: Eliza Emma Crouch, alias Cora Pearl*. British Technical & General Press; London, 1950

Holden, W.H. *They Startled Grandfather: Gay Ladies and Merry Mashers of Victorian Times*. British Technical & General Press; London, 1950

Holden, W.H. *Second Empire Medley*. British Technical & General Press; London, 1952

Houssaye, Arsène. *The Confessions of Arsène Houssaye* (translated by Henry Knepler). Victor Gollancz; London, 1972

Hutten, the Baroness von. *The Courtesan: The Life of Cora Pearl*. Peter Davies; London, 1933

Jackson, Patrick. *The Last of the Whigs: A Political Biography of Lord Hartington, Later Eighth Duke of Devonshire (1833–1908)*. Associated University Presses; London, 1994

Johnstone, Julia. *Confessions of Julia Johnstone: written by herself in contradiction to the fables of Harriette Wilson*. Benbow; London, 1925

Jordan, Jane. *Josephine Butler*. John Murray; London, 2001

Leckie, Barbara. *Culture and Adultery: The Novel, the Newspapers and the Law 1857–1914*. University of Pennsylvania Press; Pennsylvania, 1999

Loliée, Frédéric, *The Gilded Beauties of the Second Empire* (adapted by Bryan O'Donnell). John Long Ltd; London, 1909

Longford, Elizabeth. *A Pilgrimage of Passion: The Life of Wilfrid Scawen Blunt*. Weidenfeld & Nicolson; London, 1979

Lytton, Earl of. *The Life of Edward Bulwer, First Lord Lytton.* Macmillan & Co.; London, 1913

Mclaren, Angus. *Birth Control in Nineteenth Century England.* Croom Helm Ltd; London, 1978

Macleod, Catharine and Alexander, Julia. *Painted Ladies: Women at the Court of Charles II.* National Portrait Gallery Publications; London, 2001

Magne, Emile. *Ninon de Lanclos* (translated and edited by Gertrude Scott Stevenson). Arrowsmith; London, 1926

Marly, Diana de. *Worth: Father of Haute Couture.* Elm Tree Books; London, 1980

Masson, Georgina. *Courtesans of the Italian Renaissance.* Secker & Warburg; London, 1975

Mayhew, Henry. *London Labour and the London Poor.* Vol. 4. London, 1862

Mercy-Argenteau, Comtesse Louise de. *Last Love of an Emperor* (ed. C.L.W.) The Iris Publishing House; London, 1916

Mitchell, L.G. *Charles James Fox.* Oxford University Press; Oxford, 1992

Murray, Fanny. *Memoirs of the Celebrated Miss Fanny Murray.* London, 1759

Murray, Venetia. *High Society: A Social History of the Regency Period, 1788–1830.* Viking; London, 1998

Myer, V.G. *Harriette Wilson: Lady of Pleasure.* Fern House; Ely, 1999

Osgood Field, Julian. *Things I Shouldn't Tell.* Eveleigh Nash & Grayson Ltd; London, 1929

Otero, Carolina. *My Story.* A.M. Philpot Ltd; London, 1927

Pearl, Cora. *Mémoires de Cora Pearl.* Jules Lévy; Paris, 1886

Pearl, Cora. *The Memoirs of Cora Pearl: The English Beauty of the French Empire.* George Vickers; London, 1886

Pearl, Cyril. *The Girl with the Swansdown Seat.* Frederick Muller; London, 1955

Pearsall, Ronald. *The Worm in the Bud: The World of Victorian Sexuality.* Weidenfeld & Nicolson; London, 1969

Porter, Roy and Teich, Mikulás (eds). *Sexual Knowledge, Sexual Science: The History of Attitudes to Sexuality.* Cambridge University Press; Cambridge, 1994

Quennell, Peter. *London's Underworld.* Spring Books; London, 1950

Richards, Sandra. *The Rise of the English Actress*. Macmillan; London, 1993

Richardson, Joanna. *The Courtesans: The Demi-Monde in Nineteenth Century Paris*. Weidenfeld & Nicolson; London, 1967

Richardson, Joanna, *Gustave Doré: A Biography*. Cassell; London, 1980

Robinson, 'Perdita'. *Memoirs of Mary Robinson: 'Perdita'* (from the edition edited by her daughter with Introduction and notes by J. Fitzgerald Molloy). J.B. Lippincott Company; Philadelphia, 1894

Roger, Samuel. *Recollections*. Longman, Green, Longman & Roberts; London, 1859

Rosenthal, Margaret F. *The Honest Courtesan: Veronia Franco – Citizen and Writer in Sixteenth Century Venice*. University of Chicago Press; London, 1992

St Helier, Lady (Mary Jeune). *Memories of Fifty Years*. Edward Arnold; London, 1909

Sitwell, Sacheverell. *Selected Works*. Robert Hale Ltd; London, 1955

Stauffer, Donald A. *The Art of Biography in Eighteenth Century England*. Princeton University Press; Princeton, 1941

Steele, Mrs Elizabeth. *The Memoirs of Mrs Sophia Baddeley late of Drury Lane*. London, 1787

Stokes, Hugh. *The Devonshire House Set*. Herbert Jenkins Ltd; London, 1917

Stone, Lawrence. *Uncertain Unions and Broken Lives: Intimate and Revealing Accounts of Marriage and Divorce in England 1600–1857*. Oxford University Press; Oxford, 1955

Tannahill, Reay. *Sex in History*. Scarborough House; London, 1992

Thirkell, Angela. *The Fortunes of Harriette: The Surprising Career of Harriette Wilson*. Hamish Hamilton; London, 1936

Thompson, F.M.L. *The Rise of Respectable Society: A Social History of Victorian Britain*. Fontana; London, 1988

Tillyard, Stella. *Aristocrats*. Vintage; London, 1995

Trevelyan, Sir George Otto. *Early History of Charles James Fox*. Thomas Nelson & Sons; London, 1881

Vauzat, Guy. *Blanche d'Antigny (Actrice et demi-mondaine) 1840–1874*. Charles Bosse; Paris, 1933

Walker, Captain Charles. *Authentick Memoirs of the Life, Intrigues, and Adventures of the Celebrated Sally Salisbury with True Characters of her Most Considerable Gallants*. London, 1723

Wallace, Irving. *The Nympho and Other Maniacs: The Stories of Some Scandalous Women*. Cassell; London, 1971

Wilson, Harriette. *Harriette Wilson's Memoirs* (selected and edited with an introduction by Lesley Blanch). Century Publishing: London, 1985

'Zed' (le Comte de Maugny). *Le Demi-monde sous le second empire: Souvenirs d'un sybarite*. Ernest Kolb; Paris, 1892

Zola, Émile. *Nana*. Penguin Classics; Harmondsworth, 1972

Journals

Baird, John D. 'Divorce and Matrimonial Causes: An Aspect of "Hard Times" ', *Victorian Studies*, Vol. 20, 1977

Gordon, Eleanor and Nair, Gwyneth. 'The Economic Role of Middle Class Women in Victorian Glasgow', *Women's History Review*, Vol. 9, No. 4, 2001

Jackson, Patrick. 'Skittles and the Marquis', *History Today*, December 1995

Mclaren, Angus. 'Abortion in England, 1890–1914', *Victorian Studies*, Vol. 20

Santore, Cathy. 'Julia Lombardo, "Somtuosa Meretrize": A Portrait by Property', *Renaissance Quarterly*, Vol. 41, Issue 1, spring 1988

Periodicals

The Bon-Ton Gazette
The Crim-Con Gazette
Daily Telegraph
Gazeteer and London Daily Advertiser
Morning Post and Daily Advertiser
The Times
Town and Country Magazine
The Truth

INDEX

Leinster, Augustus Frederick Fitzgerald, 3rd Duke of, 166 & n, 168, 196, 198–9
Leinster, Emily, Duchess of (*née* Lennox), 118, 137–8, 166n
Lely, Sir Peter, 40–1
l'Enclos, Henri de, 19
l'Enclos, Ninon de, 19–20
Leslie, Anita: *Edwardians in Love*, 292n
Letessier, Caroline, 240, 274, 332n
Lewis, Matthew, 210
Lilford, Mary, Lady (*née* Fox), 146
Lilford, Thomas Atherton Powys, 3rd Baron, 147
Linley, Elizabeth, xvii
lit de parade, 258 & n
Loliée, Frédéric, 3n, 24, 239, 247, 251n, 253, 256, 258
Lombardo, Julia, 9–10, 16n, 17
London: Victorian social life in, 317–20
Long, Sir William, xvii
Longford, Elizabeth, Countess of, 300, 308, 315n, 316n, 325n
Lorne, George William Campbell, Marquis of (*later* 6th Duke of Argyll), 157 & n, 158, 170, 173, 175–6, 193–4, 196
Louis XVI, King of France: executed, 122
Louis (Bonaparte), King of Holland, 232n, 245n
Louis-Philippe, King of the French, 216n
Lucan, Lady Margaret, 95
Lullin de Châteauvieux, Michel, 191
Lumley, Sir Augustus, 2
Luttrell, Colonel Henry, 69, 71
Luttrell, Henry (poet), 169
Lytton, Edward Bulwer-, Baron, 150n

'macaronis', 31 & n, 103
Mclaren, Angus: *Birth Control in Nineteenth-Century England*, 195n
madams *see* brothels
Madden, General Sir George, 150, 154
Mahon, Gertrude ('The Bird of Paradise'), 7, 91, 95, 188
Maison d'Or, Paris, 250
make-up *see* cosmetics
Mann, Eliza, 55
Mann, Sir Horace, 129
Marche, Marie-Barbe de la, 19
Marelli, Niccolo, 16
Marie Antoinette, Queen of Louis XVI of France, 134

Marlborough, George Spencer Churchill, 4th Duke of, 112n
marriage: for courtesans and prostitutes, 126–30, 186–7; and women's role, 312–13
Married Women's Property Act (1882), 309, 310
Marryat, Captain Frederick, 169n
Marston, Elizabeth, 146
Marten, John: *Treatise of all the Degrees and Symptoms of the Venereal Disease in Both Sexes*, 192
Mason, Jem, 281
masquerades, 29–32
Massena, Victor, Duc de Rivoli (*later* Prince of Essling): relations with Cora Pearl, 229–31, 233–5, 244, 258
Masson, Georgina, 9n
Matrema (Rome courtesan), 8–9 & n
Matthews, Mrs (brothel-keeper), 91
Maugny, Comte de ('Zed'): on Cora Pearl, 1 & n, 5, 12, 217, 235, 278; on courtesans' style and manners, 10–11, 239, 242–4, 248–9; as chronicler, 24, 247; on Paris, 216; on separation of *monde* and *demi-monde*, 238; on courtesans' patrons, 258–9; on Catherine Walters, 277–9; *Souvenirs d'un sybarite*, 216
Maximilian, Emperor of Mexico, 271
Maycock, Sir Willoughby: *Annals of the Billesdon Hunt*, 281
Mayhew, Henry: *London Labour and the London Poor*, 226
Maynard, Charles Maynard, 2nd Viscount, 110n, 128–9
Melbourne, Elizabeth, Lady (*née* Milbanke), 43n, 59, 134
Melbourne, Peniston Lamb, 1st Baron: and Sophia Baddeley, 43 & n, 44–7, 49–52, 59, 62, 64, 66, 71, 74, 194; and Harriet Powell, 93n, 98; Hariette Wilson on, 156
Melbourne, William Lamb, 2nd Viscount, 44n
Melville, Robert Saunders Dundas, 2nd Viscount, 210
Mendez, Mr (admirer of Sophia Baddeley), 36, 37n, 38
Mendoza, Maia, 22
Mercy–Argenteau, Comtesse Louise de, 239, 270

INDEX

St Albans, Harriet, Duchess of (*formerly* Mellon), 127
St Anne's Hill, near Chertsey, Surrey, 109, 111–13, 116–18, 122–3, 132–3, 136, 138, 142, 145
Saint-Evremond, Charles de Marguetel de Saint Denis, Seigneur de, 19
St Helier, Mary, Lady (*née* Stewart-Mackenzie), 317–20; *Memories of Fifty Years*, 290–1
St James's (London district), 88–9, 94
St John, Charles, 146
St John, Frederick, 99
St John, George, 99
St John, Henry, 147
St John's Wood, London, 289 & n
Sainte-Beuve, Charles-Augustin, 253
Salé (Cora Pearl's chef), 230–2
Salisbury, Sally, 55
Santore, Cathy, 16n
Sari, Antonia, 239
Sayer, Stephen, 76–8, 193
Scholl, Aurelien, 250
Scott, Sir Walter, 5, 127, 210
Seaforth, Kenneth Mackenzie, 1st Earl of, 93n
Senate, E., 195
Sévigné, Marquis de, 19
Shelburne, 2nd Earl of *see* Lansdowne, 1st Marquis of
Sheridan, Richard Brinsley, 138
Siddons, Sarah, 43
Sitwell, Sir Sacheverell: *La Vie Parisienne*, 1, 237–8, 264
'Skittles' *see* Walters, Catherine
Sligo, John Denis Browne, 1st Marquis of, 167–8
Smith, Captain Alexander, 55
Smith, General Richard ('Sir Matthew Mite'), 100, 101n
Snow, Jonathan, 33
Snow, Mary, 33
Snow, Moses, 33
Snow, Robert, 34
Snow, Valentina, 34
Snow, Valentine, 33
Society for the Protection of the Young Female, 225
Socrates, 13
Somerset, Lord Charles, 203
Spencer, George John, 2nd Earl, 138

Spencer, Margaret Georgiana, Dowager Countess (*née* Poyntz), 135
Spencer, Lord Robert ('Bob'), 105, 117, 134, 144
Spinke, J., 192
Stamford, Catherine, Countess of, 282
Stamford, George Harry Grey, Earl of, 282
Stanley, Lord *see* Derby, 14th Earl of
Steele, Eliza: on Sophia Baddeley at theatre, xviii–xix, 25; on Sophia's attendance at masquerade, 29, 32; on Sophia's character, 33; on Sophia's education, 34; on Sophia's stage career, 35–6; on Sophia's health, 37; resumes friendship with Sophia, 38; on Gaby Hanger, 39; on Sophia's extravagance, 44, 62–5; Melbourne buys horse for, 45; on Melbourne, 46–7, 52; hires country house with Sophia, 48; as companion and intimate to Sophia, 49–50, 65–8; and Sophia's settlement, 52–4; on Sophia's admirers, 61–2; and Sophia's lovers and intrigues, 66–7; behaviour and dress, 68–70; on Sophia's break with Melbourne, 71–2; and Sophia's debts, 72–4; and Sophia's decline, 75–6; and Stephen Sayer, 76; leaves Sophia, 77; moralises over Sophia, 334–5; *Memoirs of Mrs Sophia Baddeley*, 25, 54–9, 67, 69, 331
Stockdale's bookshop, Haymarket, 209, 211
Stoker, Hugh: *The Devonshire House Circle*, 106n
Stone, Lawrence, 188n; *Uncertain Unions and Broken Lives*, 310n
Storer, Anthony, 118
Storer, Mr (Sophia Baddeley's lover), 67
Storer, Mrs (Julia Johnstone's mother), 189
Stracey, General Sir Henry, 3
Sydenham, Colonel, 177–8

'Tahitian Feast of Venus', 94–5
Tankerville, Charles Augustus Bennet, 5th Earl of, 211–12
Taylor, Tom: *Our American Cousin*, 286
Temple, George Grenville, 3rd Earl, 113
theatre: and vice, 39–40, 88

BOOKS BY KATIE HICKMAN

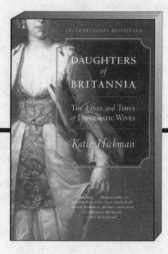

COURTESANS
Money, Sex and Fame in the Nineteenth Century
ISBN 0-06-093514-6 (paperback)

Katie Hickman reveals the extraordinary lives and times of four courtesans in Britain in the nineteenth century—including their stints in Paris, New York, and California—and offers a social history of the minutiae of courtesan life.

"Full of delicious anecdotes and superb insights. . . . This outstanding work is part history, part travelogue, and fully enjoyable." —*Booklist*

DAUGHTERS OF BRITANNIA
The Lives and Times of Diplomatic Wives
ISBN 0-06-093423-9 (paperback)

Drawing on letters, private journals, and memoirs, as well as oral history, this brilliantly written book reveals the experiences, lives, and trials of diplomatic wives.

"Fascinating. . . . Looks beyond the pomp and paegantry of the British foreign service and into the reality of making a life abroad in foreign lands."
—*Vogue*